TUBERCULOSIS

Clinical Management
and New Challenges

NOTICE

TUBERCULOSIS

Clinical Management and New Challenges

Milton D. Rossman, M.D.

Associate Professor of Medicine
Pulmonary and Critical Care Division
Department of Medicine
Hospital of the University of Pennsylvania
University of Pennsylvania Medical Center
Philadelphia, Pennsylvania

Rob Roy MacGregor, M.D.

Professor of Medicine
Director of AIDS Clinical Trial Unit
Infectious Diseases Division
Department of Medicine
Hospital of the University of Pennsylvania
University of Pennsylvania Medical Center
Philadelphia, Pennsylvania

McGRAW-HILL, INC.
Health Professions Division

New York   St. Louis   San Francisco   Auckland   Bogotá
Caracas   Lisbon   London   Madrid   Mexico City   Milan   Montreal
New Delhi   San Juan   Singapore   Sydney   Tokyo   Toronto

Tuberculosis: Clinical Management and New Challenges

1234567890   KGPKGP   987654

ISBN 0-07-053950-2

This book was set in Times Roman by Digitype, Inc.
The editors were J. Dereck Jeffers and Susan Finn;
the production supervisor was Clare Stanley;
the cover designer was Karen Quigley.
Quebecor Printing/Kingsport Press was printer and binder.
The book is printed on acid-free paper

Library of Congress Cataloging-in-Publication Data

Tuberculosis: clinical management and new challenges / [edited by] Milton D.
  Rossman, Rob Roy MacGregor.
      p.   cm.
  Includes bibliographical references and index.
  ISBN 0-07-053950-2 :
  1. Tuberculosis.   I. Rossman, Milton D.   II. MacGregor, Rob Roy.
  [DNLM: 1. Tuberculosis.   WF 200 T8803 1994]
  RC311.T825   1994
    616.9′95 — dc20
    DNLM/DLC
    for Library of Congress   94-12125

To our teachers who taught us a fascination with disease and a respect for patients. To our wives and family who patiently put up with the time demands of medicine and book editing. To the countless millions of famous and anonymous fellow humans who have been victim to *M. tuberculosis* over the millenia.

CONTENTS

CHAPTER 24   *C. ROBERT HORSBURGH, JR.*

CONTRIBUTORS*

Constance A. Benson, M.D. [14]
Associate Professor of Medicine
Infectious Diseases Division
Rush-Presbyterian-St. Luke's Medical
  Center
Chicago, Illinois

Barbara A. Body, Ph.D. [3]
Director of Microbiology and Serology
Roche Biomedical Laboratories, Inc.
Burlington, North Carolina

Patrick J. Brennan, M.D. [20]
Hospital Epidemiologist
Hospital of the University of
  Pennsylvania
Philadelphia, Pennsylvania

R. Michael Buckley, M.D. [10]
Chief, Infectious Diseases Section
Pennsylvania Hospital
Philadelphia, Pennsylvania

Richard E. Chaisson, M.D. [14]
Director, AIDS Service
Division of Infectious Diseases
Johns Hopkins University School of
  Medicine
Baltimore, Maryland

Jack T. Crawford, Ph.D. [16]
Chief, Mycobacteriology Laboratory
National Center for Infectious Diseases
Centers for Disease Control and
  Prevention
Atlanta, Georgia

H. Gerard Ten Dam [7]
Scientist, Tuberculosis, World Health
  Organization
Coppet, Switzerland

Samuel W. Dooley, M.D., M.P.H.
  [18]
Associate Director for Science
Division of Tuberculosis Elimination
National Center for Prevention Services
Centers for Disease Control and
  Prevention
Atlanta, Georgia

Asim K. Dutt, M.D. [15]
Chief, Medical Service
Veterans Administration Hospital
Murfreesboro, Tennessee;
Professor and Vice Chairman
Department of Medicine
Nashville, Tennessee

Jerrold J. Ellner, M.D. [2]
Chief, Division of Infectious Diseases
Professor of Medicine and Pathology
Case Western Reserve University
  Hospital
Cleveland, Ohio

David W. Haas, M.D. [12]
Director, Inpatient Infectious Disease
  Services
Assistant Professor of Medicine
Vanderbilt University Medical Center
Nashville, Tennessee

Alan R. Hinman, M.D., M.P.H.
  [21]
Director, National Center for
  Prevention Services
Centers for Disease Control and
  Prevention
Atlanta, Georgia

---

*The numbers in brackets following the contributor name refer to chapter(s) authored or co-authored by the contributor.

C. Robert Horsburgh, Jr., M.D. [24]
Special Assistant for Infectious Diseases
Division of HIV/AIDS
Centers for Disease Control and
Prevention
Atlanta, Georgia

Robin E. Huebner, Ph.D., M.P.H. [5]
Medical Microbiologist and
Epidemiologist
Division of Tuberculosis Elimination
Centers for Disease Control and
Prevention
Atlanta, Georgia

James M. Hughes, M.D. [21]
Director, National Center for Infectious
Diseases
Centers for Disease Control and
Prevention
Atlanta, Georgia

Richard F. Jacobs, M.D. [8]
Chief, Division of Pediatric Infectious
Diseases
Horace C. Cabe Professor of Pediatrics
Arkansas Children's Hospital
Little Rock, Arkansas

Rob Roy MacGregor, M.D. [20]
Professor of Medicine
Director of AIDS Clinical Trial Unit
Infectious Diseases Division
Department of Medicine
Hospital of the University of
Pennsylvania
University of Pennsylvania Medical
Center
Philadelphia, Pennsylvania

Robert L. Mayock, M.D. [9]
Professor of Medicine
Hospital of the University of
Pennsylvania
Philadelphia, Pennsylvania

Wallace T. Miller, M.D. [17]
Professor and Vice-Chairman of
Radiology
Hospital of the University of
Pennsylvania
Philadelphia, Pennsylvania

Thomas S. Moulding, M.D. [6]
Associate Clinical Professor of Medicine
Harbor-UCLA Medical Center
Torrance, California

Edward A. Nardell, M.D. [4]
Tuberculosis Control Officer
Division of Tuberculosis Control
Massachusetts Department of Health
Assistant Professor of Medicine
Harvard Medical School
The Cambridge Hospital
Cambridge, Massachusetts

Anne H. Norris, M.D. [10]
Fellow, Infectious Diseases
Hospital of the University of
Pennsylvania
Philadelphia, Pennsylvania

Ida M. Onorato, M.D. [1]
Chief, Surveillance and Epidemiologic
Investigations Branch
National Center for Prevention Services
Centers for Disease Control and
Prevention
Atlanta, Georgia

Donald D. Peterson, M.D. [22]
Clinical Associate Professor of Medicine
Jefferson Medical College
Philadelphia, Pennsylvania

Roger M. Des Prez, M.D. [12]
Professor of Medicine
Vanderbilt University School of
Medicine
Nashville, Tennessee

Richard L. Riley, M.D. [4]
Emeritus Professor of Medicine
Johns Hopkins University School of
Medicine
Baltimore, Maryland

Milton D. Rossman, M.D. [9]
Associate Professor of Medicine
Pulmonary and Critical Care Division
Department of Medicine
Hospital of the University of
  Pennsylvania
University of Pennsylvania Medical
  Center
Philadelphia, Pennsylvania

Jan B. Sbarbaro, Esq. [19]
Attorney at Law
Morrison and Foerster
Denver, Colorado

John A. Sbarbaro, M.D., M.P.H.
  [19]
Professor of Medicine and Preventive
  Medicine
University of Colorado
Denver, Colorado

Maybelle F. Schein, R.N., B.S. [5]
Nurse Consultant
Division of Tuberculosis Elimination
Centers for Disease Control and
  Prevention
Atlanta, Georgia

Patricia M. Simone, M.D. [18]
Medical Epidemiologist
Division of Tuberculosis Elimination
Centers for Disease Control and
  Prevention
Atlanta, Georgia

Hillas Smith, M.A., M.D.,
  F.R.C.P. [13]
Consultant Physician (Retired)
Lister Unit
Northwick Park Hospital
Harrow, England

Dixie E. Snider, Jr., M.D. [1]
Acting Associate Director for Science
National Center for Prevention Services
Centers for Disease Control and
  Prevention
Atlanta, Georgia

William W. Stead, M.D. [15]
Director, Tuberculosis Program
Arkansas Department of Health
Little Rock, Arkansas

George F. Thornton, M.D. [11]
Clinical Professor of Medicine
Director, Department of Medicine
Waterbury Hospital
Waterbury, Connecticut

Richard J. Wallace, Jr., M.D. [23]
Chairman, Department of Microbiology
Professor of Medicine
John Chapman Professorship in
  Microbiology
University of Texas Health Center
Tyler, Texas

Nancy G. Warren, Ph.D. [3]
National Tuberculosis Training Advisor
Association of State and Territory
  Public Health Laboratory Directors
Washington, DC

Paul W. Wright, M.D. [23]
Professor of Family Practice Medicine
University of Texas Health Center
Tyler, Texas

PREFACE

The current resurgence of tuberculosis might not have happened had intense control efforts been maintained (see Chapter 15). We hope that the information contained in this book will be helpful for clinicians, as they will be on the front line in the battle with this disease. However, the conquest of tuberculosis will require not only knowledgeable caregivers, but also a political agenda that will ensure public health casefinding, treatment, and renewed research support for the development of additional therapies against a disease that has plagued society since the beginning of the human race.

This book should serve as a guide to management of patients (Chapters 8 to 13) and will highlight areas of controversy (i.e., skin testing and preventive chemotherapy, Chapters 5 and 6) and areas where change is expected. These spheres of change reflect not only the changing epidemiology of the disease (Chapters 1, 14, 15, and 18) but also the impact of molecular biology (Chapters 3 and 16) and newer radiologic techniques (Chapter 17) on the identification and diagnosis of tuberculosis. With the decline of specialized hospitals for the care of patients with tuberculosis, general hospitals must learn how to manage these infectious patients (Chapters 4 and 20) and prevent the spread of tuberculosis to hospital personnel and to the many immunocompromised patients that are being cared for within these institutions. To understand tuberculosis adequately, one must also have some understanding of the nontuberculous mycobacterial diseases that may simulate tuberculosis (Chapters 22 to 24). We have created this book to be a handy straightforward guide through all these areas for the practicing physician wishing to be abreast of the newest information and most current recommendations regarding the diagnosis and management of this ageless foe of humanity. In this way, we and all contributing authors hope that our text will be a helpful companion to the reader dealing with *Tuberculosis – Clinical Management and New Challenges*. Finally, we hope that this book will convey not only this information but also our own fascination and interest in this disease.

ACKNOWLEDGMENTS

We would like to thank all of the authors who diligently contributed to the task of constructing this book. Special thanks to Mary McNichol for her invaluable help with all the little details, to Dara Rossman for assisting with the editing of several drafts, and to the entire staff at McGraw-Hill, especially J. Dereck Jeffers.

INTRODUCTION AND
BRIEF HISTORY

The story of tuberculosis in the nineties is only the latest chapter in a long and momentous history of the impact of a bacterium on the human race. Because we believe that history teaches valuable lessons to the present and because the lore of tuberculosis is such an integral part of the history of medicine, we have chosen to begin our handbook with a brief review of the history of tuberculosis.

Tuberculosis is older than recorded history. Spinal lesions characteristic of tuberculosis have been found in neolithic human remains, and Egyptian tomb paintings demonstrate the classic gibbus formation of Pott's disease. The earliest writings suggestive of tuberculosis are from India, approximately 700 B.C., describing a chronic pulmonary disease with wasting. In about 380 B.C., Hippocrates provided a detailed description of a pulmonary disorder called *phthisis*—literally, "to melt" or "to waste away." Aristotle, noting that close contacts of patients with phthisis tended to develop the disease, suggested that it was caused by some disease-producing substance exhaled into the air in a patient's breath! This flash of insight had to wait for 2000 years to be confirmed by Robert Koch. The Greek physician Galen, practicing and writing in Rome during the second century A.D., outlined treatment principles that were not modified over the next millennium: rest, restraint of cough, chest plasters, astringents for bleeding (gargles of tannic acid mixed with honey), opium for violent coughing, and emphasis on diet. The Middle Ages added the custom of curing phthisis by the royal touch (few supplicants complained of royal failure!).

The Renaissance brought a new interest in observation and empiricism. Andreas Vesalius published the first accurate human anatomy text in 1478, based on actual dissections. Thereafter, postmortem examinations of patients with known phthisis (also then called *consumption*) indicated that most had cavitary disease of the lungs. Two hundred years later, the Dutch anatomist Franciscus Sylvius described small, hard nodules in lungs of consumptives, which he called tubercles, and theorized that phthisis developed from ulcers (cavities) in the lung. Beginning in the 1600s, public health records began to note causes of death, and consumption was usually among the top three; for example, in 1667, 25 percent of deaths in London were ascribed to the disease. By the year 1800, consumption was rampant in all areas where health statistics were being kept; most physicians believed it to be a hereditary disorder, although a number of far-sighted observers argued that it was communicable and even convinced some governments to pass quarantine laws to protect the public. The pathological features were well-described, although the origin of tubercles remained unknown, and no effective therapy existed. In 1839, Johann Schönlein first suggested the name *tuberculosis*, and in 1861, Oliver Wendell Holmes used the term *the white plague* to bring attention to the devastating prevalence of tuberculosis in society.[1] The pace of discovery quickened in 1865 when Jean Antoine Villemin demonstrated that rabbits inoculated with pus from consumptives' lung cavities developed tubercles. The simultaneous birth of the science of bacteriology prepared the way for Robert Koch's historic report in 1882 describing *Mycobacterium tuberculosis* and its success in fulfilling Koch's postulates as the cause of tuberculosis.

During the nineteenth century, a peculiar cultural sense of romance became associated with tuberculosis. Perhaps because it afflicted so many artists, poets, and writers (Keats, Thoreau, the Brontë sisters, Chopin, Byron, and many others), to be consumptive became almost a mark of distinction, and the pallor caused by the disease was part of the standard of beauty.[2] The Pre-Raphaelite painters romanticized asthenic, pale, ethereal heroines, and operas such as *La Bohéme* celebrated the tragedy of premature death by consumption. Scholars wrote about the *spes phthisica*, a state of psychic excitation that "not only enabled the individual victims of tuberculosis to bear their burdens of disease most cheerfully, but has been a means of quickening genius, a fact wherefrom have flowed benefits that concern the whole world of intellect."[3] It is true that, due to the ubiquitous nature of the organism, tuberculosis was no respecter of persons, afflicting significant numbers of people from all strata of society. In fact, however, most victims of tuberculosis were not aristocrats and artists, but common folk, disproportionately those who were poor, malnourished, and living and working in polluted and unsanitary conditions characteristic of late industrial revolution cities. As throughout history, the struggles of the rich and famous were recorded, while the larger anonymous group of society's indigent suffered in silence.

The nineteenth century also witnessed both the worst and the best of therapeutic approaches: from 1800 to 1860, patients endured the era of *antiphlogistic* and *counterirritant therapy*, in which physicians employed blistering over affected chest areas, emetics, cathartics, astringents, bleeding, and dietary manipulation that often contributed to a state of malnutrition. The regimen was summarized in 1853 by John Bennett from the University of Edinburgh: "Therapy consisted of antimonials, cough mixtures and opiates, leeches applied frequently to the chest and occasionally general bleeding; sulphuric acid to relieve the sweating; astringents to stop diarrhea or hemoptysis; now and then counter-irritants and, towards the termination of the disease, wine and stimulants. Under such a system of practice, it need not be wondered that consumption should be regarded as almost a uniformly fatal disorder."[4] A growing dissatisfaction with this approach led to the advocacy of country living, horseback riding, exercise, bland diets, and use of health spas. Convinced that fresh, cool mountain air could stimulate cardiopulmonary activity, improve circulation, and enhance healing, Hermann Brehmer established the first sanatorium for tuberculosis in Gorbesdorf, Germany, in 1854. His regimen included a rich diet, gentle exercise, and hydrotherapy and, equally important, avoided the damaging procedures of the antiphlogistic approach. Dettweiler modified Brehmer's regimen by insisting on six meals a day and 8 to 12 h of daily exposure to fresh air, accomplished by initiating the pavilion style of hospital architecture, in which patients' beds were wheeled out onto balconies and verandas in all seasons.

The impressive clinical success of this approach produced a worldwide sanatorium movement based on rest, fresh air, good diet, and avoidance of toxic treatments. In the United States, Edward Livingston Trudeau, himself healed of tuberculosis in the Adirondack Mountains of New York, read of Brehmer's work and, in 1885, established the first tuberculosis sanatorium in the United States, the Saranac Lake Cottage Sanatorium. He built a laboratory there to apply the bacteriological tools developed by Koch and was quick to recognize the diagnostic value of Wilhelm Roentgen's x-ray, first reported in 1896. The contribution of the Trudeau Institute and Cottage Sanatorium to the crusade against tuberculosis was immense: by 1925, 261 physicians had "cured" and/or studied there and subsequently become sanatorium workers worldwide.

Sanatoria became the focal point of tuberculosis treatment and clinical research. Therapy was aided by fluoroscopy, which allowed accurate assessment of intrathoracic pathological changes, proving particularly useful in directing interventions aimed at collapsing diseased and sometimes bleeding lung segments. *Collapse therapy* began around 1900, stimulated by the observation that spontaneous pneumothorax often led to healing. The first attempts to create artificial pneumothorax employed injected nitrogen and were often stymied by apical pleural adhesions. This problem was first addressed by *closed intrapleural pneumonolysis*, in which a pneumoscope was used to separate pleural surfaces. Surgeons achieved longer lasting results with *extrapleural pneumothorax*, separating the parietal pleura from the chest wall and filling the cavity with fat, paraffin wax, or inert spheres. Pneumoperitoneum and phrenic nerve crushing provided relatively safe methods of temporary collapse. As surgical technique and support improved, *thoracoplasty* became the dominant method of achieving permanent collapse, by removing the posterior segments of the upper ribs on the affected side. All of the elements of collapse and rest therapy were in place by the beginning of World War I, and the period following 1918 was the heyday of the sanatorium. By 1931, the United States had 633 specialized tuberculosis hospitals, with a total bed capacity of 80,054, 78 percent publicly supported. Patients received integrated medical-surgical care, abetted by modern laboratory and radiological techniques, and mortality rates from the disease dropped steadily. An unanticipated negative effect of this specialization was the isolation of expertise and patients away from the mainstream of medical experience, with the result that those choosing to learn more about tuberculosis were required to seek this experience separately.

Developing in parallel to, and integrated with, the sanatorium movement were public health efforts focused on tuberculosis control. The National Tuberculosis Association was established in the United States in 1904 to promote public awareness of the cause, methods of transmission, and new treatments for tuberculosis and to raise funds for public health efforts to identify and treat patients with disease regardless of their ability to pay. It became the norm for states to support tuberculosis treatment, to mandate case registration, and to provide sanatoria for the care of their citizens. Use of old tuberculin and later purified protein derivative (PPD), developed by Florence Seibert at the Phipps Institute in Philadelphia, contributed to the realization that most clinical cases of tuberculosis were the result of reactivation of previous infection, not immediate contagion. The tuberculin skin test also created awareness of the large pool of people who had been infected with *M. tuberculosis* but who had no evidence of active disease. This group would have to wait until the 1950s for the development of safe and effective preventive therapy. Increased use of radiographs also identified the phenomenon of active disease with few or no clinical symptoms. The prohibitive cost of population screening with chest radiographs stimulated development of miniature radiography machinery that took photographs of fluoroscopic images. Immediately following World War II, mass campaigns to screen populations with mobile units taking miniature 35 mm fluorograms were initiated in many countries, with considerable success in case detection. For example, by 1950, almost 6 million Britons had been radiographed, and 3.7/1000 were found to have unsuspected tuberculosis. Such patients were admitted to sanatoria where combined medical-surgical care now promised great hope for control of their disease. However, clinicians and patients alike still awaited effective chemotherapy capable of arresting or killing the tuberculosis bacillus.

In the 1920s and 1930s, it was becoming increasingly clear that the growing science of microbiology would allow the development of drugs effective against human pathogens. Because tuberculosis was considered the most important infectious disease of the day, research laboratories in universities and pharmaceutical companies around the world were in a race to develop effective drug therapy.

In the mid 1940s, human trials were begun for the first two effective drugs against *M. tuberculosis*. Streptomycin was discovered by a doctoral student, Albert Schatz, working in the laboratory of Selman Waksman at Rutgers Agricultural College in New Jersey. Schatz observed that a culture of what had been called *Actinomyces griseus* produced a substance that inhibited the growth of *M. tuberculosis*. This organism had been recently renamed *Streptomyces*, and the active product was called streptomycin. Waksman developed a collaboration with Corwin Hinshaw and William Feldman of the Mayo Clinic to begin animal and possibly human testing of the new drug. In April 1944, the first animal experiments were started and were so successful that in November of the same year streptomycin was first successfully used in a patient. Streptomycin was the first successful antituberculous drug reported in the literature.[5]

Almost simultaneously with the development of streptomycin, Jorgen Lehmann conceived of the chemical modifications of aspirin that would result in a second successful antituberculous drug, para-aminosalicylic acid (PAS). Working with the Swedish pharmaceutical company Ferrosan and its senior chemist, Karl-Gustav Rosdahl, the initial in vitro experiments with PAS began in December 1943. Their success led, in March 1944, to human trials of PAS with local application to open sores from tuberculous osteomyelitis. In October 1944, the first systemic trial of PAS was begun in a patient with pulmonary tuberculosis. However, the first publication on the success of PAS was not until after the report of the success of streptomycin.[6]

With the report of two effective drugs against tuberculosis, the impression was created that scientific advances would defeat an illness that had plagued humankind for centuries. However, the ability of *M. tuberculosis* to mutate and develop resistance to antibiotics would prove the downfall of single drug therapy for tuberculosis (see Chapter 18). Within a few years of the first reports of the success of streptomycin, the rapid development of resistance was recognized. Drug-resistant organisms could appear as early as 4 weeks, and after 4 months of treatment over 90 percent of patients would have drug-resistant organisms. As a consequence of the emergence of drug resistance, the 5-year survival rate of patients treated with streptomycin was no better than that of patients undergoing sanitarium treatment alone.

In 1949, studies were conducted simultaneously in the United States and England to address the issue of drug resistance. PAS and streptomycin were combined to determine whether multidrug treatment could alter the incidence of drug resistance.[7,8] After 6 months of combined therapy, the numbers of drug-resistant organisms were markedly reduced. The ability of *M. tuberculosis* to become drug-resistant and the means of subverting this tendency have been lessons that have had to be learned and relearned. The current fear of an epidemic from a multidrug-resistant form of *M. tuberculosis* is a direct result of failure to learn from these lessons.

With the medical world aware that single-drug therapy was only temporarily effective and that double-drug therapy might not bring a lasting cure, medical researchers throughout the world searched for additional drugs against *M. tuberculosis*. In 1951, three pharmaceutical companies — in the United States, Squibb and Hoffman La Roche, and in Germany, Bayer — almost simultaneously reported the effectiveness of isoniazid against tuberculosis. The lesson of the failure of single-drug therapy due to the emergence of resistant organisms had been learned, and the introduction of isoniazid also began the era of effective multidrug treatment of tuberculosis. The effectiveness of isoniazid was due to its ability to penetrate into all tissues, its bactericidal activity against both intra- and extracellular organisms, and its low toxicity. Specific details on the action, distribution, and effectiveness of isoniazid are given in Chapter 12.

A variety of other drugs would also become available (see Chapter 12), but with the introduction of rifampin in the 1970s, a second bactericidal drug, and the subsequent development of both intermittent and short-course regimens of chemotherapy, the impression was again created that the battle against tuberculosis had been won. Because rest and sanatorium treatment no longer were felt to alter the course of the disease,[9] tuberculosis sanatoria were either closing or being taken over by other health agencies. Chemotherapy for tuberculosis was so effective that surgical removal of residual cavities was no longer recommended.[10] The incidence of tuberculosis and the death rate from tuberculosis seemed to be relentlessly declining. Hope began to arise that soon tuberculosis would be relegated to history books and take its place next to smallpox as a scourge of humankind that had been eliminated from the earth.

However, the early lessons were either forgotten or never learned. The failure to ensure that patients completed therapy and the impact of human immunodeficiency virus (HIV) infection on the incidence of tuberculosis (see Chapter 14) have helped to make tuberculosis the leading cause of death from infectious disease globally (see Chapter 1). In addition, despite the availability of numerous effective drugs, the global incidence of tuberculosis is predicted to increase by 57.6 percent between 1990 and 2005. Even in western Europe, the United States, Canada, Japan, Australia, and New Zealand, the incidence of tuberculosis is likely to increase by more than 10 percent between 1990 and 2005.[11]

REFERENCES

1. Savacool JW: Philadelphia and the white plague. *Trans Stud Coll Physicians Phila* 8:147 – 182, 1986.
2. Dubos R: The romance of death. *Am Lung Assoc Bull* March 1982:5 – 6.

3. Jacobson AC: Tuberculosis and the creative mind, in *Genius: Som Revelations*. Brooklyn, N Y, Albert T Huntington, 1909.

4. Keers RY: *Pulmonary Tuberculosis: A Journey down the Centuries*. London, Bailliere Tindall, 1978.

5. Hinshaw HC, Feldman WH: Streptomycin in treatment of clinical tuberculosis: a preliminary report. *Proc Staff Meet Mayo Clin* 20:313–318, 1945.

6. Lehmann J: Para-aminosalicylic acid in the treatment of tuberculosis. *Lancet* 1:15–16, 1946.

7. Karlson AG, Pfuetze KH, Carr DT, Feldman WH, Hinshaw HC: The effect of combined therapy with streptomycin, para-aminosalicylic acid and promin on the emergence of streptomycin resistant strains of tubercle bacilli: a preliminary report. *Proc Staff Meet Mayo Clin* 24:510–515, 1949.

8. Treatment of pulmonary tuberculosis with para-aminosalicylic acid and streptomycin: a preliminary report. *Br Med J* 2:1521, 1949.

9. Fox W: The John Barnwell lecture: changing concepts in the chemotherapy of pulmonary tuberculosis. *Am Rev Respir Dis* 97:767–790, 1968.

10. Corpe RF, Blalock FA: A continuing study of patients with "open negative" status at Battey State Hospital. *Am Rev Respir Dis* 98:954–964, 1968.

11. Dolin PJ, Raviglione MC, Kochi A: Estimates of future global tuberculosis morbidity and mortality. *MMWR* 42:961–963, 1993.

TUBERCULOSIS

Clinical Management
and New Challenges

PART I
Basic Science

CHAPTER 1

Epidemiology

DIXIE E. SNIDER, JR. / IDA M. ONORATO

The purpose of this chapter is to review the current epidemiology of tuberculosis (TB) in the world: the number of new cases and deaths due to TB each year and their demographic characteristics and geographic distribution, trends in cases and deaths over time, and the number of persons infected but without current disease. Unfortunately, this kind of information is unavailable except in a few industrialized countries. Much of the population of developing countries still does not have access to health care services.[1] Even when such services are available, cases may not be reported to health authorities, or there may be no public health surveillance system in place for the collection and analysis of the information.[2] Furthermore, the major, and often only, diagnostic tool used in developing countries is sputum microscopic examination, which does not detect cases of smear-negative, culture-positive TB or cases of extrapulmonary TB. Thus, many TB cases in developing countries remain undetectable. Because of these limitations, the global burden of TB can be examined only indirectly.[1,3]

MORBIDITY AND MORTALITY IN DEVELOPING COUNTRIES

From a global perspective, the magnitude of the TB problem appears to be huge. Murray et al.[3] estimated that, in 1990, the number of new cases of all forms of TB in developing countries was 7.1 million. More recently, Kochi[1] estimated that there were 7.6 million new cases of TB in developing countries and an additional 400,000 new cases in industrialized countries, bringing the total number of new TB cases occurring annually to 8 million. Thus, 95 percent of the TB cases are estimated to occur in developing countries and only 5 percent in industrialized countries. The largest estimated number of cases (about 5 million) are believed to occur in Asia;[1,3] however, the highest estimated case rates are in Africa. Murray et al.[3] estimated a case rate of 229 per 100,000 population in sub-Saharan Africa, and Kochi[1] has estimated a case rate of 272 cases per 100,000 population in the World Health Organization's (WHO) African Region.

Kochi[1] has estimated that about one-third of the world's population (1.7 billion people) is infected with *Mycobacterium tuberculosis*. The majority of infected persons reside in developing countries. Furthermore, in industrialized countries, 80 percent of infected individuals are aged 50 years or more; in developing countries, 75 percent of infected persons are thought to be less than 50 years of age, indicating that transmission continues to each new generation.

Murray et al.[3] have estimated that about 2.5 million people died from all forms of TB in developing countries in 1990. Kochi[1] has estimated that, worldwide, TB caused 2.9 million deaths in 1990; all but 40,000 of these deaths occurred in developing countries. The largest number of deaths (1.7–1.8 million) is estimated to occur in Asia, but the death rate is thought to be highest in Africa.

According to a 1989 WHO report,[4] 1.3 million cases and 450,000 deaths from TB in developing countries occur in children under the age of 15 years. However, the greatest number of cases and deaths is concentrated in the economically most productive age group of the population (15–59 years); 70–80 percent of the TB cases in developing countries fall into this age group.[1] Murray et al.[3] stated that TB appears to be the largest cause of death from a single pathogen in the world and estimated that TB accounts for 7 percent of all deaths and 26 percent of potentially preventable deaths in the world.

THE IMPACT OF THE HIV/AIDS EPIDEMIC

The pandemic of human immunodeficiency virus (HIV) infection has had a profound impact on the global TB problem.[5] Due to its ability to destroy the immune system, HIV has emerged as the most significant risk factor for progression of dormant TB infection to clinical disease.[6] As a result, the global TB problem has worsened, and it poses an unprecedented medical, social, and economic threat, especially in developing countries.

The Global Programme on AIDS of the WHO estimated that, in 1992, at least 9–11 million adults and 1 million children had been infected with HIV worldwide. Nearly 85 percent of the HIV infections occurred in developing countries, and the vast majority of infections occurred in the age group 15–49 years.[7] WHO's Tuberculosis Program has estimated that about 1.7 billion people are infected with *M. tuberculosis*.[1] The impact of HIV infection on the TB situation is greatest in those populations where the prevalence of TB

FIGURE 1-1. Estimated global distribution of adults who have been infected with HIV and TB, mid-1992. (*Courtesy of the World Health Organization.*)

infection in young adults (who are at highest risk of HIV infection) is high. It has been estimated that, in early 1992, there were more than 4 million persons with dual HIV and TB infection worldwide, >3 million of whom lived in sub-Saharan Africa (Fig.1-1).[5]

The annual risk of progression to active TB among individuals infected with both HIV and TB and who have not received chemoprophylaxis is 5–8 percent.[6,8-10] Thus, Narain et al.[5] estimated that, in 1992, 150,000–250,000 more cases of TB occurred in sub-Saharan Africa than would have been expected had the HIV epidemic not occurred.

In recent years, the number of reported cases of TB has increased dramatically in many countries of sub-Saharan Africa.[5] For example, Tanzania recorded 22,544 cases in 1990, an increase of 86 percent over the 12,089 cases reported in 1984. Increases in Burundi, Malawi, and Zambia during the same period were even greater: 140, 180, and 154 percent, respectively (Fig.1-2). Among patients with TB in many African countries, HIV seroprevalence rates of greater than 40 percent are common (Table 1-1).[11-26]

HIV infection is increasing in several Asian countries, especially Thailand, India, and Myanmar,[7] and in some areas the proportion of TB patients coinfected with HIV is on the increase. In Chiang Mai, Thailand, the proportion increased from 5.1 percent in late 1989 to 13.8 percent in early 1991.[5] In

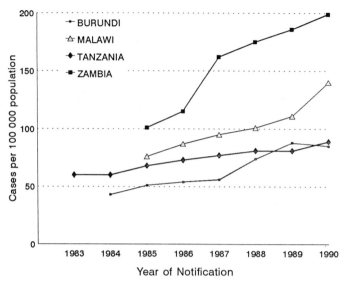

FIGURE 1-2. Annual TB notification rates in selected African countries, 1985–1991. (*Used with permission. From Narain et al.[5]*)

TABLE 1-1. HIV Seroprevalence among Patients with TB in Developing Countries

Selected Country	Year	Total No. of TB Cases	HIV-Positive, %
Zaire[4]	1985	159	33.0
Zaire (sanitorium)[15]	1985–87	465	38.0
Zaire (outpatients)[15]	1985–87	509	17.0
Burundi[13]	1986	328	54.0
Central African Republic	1986–87	72	54.0
Central African Republic (adults)[12]	1987–88	183	31.1
Central African Republic (children)[12]	1987–88	37	10.8
Malawi[18]	1988	125	26.0
Zambia[16]	1988–89	346	60.0
Malawi[17]	1988–89	153	52.0
Uganda[19]	1988–89	59	66.0
Burkina Faso*[21]	1988–89	573	22.7
Zimbabwe*[24]	1988–89	591	40.6
Ivory Coast*[25]	1989–90	2043	40.2
Ivory Coast*[22]	———	4221	34.3
Haiti[25]	1988–89	274	24.0
Haiti[23]	1989–90	143	39.0
Kenya[20]	1989–90	240	30.4

Note: In some studies, confirmed and presumed pulmonary TB cases were combined.

*Including HIV-2–infected patients.

India, 12 of 183 (6.3 percent) TB patients admitted to a hospital in Bombay were found to be HIV-infected.[5] Data from a hospital in Buenos Aires, Argentina, showed that the proportion of tuberculosis patients coinfected with HIV increased from 3 percent in 1988 to 6 percent in 1990.[5]

In many developing countries, TB has emerged as the most common opportunistic disease associated with HIV infection. Twenty to forty-four percent of AIDS patients in Africa, 18 percent of patients in Haiti, and up to 25 percent of patients in Brazil, Mexico, and Argentina had clinical TB during the course of HIV infection.[5]

It is still unclear how the increasing numbers of HIV-positive patients with TB will affect the transmission of TB in the community. It is possible that the increase in the number of TB cases will increase TB transmission both to the HIV-positive and HIV-negative populations. However, data from Tanzania indicate that the increase in TB cases among adults has so far not led to a detectable increase in transmission of TB infection to schoolchildren.[5] Because of their high mortality rates, HIV-infected patients with TB may not transmit infection to as many people as non-HIV-infected persons with TB.[14,16,26,27] It has been estimated that each untreated, HIV-uninfected TB patient infects an average of 12 other persons over a 2-year period.[28] Since HIV-infected TB patients may survive for a much shorter period of time,[29] they may infect fewer persons. The reason for higher mortality among patients with HIV infections who receive treatment for their TB is probably related to other HIV-associated complications,[30] since they do respond well to therapy if infected with drug-susceptible organisms.[29]

The future of the HIV/TB epidemic in developing countries depends to a large extent on the success of efforts to control and prevent the spread of HIV. A mathematical model has been developed using a variety of scenarios giving a range of risks for HIV infection and TB infection for the period 1980–2000.[31] The four scenarios included (1) a low rate of 1 percent risk of TB infection in year zero (1980) with a 45 percent TB infection prevalence and a 2 percent HIV prevalence in 1989; (2) a 2 percent risk of TB infection in year zero with a 60 percent TB infection prevalence and 2 percent HIV prevalence in 1989; (3) a 2 percent risk of TB infection in year zero with a 60 percent TB infection prevalence and a 10 percent HIV prevalence in 1989; and (4) a 2 percent risk of TB infection in year zero with 60 percent TB infection prevalence and a 20 percent HIV prevalence in 1989.

Under scenarios 1 and 2, a 50–60 percent increase in smear-positive rates in 15–45-year-olds was predicted for the year 2000; under scenario 3, smear-positive rates in 15–45-year-olds in the year 2000 are expected to increase 4-fold from the 1980 baseline. Under scenario 4, a 10-fold increase in smear-positive rates in the year 2000 is expected.

TB IN THE UNITED STATES AND OTHER INDUSTRIALIZED COUNTRIES

The United States

Since 1953, when national surveillance began, through 1984, the United States experienced a significant decline in TB cases—from 84,304 cases in 1953 to only 22,225 cases in 1984. The average annual decline in cases was about 5.3 percent per year. From 1985 to 1991, however, the number of reported cases has increased by 18 percent. Using the trend for 1980–1984 to calculate expected cases, the Centers for Disease Control and Prevention (CDC) estimates that from 1985 through 1992 about 51,700 excess cases have accumulated (Fig. 1-3).

The average annual case rate for the period 1985–1990 in urban areas (i.e., cities with >100,000 population) was nearly 3-fold higher than the case rate in rural areas. Rural areas, which have 75 percent of the population, contributed 52 percent of the cases, while urban areas, which have 25 percent of the population, contributed 48 percent of the cases. In addition, case rates in urban areas have increased more rapidly than they have in rural areas.

Of the 25,701 TB cases reported to the CDC in 1991, 71 percent occurred in racial and ethnic minorities. Data from 1990 show that, compared

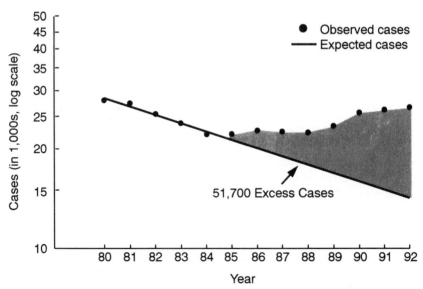

FIGURE 1-3. Expected and observed TB cases, United States, 1980–1992.

to the case rate of 4.2 per 100,000 population among non-Hispanic whites, case rates were 10-fold higher among Asians, 8-fold higher among African-Americans, and about 5-fold higher among Hispanics and Native Americans.

From 1985 to 1991, TB cases declined about 9 percent among non-Hispanic whites and 13 percent among Native Americans (Table 1-2). However, cases increased 26 percent among African-Americans, 32 percent among Asians/Pacific islanders, and 72 percent among Hispanics. All age groups, except those 65 years of age and older, experienced an increase. The largest percentage increase, 52 percent, was seen among persons 25–44 years of age. However, there was a 28 percent increase in cases among 0–4-year-olds and a 39 percent increase among children 5–14 years old. In the age group 25–44

TABLE 1-2. Reported Cases of TB by Sex, Age Group, Race / Ethnicity, and Country of Origin, United States, 1985 and 1991

Characteristic	1985	1991	% Change
Totals	22,201	26,283	+18.4
Sex			
Male	14,496	17,069	+17.7
Female	7,704	9,214	+19.6
Unknown	1	0	———*
Age			
0–4	789	1,006	+27.5
5–14	472	656	+39.0
15–24	1,672	1,971	+17.9
25–44	6,758	10,263	+51.9
45–64	6,138	6,297	+2.6
65+	6,356	6,068	−4.5
Unknown	16	22	———*
Race / ethnicity			
White, non-Hispanic	8,453	7,709	−8.8
Black, non-Hispanic	7,592	9,536	+25.6
Hispanic	3,092	5,330	+72.4
Asian / Pacific Islander	2,530	3,346	+32.3
American Indian / Alaskan native	397	345	−13.1
Unknown / other	137	17	———*
Country of origin			
Foreign-born	4,925†	6,982	+41.8
U.S.-born	17,712†	19,161	+8.2
Unknown	131†	140	———*

*Not calculated.

†Statistics are for 1986, the first year of uniform reporting.

years, increases have been observed in all racial and ethnic groups, but the largest increases have occurred among African-Americans and Hispanics. The situation is different among 0–14-year-olds. In this age group, Hispanics contributed most of the increased number of cases.

Among all cases of TB reported to the CDC in 1991, 27 percent were born outside the United States. The number and percentage of patients who were foreign-born increased from 4925 (22 percent) in 1986 to 6982 (27 percent) in 1991. By race/ethnicity, the largest numbers of cases among the foreign-born in 1991 occurred among Asians (2979) and Hispanics (2952), but Hispanics showed the largest percentage increase since 1986 (86 percent). In 1991, 55 percent of Hispanics with TB were foreign-born; among Asians/ Pacific islanders with TB, 89 percent were foreign-born. Increases in cases among the foreign-born were seen in all age groups. The largest numerical increase in cases occurred in the 25–44 age group, but the largest percentage increase occurred among 0–4-year-olds and the next largest among 5–14-year-olds.

In the 25–44 age group, substantial percentage increases in cases have occurred among both the U.S.-born and the foreign-born. However, the foreign-born accounted for only 27 percent of the increase in this age group when comparing data from 1991 with data from 1986, the first year all states reported country of origin.

The situation was quite different among 0–14-year-olds. Comparing 1986 to 1991, there was a 92 percent increase in cases among the foreign-born, and the foreign-born accounted for 48 percent of the increase in cases in this age group.

Among males, the foreign-born contributed 54 percent of the total increase in cases, whereas among females, the foreign-born contributed 67 percent of the increase in cases.

Although the CDC has not routinely collected data on the HIV serostatus of reported TB patients, there is evidence that the HIV epidemic is, at least in part, contributing to the change in the TB morbidity trend. The largest increases in reported TB cases have occurred in geographic areas heavily affected by the HIV epidemic, for example, New York City. Examining the trends in reported U.S.-born TB patients from 1985 to 1991 in clusters of states with high, medium, and low cumulative AIDS incidence rates reveals that the group of states with the highest AIDS incidence had the largest increase in cases. In fact, TB cases actually declined in states with low cumulative AIDS rates and remained flat in states with intermediate rates (Fig. 1-4).

A second piece of evidence that the HIV epidemic is contributing to the increase in TB cases is the fact that the largest increases in TB cases have occurred in the age group in which the largest number of AIDS cases have been reported: 25–44 years of age.

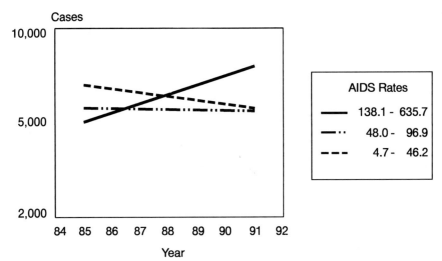

FIGURE 1-4. U.S.-born TB patients in states with high, intermediate, and low cumulative AIDS rates, 1985–1991. (*Courtesy of George Cauthen.*)

Third, there is a high prevalence of TB among AIDS patients. Matching of TB and AIDS registries through 1990 revealed that 4.9 percent of reported AIDS cases were also in the TB registry.

Fourth, CDC HIV seroprevalence surveys *in TB clinics* have shown a high prevalence of HIV coinfection among TB patients. In 1989, 20 TB clinics in 14 cities tested at least 50 sera from confirmed and suspected TB patients. HIV seroprevalence by clinic ranged from 0 to 46 percent, with the highest rates in New York City. The median rate was 3.4 percent. In 1990, 35 TB clinics in 18 cities conducted the surveys. HIV seroprevalence ranged from 0 to 58 percent, with a median of 5.9 percent. Preliminary analysis from the 1991 survey includes 32 clinics in 20 cities. The range of clinic rates was 0 to 61 percent, with a median rate of 10.3 percent.

Trend data were available from 13 cities that tested at least 50 sera per year for 1989, 1990, and 1991. Pooled seroprevalence rates were 13.1 percent in 1989, 17.8 percent in 1990, and 21.4 percent in 1991. Trend analysis from 1989 through 1991 also showed that there were significant increases in HIV coinfection among African-American, Hispanic, and white males with TB or suspected TB (Fig. 1-5*A*). Among females, the trend was significant only for African-Americans (Fig.1-5*B*).

The epidemiologic data from the United States suggest that there is no single cause for the recent increase in reported TB cases. Immigration appears to be a relatively important cause of the increase among Asians, Hispanics, and children. Among African-Americans, young adults, and males, another factor

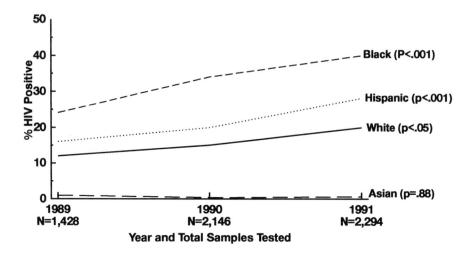

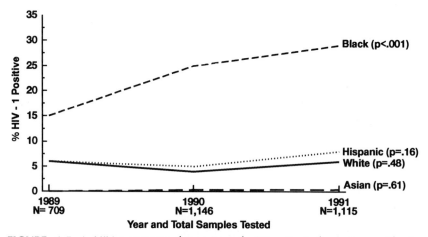

FIGURE 1-5. *A.* HIV-1 seroprevalence in male TB patients from areas with at least 50 samples tested each year, United States, 1989–1991 *B.* HIV-1 seroprevalence in female TB patients from areas with at least 50 samples tested each year, United States, 1989–1991.

(or factors)—most likely HIV infection—plays a relatively more important role.

The effect of recent outbreaks and recent transmission of infection, especially to immunosuppressed persons, on morbidity trends is difficult to ascertain. Certainly these outbreaks appear to be occurring with increasing frequency. Outbreaks have occurred in a variety of settings, including hospitals, correctional facilities, shelters for the homeless, residential care facilities for patients with AIDS, nursing homes, and even crack houses.

The most serious concern has been the outbreaks of multidrug-resistant TB (MDRTB), that is, TB due to organisms resistant to both isoniazid and rifampin (and often other drugs). During 1990–1992, the CDC investigated outbreaks of MDRTB in eight hospitals and a state correctional system. As of October 1992, nearly 300 cases of MDRTB had been identified in these outbreak investigations. Most, but not all, of the cases occurred in persons with HIV infection. Among such patients, mortality has been high (≥72 percent), and the median interval from TB diagnosis to death has been short (4–16 weeks).

The investigations demonstrated transmission of MDRTB to health care workers. In three of the hospitals, positive tuberculin skin test reactions were recorded after outbreak exposure in 13 (33 percent) of 39, 6 (50 percent) of 12, and 24 (22 percent) of 108 health care workers. In most hospitals, there were no baseline skin test data available; thus, in some cases it was not possible to determine the extent of transmission of infection to health care and other workers.

At least 17 health care and correctional workers at these institutions have developed active TB with multidrug-resistant organisms. Ten of these individuals were immunocompromised—nine with HIV infection and 1 with cancer therapy.

Factors contributing to nosocomial outbreaks include the convergence of highly susceptible, immunocompromised patients and patients with TB; the delayed recognition of TB (because the diagnosis was not considered, the patient had nonclassical radiographic findings, and/or there were delays in receiving laboratory results); the delayed recognition of drug resistance; and the delayed initiation of effective anti-TB treatment. Other factors contributing to nosocomial transmission include delayed initiation of isolation, inadequate ventilation for acid fast bacilli (AFB) isolation, lapses in maintaining AFB isolation, inadequate duration of AFB isolation, and inadequate precautions during cough-inducing procedures.

TB in Other Industrialized Countries

Data on TB morbidity in other industrialized countries were provided by the WHO (M. Raviglione, personal communication).

Seven of 14 western European countries (Austria, Denmark, Ireland, Italy, the Netherlands, Norway, and Switzerland) have also recently experienced increases in reported cases. The major factor responsible for most of these increases appears to be immigration from higher-prevalence countries. However, in Italy, 11.4 percent of AIDS cases reported during the biennium 1988–1989 had TB.

Several other industrialized countries have experienced a stagnation or increase in morbidity. In Australia, case rates slightly increased from 5.56 per 100,000 in 1986 to 5.95 per 100,000 in 1990. Immigrants (mainly from southeast Asia) constituted 66 percent of all cases in 1991. Only 2.5 percent of patients in New South Wales were HIV seropositive in 1991, and only 0.4 percent of all AIDS patients reported had TB. In New Zealand, reported cases have recently leveled off after reaching a nadir in 1988 with 295 cases reported. In 1991 there were 304 cases. In Canada, a plateau in case rates has been observed over the past 6 years. The foreign-born constituted 48 percent of all cases in 1989. In Israel, TB notifications, after having been stable (average rate, 5.6 in the 1980s), have recently increased to 505 in 1991 (rate, 10.2). Ethiopian immigrants constituted 50 percent of all cases in 1985 and 55 percent of all cases in 1991, following two waves of migration (Operation Moses and Operation Shalom).

In Japan, the downward trend in TB morbidity continued at an average rate of 3 percent per year between 1980 and 1991. However, this decline is smaller than that of the period 1970–1980 (6.5 percent per year).

DRUG RESISTANCE

Information on resistance to anti-TB drugs in developing countries was provided by the WHO (B. Vareldzis, personal communication). Data were taken from national TB control programs in countries that had resistance data from several points in time, including Tanzania, Korea, Chile, and Algeria. The overall trend is stable to slightly decreasing when one looks at initial resistance to one or more drugs. (Initial drug resistance is drug resistance in a patient who has no history of having received antituberculosis therapy.) However, of concern is the suggestion of an increase in initial rifampin resistance and multidrug resistance in some countries. The data suggest that initial rifampin resistance is a new phenomenon that has become significant since 1985. However, the data are extremely limited at this time, and only two countries have reported these trends (Thailand and Tanzania). Thus, overall initial drug resistance is decreasing due in large part to the decrease in isoniazid resistance, while resistance to rifampin may be increasing.

As for acquired resistance, which is indicative of past treatment failure, the available information is also limited. On the whole, the data suggest that, with three major exceptions, acquired resistance has decreased over the last 30 years. Developing countries have experienced decreases in acquired resistance to one or more drugs from about 50 percent to about 25 percent during the 1980s. The notable exceptions are in India and Argentina, which have reported increases in acquired rifampin resistance. Argentina has also reported increases in MDRTB.

In the United States, a survey of drug resistance was conducted among all TB cases reported from January through March 1991.[33] Provisional analyses revealed that drug susceptibility results were available for 3352 (82.7 percent) of 4051 culture-positive cases. The overall rate of resistance to one or more drugs was 13.9 percent. Among new cases, 13.0 percent were reported as being resistant to at least one drug, and 3.2 percent were resistant to both isoniazid and rifampin. Among recurrent cases, 26.2 percent were reported as being resistant to at least one drug, and 6.8 percent were resistant to both isoniazid and rifampin.

There is a need for better *systematic* surveillance of drug resistance in the world.

CONCLUSION

Tuberculosis is the leading cause of death in the world today from any single infectious agent. It is estimated to cause about 7 percent of all deaths and about 26 percent of all preventable deaths in the world; most of these deaths occur among young adults. Thus, the toll that TB exacts in both economic and human terms is enormous. The emergence of the HIV epidemic during the past decade has not only greatly exacerbated the TB problem but has raised questions about the adequacy of current methods of diagnosis, treatment, and prevention. In addition, the increasing occurrence of multidrug-resistant TB, a highly lethal disease, especially among HIV-infected persons, has unmasked the deficiencies of current control methods and their application. The global TB problem is clearly worsening and is not being adequately addressed. Additional resources, along with a long-term commitment, will be indispensable to successfully controlling TB worldwide.

REFERENCES

1. Kochi A: The global tuberculosis situation and the new control strategy of the World Health Organization. *Tubercle* 72:1, 1991.
2. Styblo K, Rouillon A: Estimated global incidence of smear-positive pulmonary tuberculosis: unreliability of officially reported figures on tuberculosis. *Bull Int Union Tuberc Lung Dis* 56:3, 1981.
3. Murray CJL, Styblo K, Rouillon A: Tuberculosis in developing countries: burden, intervention and cost. *Bull Int Union Tuberc Lung Dis* 65:6, 1990.

4. *Childhood Tuberculosis and BCG Vaccine.* EPI update supplement. Geneva, World Health Organization, 1989.
5. Narain JP, Raviglione MC, Kochi A: HIV-associated tuberculosis in developing countries: epidemiology and strategies for prevention. *Tubercle Lung Dis* 73:311, 1992.
6. Selwyn PA, Hartel D, Lewis IA: A prospective study of the risk of tuberculosis among intravenous drug abusers with human immunodeficiency virus infection. *N Engl J Med* 320:545, 1989.
7. Geneva, World Health Organization: *Global Programme on AIDS. Current and Future Dimensions of the HIV/AIDS Pandemic: A Capsule Summary.* January 1992. WHO/GPA/RES/SF/92.1.
8. Braun MM, Badi N, Ryder RW, et al.: A retrospective cohort study of the risk of tuberculosis among women of childbearing age with HIV infection in Zaire. *Am Rev Respir Dis* 143:501, 1991.
9. Kagame A, Batungwanayo J, Allen S, et al.: Prospective study of tuberculosis risk in a cohort of HIV seropositive women in Kigali, Rwanda. VII International Conference on AIDS, Florence, Italy, 16–21 June 1991. *Abstr Th C* 94:80.
10. Kaseka N, Batter W, Eleka M, et al.: Incidence of extramarital sex, STDs, HIV-1 infection and tuberculosis (TB) in 10,325 individuals followed for 2 years in Kinshasa, Zaire. VII International Conference on AIDS, Florence, Italy, 16–21 June 1991. *Abstr W C* 101:49.
11. Mann J, Snider DE, Francis H, et al.: Association between HTLV-III/LAV infection and tuberculosis in Zaire. *JAMA* 256:346, 1986.
12. Cathebras P, Vohito JA, Yete ML, et al.: Tuberculose et infection par le virus de l'immunodeficience humaine en Republique Centrafricaine. *Med Trop* 48:401, 1988.
13. Standaert B, Niragira F, Kadende P, Piot P: The association of tuberculosis and HIV infection in Burundi. *AIDS Res Hum Retroviruses* 5:247, 1989.
14. Lesbordes JL, Baquillon G, Georges MC, et al.: La tuberculose au cours de l'infection par le virus de l'immunodeficience humaine (VIH) a Bangui (Republique Centrafricaine). *Med Trop* 48:21, 1988.
15. Colebunders RL, Ryder RW, Nzilambi N, et al.: HIV infection in patients with tuberculosis in Kinshasa, Zaire. *Am Rev Respir Dis* 139:1082, 1989.
16. Elliot AM, Luo N, Tembo G, et al.: Impact of HIV on tuberculosis in Zambia: a cross sectional study. *Br Med J* 301:412, 1990.
17. Kelly P, Burnham G, Radford C: HIV seropositivity and tuberculosis in a rural Malawi hospital. *Trans R Soc Trop Med Hyg* 84:725, 1990.
18. Kool HEJ, Bloemkolk D, Reeve PA, Danner SA: HIV seropositivity and tuberculosis in a large general hospital in Malawi. *Trop Geogr Med* 42:128, 1991.
19. Eriki PP, Okwera A, Aisu T, et al.: The influence of human immunodeficiency virus infection on tuberculosis in Kampalam, Uganda. *Am Rev Respir Dis* 143:185, 1991.
20. Long R, Scalcini M, Manfreda J, et al.: Impact of human immunodeficiency virus type 1 on tuberculosis in rural Haiti. *Am Rev Respir Dis* 143:69, 1991.
21. Malkin JE, Yameogo M, Prazuck T, et al.: HIV infection in a cohort of tuberculosis patients in Burkina Faso: final results. VII International Conference on AIDS, Florence, Italy, 16–21 June 1991. *Abstr M C* 3199:347.
22. Gnaore E, Yesso G, Sidibe K, et al.: Comparison of HIV-1 and HIV-2 infections in tuberculosis patients in Abidjan, Coté d'Ivoire. VII International Conference on AIDS, Florence, Italy, 16–21 June 1991. *Abstr M B* 2449:294.
23. Clermont HC, Chaisson RE, Davis HA, et al.: HIV-1 infection in adult tuberculosis patients in Cite Soleil, Haiti. VI International Conference on AIDS, San Francisco, California, 20–24 June 1990. *Abstr Th B* 490:244.
24. Mahari M, Legg W, Houston H, et al.: Association of tuberculosis and HIV infection in

Zimbabwe. VI International Conference on AIDS, San Francisco, California, 20–24 June 1990. *Abstr Th B* 494:245.

25. De Cock KM, Gnaore E, Adjorlolo G, et al.: Risk of tuberculosis in patients with HIV-II infections in Abidjan, Ivory Coast. *Br Med J* 302:496, 1991.

26. Nunn P, Wasunna K, Galtha S, et al.: Cohort study of HIV among tuberculosis patients in Nairobi, Kenya: baseline features. VI International Conference on AIDS, San Francisco, California, 20–24 June 1990. *Abstr Th B* 486:243.

27. Perriens J, Colebunders RL, Karahunga C, et al.: Increased mortality and tuberculosis treatment failure rate among human immunodeficiency virus (HIV)-seropositive compared to HIV-seronegative patients with pulmonary tuberculosis treated with "standard" chemotherapy in Kinshasa, Zaire. *Am Rev Respir Dis* 144:750, 1991.

28. Styblo K: Recent advances in epidemiological research in tuberculosis. *Adv Tuberc Res* 20:1, 1980.

29. Chaisson RE, Schecter GF, Theurer CP, et al.: Tuberculosis in patients with the acquired immunodeficiency syndrome. *Am Rev Respir Dis* 136:570, 1987.

30. Nunn P, Kibuga D, Elliott A, Gathua S: Impact of human immunodeficiency virus on transmission and severity of tuberculosis. *Trans R Soc Trop Med Hyg* 84(suppl 1):9, 1990.

31. Schulzer M, Fitzgerald JM, Enarson DA, Grzybowski S: An estimate of the future size of the tuberculosis problem in sub-Saharan Africa resulting from HIV infection. *Tubercle Lung Dis* 73:52, 1992.

32. Selwyn PA, Sckell BM, Alcabes P, Friedland GH, Klein RS, Schoenbaum EE: High risk of active tuberculosis in HIV-infected drug users with cutaneous anergy. *JAMA* 268:504, 1992.

33. Dooley SW, Simone PM: Drug resistant tuberculosis in the United States, in Davies P (ed), *Tuberculosis*. London, Chapman and Hall, in press.

CHAPTER 2

Pathogenesis and Immunology

JERROLD J. ELLNER

After decades of relative lack of interest, the current tools of molecular genetics and cellular immunology are being applied at a headlong pace to the study of the pathogenesis of tuberculosis (TB) and the basis for the protective immune response. This renaissance in research on TB will provide a tremendous boost to basic, fundamental understanding of the disease process. It is certain that new approaches to prevention, diagnosis, and treatment of TB will spring from this arena.

The pathogenesis of TB has been reviewed recently[1] and is only summarized here. Initial infection with the tuberculous bacilli occurs by the airborne route. Since *Mycobacterium tuberculosis* contains no enzymes that allow it to penetrate mucus, the organisms must be in a particle small enough (<5 μm) to penetrate to the alveolar zone, where no mucus is present. While for humans the minimal infecting dose of *M. tuberculosis* is unknown, in rabbits and guinea pigs one to three live organisms may be sufficient.[2,3] These initial organisms will be ingested by alveolar macrophages. Since resident alveolar macrophages and nonactivated, recently arrived monocytes cannot kill intracellular *M. tuberculosis*, the organisms replicate within macrophages and rapidly increase in number. It is during this period, before the development of specific immunity, that the organisms will appear in draining lymph nodes. Subsequently, a bacteremia or hematogenous dissemination will occur.

After several weeks of uninhibited growth of *M. tuberculosis*, an immune response develops (see below) that results in a cessation of bacillary growth. At the site of initial infection (primary infection), the organisms may be completely eliminated. However, at the sites of bacillary spread through hematogenous dissemination, the organisms may persist but with arrested growth. Months to years later, for reasons that are not entirely known, the organism may begin to grow more rapidly, resulting in the development of symptomatic tuberculosis. While these lesions may be anywhere, they are most frequently in the apices of the lungs, the bones, the lymph nodes, the meninges, and the kidneys. It is believed that high tissue tensions of oxygen may be an important factor in the localization and continued growth of *M. tuberculosis* in these locations.

Several themes emerge from current knowledge and are discussed in some detail:

1. Virulence. The basis for virulence is poorly understood, and existing models are ultimately inadequate to the task of clarifying molecular mechanisms.
2. Protective immunity. In experimental models, protective immunity and delayed-type hypersensitivity (DTH) are mediated by separate lymphocyte populations, with CD4 cells expressing a predominant role in both.
3. Targets of the human immune response. The human immune response displays enormous heterogeneity, complicating identification of key protective antigens. The best may be yet to come in terms of characterizing dominant antigens.
4. Effector function of mononuclear phagocytes. New modalities of adjunctive therapy may emerge from the recognition that cytokines have bidirectional effects on the killing of mycobacteria.
5. Regulation of the immune response in TB. Active TB is associated with hyporesponsiveness to mycobacterial antigens. Specific immunosuppressive pathways have only been partially elucidated. Genetic and acquired factors (including infection with human immunodeficiency virus type 1, or HIV-1) further modulate immune reactivity.

VIRULENCE FACTORS

Virulence factors may be defined in three ways. They may be directly toxic to host cells, thwart effector mechanisms that normally control intracellular replication, or modulate the balance between growth enhancing and growth inhibitory cytokines. Progress in the identification of virulence factors has been somewhat retarded by the absence of good in vitro models. Three constituents of the outer layers of the complex cell walls of *M. tuberculosis*— cord factor, sulfolipids, and mycosides—have been considered virulence factors, although the supportive evidence is less than clearcut. Cord factor, now known to be trehalose dimycolate, has toxic activities,[4] but its role as a virulence factor is questionable, given its occurrence in nonpathogenic mycobacteria.[5] Sulfolipids are found in virulent strains of *M. tuberculosis* and enhance the toxicity of cord factor.[5] Species-specific surface mycosides (glycolipids and glycopeptidolipids) constitute an electron-transparent zone around intracellular organisms, conferring protection against the hostile intracellular environment.

Lipoarabinomannan (LAM) is a major cell wall polysaccharide constituent that may act as a virulence factor by a number of documented interactions with the host immune system. LAM from virulent *M. tuberculosis* differs from LAM from nonpathogenic mycobacteria in its enhanced capacity to stimulate production of tumor necrosis factor alpha (TNFα) by mononuclear phagocytes.[6] LAM also inhibits the production of interferon-gamma (IFNγ) and serves as a scavenger for oxygen free radicals,[7] among its other properties. The relevance of the interactions of LAM with the immune system is not precisely clear, but the widespread distribution of LAM among nonpathogenic mycobacteria makes it a poor candidate as a virulence factor.

In vitro models of bacterial invasion of epithelial cells have been used to great advantage by Falkow and others to define virulence factors of enteric bacilli. Initial observations have been made with mycobacteria in similar systems. For example, attachment to (and invasion of) a bladder transitional cell carcinoma cell line by bacille Calmette-Guérin (BCG) required binding by a 55 kilodalton mycobacterial protein to fibronectin on the carcinoma cells.[8]

PATHOGENESIS OF TB: DTH VERSUS PROTECTIVE IMMUNITY

DTH and protective immunity may be separable immunologic events responsible for a variety of observations in humans and experimental animals. The *Koch phenomenon* refers to the difference in response to challenge with *M. tuberculosis* of the immune as compared to the naive host. Primary infection following subcutaneous inoculation of guinea pigs produces a nonhealing ulcer; a second injection induces an indurated lesion that ulcerates and heals rapidly and completely. The Koch phenomenon may be related to a protective immune response. However, the response of the sensitized host to mycobacteria and their products is clearly a two-edged sword. In contrast to the inoculation with organisms, the intravenous injection of tuberculin into an infected animal produces *tuberculin shock*, and similar injections into TB patients (by Koch) were followed by exacerbation of the pulmonary disease.

A great deal of effort has been devoted to dissecting apart DTH and protective immunity. Dannenberg has proposed that both DTH and cell-mediated immunity (CMI) inhibit the intracellular growth of tubercle bacilli.[9] In CMI, monocytes first are recruited to the tubercle (i.e., granuloma) by cytokines produced by sensitized T cells and then are activated by other cytokines to destroy intracellular organisms. The monocytes differentiate into epitheliod cells in this process. DTH is a mechanism whereby bacilli-laden, nonactivated macrophages are killed. This eliminates a favorable environment for bacillary growth but is accomplished by the process of caseation necrosis and at the cost of host tissue. If the caseous focus liquefies, the milieu then becomes supportive of extracellular growth of *M. tuberculosis*. The organism proliferates to extraordinary numbers (10^{10}/ml) in cavitary lung disease and results in enhanced infectivity. Dannenberg's definitions are based in large measure on bacillary growth curves and histopathology of TB in inbred resistant and susceptible rabbits developed by Lurie.

A number of other experimental infection models support the separability of DTH and protective immunity as they can be elicited by various immunizations and are transferable by different subpopulations of T cells (see below). In these studies, in contrast to those of Dannenberg, DTH usually is defined by skin test reactivity and protective immunity by resistance to a challenge with viable *M. tuberculosis*. Similarly, in vitro studies indicate that sensitized T cells not only secrete macrophage-activating factors (MAFs), but also destroy infected macrophages. How these dual effector mechanisms are regulated or what their relative importance is in the host-parasite balance is not yet clear. The relationship of cytolysis to DTH also remains largely unexplored. Nonetheless, current speculation is consistent with the ideas of Dannenberg, namely, that killing of infected macrophages occurs at higher bacillary burdens and allows monocytes newly recruited to the fray to ingest the organisms and kill them.

PROTECTIVE IMMUNITY

Experimental Studies

After immunization of mice with BCG or Erdman strain of *M. tuberculosis*, splenic lymphocytes adoptively transfer protective immunity to naive mice against an aerogenic challenge with virulent *M. tuberculosis*.[10] The transfer of protective immunity and DTH is dissociable, each being mediated by different populations of splenic lymphocytes.[11] CD4+ lymphocytes can be divided functionally into protective T cells, which appear early, produce large quantities of INFγ, and are associated temporally with the onset of bacterial elimination, and cytolytic T cells, which peak later.[12] The CD8+ cells also produce IFNγ[12] and appear to play a role, possibly minor, in protective immunity.[13]

Further, immunization with live organisms generates splenic T cells capable of adoptively transferring protective immunity, whereas killed vaccines induce splenic T cells that transfer nonspecific resistance and DTH.[14] This finding implicates antigens requiring metabolic activity of the organism, such as secretory products, as key targets of the protective response. Recent studies, in fact, indicate that midlogarithmic growth phase culture filtrates (CF) of

M. tuberculosis, when used as an immunogen, protect guinea pigs against aerosol challenge with virulent organism.[15] The adoptive transfer of T lymphocytes from mice infected with *M. tuberculosis* to T-cell deficient recipients also confers resistance against other mycobacteria.[16] This suggests that epitopes identified by these T cells may be shared rather than unique to virulent *M. tuberculosis*.

Although protective immunity and DTH may be dissociable experimentally, tuberculin-positive humans are relatively resistant to exogenous reinfection.[17] Moreover, the remarkably increased risk (117-fold) of progressive primary TB or reactivation TB in HIV-infected persons highlights the vital contribution of CD4+ cells to protection.

T-Cell Subpopulations

Two populations of CD4+ cells play a role in resistance to intracellular infections in murine models. Th1 cells produce interleukin 2 (IL-2) and IFNγ and mediate resistance against *Leishmania*, *Candida*, and *Schistosoma* species; whereas Th2 cells produce IL-4 and mediate resistance to *Trichinella* and *Trichuris*. Lymphocytes from mice vaccinated with mycobacteria and showing resistance to *Mycobacterium bovis* express IL-2 and IFNγ but not IL-4; while mice lacking resistance produced IL-4 only.[18] In addition, CD4+ T-cell clones reactive with *M. tuberculosis* and *Mycobacterium leprae* produce mainly IFNγ.

In humans, there is a less-restricted cytokine profile of CD4+ T-cell clones obtained by stimulation of T lymphocytes from healthy tuberculin-positive donors with soluble mycobacterial antigens.[19] In addition to production of cytokines, CD4+ T-cell lines and clones are cytotoxic for *M. tuberculosis*-infected or antigen-pulsed monocytes (MNs). Another T-cell subpopulation ($\gamma\delta$ cells) may play a role in protective immunity. $\gamma\delta$ T cells appeared to be overrepresented at the site of mycobacterial infection.[21] Accumulation of $\gamma\delta$ T cells is more pronounced during primary infection than in an anamnestic response. In addition, stimulation with live mycobacteria[20] and a low–molecular weight product derived from them leads to selective induction of $\gamma\delta$ T cells.

Mycobacterial Targets of T-Cell Responses: Molecularly Characterized Antigens

Galvanized by advances in molecular genetics and spurred on by public health concerns, progress in the molecular characterization of potentially protective antigens of *M. tuberculosis* has moved at an unprecedented pace during the last 5 years. A recent review compiles the extensive literature now available concerning the immunologic properties of mycobacterial antigens.[22] The most widely studied mycobacterial products are of molecular weights 12, 14, 19, 38, 65, and 71 kilodaltons[23] and initially were identified using murine monoclonal antibodies. These mycobacterial products elicit some T-cell responses but in general appear to be targets of the humoral, rather than cellular, immune response and are less relevant in humans than in mice.[24] The primary structure of several of these proteins is similar to that of heat shock proteins (HSPs) found not only in other mycobacteria but also in other prokaryotic and in eukaryotic cells.[25]

Although T lymphocytes from healthy individuals responded to purified recombinant 12, 19, 65, and 71 kilodalton antigens, such reactivity is in fact infrequent.[24] The 10 kilodalton antigen of *M. leprae* is homologous to GroES HSP, has 90 percent homology to the BCG-a protein, and appears to be an important T-cell stimulus.[26] The homologous antigen of *M. tuberculosis* is identical to the BCG-a antigen and immunoreactive in terms of induction of blastogenesis and IFNγ expression by peripheral blood mononuclear cells (PBMC) and pleural fluid mononuclear cells.[27] The 14 kilodalton antigen is an HSP that elicits DTH and in vitro lymphocyte blastogenesis in immunized mice and guinea pigs.[28] An additional protein of potential importance in the human immune response is MTP40, a 14 kilodalton protein. Humoral and cellular responses were noted to synthetic peptides derived from this protein.[29] Cloning of the gene for the MTP40 protein suggests that it may be restricted to *M. tuberculosis*.[30]

Secreted antigens of *M. tuberculosis* are of particular interest as protective antigens in view of the induction of protective immunity by live organisms[14] and by culture filtrates (CFs).[15] The "85 complex" of *M. tuberculosis* is a group of three major extracellular antigens of *M. tuberculosis* encoded by separate genes and secreted by actively proliferating cultures[25]; there also is convincing evidence for cell wall localization of the "85 complex."[32] Two of these antigens bind fibronectin,[33] and all three are major secretory products of growing bacteria. Antigens 85A and 85B are of molecular weights 30–32 kilodaltons but differ in electrophoretic mobility; together they constitute 60 percent of total protein in CF generated with minimal cell lysis.[34] Antigen 6 and the α-antigen, the gene for which was cloned by Matsuo et al.,[35] appear to be identical[36] and represent the 85B antigen. The α-antigen contains specific as well as cross-reactive determinants,[37] stimulates blastogenesis and IFNγ production by T cells from healthy donors, and elicits DTH in sensitized guinea pigs.[34] A major recent finding by our group[24] and by Sada et al. (personal communication) is that patients with pulmonary TB fail to respond to the α-antigen.

The 38 kilodalton antigen is a lipoprotein secreted into CF[38]; it elicits

DTH in sensitized guinea pigs[39] and blastogenic reactions in approximately 60 percent of TB patients and BCG vaccinees.[40] The 46 kilodalton dimeric protein is the most abundant protein in supernatants from 5 day cultures of some BCG strains, is identical to MPB70,[37] and elicits DTH and lymphoproliferative responses in guinea pigs sensitized with high-producer BCG strains.[41]

Although this litany is impressive in terms of the number of characterized antigens with some immunologic activity, no single antigen induces responses of the same magnitude as those elicited by crude products such as tuberculin purified protein derivative (PPD).

Mycobacterial Targets of the T-Cell Response: Fractionation of Crude Microbial Products and Other Approaches

A complementary approach to the study of discrete purified products is assessment of the relative reactivity of T cells to constituents of mycobacterial lysates and filtrates fractionated by physicochemical techniques. Collins et al. demonstrated that midlogarithmic-phase CF of *M. tuberculosis* contained a major protein band at 68 kilodaltons and fainter bands in the 24–38 kilodalton range; these CF elicit DTH in infected mice and in vitro responses in T cells from tuberculin-positive donors.[42] Barnes et al. assessed antigenic reactivity by T-cell western blotting of sonicates of *M. tuberculosis*.[43] T-cell lines produced by stimulation of PBMC with purified protein-peptidoglycan complex recognized antigens of molecular weights 10, 19, 23, 28, 30, 40–50, and 65 kilodaltons. We found that T cells from tuberculin-positive, healthy donors showed peaks of reactivity to fractions of CF of *M. tuberculosis* H37Rv of 30, 37, 44, 57, 64, 71, and 88 kilodaltons (Fig. 2-1).[24] Extensive heterogeneity in terms of the targets of human T cells also was demonstrated by Schoel et al., who examined responses to 400 fractions prepared by two-dimensional gel electrophoresis of lysates of *M. tuberculosis*.[44]

In an attempt to identify mycobacterial antigens expressed at sites of infection, we have produced human monoclonal antibodies by Epstein-Barr virus transformation of pleural fluid cells and used them to probe the *M. tuberculosis* library in λgt11. This has led to cloning, sequencing, and expression of an antigen designated P1 (unpublished), which may be the target of a local, potentially protective immune response.

Another novel strategy seeks to characterize peptides of *M. tuberculosis* that may possess adjuvanticity or a role in immunopathogenesis by virtue of direct stimulation of mononuclear phagocytes.[45] Currently, a 58 kilodalton monocyte (MN)-stimulatory protein has been isolated, a monoclonal antibody produced that is reactive with it, and N-terminal sequencing performed.[46]

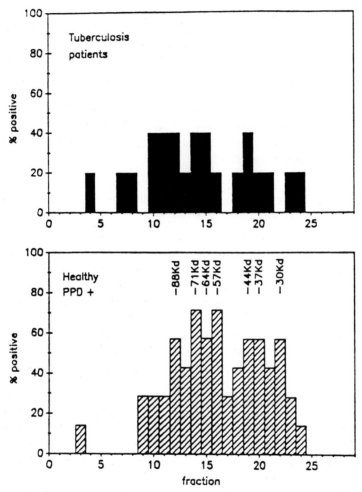

FIGURE 2-1. T-cell western blot reactivity for TB patients ($n = 5$) and PPD-positive subjects ($n = 7$) to *M. tuberculosis* culture filtrate. Vertical bars represent the percentage of subjects with positive responses (stimulation > 2 and Δcpm > 3,000) for each fraction tested. Note the lack of response of TB patients to the 30 kD fraction. (Reproduced with permission from reference 55.)

Mononuclear Phagocyte Effector Function against *M. tuberculosis*

As a facultative intracellular pathogen, *M. tuberculosis* replicates within mononuclear phagocytes. IFNγ, although the traditional macrophage activating factor (MAF) for *Toxoplasma gondii*, *Leishmania*, and other model intracellular organisms, appears to have divergent effects on murine macrophages and human MN.[47] IFNγ enhances intracellular killing of *M. tuberculosis* by mouse bone marrow – derived macrophages, possibly through increased production of reactive nitrogen intermediates.[48] Moreover, IFNγ was produced by murine T cells that conferred protective immunity against *M. tuberculosis* in adoptive transfer models.[49] Various investigators have shown that IFNγ enhances or suppresses the intracellular growth of *M. tuberculosis* in human MN.[47] The data are complicated because cytokines may induce other cytokines in addition to modulating cytokine surface receptors. Cytokine-cytokine interactions may be either antagonistic or synergistic.[50]

Given the complex interaction of cytokines in regulating mononuclear phagocyte effector function against mycobacteria, it is of substantial interest that ingestion of mycobacteria induces expression of macrophage-activating and -deactivating cytokines.[51] Bermudez has demonstrated that ingestion of *Mycobacterium avium* induces expression of transforming growth factor β (TGFβ) and that neutralizing antibody to TGFβ restores macrophage activating factor (MAF) activity of IFNγ for *M. avium.*[52] Recently, we have shown that TNFα stimulates monocyte activation to limit the intracellular growth of *M. tuberculosis*, whereas TGFβ deactivates monocytes (unpublished).

Regulation of T-Cell Responses in TB

From 17 – 25 percent of patients with newly diagnosed pulmonary TB are unresponsive to tuberculin skin tests.[53] In vitro PPD-induced blastogenesis is decreased in 40 to 60 percent of these patients, including almost all skin test – negative and some skin test – positive individuals.[54,55] Hyporesponsiveness seems to be relatively selective for mycobacterial antigens, since responses to mitogens and to other antigens remain intact.[54] Besides blastogenesis, PPD-stimulated production of IL-2 and expression of IL-2 receptors are decreased.[55] Depressed in vitro responses to PPD also have been observed in developing countries with a background of immunization with BCG and appear to be a relatively constant finding in TB. Understanding the basis for the systemic hyporesponsiveness to PPD is of interest in its own right, since it may shed light on the pathogenesis and pathophysiology of TB.

Researchers at Case Western Reserve University have elucidated the role of mononuclear phagocytes in suppressing the T-cell response to PPD in active TB. MNs expanded and primed during the course of TB are stimulated directly by mycobacterial peptides to increased expression of cytokines such as IL-1α, TNFα,[56] and IL-1β and of molecules with potential inhibitory activity, that is, receptors for IL-2,[57] and TGFβ.[58] Zabel et al. have demonstrated that patients with TB and systemic symptoms have elevated levels of serum TNFα and IL-6;[59] it is interesting to note that treatment with the

TNFα inhibitor pentoxifylline lowered serum TNFα, induced well-being, and stopped the weight loss.

During TB, CD16+ lymphocytes are increased,[60] CD4+ and CD8+ cells remain normal,[61] and $\gamma\delta$T cells remain normal in number[62] but are hyporesponsive to mycobacterial antigens.[63] CD16+ cells show suppressive activity,[60] whereas CD4+, CD8+,[61] and $\gamma\delta$T cells[62] do not.

The T-cell response to certain mycobacterial products is selectively depressed during the course of tuberculosis. Falla et al. demonstrated that, despite comparable responses to sonic extracts of H37Rv, 84 percent of healthy household contacts and only 52 percent of treated and 48 percent of untreated TB patients respond to peptides of the MTP40 (14 kilodalton) antigen.[64] PBMC from patients with TB also show hyporesponsiveness to an A60 complex of *M. bovis* in terms of blastogenesis and production of IFNγ and concurrent increased production of TNFα;[65] during treatment, 60 percent of patients become responsive to A60. Hyporesponsiveness of patients with TB to the α-antigen has been described above.

Studies in twins have clearly indicated that genetic factors influence the occurrence of TB and may do so by modifying the immune response.[66] Although a number of associations have been reported between class I and class II loci and TB, the loci in question have varied from population to population.[67] More promising was the demonstration of the *Bcg* gene on chromosome 1 in the mouse, which may regulate the priming of macrophages for increased killing of a variety of intracellular organisms, including BCG. The linkage group containing the *Bcg* gene shows structural homology to a conserved region on human chromosome 2.

Two studies have demonstrated a correlation between HLA phenotype and patterns of immune response. HLA-DR2 was associated both with the occurrence of TB in an Indonesian population as well as high titers of antibody to two epitopes of the 38 kilodalton antigen of *M. tuberculosis*.[68] Cox et al. described an association between the haplotype HLA-B14-DR1 and low in vitro lymphocyte blastogenic responses to PPD.[69] This is particularly notable, since the same haplotype is associated with the gene for nonclassic steroid 21-hydroxylase deficiency[70]; the gene for this abnormality maps within the MHC, and the trait is associated with altered expression of HLA-DR1, resulting in failure to activate alloreactive T-cell clones or to provide accessory function for class II major histocompatibility complex (MHC)-restricted T-cell clones. A closer look at genetic factors that may be expressed as dysregulation of the T-cell response to *M. tuberculosis* appears to be warranted.

Acquired factors have tremendous impact on the occurrence of TB. The greatest known risk factor is infection with HIV. Most patients in the United States develop TB before an AIDS-defining complication, at a time that tuberculin reactivity is likely to be retained.[71] The basis for reactivation at this early point is uncertain but indicates the importance of an intact CD4 population in maintaining tuberculous foci as latent.

Of patients with active TB in Uganda, over 80 percent are tuberculin skin test–positive.[72] The skin test–positive patients show augmented PPD-stimulated lymphocyte blastogenesis as well as production of IL-2 and TNFα (Fig. 2-2).[73] These data are of some interest because of the pivotal role of TNFα in mycobacterial immunity as well as expression of HIV. TNFα is an MAF for mycobacteria and a key element in granuloma formation.[74] TNFα, however, can activate HIV replication through NFκB-mediated effects on the viral long terminal repeat (LTR).[75] These findings raise the spectre that TB may accelerate the course of HIV disease. There is some evidence to support

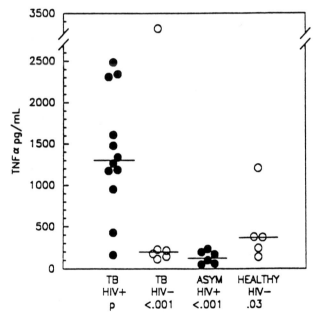

FIGURE 2-2. *M. tuberculosis* purified protein derivative (PPD)-induced production of tumor necrosis factor α factor (TNFα) in HIV-1-seropositive patients with TB and asymptomatic tuberculin positive (ASYM) controls. TNFα was measured by EIA; median values are indicated by horizontal lines. Significance was determined by one-tailed nonparametric test using medians. Simultaneous 95% confidence intervals (consecutive test for multiple comparisons) of means of HIV-1-seropositive TB and asymptomatic HIV-1-seropositive subjects did not overlap. (Reproduced with permission from reference 73.)

this hypothesis. Recent data from the United States indicate that HIV-infected patients with TB have a shortened length of survival and greater subsequent frequency of other opportunistic infections than do CD4-matched HIV-infected control patients.[76] In the study in Uganda, patients with HIV and TB had higher levels of $\beta2$-microglobulin, a surrogate marker of HIV disease activity, than did HIV alone or TB alone or healthy control subjects.[73] Recent data also indicate that monocytes from patients with TB show increased infectability with HIV[77] (Fig. 2-3) and that *M. tuberculosis* and its soluble products activate expression of HIV from latently infected U1 cells.[78]

The hypothesis that TB accelerates the natural history of HIV disease is under prospective study in Uganda. If that hypothesis is confirmed, HIV and TB would have bidirectional amplifying effects leading to a vicious cycle of immunosuppression, TB, and other complications of AIDS. This scenario would provide further impetus to the application of preventive therapy, particularly in developing countries in which dual infection is common.

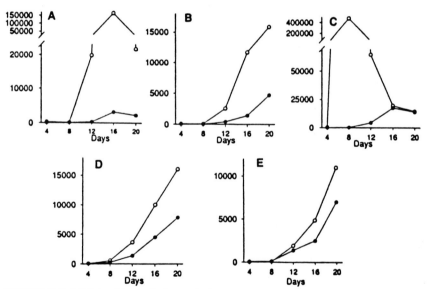

FIGURE 2-3. HIV-1 p24 levels (in pg/ml) in supernatants of monocytes from patients with TB and healthy control subjects. Monocytes from each patient-control pair were infected with HIV-1 JR-FL and culture by ELISA. Each panel demonstrates results for one patient-control pair. Patient (o); control (•). (Reproduced with permission from reference 77.)

REFERENCES

1. Nardell EA: Pathogenesis of tuberculosis, in Reichman LB, Hershfield ES (eds), *Tuberculosis: A Comprehensive International Approach*, Lung Biology in Health and Disease, vol 66. New York, Dekker, 1993, pp 103.

2. Ratcliffe HL: Tuberculosis induced by droplet nuclei infection: pulmonary tuberculosis of predetermined initial intensity in mammals. *Am J Hyg* 55:36, 1952.

3. Lurie MB, Heppleston SA, Swartz IB: An evaluation of the method of quantitative airborne infection and its use in the study of the pathogenesis of tuberculosis. *Am Rev Tuberc* 61:765, 1950.

4. Artman M, Bekierkunst A, Goldenberg I: Tissue metabolism in infection: biochemical changes in mice treated with cord factor. *Arch Biochem Biophys* 105:80, 1964.

5. Goren MB, Brennan PJ: Mycobacterial lipids: chemistry and biologic activity, in Youmans GP (ed), *Tuberculosis*. Philadelphia, Saunders, 1979, pp 63.

6. Roach TIA, Barton CM, Chatterjee D, Blackwell JM: Macrophage activation: lipoarabinomannan from avirulent and virulent strains of *Mycobacterium tuberculosis* differentially induces the early genes c-fos, KC, JE and tumor necrosis factor alpha. *J Immunol* 150:1886, 1993.

7. Chan J, Fan X, Hunter SW, Brennan PJ, Bloom BR: Lipoarabinomannan: a possible virulence factor involved in persistence of *Mycobacteriurm tuberculosis* within macrophages. *Infect Immun* 59:1755, 1991.

8. Kuroda K, Brown EJ, TeIIe WB, Russell DG, Ratliff TL: Characterization of the internalization of bacillus Calmette-Guerin by human bladder tumor cells. *J Clin Invest* 91:69, 1993.

9. Dannenberg AM Jr: Delayed-type hypersensitivity and cell-mediated immunity in the pathogenesis of tuberculosis. *Immun Today* 12:228, 1991.

10. Orme IM, Collins FM: Adoptive protection of the *M. tuberculosis*-infected lung: dissociation between cells that passively transfer protective immunity and those that transfer delayed-type hypersensitivity to tuberculin. *Cell Immunol* 84:113, 1984.

11. Orme IM: The kinetics of emergence and loss of mediator T lymphocytes acquired in response to infection with *M. tuberculosis*. *J Immunol* 138:293, 1987.

12. Orme IM, Miller ES, Roberts AD, Furney SK, Griffin JP, Dobos EM, Chi D, Rivoire B, Brennan JP: T lymphocyte mediating protection and cellular cytolysis during the course of *M. tuberculosis* infection. *J Immunol* 148:189, 1992.

13. Muller I, Cobbold S, Waldmann H, Kaufmann SME: Impaired resistance to *M. tuberculosis* after selective in vivo depletion of L3T4+ and Lyt-2+ T cells. *Infect Immun* 55:2037, 1987.

14. Orme IM: Induction of nonspecific acquired resistance and delayed type hypersensitivity, but not specific acquired resistance, in mice inoculated with killed mycobacterial vaccines. *Infect Immun* 56:3310, 1988.

15. Pal PG, Horowitz MA: Immunization with extracellular proteins of *M. tuberculosis* induces cell-mediated immune responses with substantial protective immunity in a guinea pig model of pulmonary tuberculosis. *Infect Immun* 60:4782, 1992.

16. Orme IM, Collins FM: Cross protection against nontuberculosis mycobacterial infection by *M. tuberculosis* memory immune T-lymphocytes. *J Exp Med* 163:213, 1988.

17. Stead WW: Tuberculosis among elderly persons: an outbreak in a nursing home. *Ann Intern Med* 94:606, 1981.

18. Singh IG, Mukherjee R, Talwar GP, Kaufmann SHE: In vitro characterization of T cells from mycobacterium-vaccinated mice. *Infect Immun* 60:257, 1992.

19. Boom WH, Wallis RS, Chervenak KA: Human *M. tuberculosis*-relative CD4+ T-cell clones: heterogeneity in antigen recognition, cytokine production, and cytotoxicity for mononuclear phagocytes. *Infect Immun* 59:2737, 1991.

20. Havlir DV, Ellner JJ, Chervenak KA, Boom WH: Selective expansion of human $\gamma\delta$ T cells by monocytes infected with live *M. tuberculosis. J Clin Invest* 87:729, 1991.

21. Janis EM, Kaufmann SHE, Schwatz RH, Pardoll DM: Activation of $\gamma\delta$ T-cells in the primary immune response to *M. tuberculosis. Science* 244:713, 1989.

22. Young DB, Kaufmann SHE, Hermans PWM, Thole JER: Mycobacterial proteins: a compilation. *Mol Microbiol* 6:133, 1992.

23. Husson RW, Young RA: Genes for the major protein antigens of *M. tuberculosis*: the etiologic agents of tuberculosis and leprosy share an immunodominant antigen. *Proc Natl Acad Sci (U S A)* 84:1679, 1987.

24. Havlir DV, Wallis RS, Boom WH, Daniel TM, Chervenak K, Ellner JJ: Human immune response to *M. tuberculosis* antigens. *Infect Immun* 59:665, 1991.

25. Young D, Lathigra R, Sweetser D, Young RA: Stress proteins are immune targets in leprosy and tuberculosis. *Proc Natl Acad Sci (U S A)* 85:4267, 1988.

26. Barnes PF, Mehra V, Rivoire B, Fong SJ, Brennan PJ, Voegtline MS, Minden B, Houghten RA, Bloom BR, Modlin RL: Immunoreactivity of 10-kDa antigen of *M. tuberculosis. J Immunol* 148:1835, 1992.

27. Reynolds SR, Kunkel SL, Thomas DW, Higashi GI: T cell clones for antigen selection and lymphokine production in murine *Schistosomiasis mansoni. J Immunol* 144:2757, 1990.

28. Kingston AE, Salgame P, Mitchison NA, Colston MJ: Immunological activity of a 14-kilodalton recombinant protein of *M. tuberculosis* H37Rv. *Infect Immun* 55:3149, 1987.

29. Falla JC, Parra CA, Mandoza M, Franco LC, Guzman F, Forero J, Orozco O, Patarroyo ME: Identification of B- and T-cell epitopes within the MTP40 protein of *M. tuberculosis* and their correlation with the disease course. *Infect Immun* 59:2265, 1991.

30. Parra CA, Londono LP, DePortillo P, Patarroyo ME: Isolation, characterization, and molecular cloning of a specific *M. tuberculosis* antigen gene: identification of a species-specific sequence. *Infect Immun* 59:3411, 1991.

31. Wiker HG, Sletten K, Nagai S, Harboe M: Evidence for three separate genes encoding the proteins of the mycobacterial antigen 85 complex. *Infect Immun* 58:272, 1990.

32. Rambukkan A, Das PK, Chand A, Baas JG, Grothuis DG, Kold AHJ: Subcellular distribution of monoclonal antibody-defined epitopes on immunodominant 33-kilodalton proteins of *M. tuberculosis*: identification and localization of 29/33 kilodalton doublet proteins in mycobacterial cell walls. *Scand J Immunol* 33:763, 1991.

33. Abou-Zeid C, Ratliff TL, Wiker HG, Harboc M, Bennedsen J, Rook GAW: Characterization of fibronectin-binding antigens released by *M. tuberculosis* and *M. bovis* BCG. *Infect Immun* 56:3046, 1988.

34. Wiker HG, Harboe M: The antigen 85 complex: a major secretion product of *M. tuberculosis. Microbiol Rev* 56:648, 1992.

35. Matsuo K, Yamaguchi A, Yamakazi A, Tasaka H, Yamada T: Cloning and expression of the *M. bovis* BCG gene for extracellular alpha antigen. *J Bacteriol* 170:3847, 1988.

36. Salata RA, Sanson AJ, Malhotra I, Wiker HG, Harboe M, Phillips NB, Daniel TM: Purification and characterization of the 30,000 dalton native antigen of *M. tuberculosis* and characterization of six monoclonal antibodies reactive with a major epitope of this antigen. *J Lab Clin Med* 168:589, 1991.

37. Abou-Zeid C, Harboe MN, Rook GAW: Characterization of the secreted antigens of *M. bovis* BCG: comparison of the 46-kilodalton dimeric protein with proteins mpb64 and mpb70. *Infect Immun* 55:3213, 1987.

38. Lamb JR, Rees ADM, BaI V, Ikeda H, Wilkinson D, I de Vries RRP, Rothbard JB: Prediction and identification of an HLA-DA-restricted T cell determinant in the 19-KDa protein of *M. tuberculosis. Eur J Immunol* 18:973, 1988.

39. Haslou K, Andersen AB, Lundquist N, Weis-Bentzon M: Comparison of the immunological

activity of five identified antigens from *M. tuberculosis* in seven inbred guinea pig strains: the 38-KDa antigen is immunodominant. *Scand J Immunol* 31:503, 1990.

40. Young D, Kent L, Rees A, Lamb J, lvanyi J: Immunological activity of a 38-kilodalton protein purified from *M. tuberculosis. Infect Immun* 54:177, 1986.

41. Miura K, Nagai S, Kinomoto M, Haga S, Tolunaga T: Comparative studies with various substrains of *M. bovis* BCG on the production of an antigenic protein mpb70. *Infect Immun* 39:540, 1983.

42. Collins FM, Lamb JR, Young DB: Biological activity of protein antigens isolated from *M. tuberculosis* culture filtrate. *Infect Immun* 56:1260, 1988.

43. Barnes PF, Mehra V, Hirschfield GR, Fong S-J, Abou-Zeid C, Rook GAW, Hunter SW, Brennan PJ, Moldin RL: Characterization of T cell antigens associated with the cell wall protein-peptidoglycan complex of *M. tuberculosis. J Immunol* 143:2656, 1989.

44. Schoel B, Gulle M, Kaufmann SHE: Heterogeneity of the repertoire of T cells of tuberculosis patients and healthy contacts to *M. tuberculosis* antigens separated by high resolution techniques. *Infect Immun* 60:1717, 1992.

45. Wallis RS, Amir-Tahmasseb M, Ellner JJ: Induction of interleukin-1 and tumor necrosis factor by mycobacterial proteins: the monocyte western blot. *Proc Natl Acad Sci U S A* 87:3348, 1990.

46. Wallis RS, Raranjape A, Phillips M: Identification by 2-D gel electrophoresis of a 47 kD TNF-reducing protein of *M. tuberculosis. Infect Immun* 61:627, 1993.

47. Ellner JJ: Sources of variability in assays of the interaction of mycobacteria with mononuclear phagocytes of mice and men. *Res Microbiol* 141:237, 1990.

48. Flesch I, Kaufmann SHE: Mycobacterial growth inhibition by interferon-γ activated bone marrow macrophages and differential susceptibility among strains of *M. tuberculosis. J Immunol* 138:4408, 1987.

49. Kawamura I, Tsukada H, Yoshikawa H, Fujita M, Nomoto K, Mitsuyama M: IFN-γ-producing ability as a possible marker for the protective T cells against *M. bovis* BCG in mice. *J Immunol* 148:2887, 1992.

50. Shiratsuchi H, Johnson JL, Ellner JJ: Bidirectional effects of cytokines on the growth of *M. avium* within human monocytes. *J Immunol* 146:3165, 1991.

51. Valone SE, Rich EA, Wallis RS, Ellner JJ: Expression of tumor necrosis factor in vitro by human mononuclear phagocytes stimulated with whole *M. bovis* BCG and mycobacterial antigens. *Infect Immun* 56:3313, 1988.

52. Bermudez LE: Production of transforming growth factor-β by *M. avium*-infected human macrophages is associated with unresponsiveness to IFN-γ. *J Immunol* 150:1838, 1993.

53. Daniel TM, Oxtoby MJ, Pinto E, Moreno E: The immune spectrum in patients with pulmonary tuberculosis. *Am Rev Respir Dis* 123:556, 1981.

54. Kleinhenz ME, Ellner JJ: Antigen responsiveness during tuberculosis: regulatory interaction of T-cell subpopulations and adherent cells. *J Lab Clin Med* 110:31, 1987.

55. Toossi Z, Kleinhenz ME, Ellner JJ: Defective interleukin-2 production and responsiveness in human pulmonary tuberculosis. *J Exp Med* 163:1162, 1986.

56. Ogawa T, Uchid H, Kusumoto Y, Mori Y, Yamamura Y, Hamada S: Increases in tumor necrosis factor alpha and interleukin 6-secreting cells in peripheral blood mononuclear cells from subjects infected wtih *Mycobacterium tuberculosis. Infect Immun* 59:3021, 1991.

57. Toossi Z, Lapurga JP, Ondash RJ, Sedor JR, Ellner JJ: Expression of functional interleukin 2 receptors by peripheral blood monocytes from patients with active pulmonary tuberculosis. *J Clin Invest* 85:1777, 1990.

58. Toossi Z, Gogate P, Shiratsuchi M, Young T, Ellner JJ: Enhanced expression of TGFβ by blood monocyte and lung macrophages of patients with active tuberculosis, submitted.

59. Zabel P, Greinert U, Entzian P, Schlaak M: Effects of pentoxifylline on circulating cytokines

(TNF and IL-6) in severe pulmonary tuberculosis, in Basel K (ed), *Tumor Necrosis Factor* 4:1992.

60. Toossi Z, Edmonds KE, Tomford WJ, Ellner JJ: Suppression of PPD-induced interleukin-2 production by interaction of Leu-11 (CD16) positive lymphocytes and adherent mononuclear cells in tuberculosis. *J Infect Dis* 159:352, 1989.

61. Kleinhenz ME, Ellner JJ: Antigen responsiveness during tuberculosis: regulatory interaction of T-cell subpopulations and adherent cells. *J Lab Clin Med* 110:31, 1987.

62. Tazi A, Bouchonnet F, Valeyre D, Cadranel J, Battesti JP, Hance AJ: Characterization of γ/δ T-lymphocytes in the peripheral blood of patients with active tuberculosis. *Am Rev Respir Dis* 146:1216, 1992.

63. Barnes PF, Grisso CE, Abram JF, Band H, Rea TM, Modlin RC: $\gamma\delta$ T-1 lymphocytes in human tuberculosis. *J Infect Dis* 165:506, 1992.

64. Falla JC, Parra CA, Mendoza M, Franco LC, Guzman F, Forero J, Orozco O, Patarroyo ME: Identification of B- and T-cell epitopes within the MTP4O protein of *M. tuberculosis* and their correlation with the disease course. *Infect Immun* 59:2265, 1991.

65. Carlucci S, Beschin A, Tuosto L, Ameglio F, Gandolfo GM, Cocito C, Fiorucci F, Saltini C, Piccolella E: Mycobacterial antigen complex A60-specific T-cell repertoire during the course of pulmonary tuberculosis. *Infect Immun* 61:439, 1993.

66. Comstock GW: Tuberculosis in twins: a re-analysis of the prophit survey. *Am Rev Respir Dis* 117:621, 1978.

67. Skamene E: Genetic control of susceptibility to mycobacterial infections. *Rev Infect Dis* 2:S394, 1989.

68. Bothamley GM, Beet JJ, Schrender GMTH, D'Amaro J, DeVries RRP, Kardjits T, Ivanyi J: Association of tuberculosis and *M. tuberculosis*-specific antibody levels with HLA. *J Infect Dis* 159:549, 1989.

69. Cox RA, Downs M, Neimes RE, Ognibene AJ, Yamashita TS, Ellner JJ: Immunogenetic analysis of human tuberculosis. *J Infect Dis* 158:1302, 1988.

70. Davis JE, Rich RR, Van M, Le MV, Pollach MS, Cook RG: Defective antigen presentation and novel structural properties of DR1 from an HLA haplotype associated with 21-hydroxylase deficiency. *J Clin Invest* 80:998, 1987.

71. Ellner JJ: Tuberculosis in the time of AIDS: the facts and the message (editorial). *Chest* 98:1051, 1990.

72. Eriki PP, Okwera A, Aisu T, Morrissey AB, Ellner JJ, Daniel TM: The influence of human immunodeficiency virus (HIV) on expression of tuberculosis in Kampala, Uganda. *Am Rev Respir Dis* 145:185, 1991.

73. Wallis RS, Vjecha M, Amir-Tahmasseb M, Okwera A, Byekwaso F, Nyole J, Kabengera J, Mugerwa RD, Ellner JJ: Influence of tuberculosis on HIV: enhanced cytokine expression and elevated $\beta2$ microglobulin in HIV-1 associated tuberculosis. *J Infect Dis* 167:43, 1992.

74. Kindler V, Sappino AAP, Grua GE, Piquet Pl, Vassali P: The inducing role of tumor necrosis factor in the development of bactericidal granulomas during BCG infection. *Cell* 56:731, 1989.

75. Fauci AS: The human immunodeficiency virus: infectivity and mechanisms of pathogenesis. *Science* 239:617, 1988.

76. Whalen C, Horsburgh CR, Hom D, Lahart C, Simberkoff M, Ellner J: Accelerated clinical course of human immunodeficiency virus infection following active tuberculosis, submitted.

77. Toossi Z, Sierra-Madero JG, Blinkhorn RA, Mettler MA, Rich EA: Enhanced susceptibility of blood monocytes from patients with pulmonary tuberculosis to productive infection with human immunodeficiency virus-1 (HIV-1). *J Exp Med* 177:1511, 1993.

78. Lederman MM, Georges D, Kushner D, Giam CZ, Toossi Z: *Mycobacterium tuberculosis* and its purified protein derivative activate expression of the human immunodeficiency virus, submitted.

CHAPTER 3

Bacteriology and Diagnosis

NANCY G. WARREN / BARBARA A. BODY

BACTERIOLOGY

The Genus

Members of the genus *Mycobacterium* are shaped as straight to slightly curved rods, ranging in size from 0.2–0.6 × 1.0–10 μm. Some branching and filamentous extensions may be observed, but they usually fragment into rods or coccobacillary forms upon manipulation. Mycobacteria are aerobic, acid-fast, nonmotile bacteria that produce no endospores, conidia, or aerial mycelia.[1] While generally considered to be gram-positive, mycobacteria do not accept Gram's stain readily. The acid-fast stain, using either fuchsin or fluorochrome procedures, is the stain of choice to demonstrate the organisms by microscopy.

The lipid content of the cell wall is high and is made up of high–molecular weight α-alkyl, β-hydroxy fatty acids. These mycolic acids are not unique to the genus but are also found in the genera *Nocardia, Corynebacterium,* and *Rhodococcus.* The length of the chains differs among these genera, with mycobacteria having the largest number of carbon atoms (60–90) in the structure.[2]

Mycobacterium is the sole genus in the family *Mycobacteriaceae.* The genus contains species that are obligate parasites as well as saprophytes and various intermediate forms. Most species are free-living in the environment, but for some, notably *Mycobacterium tuberculosis*, the ecologic niche is diseased tissue of warm-blooded hosts.

The Species

The type species of the genus is *M. tuberculosis*, and at least 53 other species are recognized today.[1] From a clinical point of view, *M. tuberculosis* is the most important member of the genus due to its disease potential and its associated public health concerns. Sometimes it is convenient to place several like species, with similar significance, together to form a complex. Thus, *M. tuberculosis, Mycobacterium bovis, Mycobacterium africanum, Mycobacterium microti,* and bacille Calmette-Guérin (BCG) comprise the *tuberculosis (TB)*

35

complex. The other mycobacteria comprise the *nontuberculous mycobacteria (NTM).* This group has had several other names in the past, the least appropriate (but perhaps most common) being *atypicals.*

The NTM were further divided into groups based on their rate of growth and pigment production (Table 3-1) by Runyon. The photochromogens (group I) are slowly growing mycobacteria (>7 days) that are buff-colored when grown in the dark but turn a bright lemon yellow when exposed to light. The scotochromogens (group II) are also slow growers, but they have an orange pigment regardless of the light conditions. The group III nonphotochromogens are slow growers that do not react quickly to light and are usually nonpigmented but may develop some pigment with age. The rapid growers (group IV) develop fully mature colonies in less than 7 days and can exhibit the full spectrum of pigment possibilities. Each group contains species with pathogenic potential, but the largest number of cases of nontuberculous disease is attributable to the group III nonphotochromogens.

DIAGNOSIS

Clinical Laboratory Considerations

The algorithm in Fig. 3-1 gives an overview of the work flow in a mycobacteriology laboratory. Indispensable for all mycobacteriology laboratories are good references, such as the mycobacteriology manuals published by the U.S. Department of Health and Human Services and manuals published by the American Society for Microbiology.[3-6] These references include the usual topics of microscopy, processing specimens for culture, incubation, and biochemical testing for identification but also include details of laboratory design and appropriate packaging for sending specimens through the mail.

The routine cultivation and detection of mycobacteria have undergone a number of dramatic changes during the last two decades. Microscopy for direct detection has gone from conventional fuchsin-based stains to fluorescent stains, culture practices have progressed to include the routine use of broth media, and identification of several mycobacteria by nucleic acid probes has become routine rather than being limited to a few reference laboratories.[4,6] These technical advances in mycobacteriology come at a time when there is greater awareness than ever of disease due to nontuberculous mycobacteria, such as *Mycobacterium kansasii*, *Mycobacterium xenopi*, and *Mycobacterium avium* complex.[7,8,9,10,11] In addition, the incidence of TB is increasing, and multidrug-resistant (MDR) isolates of *M. tuberculosis* have been responsible for a number of outbreaks of the disease.[12,13] With the increased risk of TB

TABLE 3-1. Salient Characteristics of Mycobacteria Commonly Encountered in the Clinical Laboratory

Species	Runyon Group	Growth Rate	Pigment	Commercial Probe Available	Key Tests or Properties
M. tuberculosis	TB complex	S	N	Yes	Niacin +, nitrate +, 68°C catalase −
M. bovis	TB complex	S	N	Yes	Niacin −, nitrate −, inhibited by 10µg/ml TCH
M. kansasii	I	S	P	Yes	Nitrate +
M. marinum	I	—	P	No	Nitrate −
M. asiaticum	I	S	P	No	Tween hydrolysis slow +
M. simiae	I	S	P, N	No	Tween hydrolysis −, niacin may be +
M. scrofulaceum	II	S	Sc	No	Nitrate −, Tween hydrolysis −, urease +
M. szulgai	II	S	P, Sc*	No	Nitrate +, Tween hydrolysis slow +
M. gordonae	II	S	Sc	Yes	Nitrate +, Tween hydrolysis +, urease −
M. flavescens	II	—	Sc	No	Nitrate +, Tween hydrolysis +, urease +
M. xenopi	III	S	N, Sc	No	Produces X colonies on 7H-10, grows well at 42°C
M. avium	III	S	N, Sc	Yes	Nitrate −, Tween hydrolysis −
M. intracellulare	III	S	N, Sc	Yes	Nitrate −, Tween hydrolysis −
M. malmoense	III	S	N	No	Nitrate −, Tween hydrolysis +, urease −
M. haemophilum	III	S	N	No	Grows best at 25–30°C and requires hemin
M. gastri	III	S	N	No	Nitrate −, Tween hydrolysis +, urease +
M. terrae complex	III	—	N, Sc	No	Nitrate +, Tween hydrolysis +, urease −
M. triviale	III	S	N	No	Nitrate +, Tween hydrolysis +, urease −, 5% NaCl −
M. fortuitum	IV	R	N	No	Nitrate +, iron uptake +, MacConkey's +, mannitol −
M. peregrinum	IV	R	N	No	Nitrate +, iron uptake +, MacConkey's +, mannitol +
M. chelonae	IV	R	N	No	Nitrate −, iron uptake −, 5% NaCl −
M. abscessus	IV	R	N	No	Nitrate −, iron uptake +, 5% NaCl +

Note: S = slow; I = Intermediate; R = rapid; N = nonphotochromogen; P = photochromogen; Sc = scotochromogen; TCH = thiophene-2-carboxylic acid hydrazide.

*Sc at 37°C and P at 25°C

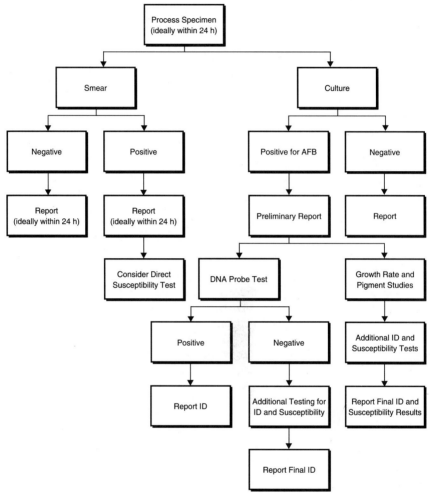

FIGURE 3-1. Work flow in a mycobacteriology laboratory.

transmission and outbreaks of MDR TB, new emphasis is being placed on rapid detection, identification, and susceptibility testing of *M. tuberculosis*, and that will also be the focus of this discussion.

There is a resurgence of interest in mycobacteriology, and many laboratory managers are being asked to consider adding or reinstituting mycobacteriologic services to their clinical laboratories. A pertinent discussion of laboratory services can be found in the guidelines for the practice of mycobacteriology in the form of the levels of laboratory service concept proposed by the American Thoracic Society (ATS) and summarized in Table 3-2.[4,12,14] These guidelines advocate classification of laboratories based on the demand and level of mycobacteriologic services offered. The levels of service correspond roughly to those of the College of American Pathologists (CAP)

TABLE 3-2. The Levels of Service Concept

All laboratories

- Routinely include quality-control checks.
- Participate in recognized proficiency testing programs.
- Establish levels of service based on quality of performance demonstrated in these examinations.

Level I

- Collect adequate clinical specimens.
- Transport specimens to a higher-level laboratory for isolation and identification.
- *May* prepare and examine smears.

Proficiency in reading smears may be maintained by examination of 10–15 specimens per week.

Level II

- Perform functions of a level I laboratory.
- Process specimens as necessary for culture on two media.
- Identify *M. tuberculosis*.
- *May* perform susceptibility studies against *M. tuberculosis*.
- Retain mycobacterial cultures for additional or repeat tests (6 months).

Proficiency in culture and identification of *M. tuberculosis* may be maintained by digestion and culture of 20 specimens per week.

Level III

- Perform functions of laboratories at levels I and II.
- Identify all *Mycobacterium* species from clinical specimens.
- Should perform drug susceptibility studies against all mycobacteria.
- *May* conduct research and provide training.

Summary
The American Thoracic Society recommends that the full spectrum of mycobacteriologic support be concentrated in only a few laboratories in a given community or region where professional expertise and complete and safe facilities are available.

Source: Adapted from Master[4] and Bass et al.[12]

for proficiency testing (CAP levels are generally rated one level higher for comparable levels of service; e.g., CAP level 4 = ATS level III). Laboratory managers and physicians who are interested in reinstituting services for mycobacteriology in their laboratories may wish to refer to these figures when justifying a decision.

Safety Considerations

All specimens received for acid-fast culture must be handled as though they contained mycobacteria. The Centers for Disease Control and Prevention (CDC) and the National Institutes of Health recommend the use of biosafety level 2 practices for the preparation of acid-fast smears and culture of specimens.[15] In addition to the use of a class I or II biological safety cabinet for aerosol-generating processes, level 2 practices include recommendations for containment equipment, clothing, and facilities. If the laboratory work includes manipulation of *M. tuberculosis*, biosafety level 3 containment facilities are recommended, including a controlled access room, suitable protective clothing for workers, and decontamination of all infectious waste.

Independent of the above mentioned recommendations, the National Institute of Occupational Health and Safety (NIOSH) published recommendations in 1992 based on the Occupational Health and Safety Act of 1970.[16] This act required the director of NIOSH to develop criteria for exposure levels to any agent so that workers will not have impaired health, functional capabilities, or diminished life expectancy due to their work. The CDC position is that no combination of methods can completely eliminate the risk of TB but that these risks can be substantially reduced. One of the unresolved issues under discussion by the CDC and NIOSH is the need for self-powered respirators, advocated by NIOSH, versus the use of high-efficiency particle masks, recommended by the CDC, for workers who may be exposed to *M. tuberculosis* by laboratory work or through contact with patients. In either case, it would seem that the use of surgical masks as respiratory protection for health care workers in the mycobacteriology laboratory or in the care of patients is no longer considered adequate respiratory protection.

Specimen Collection

The first step in the detection of *M. tuberculosis* and other mycobacteria is the suspicion by the physician who will order the appropriate cultures. General guidelines for specimen collection and transport to the laboratory are shown in Table 3-3. In addition, most standard references review procedures for collection to ensure good-quality sputum (and other) specimens.[3,4,5] How well this information is conveyed to the physician is a major concern. In this

TABLE 3-3. General Guidelines for Specimen Collection

Specimen	Quantity	Collection	Container and Transport	Special Instructions
Blood	10 ml	Collect specimen for routine blood culture and an additional specimen for recovery of AFB.	Use SPS, heparin, or Isolator blood collection tubes	Do not send conventional blood culture bottles.
Bone marrow	As much as possible	Collect aseptically; mix with transport media as soon as possible.	Collect in SPS tube, Pediatric Isolator, or BACTEC 13A	
Gastric aspirate/lavage	40–50 ml	Collect specimen early in the morning before the patient has eaten or gotten out of bed.	Use sterile, leakproof container, such as a rigid plastic jar with a metal lid or 50 ml conical centrifuge tubes.	The specimen should be neutralized with disodium phosphate if transport will be delayed more than 4 h.
Respiratory specimens Sputum	5–10 ml	Collect 3–6 specimens. First morning specimens are preferable. Do not send pooled collections or saliva.	Use sterile, leakproof container, such as a rigid plastic jar with a metal lid or 50 ml conical centrifuge tubes. Refrigerate if transport to laboratory is delayed and during transport if possible.	Do not send tracheal suction collection devices with suction ports in the cap, since they will leak in transit to the laboratory. Most devices are packaged with a cap to be replaced with ports.

TABLE 3-3 (*Continued*). **General Guidelines for Specimen Collection**

Specimen	Quantity	Collection	Container and Transport	Special Instructions
Induced sputum	5–10 ml	Collect specimen after instillation of aerosolized hypertonic saline. After induction, patients may cough and produce additional good-quality specimens, which should also be submitted to the laboratory.	As for sputum	Because these specimens are watery, it is important to indicate that the specimen is "induced sputum" on a history sheet or in a clinical information section of a request form.
Bronchial washings, brushings, and transtracheal aspirates	Variable		As for sputum	Do not send tracheal suction collection devices with suction ports in the cap, since they will leak in transit to the laboratory. Most devices are packaged with a cap to be replaced with ports.
Pus drainage	1–2 ml	Use aseptic technique; aspirate with sterile saline. Do not use swabs.	As for sputum	

Sterile tissue	Whatever is collected	Specimen should be collected using aseptic technique. About 1 ml of sterile saline solution should be added to maintain moisture.	As for sputum	It is important to include the site from which tissue was collected, since skin sites require inoculation of additional media for recovery of *M. marinum* and *M. haemophilum*.
Sterile body fluids	1 – 10 ml	Use aseptic technique. Collect without contamination by urine.	As for sputum	
Stool	5 – 10 ml		As for sputum	
Urine	40 – 50 ml	Wash external genitalia before collection, as for a routine urine culture. Collect first morning specimens on 3 – 6 consecutive days; do not pool specimens.	As for sputum Refrigerate immediately and during transport as soon as possible.	

Note: AFB = acid-fast bacilli; SPS = sodium polyanethol sulfonate.

43

regard, it is important to note the results of a study by Kramer et al., who examined the differences between patients for whom a timely diagnosis was made and those whose diagnosis of TB was delayed.[17] Errors in management by the physician were responsible for the delay in 21 of 25 patients for whom the diagnosis was delayed; the most common error was the failure to obtain three sputum specimens for acid-fast smear and culture in patients with clinical and chest radiograph findings compatible with TB. It may be easy for the laboratorian to read this article and deny responsibility, but it might have been possible to alert the physician who ordered the test that three specimens are recommended through a note in the medical information system at the time of ordering or as part of an initial smear report.

Specimen Processing

Mycobacteria grow slowly, with doubling times on the order of 12–24 h, compared to most other bacteria, which reproduce in less than 1 h.[5] Therefore, in order to recover mycobacteria from specimens that contain large numbers of normal flora, decontamination of the specimens is needed. The decontamination process exploits the relative chemical resistance of the mycobacteria (compared to the normal flora) due to the high lipid content of their cell envelopes. However, since the decontamination process also decreases the number of mycobacteria present, it should not be used on specimens that are considered sterile, such as cerebrospinal fluid, blood, and tissue. Because many specimens are nonuniform, it has also been found to be preferable to liquefy, or "digest," specimens so that the number of mycobacteria can be concentrated by centrifugation of a liquid specimen.

The aim of the digestion-decontamination procedure is to keep the rate of contamination between 2 and 5 percent.[3,5] If contamination is above 5 percent, the decontamination part of the process is inadequate; if it is below 2 percent, then too many mycobacteria are being killed. Several procedures have been developed for digestion and decontamination; the one most commonly used in the United States is the N-acetyl-L-cysteine (NALC)–sodium hydroxide (NaOH) method. Some specimens require special handling. Those from patients known to be colonized with *Pseudomonas* species should be treated with oxalic acid, since *Pseudomonas* is not adequately destroyed by NALC-NaOH.[3,5]

The NALC-NaOH method uses a final concentration of 2 percent NaOH for 15 min, followed by centrifugation at 3000 $\times g$.[3,4,18] Once concentrated by centrifugation, the supernatant is carefully decanted, and the pellet is used to prepare smears and inoculate culture media. The amount of centrifugal force, or g's, and the temperature of centrifugation are important variables in the recovery of mycobacteria. The high lipid content of the mycobacteria works to keep them buoyant and prevent their concentration if the centrifugal force is too low. Some sources recommend only 2200 $\times$ g, but use of 3000 $\times$ g has been shown to increase recovery of mycobacteria.[3,4,5,18] If the centrifuge is run repeatedly, heat will build up, and the increase in temperature can dramatically reduce the recovery of mycobacteria; therefore, it may be best to use a centrifuge with refrigeration capabilities to prevent temperature increases if multiple runs are needed.[3]

Microscopy

Smears for the direct detection of mycobacteria can provide the first confirmation of a clinical diagnosis and can often be accomplished within a few hours after collection of an early morning sputum specimen. Smears should be prepared after digestion and decontamination and concentration of specimens likely to be contaminated with normal flora or directly from sterile specimens after grinding or concentration procedures.[3,4,5] At one time, the Ziehl-Neelsen stain was the stain of choice, but it is now preferable to use one of the fluorescent stain preparations. Fluorescent stains are more sensitive for the detection of acid-fast bacilli based on the amount of time required to review the slide.

It is recommended that the smear occupy an area on the slide that is 1 $\times$ 2 cm.[3] Rather than stating a time period for examination, most standard references state that the slide should be examined in a pattern consisting of either three zig-zag passes over the entire 2 cm length or nine zig-zag passes over the 1 cm width. Fluorescent smears can be examined at 250–450$\times$, while the conventional Ziehl-Neelsen or Kinyoun stains require the use of magnifications of 800 to 1000$\times$. If fluorescent smears are examined, it is best for the laboratory to convert the number of acid-fast bacilli seen to this scale (Table 3-4). The laboratory report should contain a key to the scale.

Culture

Traditionally, mycobacteriology has employed both egg-based (Lowenstein-Jensen) and agar-based (Middlebrook 7H10 or 7H11) media incubated in 5–10% CO_2 for 6–8 weeks. Each medium has advantages and disadvantages, and they compliment each other. The BACTEC (Becton Dickinson Diagnostic Systems, Sparks, MD) system for radiometric detection of mycobacteria was introduced in the late 1970s and has joined the ranks of conventional alternatives rather than being considered new.[19] It has advantages of increased recovery, especially when combined with one of the conventional culture media, and decreased time to detection of positive cultures, with many laboratories reporting an average time to detection of 8–14 days.[5,20] It also has the

TABLE 3-4.   Correlation of Smear Quantitation for Fluorescent and Conventional Smears

Fuchsin Stain: No. of AFB Observed at 1000×	Fluorescent Stain: No. of AFB Observed at 250×	Report
None	None	No AFB seen
1–2 per 300 fields	1–2 per 30 fields (1 × 2 cm sweep) (3 × 1 cm sweep)	Doubtful, please resubmit
1–9 per 100 fields	1–9 per 10 fields	1+
1–9 per 10 fields	1–9 per field	2+
1–9 per field	10–90 per field	3+
>9 per field	>90 per field	4+

Note: AFB = acid-fast bacilli.

advantage of being suitable for direct use with nucleic acid probe tests, thus further reducing the time required for identification of the acid-fast organisms once detected.[21] The major drawback of the BACTEC system is the use of radioactive substrates and the necessity of specialized instrumentation. It has also suffered from problems with needle-heater defects, leading to cross-contamination of bottles and one pseudo-outbreak of *Mycobacterium gordonae* due to an additive that was contaminated.[22,23] The most recent addition to the culture alternatives has been the adaptation of the Septi-Chek (Becton Dickinson Microbiology Systems, Hunt Valley, MD) system for mycobacteriology.[24] This system employs a Middlebrook broth–based system with a paddle that has chocolate agar, Middlebrook agar, and an egg-based medium similar to Lowenstein-Jensen agar. Several studies have demonstrated the recovery in this system to be comparable or superior to that with BACTEC and better than that with a conventional medium; it can also be combined with an additional medium to increase overall recovery.[24] From the limited studies available at present, the speed of recovery does not appear to be as fast as with the BACTEC system, but it is faster than with conventional media. This system does not use radioactive substrates and requires no instrumentation.

Mycobacteria can be effectively recovered from blood either by use of the BACTEC 13A system, which is designed specifically for the detection of mycobacteria in blood, or by a combination of lysis centrifugation (either "homemade" or Isolator; Wampole Laboratories, Cranbury, NJ) and the BACTEC 12B system, the Septi-Chek system, or a conventional medium.[5,24,25,26] It should be noted that the packaging of the Septi-Chek system does not currently list blood as a suitable specimen, but when combined with the Isolator it was found to have good performance.[24]

Conventional Identification Techniques

Traditionally, the recognized techniques for identification of mycobacteria have consisted of a combination of growth rate determination, pigment production, macroscopic colony morphology, and reactions to biochemical tests.[3] All these techniques have several common characteristics: they are time-consuming, labor-intensive, and, depending on the "level of service" (Table 3-2), may require highly skilled cognitive capabilities on the part of the mycobacteriologist. Regardless of these potential drawbacks, these techniques have served the clinical laboratory well and continue to be the comparative reference standards for new technology development.

Growth Rate Determination
Carefully controlled growth rate tests will aid in the identification of myco-bacteria. Growth rate tests are best performed by preparing subcultures of growth using standardized dilute inocula. Growth rate based solely on recovery time of mycobacteria from primary isolation may give a false impression. A specimen containing very large numbers of slowly growing acid-fast bacilli may grow cultures too quickly, giving the false impression of the presence of a rapid grower, or, conversely, alkali treatments of the clinical specimen may damage some rapidly growing mycobacteria, causing them to take weeks to grow. Members of group IV, or the rapid growers, such as *Mycobacterium fortuitum* complex, will produce mature colonies on standard media (Lowenstein-Jensen) in less than 7 days (often in 3 – 5 days). Most other mycobacteria (including *M. tuberculosis*) require longer than 1 week for growth. A notable exception is *Mycobacterium marinum*, which often has an intermediate growth rate of 5 – 7 days.

Pigment Production
Colony color and the production of pigment help to differentiate the mycobacteria. Mycobacteria such as *M. tuberculosis*, *M. avium* complex, and *M. fortuitum* are considered buff-colored and usually do not have any significant pigment. Occasionally, a strain of *M. fortuitum* may have a noticeable green color, but this is not true cell wall pigment; rather, it is a result of malachite green absorption from the culture medium. Pigment in some of the nonphotochromogenic mycobacteria may intensify with age, resulting, for example, in strains of *M. avium* complex with a distinct yellow color. Members of the photochromogenic mycobacteria, such as *M. kansasii* and *M. marinum*, are initially buff-colored when grown in the dark, but 1 h of exposure to light activates cell wall carotnoid pigments, and the cultures turn a bright lemon yellow. While *Mycobacterium simiae* and *Mycobacterium asiaticum* are considered photochromogenic mycobacteria, their pigment production can be much more subtle than that of *M. kansasii* and can take longer to appear. *M.*

gordonae, *Mycobacterium scrofulaceum*, and other scotochromogenic mycobacteria are orange-colored, and this color may deepen to a dark brick orange with age. *Mycobacterium szulgai* is somewhat of an exception, since it can be a photochromogen or a scotochromogen, depending on incubation temperature. At 25°C the colonies are photochromogenic, but at 37°C the culture is orange whether grown in the light or in the dark.

Colony Morphology
The macroscopic appearance of mycobacterial colonies on solid media aids in the identification of the organism and can also suggest the presence of more than one species. Colony morphology is best determined on translucent Middlebrook 7H-10 agar, where texture, edge entirety, colony thickness, and color can be viewed using a stereoptic microscope. A typical description of *M. tuberculosis* would be rough, with an irregular edge; *M. gordonae* would be orange, smooth, and domed, with an entire edge; and *Mycobacterium terrae* complex would be smooth and domed, with an aproned edge. The *M. avium* complex can have up to three colony types: smooth and domed, transparent with starlike edges, and rough with a spot in the center. Familiarity with various colony morphologies will aid the mycobacteriologist in searching for more than one species in a clinical specimen. Dual infections are not common but are being found with more frequency today.

Biochemical Tests
The mainstay of the biochemical tests in the mycobacteriology laboratory is the niacin test. All mycobacteria produce niacin, but most mycobacteria continue to process this metabolite to an end product that is not detectable. *M. tuberculosis* does not have this capability, and niacin accumulates as a result of a blocked metabolic pathway. The accumulated niacin is deposited in the medium on which the culture is growing. Because niacin is deposited in the medium and is not a constituent of bacterial cell wall, the test to detect niacin accumulation is an extraction test. In order to avoid handling hazardous chemicals associated with this test, many laboratories use a paper strip modification that eliminates the use of cyanogen bromide and aniline. Nearly 99 percent of *M. tuberculosis* strains are niacin-positive. Because some strains of *M. simiae* and *M. kansasii*[27] are also niacin-positive, it is best to consider niacin positivity as presumptive for *M. tuberculosis* and follow up with additional biochemical tests. The combination of positive niacin, positive nitrate reduction, and negative heat stable catalase test results is definitive for the species. False-positive results can be obtained if the culture is pigmented (pigment, not niacin, is extracted), and false-negative results can occur when too little niacin is present (in young cultures, cultures with too few colonies, or cultures with confluent colony mass that blocks extraction).

Nearly 20 other biochemical tests are routinely used in level 3 laboratories to identify mycobacteria recovered from clinical specimens. These tests can require from 20 min (heat stable catalase) to several weeks (semiquantitative catalase) for completion and frequently require subculture to additional selective media. Key differential tests for the NTM are often associated with a specific NTM group. For example, once a culture has been determined to be a rapid grower (group IV), then positive 3 day arylsulfatase and MacConkey's agar test results place the organism in the *M. fortuitum* complex. Additional tests to determine nitrate reduction, iron uptake, ability to grow in the presence of 5 percent NaCl, and carbon source utilization are needed for speciation. Table 3-1 lists some of the notable biochemical reactions of the commonly encountered mycobacteria, and several laboratory-oriented publications offer in-depth instructions on the preparation, performance, and interpretation of mycobacterial biochemical tests.[3,5,28]

Rapid Identification Techniques

Clinical mycobacteriology has undergone major changes in the last several decades, with the result that it is now possible to apply rapid speciation methods to the identification of mycobacteria. A recent commentary[19] summarizes these methods and encourages all clinical mycobacteriology laboratories to incorporate fluorescent microscopy, broth cultures, and DNA probes for the rapid detection, isolation, and identification of mycobacteria (Table 3-5). Refer to Chapter 15 for a discussion of new methods that clinical laboratories of the future will incorporate into their testing schedules.

BACTEC Identification
Once an acid-fast organism has been detected in the BACTEC system, as evidenced by an increase in the daily growth index value and a positive acid-fast smear result, it is possible to use the BACTEC system to obtain preliminary identification. Organisms are inoculated into BACTEC 7H-12 medium with and without NAP (*p*-nitro-α-acetylamino-β-hydroxypropiophene). Growth of the culture is monitored daily, with the outcome that *M. tuberculosis* complex is inhibited by NAP while NTM continue to grow in the presence of the compound. Results are usually obtained in 5–7 days, making this test quicker than conventional methods and a good screening test for TB complex versus NTM. Limitations of the test include the following: (1) the test medium contains a radiolabel, (2) the test is unable to separate the members of the TB complex, and (3) some isolates of *M. kansasii* are slow to grow in the presence of NAP, giving a false interpretation in favor of the TB complex. NAP testing should be followed by confirmatory testing to identify

TABLE 3-5. **Expected Time to Obtain Results of Mycobacterial Laboratory Procedures**

Method/ Organism	Smear	Average Time to Detection, Days (range)	Average Time to Identification, Days*	Average Time to Susceptibility, Days*
Conventional				
M. tb	Same day	17 (11–42)	21	21
NTM	Same day	21 (2–48)	42	
BACTEC				
M. tb		7.3 (2–21)		7
NTM		4.8 (1–21)		7
Probes				
M. tb			Same day detected	
NTM			Same day detected	

Note: M. tb = M. tuberculosis; NTM = nontuberculous mycobacteria.

*Time required after inital detection.

Source: Compiled during 1972–1990 at the Department of General Services, Division of Consolidated Laboratory Services, Richmond, VA.

specific members of the TB complex and to rule out the presence of mixed mycobacterial populations.

DNA Probe Identification
A major step toward the rapid identification of mycobacteria was realized when DNA probes were introduced into the clinical laboratory.[29] Currently, only one commercial company markets DNA probes. The Gen-Probe Accu-probe test system (Gen-Probe Inc., San Diego, CA) is based on the hybridization of known labeled DNA with ribosomal RNA (rRNA) in the target (or "unknown") culture genome. The test system uses an acridinium ester attached to the known DNA probe as a detector. Light is produced when this ester is oxidized by hydrogen peroxide and hydrolyzed by strong alkali, and detection is accomplished by measuring this chemiluminescent reaction.

Numerous studies have indicated a high performance of the mycobacterial probes.[30] The sensitivity and specificity of this test system is achieved due to a number of factors: the detection system is very sensitive, since chemiluminescence is about a million times more sensitive than fluorescence; temperature and salt concentration of the reaction are controlled to provide stringency of hybridization; the use of rRNA as target nucleic acid allows a 1000-fold amplification of target molecules; and rRNA is very highly conserved across phylogenetic lines, thus minimizing effects of mutational changes. The TB complex probe approaches 100 percent specificity and sensitivity, with only rare mismatches reported.[30] Additional probes are available for *M. avium* complex, *M. kansasii*, and *M. gordonae*, and they also show good performance, with sensitivity and specificity usually reported as over 95 percent. When combined with early detection in the BACTEC system, identification of mycobacteria by probe can be a powerful tool for rapid testing.[21]

Drug Susceptibility Testing

Several variations of drug susceptibility testing are available in the clinical laboratory today. Direct susceptibility testing is performed on concentrated sediments of smear-positive specimens; indirect testing utilizes the cultures grown from clinical specimens. The direct test has the advantages of providing earlier results and being more representative of the bacillary population within lesions of the diseased patients. The indirect test is more appropriate when specimens have negative concentrated smears, when the specimen is heavily contaminated with non–acid-fast bacilli, or when a culture is submitted to a reference laboratory. The two most commonly used drug susceptibility testing techniques in the United States are the proportion method in solid media (i.e., "conventional" testing) and BACTEC ("rapid") in broth. Because it is more difficult to adjust the inoculum and avoid contamination in the BACTEC system, with specimen concentrates, conventional testing remains the method of choice for direct susceptibility testing, even though it can take up to three times as long to obtain results. Rapid testing in the BACTEC system is more applicable to indirect testing, either from primary BACTEC isolation broths or solid culture.

Conventional Drug Susceptibility Testing

The conventional test utilizes the proportion method of Canetti et al.[3] and requires an incubation time of 3 weeks. The test is usually performed on Middlebrook 7H-10 agar plates in which liquid drug or disk-containing drug is incorporated. Results are expressed as a percentage of colonies found growing on drug-containing media compared to those growing on drug-free media. Any result found to be in excess of 1 percent is considered an indication of emerging resistance. Careful attention to media preparation, drug storage, inoculation, incubation conditions, and interpretation of results renders this testing more suitable for at least a level II laboratory and more likely a level III laboratory. If drug susceptibility testing is performed in a level II laboratory, then most likely the drug battery offered will be the "first-line drugs," isoniazid, rifampin, ethambutol, and streptomycin. The other drugs, including pyrazinamide (PZA), are more likely to be tested in a level III laboratory.

BACTEC Susceptibility Testing

In addition to rapid detection of mycobacteria, the BACTEC system can also be used for drug susceptibility testing. The major advantage of this type of testing is turnaround time: BACTEC drug susceptibility results are usually ready in 5–7 days, compared to 21 days required for conventional testing. Like conventional testing, the BACTEC method is also designed to detect the emergence of drug resistance at the 1 percent level. To date, the only drugs for which a standardized method is available are the first-line drugs, including PZA.

REFERENCES

1. Wayne LG, Kubica GP: Family Mycobacteriaceae, in Holt JG, Sneath PHA (eds), *Bergey's Manual of Determinative Bacteriology*, section 16, 9th ed. Baltimore, Williams & Wilkins, 1986, pp 1435.
2. Takayama K, Qureshi N: Structure and synthesis of lipids, in Kubica GP, Wayne LG (eds), *The Mycobacteria: A Sourcebook*, part A. New York, Dekker, 1984, pp 319.
3. Kent PT, Kubica GP: *Public Health Mycobacteriology: A Guide for the Level III Laboratory*. Atlanta, Centers for Disease Control, 1985.
4. Master RN: Mycobacteriology, in Isenberg HD (ed), *Clinical Microbiology Procedures Handbook*, vol 1. Washington, DC, American Society for Microbiology, 1992, pp 3.0.1.
5. Roberts GD, Koneman EW, Kim YK: Mycobacterium, in Balows A, Hausler WJ Jr, Herrmann KL, Isenberg HD, Shadomy HJ (eds), *Manual of Clinical Microbiology*, 5th ed. Washington, DC, American Society for Microbiology, 1991, pp 304.
6. Strong BE, Kubica GP: *Isolation and Identification of* Mycobacterium tuberculosis: *A Guide for the Level II Laboratory*. Washington, DC, US Department of Health and Human Services, HHS publication no (CDC) 81-8390, 1981.
7. Contreras MA, Cheung OT, Sanders DE, Goldstein RS: Pulmonary infection with nontuberculous mycobacteria. *Am Rev Respir Dis* 137:149,1988.
8. Havlik JA, Horsburgh CR Jr, Metchock B, Williams PP, Fann AS, Thompson SE III: Disseminated *Mycobacterium avium* complex infection: clinical identification and epidemiologic trends. *J Infect Dis* 165:577, 1992.
9. Levine B, Chaisson RE: *Mycobacterium kansasii*: a cause of treatable pulmonary disease associated with advanced human immunodeficiency virus (HIV) infection. *Ann Intern Med* 114:861, 1991.
10. Pringe DS, Peterson DD, Steiner RM, Gottlieb JE, Scott R, Israel HL, Figueroa WG, Fish JE: Infection with *Mycobacterium avium* complex in patients without predisposing conditions. *N Engl J Med* 321:863, 1989.

11. Reich J, Johnson RE: *Mycobacterium avium* complex pulmonary disease. *Am Rev Respir Dis* 143:1381, 1991.
12. Bass JB Jr, Farer LS, Hopewell PC, Jacobs RF, Snider DE Jr: Diagnostic standards and classification of tuberculosis. *Am Rev Respir Dis* 142:725, 1990.
13. Fischl M, Uttamchandani R, Reyes R, Cleary T, Otten J, Breeden A, Bigler W, Valdez H, Cacciatore R, Witte J, et al.: Nosocomial transmission of multi-drug resistant tuberculosis among HIV-infected persons: Florida and New York 1988–1991. *MMWR* 40:585, 1991.
14. Hawkins JE, Good RC, Gangadharam PRJ, Gruft HM, Stottmeier KD: Levels of laboratory services for mycobacterial diseases. *Am Rev Respir Dis* 128:213, 1983.
15. Centers for Disease Control and National Institutes of Health: Biosafety in microbiological and biomedical laboratories, in Richmond JY, McKinney RW (eds), HHS publication no (NIH) 88-8395, 3d ed. Washington, DC, US Government Printing Office, 1993.
16. Code of Federal Regulations. 29 Chapter XVII (7-1-92 Edition) Subpart Personal Protective Equipment. Section 1910.134. Respiratory Protection.
17. Kramer F, Modilevsky T, Waliany AR, Leedom JM, Barnes PF: Delayed diagnosis of tuberculosis in patients with human immunodeficiency virus infection. *Am J Med* 89:451, 1990.
18. Rickman TW, Moyer NP: Increased sensitivity of acid-fast smears. *J Clin Microbiol* 11:618, 1980.
19. Tenover FC, Crawford JT, Huebner RE, Geiter LJ, Horsburgh CR, Good RC: The resurgence of tuberculosis: is your laboratory ready? *J Clin Microbiol* 31:767, 1993.
20. Morgan MA, Horstmeier CD, DeYoung DR, Roberts GD: Comparison of a radiometric method (BACTEC) and conventional culture media for the recovery of mycobacteria from smear-negative specimens. *J Clin Microbiol* 18:384, 1983.
21. Body BA, Warren NG, Spicer A, Henderson D, Chery M: Use of Gen-Probe and BACTEC for rapid isolation and identification of mycobacteria. *Am J Clin Pathol* 93:415, 1990.
22. Body BA, Chery M, Warren NG, Tsang A: Report of a pseudo-outbreak of *Mycobacterium gordonae* associated with PANTA. *Abstr Annu Meet Am Soc Microbiol* (Abstr U69, p 153), 1990.
23. Murray PR: Mycobacterial cross-contamination with the BACTEC 460 TB system. *Diagn Microbiol Infect Dis* 14:33, 1991.
24. Whittier PS, Westfall K, Setterquist S, Hopfer RL: Evaluation of the Septi-Chek AFB system in the recovery of mycobacteria. *Eur J Clin Microbiol Infect Dis* 11:915, 1992.
25. Kiehn TE, Cammarata R: Comparative recoveries of *Mycobacterium avium*–*M. intracellulare* from Isolator lysis-centrifugation and BACTEC 13A blood culture systems. *J Clin Microbiol* 26:760, 1988.
26. Salfinger M, Stool EW, Piot D, Heifets L: Comparison of three methods for recovery of *Mycobacterium avium* complex from blood specimens. *J Clin Microbiol* 26:1225, 1988.
27. Nachamkin I, MacGregor RR, Staneck JL, Tsang AY, Denner JC, Willner M, Barbagallo S: Niacin-positive *Mycobacterium kansasii* isolated from immunocompromised patients. *J Clin Microbiol* 30:1344, 1992.
28. Good RC: Opportunistic pathogens in the genus *Mycobacterium*. *Ann Rev Microbiol* 39:347, 1985.
29. Walker J, Dougan, G: DNA probes: a new role in diagnostic microbiology. *J Appl Bacteriol* 67:229, 1989.
30. Goto M, Oka S, Okuzumi K, Kimura S, Shimada K: Evaluation of acridinium-ester-labeled DNA probes for identification of *Mycobacterium tuberculosis* and *Mycobacterium avium*–*Mycobacterium intracellulare* complex in culture. *J Clin Microbiol* 29:2473, 1991.

PART II
Prevention

CHAPTER 4

Precautions to Prevent Transmission

EDWARD A. NARDELL / RICHARD L. RILEY

The transmission of tuberculosis (TB) is a paradox—at once extremely simple, yet extraordinarily complex. A single inhaled tubercle bacillus can infect the susceptible host, yet most exposures are unlikely to result in infection. It has been estimated that a third of the world's population is infected with the tubercle bacillus, almost every infection the result of airborne transmission; yet TB is considered not very infectious compared to measles, varicella, and other airborne viruses. While an unlucky intern or nurse may become infected after contact with his or her first case of active TB, student nurses working on hospital wards during the 1930s and 1940s, when TB was common and not effectively treated, required an average 6–8 months' exposure to convert their tuberculin skin test from negative to positive.[1] Upon completing three years of training, however, nearly all nursing students in that era had become infected. Today, many health care workers are rarely if ever exposed to TB, others traverse entire careers periodically caring for patients with TB without becoming infected, while others, working in high-prevalence areas, are becoming infected at rates reminiscent of earlier times. In areas where multidrug-resistant (MDR) TB is common, moreover, the poor prospects for treating infection or active disease also recall the era before chemotherapy, when health care workers knowingly exposed themselves to the risk, however small, of a potentially fatal illness. Variable numbers of TB patients, variable infectiousness of individual patients, greatly reduced infectiousness of patients on effective chemotherapy, variable resistance to initial infection among those exposed, highly variable exposure times and environmental conditions, and many other factors combine to make TB transmission both difficult to predict and hard to control. Ironically, the underlying determinants of transmission are well understood based largely on experiments conducted before the availability of chemotherapy, a period when the disease was considered the most important threat to both personal and public health.[2,3] Attention to basic control principles should reduce the risk of transmission after a case has been identified or suspected. However, the greatest source of nosocomial transmission today is the undiagnosed and unsuspected TB patient. These individuals will continue to pose a threat, especially to immunocompromised persons and under crowded living conditions. This chapter reviews both the principles of transmission and the practical aspects of control.

DROPLETS AND DROPLET NUCLEI

Many respiratory maneuvers, especially coughs and sneezes, produce high air flow rates in the upper respiratory tract, sheering off minute portions of the fluid lining the mucosa, expelling respiratory droplets into the environment in large numbers.[3] When respiratory droplets are released, they range in size from relatively large particles that are easily seen and felt to microscopic particles that are imperceptible but may contain viable tubercle bacilli. The visible and larger microscopic droplets rapidly settle onto surfaces within the immediate vicinity of their source and are essentially noninfectious even if they contain tubercle bacilli. Droplets aggregate with dust and other surface materials and can no longer be readily resuspended as particles of a respirable size. However, some of the respiratory droplets released by vigorous respiratory maneuvers evaporate nearly completely before settling out, forming 1 to 5 μm *droplet nuclei*, which remain suspended indefinitely, buoyed by room air currents.[4] Patients with chronic pulmonary TB usually cough vigorously as the disease progresses, expelling large numbers of droplet nuclei containing potentially infectious tubercle bacilli. Cough frequency has been associated with infectiousness, and, not surprisingly, respiratory procedures such as bronchoscopy, sputum induction, and pentamidine aerosol treatments, which induce vigorous coughing, have also been associated with TB transmission.[5-7] Although the majority of aerosolized tubercle bacilli are believed to die in transit, under experimental conditions of controlled temperature and humidity, the half-life of aerosolized tubercle bacilli (H37Rv strain) was found to be about 6 h.[8] However, the concentration of tubercle bacilli is determined more by dilution than viability. Ventilation with only two room air changes per hour removes about 87 percent of airborne particles, and after five room air changes only 1 percent of droplet nuclei remain. The risk of TB transmission requires the ongoing presence of an infectious patient. Unlike the case with *Legionella* and certain fungal infections, buildings are neither sources nor reservoirs of TB infection.

The same aerodynamic properties that permit droplet nuclei to remain airborne allow roughly half of the particles to evade impaction on the upper respiratory tract. These droplet nuclei can carry tubercle bacilli to the alveoli and initiate infection.[3] In experiments using concentrated aerosols of cultured organisms, Wells et al. found 16 times as many tubercles in the lungs of rabbits breathing fine (2 μm) droplets as in those of rabbits breathing equal numbers of coarse aerosol suspensions (12–15 μm).[9] Fine droplets (droplet nuclei) were dragged with air into the vulnerable alveoli, whereas larger droplets were much more likely to impact the upper airways, which are highly resistant to infection. Such quantitative inhalation experiments using animals established the fundamental principle that the probability of infection is proportional to the concentration of infectious droplet nuclei in air and the volume of air breathed over the exposure time.[10,11] Within the limits of the experimental methods, complete parity was established between the number of bacilli aerosolized into air, as determined by colony counts on air centrifuge culture tubes, and the number of tubercles in the lungs of exposed animals. The minimum infective dose for highly susceptible experimental animals such as rabbits and guinea pigs was a single droplet nucleus containing one or at most several tubercle bacilli. Therefore, these animals have been used as nearly ideal quantitative samplers for infectious droplet nuclei in air.

PATTERNS OF TB TRANSMISSION WITHIN BUILDINGS: THE RELATIVE IMPORTANCE OF CONVECTION, RECIRCULATION, AND CLOSE PROXIMITY

In the absence of central heating, ventilating, and air conditioning (HVAC) systems, where forced air distributes conditioned air, droplet nuclei containing tubercle bacilli disperse rapidly throughout the air of a room or other enclosed space, exposing all occupants to the chance of infection. The primary force causing particles to disperse is convection. Within large, crowded, poorly ventilated communal spaces such as urban shelters, moreover, convection may be responsible for extensive TB transmission if conditions permit droplet nuclei to accumulate to high enough concentrations, especially where both the infectious source individuals and susceptible occupants move freely in the building.[12] Exposure in relatively small enclosed spaces, such as the naturally ventilated rooms where families live together and work places without central ventilation, is probably the most important transmission setting worldwide. In larger buildings with central HVAC systems, however, another important pattern of TB transmission has become evident. Forced-air ventilation potentially encourages airborne TB transmission for two reasons: (1) it effectively brings together greater numbers of occupants either to potentially transmit infection or to become infected, and (2) it effectively distributes and recirculates infectious air, exposing all occupants, albeit to lower concentrations as droplet nuclei are diluted within the larger volume of the ventilation circuit. Examples of TB outbreaks where either convection or recirculation appear to have predominated appear in the literature, but both transmission patterns probably contribute to infections in most institutional settings.[12-15]

Many health care workers fear being "coughed on" by patients with TB. The risk of brief, close-proximity exposures to coughing TB patients is difficult to assess compared to the risk of breathing more dilute contaminated air for many hours. In the immediate vicinity of the source patient, the concentrations of droplet nuclei are high transiently before rapidly dispersing within the available space. However, in a clinic-associated outbreak in South Florida where 17 new infections were identified, a case-control study found that the highest risk was simply being in the building 40 or more hours per week.[7] The next highest risk was associated with administering pentamidine treatments or performing diagnostic sputum inductions, both cough-generating procedures during which higher local concentrations of droplet nuclei would be expected. In an office outbreak in which 27 of 67 workers became infected after a 4-week exposure to an infectious colleague, infections were fairly evenly distributed throughout both floors of the building, and a case-control analysis failed to uncover risks related to proximity to the index patient.[16] At the National Jewish Hospital for Immunology and Respiratory Diseases in Denver, the absence of transmission to staff routinely working in close contact with MDR patients in isolation rooms over the last 10 years may also suggest that close-proximity exposure may not be as important as longer exposure to more dilute contagion.[17] National Jewish Hospital employs high-volume air disinfection within its TB isolation rooms, but such an intervention would not be likely to interrupt person-to-person transmission if close proximity (i.e., being "coughed on") was the predominant mode of transmission. The Lemuel Shattuck Tuberculosis Treatment Unit in Boston, where drug-resistant patients and those with complicated cases receive long-term treatment, has had a similar record of staff safety over the last 3 years (Dr. Marie Turner, personal communication, 1993). There have been no nosocomial infections in this naturally ventilated hospital, where air disinfection depends predominantly on upper room ultraviolet irradiation. If close-proximity contact were the most important type of exposure, one would expect higher rates of infection among intimate contacts than among other household contacts of a patient with active TB. This does not appear to be the case, although we are aware of no data to support or refute this impression. Momentary exposure to a patient's cough is probably less important epidemiologically than prolonged breathing of dispersed organisms.

ENGINEERING CONTROLS TO REDUCE THE RISK OF TRANSMISSION: EFFICACY AND LIMITATIONS

The interruption of person-to-person transmission of pulmonary TB is especially difficult because the infecting particles are airborne,[18] and, as noted, a single TB-containing particle strategically deposited in the lung is all it takes to initiate infection.[19] When guinea pigs become infected after breathing dilute aerosols of tubercle bacilli, as indicated by tuberculin skin test conversion, a single peripheral lesion is found, corresponding to the site of initial implantation of the infecting droplet nucleus. People breathe about 0.353 ft³ of air per minute, or about 500 ft³/day, yet it ordinarily takes months or even years of association with TB patients before infection occurs. Although resistance to initial infection appears to be more variable among humans than among inbred guinea pigs, it is inescapable that infectious droplet nuclei are few and far between. In a study in which a large colony of guinea pigs breathed air from a TB ward for a total of 4 years, it was estimated that there was, on average, only one infectious dose, or quantum, of tubercle bacilli in each 11,000 ft³ of ward air.[18] Because of the huge cumulative volumes of air that people breathe over time, such a dilute suspension of tubercle bacilli in the air was found adequate, by calculation, to account for the rate of infection of student nurses working on TB wards already mentioned. On average, it took about a year.[1,21] When patients produce larger numbers of airborne organisms (e.g., tuberculous laryngitis) or dilution by room ventilation is less, organisms may be less widely separated, and infection may occur more rapidly. Nevertheless, the fact that airborne tubercle bacilli are few and far between, together with the fact that a single one, when deposited in the lung, can cause infection, makes transmission of TB hard to control.

Control at the Source

As a general principle, it is more efficient to control a contaminant at the source than after it is dispersed in the environment. Effective chemotherapy is by far the most desirable form of source control, but transmission can occur before patients are suspected, diagnosed, and placed on effective therapy. The simplest mechanical method of control at the source is to cover the mouth when coughing or sneezing. At the mouth, respiratory droplets have not yet evaporated to become droplet nuclei. The droplets have enough momentum to impact the hand or tissue paper and thus be prevented from contaminating the air.[22] While potentially helpful in reducing the numbers of droplet nuclei generated, covering coughs requires cooperation and alone does not constitute effective infection control.

Patients could theoretically wear face masks continuously, assuming an unlikely degree of cooperation. However, masks cannot contain the force and volume of vigorous coughing, become wet with potentially infectious secretions, and may then become effective atomizers when struck by a blast of air during a cough. While not an adequate form of source control, masks do serve as a reminder to patients and to others that a hazard is at hand. Unfortunately, masks are stigmatizing, and patients should not be routinely required to wear them whenever there are alternative means of control.

In current terminology, face masks refer to mouth and nose covers intended to protect others from the wearer's respiratory secretions. The most common form of face mask used in hospitals is the surgical face mask, intended to prevent contamination of the surgical field by operating room staff. For decades, however, surgical masks have been routinely found outside of isolation rooms, worn for personal protection by hospital employees entering the rooms of potentially infectious patients. However, surgical face masks have neither the fit nor the filtration properties to provide protection from true airborne transmission. Mouth and nose coverings intended to protect the wearer are called *personal respirators* and are related to the devices long used in industry to protect workers from hazardous dusts, mists, and fumes.

Personal respirators worn by health care workers and visitors to protect against infection must filter out droplet nuclei, particles so small that they pass through the tiniest leaks and penetrate all but well-constructed and perfectly fitted personal protective devices. Face masks are not a reliable way of controlling TB at the source, nor do personal respirators provide practical protection for uninfected health care workers. Their use assumes that potentially infectious patients are always identified, whereas in fact transmission often results from patients in whom TB is not even suspected. Personal respirators interfere with communication and other functions, cannot be worn at all times, and cannot be worn by personnel with beards. Unlike industrial settings, where respirators can be issued to everyone in a factory, hospitals are complex places where visitors, volunteers, students, and other patients, as well as workers, must be protected. Despite these considerations and the absence of evidence of efficacy against TB, official recommendations and regulations are likely to continue to specify high-efficiency respirators for use when interacting with potentially infectious patients.[23]

Certain cough-producing procedures, such as sputum induction or pentamidine aerosol treatment, can be performed in a booth, the air of which is filtered before return to the room. High-efficiency particle air (HEPA) filters are capable of removing particles as small as droplet nuclei, and booths or comparable devices offer highly efficient source control at a time when coughing is most severe. Because the therapist does not enter the same breathing space with the patient during the cough-generating procedure, the protection afforded is primarily of importance to the therapist administering the treatment, but other building occupants may also benefit. Whereas a well-ventilated, small room with a dedicated exhaust system has been recommended as an alternative to a booth, it may fail to fully protect therapists who must enter the room between treatments. Likewise, incomplete enclosures (patient hoods) that depend on directional airflow to capture droplet nuclei cannot offer as reliable protection as a well-designed booth, although they may be useful for patients who cannot easily enter a booth.

Since other cough-producing procedures, such as bronchoscopy, cannot be easily performed in an enclosure, personal respiratory protection for the operator is advised in addition to room air disinfection. However, the personal respirator employed must allow easy communication with an awake and frightened patient.

Isolation rooms, in which known or suspected TB patients live continuously until proven noninfectious, are an extension of the booth principle. Air from isolation rooms should be vented to the outdoors or disinfected before being recirculated. Air should flow from corridors into isolation rooms, but where this is not possible, air in both rooms and corridors should be disinfected. Directional airflow into isolation rooms (i.e., negative pressure isolation) requires that the exhaust flow rate exceed intake, including both mechanical ventilation and infiltration. This is often extraordinarily difficult and expensive to achieve and maintain, primarily due to the interdependency of ventilation within buildings. Ventilation system function deteriorates over time as filters become filled, as fan pulley belts slip, and as systems are modified over the years to accommodate renovations and new construction. Opening and closing of windows and doors, outside climatic conditions, "stack" effects (i.e., airflows generated by chimney-like structures), and the air pressures generated by elevators in tall buildings can all neutralize and even reverse directional airflow. In practice, so-called negative pressure rooms are often found to be positive in relation to adjoining corridors, and outbreaks of airborne infection have been reported due to such discrepancies.[24] Sealing isolation rooms from outside air infiltration and the use of anterooms are interventions intended to preserve directional airflow. Anterooms are expensive in new construction and often impossible in renovations without losing valuable patient care or corridor space. Anterooms with closed doors may also impair observation of, care of, and communication with the patient. Effective air disinfection in both rooms and corridors should render the direction of airflow relatively unimportant and does not entail the liabilities and cost of sealed, negative pressure isolation rooms with anterooms. Negative pressure alone does not in any way protect nurses or visitors while in the patient's room. Air disinfection is required.

Air Disinfection

Ventilation

Room ventilation, whether by open windows or by forced air from a HVAC system, vents airborne organisms to the outdoors and dilutes those remaining with uncontaminated outdoor air. Under ordinary circumstances, the air entering a room is assumed to mix thoroughly, and, when the volume of outside air entering equals the volume of the room (one air change), the fraction of airborne organisms left behind equals e^{-1}, or 0.368. Thus, one air change removes about 63 percent of airborne organisms. Since recirculated air recirculates airborne organisms, only outside or disinfected air serves as a diluent.

Let us assume that room air contains one infectious dose (1 quantum) of potentially infectious droplet nuclei. Pulmonary ventilation deposits droplet nuclei on surfaces in the respiratory tract and thus, like room ventilation, removes them from the air of the room. If, over time, a susceptible person breathes an amount of air equal to the volume of the room, there will be about a 37 percent chance that the quantum of airborne TB will be left behind and not removed by being breathed. The chance of infection will be 63 percent. That is a specific example based on the general expression $P = 1 - e^{-Iqpt/Q}$, where P = probability of infection over time (t), the duration of exposure in hours, I = number of infectors (people in the infectious stage of the disease), q = number of quanta of airborne infection produced per hour per infector, p = pulmonary ventilation per susceptible person in cubic feet per minute (cfm), and Q = room ventilation with germ-free air in cfm. A simpler form of this equation was derived from basic principles by Wells, and the more refined exponential form came from Riley et al., who used it in analyzing an outbreak of measles, which, like TB, is airborne.[2,25] Figure 4-1 shows how P varied with Q in two outbreaks of TB in which I, q, p, and t were either known or calculated.[6,16] The squares show the respective values of P and Q that actually existed. Since the probability (P) applies to each susceptible person (S), the number of people infected is $P \times S$ (0.77 × 13 in the Catanzaro study; 0.40 × 67 in the Nardell study).

The curves of Fig. 4-1 become progressively steeper as germ-free ventilation is reduced to very low values, showing that poor ventilation greatly increases the probability of infection. On the other hand, the progressive flattening of the curves with increasing amounts of ventilation shows that enormous amounts of air are required to reduce an already small number of infectious particles in the air. To reduce the chance of infection to 10 percent would require a 14-fold increase in germ-free ventilation in the Catanzaro study (150–2100 cfm) and a 5-fold increase in the Nardell study (1450–7000 cfm). Such increases would produce unacceptable drafts and be outrageously expensive, and a significant number of people would still become infected. The theoretical limits of control by germ-free ventilation are clearly demonstrated. In real life, protection would be worse than predicted due to incomplete mixing.

The cost factor becomes important whenever rooms or buildings are ventilated with 100 percent outdoor air or whenever air from isolation rooms

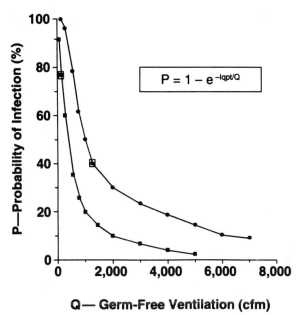

FIGURE 4-1. The effect of room ventilation on the probability of infection.
● = Nardell; ■ = Catanzaro. (*From Riley RL, Nardell EA: Controlling tuberculosis in health care facilities: ventilation, filtration, and ultraviolet air disinfection, in Controlling Occupational Exposure to Tuberculosis, Plant Technology and Safety Management Series, Oakbrook Terrace, IL, Joint Commission of Accredition of Health Care Organizations, 1993.*)

is exhausted directly to the outside. Huge demands are placed on the HVAC system to heat or cool the air under extreme weather conditions. Recirculation of air saves money but spreads airborne organisms throughout the distribution of the HVAC system and is unacceptable unless the air is disinfected in the ducts by filtration or ultraviolet germicidal irradiation (UVGI).

Filtration

High-efficiency particle air (HEPA) filters remove 99.97 percent of airborne particles over 0.3 μm in diameter. Such filters are quite capable of removing infectious droplet nuclei, whose size is believed to range between 1 and 5 μm (average, 3 μm). Outdoor air and HEPA-filtered air are equivalent in the sense that both are free of TB-containing droplet nuclei. A basic problem with HEPA filters is the resistance to moving air through them, the resulting energy costs, and the potential for leakage around the filter.[23] Filters need regular maintenance, including testing for leaks. HEPA filters can be used in ventilating ducts to prevent recirculation of airborne organisms or to provide clean air to individual rooms, such as operating rooms. They work best when they are located close to a source of contamination and when the volume of air filtered is relatively small, as in booths designed for sputum induction and pentamidine aerosol therapy.

Free-standing units designed to filter room air suffer from the disadvantages of both ventilation and filtration. As with room ventilation, large volumes of air must be moved to remove very dilute droplet nuclei. This generates uncomfortable noise and drafts and is unlikely to offer substantial protection unless room ventilation is very poor.[16] Free-standing units are likely to recirculate air in their immediate vicinity, neglecting air in other parts of the room. One popular filtration unit failed to capture smoke generated by a source held only 18 in. from the intake, the smoke rising toward the ceiling as usual (George Kubica, Ph.D., personal communication, 1993). Free-standing units using UVGI (see below) instead of HEPA filters require smaller, quieter blowers, since airflow resistance is less, but they have the same disadvantages as filter units, requiring high-volume air movement with limited potential efficacy for the entire room.[16] Units using both HEPA filters and UVGI are redundant in a way that is not helpful. No droplet nuclei should escape HEPA filtration, and HEPA-trapped organisms need not be irradiated. Although ordinary precautions are prudent in handling used HEPA filters, it is highly unlikely that retained tubercle bacilli, if viable, can easily be resuspended as particles of a respirable size.

Ultraviolet Germicidal Irradiation

Studies to demonstrate the efficacy of upper air irradiation in disinfecting air in the lower part of a room were performed by Wells in the 1930s and 1940s using *Escherichia coli* as the test organism.[2] In the 1960s and 1970s, this work was extended by Riley et al. using *Serratia marcescens* and a simple experimental protocol.[26] After atomization of *S. marcescens* into the air, the decay with time in the number of culturable test organisms in lower room air was determined with upper air UVGI on and with it off. When plotted on semilog paper, the decay curves were approximately straight lines. A decrease due to UVGI of 63 percent was called one equivalent air change, and the results were reported as equivalent air changes per hour (eq AC/h). The experiments were performed under real life conditions with people going about their normal activities and with doors in their normal positions, either open or closed. This simple experimental protocol was used to study the effects of ceiling fans, hot and cold air entering through ceiling diffusers,[27] high and low humidity,[28] corridor irradiation,[29] and UV fixtures of various types. By means of a mathematical model developed by Permutt, the rate of killing in the upper UV-irradiated part of the room and the rate of mixing between upper and lower room air were calculated to supplement the direct determinations made in the lower room air.[26]

Studies with test organisms provided much information about the factors affecting upper air disinfection but gave no quantitative indication of its effectiveness against such pathogens as the tubercle bacillus. To make this transition, it was necessary to know in absolute terms the effectiveness of UV in killing airborne TB as compared to *S. marcescens*. An apparatus was therefore constructed in which the UV intensity and duration of exposure of airborne organisms could be accurately known.[28]

Although, with knowledge of the UV susceptibility of *S. marcescens* and TB, the effectiveness of upper air UVGI against TB could be calculated using the mathematical model of Permutt, a direct demonstration by atomizing TB into the air of a room was considered necessary. It was first determined that the susceptibility of bacille Calmette-Guérin (BCG), a closely related but less virulent *Mycobacterium* than TB, was virtually the same as for TB.[30] Then, with great care to ensure safety, the usual protocol for studying upper air UVGI effectiveness in a room was carried out using BCG. The room had a floor area of 198 ft² and a ceiling height of 11.4 ft. The decay curves indicated that a 30 watt UV fixture could reduce airborne TB at a rate just under 20 eq AC/h (Fig. 4-2). Taking the volume of the room into account, calculations showed this to be equivalent to about 700 cfm of fresh air ventilation. The effect of equivalent ventilation due to UVGI is additive to the effect of fresh air ventilation. The decay of BCG without UVGI indicated fresh air ventilation of about 3 AC/h. Organisms could thus be removed from the air at a combined rate equivalent to 23 AC/h, or more than seven times the rate without upper air UVGI.

The room in which the BCG studies were carried out had a higher ceiling than most offices or corridors, and one of the UV fixtures was of a type that is not commercially available. Nevertheless, on the basis of the work with BCG in a room of approximately 200 ft² floor area, we recommend as a practical guide that one 30 W UV fixture (or two 17 W fixtures for better distribution and less chance of excessive reflection) be used for each 200 ft² of floor area, provided the fixtures are well designed. In large rooms with high ceilings and fixtures suspended from the ceiling, fewer fixtures are needed because their overlapping rays make them mutually supportive. Quantitative studies with test organisms have not been performed in large rooms or under a variety of other real life conditions.

Fixtures must be designed so that excessive UV radiation, either direct or reflected, does not impinge on people. Overexposure causes superficial irritation of skin and eyes (photokeratoconjunctivitis) that can be painful for several hours but does no lasting damage.[31] The National Institute of Occupational

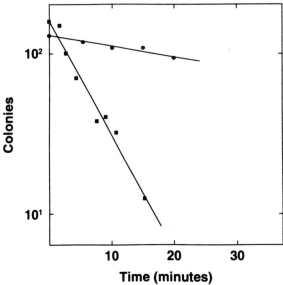

FIGURE 4-2. The effect of ultraviolet irradiation on aerosolized bacilli. Disappearance of aerosolized bacille Calmette-Guérin (BCG) from room air with and without upper air ultraviolet (UV) irradiation using one suspended fixture with a 17 W tube. AC/h = air changes per hour. ● = UV off: 2 AC/hr (12/21/74); ■ = 17 W UV: 12 AC/hr (12/21/74). (*From Riley RL, Nardell EA: Controlling tuberculosis in health care facilities: ventilation, filtration, and ultraviolet air disinfection, in Controlling Occupational Exposure to Tuberculosis, Plant Technology and Safety Management Series, Oakbrook Terrace, IL, Joint Commission of Accredition of Health Care Organizations, 1993.*)

Safety and Health (NIOSH) recognizes an upper limit of 0.2 μW/cm^2 of continuous UVGI exposure over 8 h.[32] The standard is set to avoid superficial eye irritation and is not based on any serious health hazard. At the low levels permitted in the lower room, more than 8 h "stare time" are required to produce eye irritation. The popular misconception that all UV radiation can cause cataracts and skin cancer is based on a failure to understand the differences in the biological effects of various wavelengths within the UV band. UV-A and UV-B from the sun penetrate the earth's atmosphere and penetrate skin and eye tissue sufficiently to cause serious damage after prolonged exposure. Germicidal UV (UV-C) is generated by mercury arc lamps, similar to ordinary fluorescent tubes, but 95 percent of their emission is at the 254 nm wavelength, a shorter wavelength than UV-A or UV-B, with little capacity to penetrate skin and eye tissue and cause serious damage.[33] It has been estimated

18. Riley RL, Mills CC, O'Grady F, Sultan LU, Wittstadt F, Shivpuri DN: Infectiousness of air from a tuberculosis ward. *Am Rev Respir Dis* 85:511, 1962.
19. Riley RL, Mills CC, Nyka W, Weinstock N, Storey PB, Sultan LU, Riley EC, Wells WF: Aerial dissemination of pulmonary tuberculosis: a two year study of contagion in a tuberculosis ward. *Am J Hyg* 80:186, 1959.
20. Wells WF: On air-borne infection: Part II. Droplets and droplet nuclei. *Am J Hyg* 20:611, 1934.
21. Riley RL, Wells WF, Mills CC, Nyka W, McLean RL: Air hygiene in tuberculosis: quantitative studies of infectivity and control in a pilot ward. *Am Rev Tuberc Pulm Dis* 75:420, 1957.
22. Jennison MW: Atomizing of mouth and nose secretions into the air as revealed by high-speed photography, in *Aerobiology*. Washington, DC, American Association for the Advancement of Science, publication no 17, 1942, pp 106–128.
23. Centers for Disease Control: Guidelines for preventing the transmission of tuberculosis in health-care settings, with special focus on HIV-related issues. *MMWR* 39:1, 1990.
24. Edlin BR, Tokars JI, Grieco MH, Crawford JT, Williams J, Sordillo EM, Ong KR, Kilburn JO, Dooley SM, Castro KG, Jarvis WR, Holmberg SD: An outbreak of multi-drug resistant tuberculosis among hospitalized patients with the acquired immunodeficiency syndrome. *N Engl J Med* 326:1514, 1992.
25. Riley EC, Murphy G, Riley RL: Airborne spread of measles in a suburban elementary school. *Am J Epidemiol* 107:421, 1978.
26. Riley RL, Permutt S: Room air disinfection by ultraviolet irradiation of upper air: air mixing and germicidal effectiveness. *Arch Environ Health* 22:208, 1971.
27. Riley RL, Permutt S, Kaufman JE: Room air disinfection by ultraviolet irradiation of upper air: further analysis of convective air exchange. *Arch Environ Health* 23:35, 1971.
28. Riley RL, Kaufman JE: Effect of relative humidity on the inactivation of airborne *Serratia marcescens* by ultraviolet radiation. *J Appl Microbiol* 23:1113, 1972.
29. Riley RL, Kaufman JE: Air disinfection in corridors by upper air irradiation with ultraviolet. *Arch Environ Health* 22:551, 1971.
30. Riley RL, Knight M, Middlebrook G: Ultraviolet susceptibility of BCG and virulent tubercle bacilli. *Am Rev Respir Dis* 113:413, 1976.
31. Nardell EA, Iseman MD, Kubica G, Riley RL, Stead WW, Urbach, F: Multidrug-resistant tuberculosis (letter). *N Engl J Med* 327:1173, 1992.
32. National Institute of Occupational Safety and Health: *Occupational Exposure to Ultraviolet Radiation*. Washington, DC: US Government Printing Office, 1972.
33. Bruls WAG: Transmission of human epidermis and stratum corneum as a function of thickness in the ultraviolet and visible wavelengths. *Photochem Photobiol* 40:485, 1984.
34. Urbach F: Potential carcinogenic effects for human skin of ultraviolet radiation of 253.7 nm wavelength. Presented at Centers for Disease Control Consultant Meeting on Ultraviolet Germicidal Radiation, Atlanta, Dec 10–11, 1991.
35. Jeevan A, Kripke M: Alteration of the immune response to *M. bovis* BCG in mice exposed chronically to low doses of UV irradiation. *Cell Immunol* 130:32, 1990.
36. Zmudzka BZ, Beer J: Activation of human immunodeficiency virus by ultraviolet radiation (yearly review). *Photochem Photobiol* 52:1153, 1990.

PART III
Disease Manifestations

that hundreds of years of continuous exposure to 254 nm UV of 0.2 μW/cm^2 intensity would be required to cause skin cancer.[34] Superficial irritation can be considered an early warning of overexposure, but this has not been experienced in the lower room with proper application of upper air UV. Painters or maintenance people working in the upper part of a room without turning off the UV lamps, however, have been accidently overexposed, resulting in photokeratitis. Education of workers and unmistakable warning labels on fixtures should be used to prevent these mishaps. We recommend that UV tubes not be routinely dusted under ordinary hospital conditions because dust tends to accumulate mainly on the uppermost portion of the lamp, where it interferes only marginally with the most efficacious horizontal rays. Routine maintenance might be required if experience shows that a heavy dust layer accumulates, reducing measured upper room irradiation intensity before the routine replacement time recommended by the manufacturer.

Immunosuppression and HIV activation have been produced experimentally by UV irradiation (usually by more penetrating UV-B) in thin-skinned, hairless mice and in cell culture, respectively.[35,36] The low penetration rate of germicidal UV-C and the extremely low daily exposure levels permitted in the lower room (6 mJ/cm^2) make it highly unlikely that UV fixtures will produce either of these phenomena in humans. Indeed, the daily exposure of more penetrating UV-A and UV-B (summer sunlight) outside of facilities using UVGI may be greater by a factor of more than 100-fold, and neither immunosuppression nor HIV activation has been epidemiologically associated with sunlight, despite large regional and individual differences in exposure.

Certain principles of fixture design are evolving. With ceiling heights of less than 8 ft there is little room for upper air irradiation and considerable danger of excessive reflection, exceeding permitted levels in the lower room. An enclosed air disinfecting apparatus is therefore recommended. For ceiling heights between 8 and 10 ft, multilouvered fixtures are required to prevent excessive upward or downward radiation. Louvers must be carefully constructed to control the UV beam across the top of the room without obstructing it. For high ceilings, fixtures can be open to permit free radiation above the horizontal plane of the fixture. If properly louvered, vertical UV tubes have the advantage of radiating throughout 360° in the horizontal plane. The comparative effectiveness of vertical compared to horizontal tube fixtures has not been studied.

CONCLUSIONS AND RECOMMENDATIONS

Ventilation, air filtration, and UVGI all have a place in controlling the transmission of TB. Adequate ventilation with outdoor air is essential for comfort, while poor ventilation greatly increases the probability of infection (Fig. 4-1). On the other hand, a high ventilation rate is an inefficient, uncomfortable, and costly way to reduce the chance of infection. HEPA filters add to the load on HVAC systems and, with the exception of special situations such as operating rooms, are an inefficient way to provide clean air to large spaces. HEPA filters are the method of choice for cleaning the air vented from small spaces, such as booths for cough-producing procedures. UVGI is well-suited to disinfecting the air throughout buildings where a hazard of TB transmission has been identified. Upper air UVGI has been shown to be quantitatively more effective than feasible levels of ventilation, requires little or no air-moving equipment, is silent, entails no discomfort, and is relatively cheap. A significant problem is the lack of technically qualified consultants to help with the details of installation. UVGI tubes in central ventilating ducts can disinfect recirculated air, reducing the need for costly ventilation with outdoor air, but central air disinfection does little to protect occupants of the same room as the infectious patient. When applied throughout a building, including corridors, upper room UVGI nullifies concerns regarding directional airflow in or out of patients' rooms. Whereas the current focus on negative pressure isolation rooms (and personal respiratory protection) addresses the known or suspected TB patient, it does not address the undiagnosed and unsuspected patient who may transmit in any area of a high-risk facility. Not only do patients move freely within facilities, but so do staff members and contaminated air. For these reasons, air disinfection throughout institutions serving high-risk populations is the logical approach to nosocomial TB transmission.

Specifically, in facilities where the risk of TB transmission is a concern, we recommend upper room UVGI as the primary environmental precaution, superimposed on a well-designed and functioning ventilation system. In hospital emergency departments and clinic waiting rooms, where patients with unsuspected TB may spend hours, we recommend UVGI in addition to efforts to promptly triage patients with chronic cough to isolation areas. In hospitals, clinics, and long-term facilities where infectious TB patients are likely to receive care, isolation rooms, procedure rooms, examination rooms, ordinary patient rooms, common areas, and corridors should be considered for UVGI. In facilities caring for AIDS patients, UVGI in rooms and corridors simultaneously provides isolation and reverse isolation, whereas directional airflow can be in only one direction or the other, potentially exposing highly susceptible patients to airborne infections from other infected patients. Finally, in shelters for the homeless, UVGI is often the only practical environmental precaution against TB transmission.

Unfortunately, no form of air disinfection (ventilation, filters, or UVGI) can provide total protection against airborne transmission if a highly infectious person is in the room. Control of TB ultimately depends on effective surveillance and treatment. Environmental interventions, however, can make transmission from known, suspected, and unsuspected patients less likely. Relatively inexpensive and practical interventions, such as UVGI and patient triage strategies, offer the greatest potential benefit because they can be readily implemented wherever transmission is likely. The above-mentioned recommendations represent a personal viewpoint and may not be entirely consistent with current local and federal guidelines. Because the latter may be subject to enforcement, they should be consulted before interventions are planned and implemented.

REFERENCES

1. Riley RL: Aerial dissemination of tuberculosis. *Am Rev Tuberc Pulm Dis* 76:931, 1957.
2. Wells WF: *Airborne Contagion and Air Hygiene: An Ecological Study of Droplet Infections.* Cambridge, MA: Harvard University Press, 1955.
3. Riley RL, O'Grady F: *Airborne Infection.* New York, Macmillan, 1961.
4. Wells WF: On airborne infection: II-droplets and droplet nuclei. *Am J Hyg* 20:611, 1934.
5. Loudon RG, Spohn SK: Cough frequency and infectivity in patients with pulmonary tuberculosis. *Am Rev Respir Dis* 99:109, 1969.
6. Catanzaro A: Nosocomial tuberculosis. *Am Rev Respir Dis* 125:559, 1982.
7. Daley CL, Small PM, Schecter GF, Schoolnik GK, McAdam RA, Jacobs WR, Hopewell PC: An outbreak of tuberculosis with accelerated progression among persons infected with the human immunodeficiency virus. *N Engl J Med* 326:231, 1992.
8. Loudon RG, Bumbarner LR, Lacy J, Coffman GK: Aerial transmission of mycobacteria. *Am Rev Respir Dis* 100:165, 1969.
9. Wells WF, Ratcliff HL, Crumb C: On the mechanism of droplet nuclei infection: Part 2. Quantitative experimental airborne infection in rabbits. *Am J Hyg* 47:11, 1948.
10. Lurie MB, Heppleston AG, Abramson S, Swartz IB: An evaluation of the method of quantitative airborne infection and its use in the study of the pathogenesis of tuberculosis. *Am Rev Tuberc* 61:765, 1950.
11. Ratcliff HL: Tuberculosis induced by droplet nuclei infection: pulmonary tuberculosis of predetermined initial intensity in mammals. *Am J Hyg* 55:36, 1952.
12. Nardell E, McInnis B, Thomas B, Weidhaas S: Exogenous reinfection with tuberculosis in a shelter for the homeless. *N Engl J Med* 315:1570, 1986.
13. Hutton MD, Stead WW, Cauthen GM, Bloch AB, Ewing WM: Nosocomial transmission of tuberculosis associated with a draining abscess. *J Infect Dis* 161:286, 1990.
14. Houk VN, Baker JH, Sorensen K, Kent DC: The epidemiology of tuberculosis infection in a closed environment. *Arch Environ Health* 16:26, 1968.
15. Ehrenkranz NJ, Kicklighter L: Tuberculosis outbreak in a general hospital: evidence for airborne spread. *Ann Intern Med* 38:377, 1975.
16. Nardell EA, Keegan J, Cheney SA, Etkind SC: Airborne infection: theoretical limits of protection achievable by building ventilation. *Am Rev Respir Dis* 144:302, 1991.
17. Iseman MD: A leap of faith: what can we do to curtail intrainstitutional transmission of tuberculosis? *Ann Intern Med* 177:251, 1992.

18. Riley RL, Mills CC, O'Grady F, Sultan LU, Wittstadt F, Shivpuri DN: Infectiousness of air from a tuberculosis ward. *Am Rev Respir Dis* 85:511, 1962.

19. Riley RL, Mills CC, Nyka W, Weinstock N, Storey PB, Sultan LU, Riley EC, Wells WF: Aerial dissemination of pulmonary tuberculosis: a two year study of contagion in a tuberculosis ward. *Am J Hyg* 80:186, 1959.

20. Wells WF: On air-borne infection: Part II. Droplets and droplet nuclei. *Am J Hyg* 20:611, 1934.

21. Riley RL, Wells WF, Mills CC, Nyka W, McLean RL: Air hygiene in tuberculosis: quantitative studies of infectivity and control in a pilot ward. *Am Rev Tuberc Pulm Dis* 75:420, 1957.

22. Jennison MW: Atomizing of mouth and nose secretions into the air as revealed by high-speed photography, in *Aerobiology*. Washington, DC, American Association for the Advancement of Science, publication no 17, 1942, pp 106–128.

23. Centers for Disease Control: Guidelines for preventing the transmission of tuberculosis in health-care settings, with special focus on HIV-related issues. *MMWR* 39:1, 1990.

24. Edlin BR, Tokars JI, Grieco MH, Crawford JT, Williams J, Sordillo EM, Ong KR, Kilburn JO, Dooley SM, Castro KG, Jarvis WR, Holmberg SD: An outbreak of multi-drug resistant tuberculosis among hospitalized patients with the acquired immunodeficiency syndrome. *N Engl J Med* 326:1514, 1992.

25. Riley EC, Murphy G, Riley RL: Airborne spread of measles in a suburban elementary school. *Am J Epidemiol* 107:421, 1978.

26. Riley RL, Permutt S: Room air disinfection by ultraviolet irradiation of upper air: air mixing and germicidal effectiveness. *Arch Environ Health* 22:208, 1971.

27. Riley RL, Permutt S, Kaufman JE: Room air disinfection by ultraviolet irradiation of upper air: further analysis of convective air exchange. *Arch Environ Health* 23:35, 1971.

28. Riley RL, Kaufman JE: Effect of relative humidity on the inactivation of airborne *Serratia marcescens* by ultraviolet radiation. *J Appl Microbiol* 23:1113, 1972.

29. Riley RL, Kaufman JE: Air disinfection in corridors by upper air irradiation with ultraviolet. *Arch Environ Health* 22:551, 1971.

30. Riley RL, Knight M, Middlebrook G: Ultraviolet susceptibility of BCG and virulent tubercle bacilli. *Am Rev Respir Dis* 113:413, 1976.

31. Nardell EA, Iseman MD, Kubica G, Riley RL, Stead WW, Urbach, F: Multidrug-resistant tuberculosis (letter). *N Engl J Med* 327:1173, 1992.

32. National Institute of Occupational Safety and Health: *Occupational Exposure to Ultraviolet Radiation*. Washington, DC: US Government Printing Office, 1972.

33. Bruls WAG: Transmission of human epidermis and stratum corneum as a function of thickness in the ultraviolet and visible wavelengths. *Photochem Photobiol* 40:485, 1984.

34. Urbach F: Potential carcinogenic effects for human skin of ultraviolet radiation of 253.7 nm wavelength. Presented at Centers for Disease Control Consultant Meeting on Ultraviolet Germicidal Radiation, Atlanta, Dec 10–11, 1991.

35. Jeevan A, Kripke M: Alteration of the immune response to *M. bovis* BCG in mice exposed chronically to low doses of UV irradiation. *Cell Immunol* 130:32, 1990.

36. Zmudzka BZ, Beer J: Activation of human immunodeficiency virus by ultraviolet radiation (yearly review). *Photochem Photobiol* 52:1153, 1990.

CHAPTER 5

Tuberculin Skin Testing

MAYBELLE F. SCHEIN / ROBIN E. HUEBNER

HISTORY OF TUBERCULIN SKIN TESTING

In 1890, Robert Koch announced that he had discovered a cure for tuberculosis (TB). He advocated treating TB patients with subcutaneous doses of what he called tuberculin, a brownish, transparent liquid obtained from culture filtrates of *Mycobacterium tuberculosis*. This treatment caused a febrile reaction within 4–5 h. In most patients, the fever was accompanied by vomiting, rigors, and other constitutional symptoms. Koch reported that giving patients daily increasing doses of tuberculin resulted in the rapid healing of milder cases of TB and slow, progressive improvement in more serious cases. Patients who did not have TB experienced slight pains in the limbs and transient fatigue when injected with tuberculin. Less than a year after the announcement, Koch's tuberculin was disproved as a cure for consumption.[1]

Koch did not realize that he had discovered what would become one of the more widely used diagnostic tests ever developed. The observation of differences in the responses of patients with and without TB to tuberculin led to the development of new methods of administering the antigen. These new methods eliminated the systemic symptoms, but they caused a local reaction at the injection site. Various methods of administration were tested, including a cutaneous test (von Pirquet), a percutaneous test (Moro), a conjunctival test (Calmette), an intracutaneous test (Mantoux), and others. Three methods have remained: the Pirquet cutaneous test, the Moro percutaneous patch test, and the Mantoux intracutaneous test.[1]

By the early 1930s, tuberculin skin testing had become a method of screening apparently healthy persons for infection with *M. tuberculosis*. At that time it was common practice to give a series of 4 or 5 graded doses of tuberculin before excluding the possibility of tuberculous infection. As the use of the tuberculin skin test increased, evidence began accumulating that not all reactions to tuberculin were caused by infection with *M. tuberculosis*. Furcolow et al.[2] skin-tested children and adults with a graduated series of increasing concentrations of tuberculin; individuals were retested with a more concentrated solution of the antigen if the previous skin test result was negative after

4 days. Persons with either active TB or a history of contact with a person who had active disease reacted even to the lowest doses of tuberculin. Persons who had not been exposed to TB reacted only to the large doses of tuberculin. A similar study was conducted among student nurses from 76 schools in the United States. On entering training, the students were tested with 5 tuberculin units (TU) of tuberculin; information on previous exposure to TB also was collected. Those who did not react to the initial dose of tuberculin were retested with 250 TU.[3] A dose-response relationship to the 5 TU was observed: the frequency of reactions increased as the amount of previous exposure to TB increased. The frequency of reaction to the 250 TU dose was independent of the amount of exposure to TB. Radiographic evidence of inactive or healed TB was also related to reactions to the 5 TU but not to the 250 TU dose. The percentage of students with radiographic evidence of calcification was almost 10 times higher for persons who reacted to the lower concentration of tuberculin than for persons who reacted to the higher dose. The frequency of calcification was the same for persons who reacted to the 250 TU dose as for persons who did not react to either dose of tuberculin.[4] Pulmonary calcifications in tuberculin nonreactors or in those persons who only reacted to the higher doses of tuberculin were later found to result from infection with *Histoplasma capsulatum*.[1]

The practical limitations of screening individuals with multiple concentrations of antigen and the recognition that almost all persons would react to tuberculin if large enough doses were given led to the adoption of the 5 TU test as the standard screening dose.

TYPES OF TUBERCULINS

The original method used by Koch to prepare tuberculin involved growing the tubercle bacilli in a medium of glycerinated meat broth and then heat-killing the organisms in a 100°C flowing steam cabinet. The remaining culture medium was concentrated to one-tenth of its original volume on a steam bath. Because this type of tuberculin contains meat broth derivatives, it is no longer in general use. The two types of tuberculin used today are heat-concentrated synthetic-medium tuberculin (Old Tuberculin, or OT) and purified protein derivative (PPD) of tuberculin.

Heat-Concentrated Synthetic-Medium Tuberculin (Old Tuberculin)

The method of preparing OT is virtually identical to that used by Koch, but a synthetic medium, such as Sauton's medium, is used in place of the meat broth. Some manufacturers also prefer to concentrate the culture filtrate under vacuum rather than by heat evaporation. In the United States this type of tuberculin is commonly used in veterinary medicine and as antigen in multiple puncture screening tests.[5]

Preparations of OT are standardized against the Third International Standard for Old Tuberculin. The international unit (IU) of OT is defined as the biologic activity contained in 0.011111 μl of the international standard; each milliliter of the standard contains 90,000 IU.[5]

Purified Protein Derivative of Tuberculin (PPD)

The need for a standardized and reliable preparation of tuberculin was recognized by Florence Seibert of the Henry Phipps Institute. In 1932, Seibert and Munday isolated a low–molecular weight protein by precipitating culture filtrates of tubercle bacilli with trichloroacetic acid (TCA); in low doses, this product was found to be fairly specific for tuberculous infection in both guinea pigs and humans. Efforts to produce a more purified product through ammonium sulfate (AS) precipitation resulted in PPD.[1] Today, three methods are most commonly employed for preparing PPD tuberculin: the TCA precipitation of culture media from bacilli grown in Long's synthetic medium, the AS precipitation of culture filtrates concentrated by ultrafiltration, and a combination of both methods.

The standard for all PPD preparations is tuberculin PPD, lot number 49608. Aliquots of this lot, or PPD-S, prepared in 1941 by Seibert and Glenn, were sent to the Division of Biologics Standards, at the National Institutes of Health for use as the reference standard for the United States; to various commercial and private concerns for research studies; and to the State Serum Institute, Copenhagen, Denmark. In 1952, PPD-S was adopted as the International Standard for Purified Protein Derivative of Mammalian Tuberculin by the World Health Organization.[6] PPD-S refers to only one particular lot of tuberculin; all other PPDs prepared in the United States from *M. tuberculosis* are standardized against this product.

The IU for PPD is defined as the biologic activity contained in 0.000028 mg of PPD-S, consisting of 0.00002 mg PPD plus 0.000008 mg salts. The standard is distributed as a lyophilized powder; each ampule contains 500,000 IU. In the United States and Canada, the potency of PPD preparations is expressed in U.S. units, or TU, rather than IU.[5] One TU is defined as 0.00002 mg of PPD-S.[1]

IMMUNE RESPONSE TO TUBERCULIN

After a person becomes infected with mycobacteria, T lymphocytes in the regional lymph nodes proliferate and become sensitized. Within weeks these sensitized T cells are circulating in the bloodstream. The injection of tuberculin into the skin stimulates the lymphocytes and activates the cascade that leads to a delayed-type hypersensitivity (DTH) response. This response is called "delayed" because the reaction requires 24–48 h to appear. Dermal reactivity involves vasodilation, edema, and the infiltration of lymphocytes, basophils, monocytes, and neutrophils into the site of antigen injection. Antigen-specific T lymphocytes proliferate and release lymphokines, which mediate the accumulation of other cells at the site. Maximal responses generally occur at 48 h after antigen injection.[7] The area of cellular infiltration or induration reflects DTH activity. Erythema, an acute inflammatory reaction marked by redness at the site of injection, can occur in response to a skin test antigen. Erythema is caused by vasodilation and congestion of capillaries. Erythema is not significant; alone, it does not constitute a positive reaction.

The adequate sensitization of lymphocytes to produce a detectable DTH response usually occurs 2–10 weeks after a person is initially infected with *M. tuberculosis*. This sensitivity may persist for years, although reactivity may wane with increasing age.[8]

SENSITIVITY AND SPECIFICITY OF TUBERCULIN TESTING

The tuberculin skin test is the only method of determining *M. tuberculosis* infection; however, it is neither 100 percent sensitive nor 100 percent specific. Approximately 10 percent of patients with active TB will fail to react to tuberculin, although reactivity can be variable. Of the more than 5000 TB patients tested in one study, 96 percent produced measurable induration when skin-tested with tuberculin. These reactions averaged approximately 16–17 mm; few reactions were less than 5 mm.[3] In contrast, Stead found that 20 percent of persons whose sputum was positive for *M. tuberculosis* and in whom TB was newly diagnosed had negative tuberculin test results.[9] Seventeen percent of culture-confirmed TB patients admitted to one hospital in New York had less than 4 mm of induration when tuberculin-tested.[10] In another study, 21 percent of TB patients produced 5 mm of induration or less to tuberculin at the time of diagnosis; reactivity was restored in 95 percent of the patients after 2 weeks of antituberculosis chemotherapy and nutritional supplements.[11]

The specificity of the tuberculin test is also variable. The results of tuberculin skin test surveys in population groups with varying risks of infection with *M. tuberculosis* showed that some people with reactions of less than 6 mm to tuberculin were unlikely to show radiographic evidence of pulmonary calcifications.[12] A large survey of Navy recruits in the United States found a wide range of tuberculin reaction sizes that differed markedly according to the geographic residence of the recruit.[13] In all of the geographic areas, some persons had large tuberculin reactions (≥ 10 mm) that resembled those commonly seen in TB patients. In contrast, small reaction sizes (< 10 mm) occurred with greater frequency in recruits native to the southeast and were less common in recruits from the northern United States. These small reactions are now known to be caused by infection with nontuberculous mycobacteria.[14]

The utility of the tuberculin skin test will depend on the prevalence of infection with *M. tuberculosis* and the relative prevalence of cross-reactions with the nontuberculous mycobacteria. In a population with a low prevalence of tuberculous infection, the majority of the tuberculin reactors will actually be infected with nontuberculous mycobacteria (i.e., the positive predictive value of the test will be low). The positive predictive value for a tuberculin skin test will be much higher in populations in which infection with *M. tuberculosis* is more common. For this reason, tuberculin skin testing should only be done in population groups at increased risk of tuberculous infection.

RISK OF DISEASE IN TUBERCULIN-REACTIVE PERSONS

The development of TB involves initial infection with *M. tuberculosis* and the subsequent progression to active disease. The probability of being infected depends on prolonged, close contact with a person who has active TB. Once infection has been established, the risk of progression to active disease is influenced by factors intrinsic to the individual. Age at infection is important: the very young and the elderly are at increased risk for clinical tuberculosis. Being male or 10 percent below one's ideal body weight also increases the risk of active disease after infection. For all groups, the greatest risk of disease occurs shortly after infection; active TB will develop in 5–15 percent of immunocompetent persons within 2 years of primary infection.[15-17] Although this risk diminishes with time, the additional risk during the older ages results in a cumulative lifetime risk of 10 percent.[18,19]

The suppression of cell-mediated immunity, such as that resulting from infection with human immunodeficiency virus (HIV), can accelerate the development and the progression of active TB in persons infected with *M. tuberculosis*. In recent nosocomial outbreaks of multidrug-resistant TB in Florida and New York, the estimated incubation period of TB in HIV-infected contacts ranged from 22–182 days.[20,21] Selwyn et al.[22] observed 520 injecting drug users (IDUs) enrolled in a methadone maintenance program. Active TB developed in 4 percent of the HIV-seropositive persons, whereas no cases were found in persons who were HIV-seronegative. Among the 49 HIV-seropositive tuberculin reactors, the observed rate of disease over the 2-year follow-up was 14 percent. A similar incidence rate was found among IDUs who were anergic — or nonreactive — to tuberculin and to a panel of DTH antigens.[23] These rates, far greater than the estimated 5-10 percent lifetime risk for the reactivation of latent TB in all immunocompetent persons with positive tuberculin skin test results, underscore the extraordinary risk of TB faced by persons coinfected with *M. tuberculosis* and HIV.

ADMINISTRATION OF THE TUBERCULIN TEST

Two techniques are being used in the United States for tuberculin skin testing. They are the Mantoux method and the multiple-puncture method.

Mantoux Technique

The Mantoux skin test involves the intracutaneous injection of tuberculin into the volar surface of the forearm. A tuberculin syringe with a 26- or 27-gauge needle is used to introduce 0.1 ml of antigen just beneath the top layer of skin; some resistance should be felt as the antigen is injected into the skin. If the test is applied correctly, a discrete, pale elevation of the skin (a wheal) 6-10 mm in diameter is produced. If no wheal is produced, if the antigen goes into the skin with little resistance, if most of the tuberculin leaks out of the injection site, or if the full 0.1 ml of antigen has not been delivered, the skin test has been improperly administered. Another skin test should be given immediately at a site at least 2 in from the original injection.[8]

The recommended dose of PPD to be used in skin testing is 5 TU. Other strengths of tuberculin are available commercially (e.g., 1 and 250 TU); however, they have little clinical usefulness because they can produce frequent false-negative or false-positive reactions.[8] Tuberculin is adsorbed by glass and plastics; therefore, the detergent polysorbate 80 (Tween 80) is added by the manufacturer to minimize a reduction in potency during storage. To further reduce adsorption, syringes should be filled with tuberculin just before the skin test is given. Antigen should never be stored in syringes for more than 1 h. Prolonged exposure to light also reduces the potency of the antigen. Tuberculin should be refrigerated (not frozen) and stored in the dark as much as possible.[8]

Some skill is required to perform a Mantoux skin test. Persons doing tuberculin skin testing should be adequately trained in the proper administration of the test. Poor technique in administering the test can lead to inaccurate test results.

Multiple Puncture Technique

Multiple puncture tests (MPTs) are commonly used because of the speed and ease with which they can be administrated even by unskilled personnel. MPTs introduce tuberculin into the skin through tuberculin-coated prongs on the applicator device. A limitation of this test is that the amount of tuberculin introduced into the skin cannot be precisely controlled. A number of studies have been done comparing the MPT with the Mantoux skin test. The results are conflicting: some investigators reported agreement between the two tests, and others reported many false-positive or false-negative results. This variability justifies the cautious use of the MPT for only special circumstances, namely, for screening large populations with a low expected prevalence of tuberculous infection. Vesicular reactions to MPTs should be interpreted as positive reactions: they indicate the presence of tuberculous infection. However, other reactions to MPTs must be confirmed by the Mantoux test.[8]

READING OF THE TUBERCULIN TEST

Tuberculin skin test results are read 48–72 h after the test is administered because that is the time interval required for the development of a DTH response. Readings should be done in good light, and the patient's forearm should be slightly flexed at the elbow. The margins of induration are found by drawing the index finger lightly across the reaction. When the induration merges imperceptibly with the surrounding skin, the margins can be difficult to locate. Examining the reaction in cross-light while lightly stroking the induration may help define the outer edges of the reaction. After the margins are marked, the induration is measured transversely at its widest diameter with a flexible ruler. Some readers prefer to use the pen technique for measuring tuberculin reactions: in this method a ballpoint pen is placed on the skin and then advanced toward the center of the reaction; when an increased resistance to movement is felt, the border of induration is marked. Howard and Solomon evaluated the pen method of reading and found significant differences between the pen and palpation methods for induration sizes of 5–14 mm.[24] Because the palpation method is the "gold standard," measurements made by the pen method should be interpreted cautiously.

Tuberculin skin test results should be read by persons who have received sufficient training and have had practice to become proficient in measuring DTH responses. Patients should never be allowed to read their own tuberculin test results. The study by Howard and Solomon showed that only 37 percent of patients recognized a reaction that was read as positive by two experienced readers.[24]

The results of tuberculin skin tests should be recorded in millimeters of induration; recording "positive" or "negative" provides no information on the size of the reaction and makes subsequent decisions concerning preventive therapy problematic.

Severe reactions to tuberculin, such as vesiculation or ulceration, are uncommon and are usually seen only among hypersensitive persons. Such reactions usually do not require treatment, and they disappear within several weeks without leaving scars. Anaphylactic or otherwise systemic reactions to PPD have not been documented. Immediate skin test reactions, occurring shortly after injection, have no clinical or epidemiologic significance, do not indicate tuberculous infection, and generally disappear within 48 h.

INTERPRETATION OF THE TUBERCULIN TEST

Current American Thoracic Society (ATS) and Centers for Disease Control and Prevention (CDC) criteria for a positive tuberculin skin test result are designed to increase the likelihood that those at high risk for tuberculosis are considered for preventive therapy and to exclude those with tuberculin reactions not due to *M. tuberculosis* infection from unnecessary drug treatment. These criteria are summarized in Table 5-1.[25]

TABLE 5-1. Recommended Criteria for Tuberculin Positivity by Risk Groups

Induration		
≥5 mm	*≥10 mm*	*≥15 mm*
HIV-infected persons	Foreign-born persons from	No risk factors
IDUs of unknown HIV status	high-prevalence countries	
Recent exposure to TB	Low-income populations	
Persons with chest	IDUs known to be	
radiographs that suggest	HIV-seronegative	
old, healed TB	Correctional institution/	
	nursing home residents	
	Mycobacterial laboratory	
	employees	
	Health care workers	
	Other medical conditions	
	Diabetes mellitus	
	Corticosteroid therapy	
	Gastrectomy	
	Silicosis	
	Chronic malabsorption	

Reactions in persons who have had recent close contact with a person with active TB and persons who have abnormal chest radiographs that suggest TB are likely to represent infection with *M. tuberculosis*. Also, persons infected with HIV may have a limited ability to respond to tuberculin, even if infected with tubercle bacilli. These groups are at high risk for TB; therefore, a 5 mm cutoff is appropriate to ensure that those who are infected with *M. tuberculosis* are considered for preventive therapy.

Persons who have other risk factors for TB, such as medical conditions reported to increase the risk of TB (e.g., diabetes mellitus, gastrectomy, silicosis, or IDU without concomitant HIV infection) or those who are immunocompromised because of other diseases or drug therapy, are at moderate risk for active disease. In these groups, a reaction of 10 mm or greater should be considered positive. This cutoff also is appropriate for foreign-born persons from countries with a high prevalence of TB, residents of correctional institutions and nursing homes, and hospital and mycobacterial laboratory employees.

Finally, in the remainder of the population, which has a very low likelihood of exposure to TB, a higher cutoff (15 mm) is appropriate.

FALSE-POSITIVE REACTIONS TO TUBERCULIN

A small number of tuberculin reactions may be due to errors in administering the test or reading the results; however, the more common causes of false-positive reactions are infection with nontuberculous mycobacteria or vaccination with bacille Calmette-Guérin (BCG).

Infection with Nontuberculous Mycobacteria

An important cause of misinterpreting a positive reaction as representing tuberculous infection is hypersensitivity to mycobacteria other than *M. tuberculosis*. Infection with *Mycobacterium avium* or other members of the genus *Mycobacterium* can result in tuberculin sensitivity. These cross-reactions occur in many parts of the world. Distinguishing reactions resulting from infection with *M. tuberculosis* from those occurring after infection with other mycobacteria is not possible. In general, the larger the induration size, the greater the likelihood that the reaction represents true infection with *M. tuberculosis*.[26]

BCG Vaccination

The interpretation of tuberculin skin test reactions among persons who have been vaccinated with BCG is problematic. In BCG-vaccinated children, reactions to tuberculin range from 3 – 19 mm. The presence or size of postvaccination tuberculin skin test reactions does not reliably predict the degree of protection afforded by BCG.[27]

After BCG vaccination, it is not possible to distinguish between a tuberculin skin test reaction caused by virulent mycobacterial infection or by vaccination itself. Tuberculin skin reactivity due to BCG vaccination wanes with time and is unlikely to persist beyond 10 years after vaccination. Therefore, TB should be included in the differential diagnosis of any TB-like illness, especially if the person received BCG several years before being tuberculin-tested or if the person has been recently exposed to someone who has infectious TB.

General guidelines exist for interpreting tuberculin skin test reactions among recipients of BCG vaccine. The probability that a skin test reaction results from infection with *M. tuberculosis* increases (1) as the size of the reaction increases, (2) when the patient is a contact of a person with TB, especially if that person has already infected others, (3) when there is a family history of TB or when the patient's country of origin has a high prevalence of TB, and (4) as the length of time between vaccination and tuberculin testing increases.[28]

FALSE-NEGATIVE REACTIONS TO TUBERCULIN

Potential causes of false-negative tuberculin skin test results are listed in Table 5-2.[8] A lack of reaction to tuberculin or a small induration size does not alone exclude the diagnosis of TB from consideration. An important cause of tuberculin nonreactivity in HIV-infected persons is anergy.

Anergy

There is increasing evidence that nonresponsiveness to DTH antigens such as tuberculin may be common in HIV-infected persons and that such anergy may occur before the onset of signs and symptoms of HIV infection. Of 108 prisoners in Italy who were tuberculin-tested, positive test results were noted for 28 (43 percent) of 65 HIV-seronegative persons but only for 4 (9 percent) of 43 of the HIV-seropositive persons.[29] Similar results were found in a study of pregnant women admitted to a hospital in Uganda for uncomplicated delivery. Of the 33 HIV-seronegative women, 27 (82 percent) had tuberculin reactions of 3 mm or greater, whereas 48 percent of the HIV-seropositive women had reactions of that size or greater. Differences in the median induration sizes of the two groups were statistically significant (10.6 versus

TABLE 5-2. Potential Causes of False-Negative Tuberculin Skin Test Reactions

Factors related to the person being tested
  Infections
    Viral (HIV, measles, mumps, chickenpox)
    Bacterial (typhoid fever, brucellosis, typhus, leprosy, pertussis, overwhelming TB, tuberculous pleurisy)
    Fungal (South American blastomycosis)
  Live virus vaccinations (measles, mumps, polio)
  Metabolic derangements (chronic renal failure)
  Nutritional factors (severe protein depletion)
  Diseases affecting lymphoid organs (Hodgkin's disease, lymphoma, chronic lymphocytic leukemia, sarcoidosis)
  Drugs (corticosteroids, many other immunosuppressive agents)
  Age (newborns, elderly patients whose sensitivity has waned)
  Recent or overwhelming infection with M. tuberculosis
  Stress (surgery, burns, mental illness, graft-versus-host reactions)
Factors related to the tuberculin used
  Improper storage (exposure to light and heat)
  Improper dilutions
  Chemical denaturation
  Contamination
  Adsorption (partially controlled by adding Tween 80)
Factors related to the method of administration
  Injection of too little antigen
  Delayed administration after drawing into syringe
  Injection too deep
Factors related to reading the test and recording results
  Inexperienced reader
  Conscious or unconscious bias
  Error in reading

7.5 mm, respectively). The relative risk of tuberculin nonreactivity in HIV-infected persons compared with that in non–HIV-infected persons was 2.89.[30]

General cellular hypersensitivity can be assessed by the use of bacterial, viral, and fungal antigens, such as tetanus toxoid, mumps, and *Candida* antigens; coccidioidin; and histoplasmin. These are antigens to which most healthy persons in the population are sensitized. A total of 190 HIV-seropositive and 151 HIV-seronegative IDUs were skin-tested with mumps and *Candida* antigens at the time of tuberculin testing.[31] HIV seropositivity was significantly associated with a lower frequency of tuberculin reactivity (13.8 versus 25.2 percent) and smaller mean tuberculin reaction sizes (2.6 versus 5.4 mm). Persons infected with HIV also were six times more likely to be anergic than persons not infected with HIV. In another study, 150 (31 percent) of 479 HIV-infected persons being screened for tuberculous infection produced less than 3 mm of induration to mumps and *Candida* antigens, tuberculin, and tetanus toxoid (CDC, unpublished data).

Because of these findings of apparent PPD anergy among asymptomatic HIV-infected persons who are at high risk for tuberculous infection, CDC recommends that persons infected with HIV be evaluated for DTH anergy in conjunction with PPD testing.[32]

At least two DTH skin test antigens should be given concurrently with a PPD tuberculin (5 TU) when skin-testing HIV-infected persons. Tetanus toxoid or mumps and *Candida* antigens are considered the most useful, and they should be given by the standard Mantoux method (0.1 ml). The recommended antigens and dosages are summarized in Table 5-3. Second-strength (250 TU) tuberculin is not recommended for anergy evaluation; two-step tuberculin testing also has not been found to be useful in determining immune competency (CDC, unpublished data). An induration of 3 mm or greater to one or more of the antigens (including tuberculin) is evidence of DTH responsiveness; erythema alone is not a measure of DTH reactivity. Persons who do not respond to the antigens are considered anergic. A reaction of 5 mm or greater to tuberculin is necessary to consider a person infected with *M. tuberculosis.*

TABLE 5-3. Dose and Concentrations of Antigens Recommended for Anergy Testing

Antigen	Dose, ml	Concentration	Comments
Candida	0.1	1:100 dilution*	—
Mumps	0.1	Undiluted	Contraindicated for persons with allergies to egg products. No information is available on use of this antigen in pregnant women.
Tetanus toxoid	0.1	1:5 dilution†	Use fluid toxoid; aluminum phosphate-adsorbed toxoid is not recommended.
Tuberculin	0.1	5 TU	—

*Can be purchased already diluted. Use concentration as supplied if antigen is licensed specifically for DTH testing.

†Dilute in human serum albumin. Shelf life is 90 days if refrigerated.

OTHER CONSIDERATIONS IN TUBERCULIN TESTING

Booster Phenomenon

The tuberculin skin test is valuable when used periodically for the surveillance of tuberculin-negative persons at risk for exposure to *M. tuberculosis*. The repeated testing of uninfected persons does not sensitize them to tuberculin; however, hypersensitivity to tuberculin, once established by infection with mycobacteria or BCG vaccination, may gradually wane over the years. If skin testing is done at this point, the reactions may be insignificant. However, the stimulus of the first test may boost or increase the size of the reaction to a second or subsequent test, causing an apparent tuberculin conversion.[33]

Although the booster phenomenon may occur at any age, boosting increases with age and occurs most frequently in persons over 55 years of age. When the tuberculin skin testing of adults is to be repeated periodically, as in employee health or institutional screening programs, the initial use of a two-step testing program can reduce the likelihood that a boosted reaction will be incorrectly interpreted as a recent infection. If the first tuberculin test result is negative, a second 5-TU test should be given 1 – 3 weeks later. If the second tuberculin test result is positive, it probably indicates the boosting of a remote infection. Persons who have a boosting reaction should be classified as being infected, and they are reactors, not converters. If the second test result is negative, the person should be considered uninfected. Any positive reaction to subsequent skin tests indicates recent infection with *M. tuberculosis*; the person should be classified as a converter. Conversion is defined as an increase of 10 mm or greater in skin test reaction size within a 2-year interval for persons 35 years of age or younger and an increase of 15 mm or greater in reaction size for persons 35 years of age or older.[33]

Tuberculin Testing in Infants and Children

There is no medical contraindication to administering a tuberculin skin test to infants. Because their immune systems are immature, many infants younger than 6 weeks of age who are infected with *M. tuberculosis* do not react to tuberculin tests. Older infants and children develop tuberculin sensitivity 3 – 6 weeks after initial infection. Very young children are at increased risk for active TB once infected; therefore, during contact investigations, priority for skin testing and evaluation for preventive therapy should be given to infants and young children who have been exposed to persons with active TB. Infants and young children who have been exposed to TB should be given preventive therapy if their reactions to a tuberculin skin test are 5 mm or greater. A cutoff of 10 mm is appropriate for children in groups where TB case rates are high. A cutoff of 15 mm is used for children with minimal risk of exposure to TB.[34]

Tuberculin Testing during Pregnancy

The use of the tuberculin skin test for screening pregnant women for latent or active TB is indicated in certain circumstances: women who have symptoms of TB, who have recently been exposed to TB, who are in high-risk categories, or who have medical conditions, such as HIV infection, that predispose them to TB, should be tested for tuberculin reactivity. Studies in which the same patients were tested during and after pregnancy have demonstrated that pregnancy has no effect on cutaneous tuberculin hypersensitivity. It is now accepted that tuberculin skin testing is probably valid throughout the course of pregnancy.[35] No reports of teratogenic effects have been documented among women who were tuberculin skin-tested while pregnant.

CONCLUSIONS

The tuberculin skin test is one of the more widely used diagnostic tests ever developed, and it remains the only method of determining *M. tuberculosis* infection. False-positive and false-negative reactions to tuberculin can occur, thus making decisions concerning preventive therapy sometimes problematic. Future research into the development of more sensitive and specific skin test antigens could result in a diagnostic test that distinguishes between infections resulting from individual species of mycobacteria. Clearly, much remains to be learned about tuberculin skin testing, particularly in the era of HIV infection.

REFERENCES

1. Edwards PQ, Edwards LB: Story of the tuberculin test from an epidemiologic viewpoint. *Am Rev Respir Dis* 81:1, 1960.
2. Furcolow ML, Hewell B, Nelson WE, Palmer CE: Quantitative studies of the tuberculin reaction: Part 1. Titration of tuberculin sensitivity and its relation to tuberculous infection. *Public Health Rep* 56:1082, 1941.
3. Palmer CE, Edwards LB: The tuberculin test: in retrospect and prospect. The Baker Lecture, presented at the University of Michigan School of Public Health, Ann Arbor, MI, November 21, 1966.
4. Goddard JC, Edwards LB, Palmer CE: Studies of pulmonary findings and antigen sensitivity

among student nurses: Part 4. Relationship of pulmonary calcifications with sensitivity to tuberculin and histoplasmin. *Public Health Rep* 64:820, 1949.

5. Landi S: Production and standardization of tuberculin, in Kubica GP, Wayne LG (eds), *The Mycobacteria*. New York, Dekker, 1984, pp 505–535.

6. American Thoracic Society: What is PPD-S? A statement by the committee on diagnostic skin testing. *Am Rev Respir Dis* 99:460, 1969.

7. Waksman BH: Delayed (cellular) hypersensitivity, in Samter M (ed), *Immunologic Diseases*, 2d ed. Boston, Little, Brown, 1971, pp 220–252.

8. American Thoracic Society, Centers for Disease Control: The tuberculin skin test. *Am Rev Respir Dis* 124:356, 1981.

9. Stead WW: The new face of tuberculosis. *Hosp Prac* 4:62, 1969.

10. Holden M, Dubin MR, Diamond PH: Frequency of negative intermediate-strength tuberculin sensitivity in patients with active tuberculosis. *N Engl J Med* 285:1506, 1971.

11. Rooney JJ, Crocco JA, Kramer S, Lyons HA: Further observations on tuberculin reactions in active tuberculosis. *Am J Med* 60:517, 1976.

12. Danish Tuberculosis Index: The relation of tuberculin sensitivity to pulmonary calcifications as an index of tuberculosis infection. *Bull WHO* 12:261, 1955.

13. Edwards LB, Acquaviva FA, Livesay VT, Cross FW, Palmer CE: An atlas of sensitivity to tuberculin, PPD-B, and histoplasmin in the United States. *Am Rev Respir Dis* 99:1, 1969.

14. WHO Tuberculosis Research Office: Further studies of geographic variation in naturally acquired tuberculin sensitivity. *Bull WHO* 12:63, 1955.

15. Stead WW, To T, Harrison RW, Abraham JH: Benefit-risk considerations in preventive treatment for tuberculosis in elderly persons. *Ann Intern Med* 107:843, 1987.

16. Medical Research Council: BCG and vole bacillus in the prevention of tuberculosis in adolescence and early adult life. *Bull WHO* 46:3785, 1972.

17. Zeiderberg LD, Gass RS, Dillon A: Williamson County tuberculosis study. *Am Rev Respir Dis* 87:1, 1963.

18. Comstock GW: Frost revisited: the modern epidemiology of tuberculosis. *Am J Epidemiol* 101:363, 1975.

19. Comstock GW, Livesay VT, Woolpert SF: The prognosis of a positive tuberculin reaction in childhood and adolescence. *Am J Epidemiol* 99:131, 1974.

20. Edlin BR, Tokars JI, Grieco MH, Crawford JT, Williams J, Sordillo EM, Ong KR, Kilburn JO, Dooley SW, Castro KG, Jarvis WR, Holmberg SD: An outbreak of multidrug-resistant tuberculosis among hospitalized patients with the acquired immunodeficiency syndrome. *N Engl J Med* 326:1514, 1992.

21. Fischl MA, Daikos GL, Uttamchandani RB, Poblete RB, Morena JN, Reyes RR, Boota AM, Thompson LM, Cleary TJ, Oldham SA, Saldana MJ, Lai S: Clinical presentation and outcome of patients with HIV infection and tuberculosis caused by multiple-drug-resistant bacilli. *Ann Intern Med* 117:184, 1992.

22. Selwyn PA, Hartel D, Lewis VA, Schoenbaum EE, Vermund SH, Klein RS, Walker AT, Friedland GH: A prospective study of the risk of tuberculosis among intravenous drug users with human immunodeficiency virus infection. *N Engl J Med* 320:545, 1989.

23. Selwyn PA, Sckell BM, Alcabes P, Friedland GH, Klein RS, Schoenbaum EE: High risk of active tuberculosis in HIV-infected drug users with cutaneous anergy. *JAMA* 268:504, 1992.

24. Howard TP, Soloman DA: Reading the tuberculin skin test: who, when, and how? *Arch Intern Med* 148:2457, 1988.

25. Centers for Disease Control: The use of preventive therapy for tuberculous infection in the United States: recommendations of the Advisory Committee for Elimination of Tuberculosis. *MMWR* 39:9, 1990.

26. American Thoracic Society: Diagnostic standards and classification of tuberculosis. *Am Rev Respir Dis* 142:725, 1990.

88 • PART II PREVENTION

27. Centers for Disease Control: Use of BCG vaccines in the control of tuberculosis: a joint statement by the ACIP and the Advisory Committee for Elimination of Tuberculosis. *MMWR* 37:663, 1988.
28. Snider DE: Bacille Calmette-Guérin vaccinations and tuberculin skin tests. *JAMA* 253:3438, 1985.
29. Canessa PA, Fasano L, Lavecchia MA, Torraca A, Schiattone ML: Tuberculin skin test in asymptomatic HIV seropositive carriers. *Chest* 96:1215, 1989.
30. Centers for Disease Control: Tuberculin reactions in apparently healthy HIV-seropositive and HIV-seronegative women: Uganda. *MMWR* 39:638, 1990.
31. Graham NMH, Nelson KE, Solomon L, Bonds M, Rizzo RT, Scavotto J, Astemborski J, Vlahov D: Prevalence of tuberculin positivity and skin test anergy in HIV-1-seropositive and -seronegative intravenous drug users. *JAMA* 267:369, 1992.
32. Centers for Disease Control: Purified protein derivative (PPD)-tuberculin anergy and HIV infection: guidelines for anergy testing and management of anergic persons at risk of tuberculosis. *MMWR* 40:27, 1991.
33. Thompson NJ, Glassroth JL, Snider DE, Farer LS: The booster phenomenon in serial tuberculin testing. *Am Rev Respir Dis* 119:587, 1979.
34. Starke JR, Jacobs RF, Jereb J: Resurgence of tuberculosis in children. *J Pediatr* 120:839, 1992.
35. Snider DE: Pregnancy and tuberculosis. *Chest* 86S:10S, 1984.

CHAPTER 6

Preventive Treatment of Tuberculosis: A Clinician's Perspective

THOMAS MOULDING

Isoniazid (INH) can significantly decrease the risk of developing active tuberculosis (TB), when given to persons who have positive reactions to purified protein derivative (PPD) of tuberculin. Unfortunately, INH is not a completely benign drug. A major concern is hepatitis that is occasionally fatal. The American Thoracic Society (ATS) and Centers for Disease Control (CDC) last made recommendations to balance these benefits and risks in 1986.[1] Since 1986, multiple risk-benefit and cost effectiveness analyses have been published that come to conflicting recommendations about the use of INH in persons with positive tuberculin test results.[2-7] Furthermore, the changing epidemiology of TB has provided reasons to increase the use of INH, for example, very high rates of developing TB in persons infected with the human immunodeficiency virus (HIV), in addition to the spread of TB in prisons. In contrast, concerns of increased toxicity are reasons to decrease INH use; there have been reports of INH-associated deaths in young people, primarily women. Consequently, considerable controversy exists about the proper use of INH.

The following is a glossary of terms used in this chapter:

Active TB: disease due to tuberculosis.
Tuberculin-negative: a nonreactive or negative tuberculin test result.
Tuberculin-positive: a positive tuberculin test result.
Reactor: a person who has a positive tuberculin test result.
Low-risk or low-priority reactor: a reactor without additional risk factors that increase the rate of developing TB.
Convertor: a person whose tuberculin test changes from negative to positive within 2 years.

BACKGROUND

Rates of Developing TB

The greater the risk of developing TB, the greater the justification for giving INH and risking a small chance of hepatitis. The chance of developing TB is greatest within the first few months and years after infection with the tubercle bacillus. Because of this, a high priority for using INH is given to definite recent PPD convertors and tuberculin-positive contacts of infectious patients. For the same reason, INH also should be given to tuberculin-negative children who are contacts of infectious patients, since they have a reasonable chance of having recently acquired the tubercle bacillus without having had time to convert their skin test results to positive.

For individuals who do not develop TB within 2 years after being infected, a decreased risk of developing TB probably persists for the life of the individual. Long-term (longitudinal) studies have shown that the risk continues to decrease for at least 20 years[8] and in one study for 30 years.[9] It is debatable whether the risk will continue to decrease after 30 years.[10] Cross-sectional data strongly suggest that there will be an increase in the rates of developing active TB near the end of a long-standing reactor's life,[11] but there are no longitudinal data to show how much of an increase occurs.

Cross-sectional data were used in a 1975 editorial to calculate the rates of developing TB after 20 years.[12] Such data included long-standing reactors and recent convertors. Since recent convertors have higher rates of developing TB and a group that was tuberculin-positive 20 years earlier has no recent convertors, the use of cross-sectional data artificially increases the rates of developing TB. I estimate that it increased these rates about 3-fold. Two risk-benefit analyses based on these cross-sectional data came to the conclusion that the indications for using INH should be expanded in persons over the age of 35.[2,5] Two separate risk-benefit analyses that did not use cross-sectional data and projected a decrease in case rates after 20 years concluded that the existing recommendations for using INH in young adults were at best marginally beneficial.[3,4]

The 1986 ATS-CDC recommendations allow for all reactors under the age of 35 to be given INH if there are no contraindications.[1] This recommendation makes no distinction among the widely varying rates of developing TB in children of various ages. Very young tuberculin-positive children have extremely high rates of developing TB, which frequently takes the form of TB meningitis, making preventive treatment for this group mandatory. In the period from age 5 years to adolescence, children have the lowest rates of developing TB of any time in their lives, with low case fatality rates and disease that is noncavitary and noninfectious in most cases. This calls into question the wisdom of tuberculin testing programs for entering school children at ages 5 or 6, which finds the majority of these reactors. When children reach adolescence, their chance of developing TB is approximately that of adults, and, like adults, they develop infectious cavitary TB. School epidemics due to these adolescent cases of TB have been reported on many occasions. Therefore, if resources exist to carry out a school tuberculin testing program, it should be designed to prevent adolescent cases by finding candidates for preventive treatment. Unfortunately, adolescents are rebellious and often noncompliant with medication. This makes it optimal to tuberculin-test the children and initiate preventive treatment just before adolescence.

PPD reactions are not specific for infection with *Mycobacterium tuberculosis*. Infection with nontuberculous mycobacteria (NTM) can also cause an individual to have a positive PPD reaction. Therefore, the rates of developing TB in reactors vary according to the setting from which the person comes.[13] Furthermore, in most middle-class communities in the United States, the transmission of TB has been very low in the past 30 years. This increases the chance that a reactor has a false-positive tuberculin test, that is, is not infected with the tubercle bacillus.[13] It also increases the chance that the tubercle bacillus was acquired many years in the past. Both factors decrease the risk of developing TB.

By contrast, a reactor from a developing country is much more likely to be infected with the tubercle bacillus. In some poor communities in the United States, such as ghetto areas in big cities, which have a higher than average prevalence of infectious TB cases, greater transmission of TB is more likely to occur than in middle-class communities. Therefore, PPD reactors from a ghetto area are more likely to be infected with the tubercle bacillus, more likely to be infected recently, and more likely to develop TB. The variable criteria for interpreting the tuberculin test with various cutoff points at 5, 10, and 15 mm were introduced in part to provide a better risk stratification for the development of active TB in these various settings (see Chapter 5).[14] Since the prevalence of infection with atypical mycobacteria also affects the prevalence of false-positive tuberculin test results, different cutoff points may also need to be used in various communities based on the prevalence of these nontuberculosis infections.

Infection with the HIV increases the rate of developing active TB to a degree never before seen. It is estimated that HIV infection increases the risk of TB 113-fold and that AIDS increases it 170-fold.[15] HIV infection suppresses the size of the tuberculin reaction, with many, but not all, previous reactors becoming tuberculin-negative. Therefore, preventive treatment should be given to (1) HIV-positive tuberculin reactors, even small reactors with 5 mm of induration to 5 TU of PPD; (2) HIV-positive, tuberculin-negative contacts of an infectious TB patient; and (3) HIV-positive, tuberculin-negative persons known to have been tuberculin-positive in the past. CDC has developed recommendations for giving INH to HIV-positive, tuberculin-negative persons who have been demonstrated to be anergic and come from a group where infection with the tubercle bacillus is likely.[16] The effectiveness of these expanded recommendations, which are reasonable in theory, has not been demonstrated in practice.

Prior Use of BCG

Bacille Calmette-Guérin (BCG; discussed in Chapter 7) has been shown to provide variable (0-80 percent) protection against the development of active TB. The protection provided by BCG wanes with passage of time. BCG usually leads to a positive tuberculin test result that becomes smaller with the passage of time, especially when BCG is given in infancy. For a person who has had BCG and comes from a country with a low prevalence of TB (e.g., western Europe), the tuberculin reaction is much more likely to be caused by BCG than for a person from a developing nation with a high prevalence of TB.

When deciding on the use of INH in tuberculin reactors who have had a BCG vaccination, it is difficult to determine if the reaction is due to BCG or the tubercle bacillus. The usual practice in the United States has been to disregard prior use of BCG. I believe this recommendation is correct if BCG was given in the first 2 years of life. If the BCG was given after the age of 2 years, the positive tuberculin test result has a reasonable chance of being due to BCG, and the BCG most likely gives some degree of protection against TB. Since INH-associated deaths have occurred under the age of 35, I suggest the following recommendations:

1. If a low-risk reactor is from a country with a *low* prevalence of TB and has had BCG after the first 2 years of life and within 20 years, INH should not be given.
2. If a low-risk reactor is from a country with a high prevalence of TB and has had BCG after the first 2 years of life and within the past 5 years, the use of INH is optional.

Protection Provided by INH

The use of INH in persons infected with tubercle bacilli has been shown to reduce the incidence of disease by 54-88 percent.[17] In a trial with infected adults having abnormal chest radiographs, a 12-month course of INH preventive therapy was 75 percent effective among all persons assigned to the regimen and 93 percent effective among those who were compliant with therapy.[18]

The duration of protection from INH is debatable. One study showed that 1 year of INH provides 68 percent protection against developing TB over a 20-year time span, but the protection was limited to 50 percent in the last 4 years.[19] The authors stated, "The results from this study are consistent with the hypothesis that the decrease in risk from TB produced by INH preventive therapy is lifelong." In a study that was limited to 5 years, 6 months of INH provided protection comparable to 1 year of treatment for persons with fibrotic abnormalities on their radiographs, but the number of TB cases in the INH and control group approached one another by the fifth year.[18] This suggests that 6 months of INH provides very little protection after 5 years. One could argue that 6 months of INH would provide a longer degree of protection for reactors without fibrosis on their radiograph, but a prolonged duration of protection (> 10 years) is unlikely.

Deaths Associated with INH

The occurrence of serious hepatitis and death associated with INH is infrequent but real. The incidence of hepatitis and hepatitis deaths increases with age,[20] but 33 possible INH deaths have been reported in individuals, including children, under the age of 35.[21,22] Since reporting is incomplete, there may be significantly more deaths. Furthermore, we can only grossly estimate the number of persons who have taken INH, making it very difficult to determine INH death rates.

Existing data strongly suggest that INH deaths occur more often in women, with an indication of increased rates in the period surrounding pregnancy and the postpartum period.[21,22] Two studies suggest that the risk of dying from INH-induced hepatitis during any period of time increases with the duration of treatment or at least stays constant. One of these studies showed that 84 percent of the deaths (11 out of 13) occurred in patients presenting with hepatitis 8 weeks after starting INH, while only 54 percent of the hepatitis patients presented after 8 weeks.[20] In a second study, 7 of 18 deaths occurred in the second 6 months of treatment despite the fact that many patients discontinued therapy after a few months.[21]

The reports of INH-associated deaths suggest that several drugs or conditions may have been contributing factors: use or excessive use of acetaminophen,[21,23] barbiturate anesthesia,[21,24] prolonged use of tetracycline,[21] and cholecystitis.[21,25] Epidemiologic studies suggest that INH causes chronic liver disease in women.[26,27]

Among 12 of 17 fatal INH hepatitis cases where the duration of hepatitis symptoms was known, the symptoms were present for 7 or more days before the patient presented for medical care.[21] In at least 6 out of 20 cases, the care provider who first saw the patient with symptoms of hepatitis failed to stop the INH. Presumably, most of these cases would not have been fatal if the drug had been stopped earlier. Often, when hepatitis symptoms developed, the patient went to a different health care provider, who may not have known that the patient was taking INH or that INH is hepatotoxic. *To reduce the chance of these occurrences, all patients should be given no more than a 1-month supply of medication, at which time they should be interviewed for symptoms and warned to stop the INH if symptoms occur (especially gastrointestinal complaints with or without flulike symptoms).*

Weighing INH-Associated Deaths against Preventable TB Deaths

Strong proponents of an extensive use of INH preventive treatment argue that the TB deaths prevented by INH, over the life of the patient, fully justify the occasional hepatitis death caused by INH. Opponents usually use three issues to refute this position: (1) the rate of developing TB in reactors probably decreases for most of the individual's life, (2) the duration of protection provided by INH may not be lifelong, and (3) most people view an early death due to INH as more important than a later death due to TB. If one gives significant weight to any one of these three factors, the potential long-term benefit of INH is greatly limited. However, even this limitation does not lead to a blanket rejection of INH use, since in many settings the short-term benefits are quite great.

In addition, I have proposed that a "health concern factor" affects the death rates due to TB and the decision to use INH.[28] In general, TB deaths occur for two reasons: (1) the patient's failure to present for medical care early enough to be cured or (2) a mistake in diagnosis. Patients with sufficient concern about their health to take self-administered preventive treatment would probably present for medical care early enough to be cured if they developed TB and would have less chance of dying of TB and less reason for taking INH. By contrast, clients at a methadone treatment program or inmates of a prison who developed TB at some later point in time would probably present for medical care with more advanced disease, increasing their risk of dying of TB. Since such persons can be given directly observed preventive treatment when in prison or while taking methadone, the health concern factor provides additional justification for giving preventive treatment in these settings.

Prevention of Secondary Cases

INH preventive treatment prevents the development of secondary cases, i.e., persons who would have been infected and would have developed disease if a case of TB had not been prevented by INH. While each TB patient may infect many persons, only a few infected persons develop disease. In the days before

AIDS, it was estimated that each case of TB created one-third of an additional case of TB.[29]

This estimate does not apply to all settings. Persons in prisons who develop infectious TB are in an ideal position to spread their disease efficiently because of their close living quarters. A patient in an AIDS hospice is in an even better position to cause an explosive outbreak. Settings such as these increase the justification for giving preventive treatment.

Cost Effectiveness

In my opinion, the strongest argument against the extensive use of preventive treatment is its lack of cost effectiveness for low-risk reactors. This is best shown by data from a cost-effectiveness analysis, which reveal that preventing a case of TB by giving 6 months of INH to persons with fibrotic lesions on their radiographs costs 2.5 times as much as treating a case of TB, assuming that INH provides 20 years of protection.[30] Specifically, the authors showed it cost $124,796 to prevent 12.4 cases, compared with $49,836 to treat the cases.[30] Reactors with normal radiographs have lower rates of developing TB. Persons reliable enough to take self-administered preventive treatment would probably present early for medical care if they developed TB, require minimal hospitalization, and cooperate with outpatient treatment, making them relatively inexpensive to treat. If one assumes low-risk reactors have one-third the rate of developing TB as persons with fibrotic lesions[8,18] and individuals reliable enough to take self-administered medication are 40 percent less expensive to treat if they develop disease, calculations show that it costs 12.5 times as much to prevent as to treat a case of TB by giving self-administered INH.

The literature contains two analyses that concluded that INH is modestly cost effective.[6,7] I believe these conclusions are wrong because they were (1) based on cross-sectional data; (2) assumed lifetime protection from INH, which is doubtful; and (3) did not consider the lower costs of treating persons reliable enough to take self-administered preventive treatment, plus several other erroneous assumptions.

By contrast, preventive treatment given to inmates in prisons and clients at methadone treatment programs is more likely to be cost effective. If these patients develop TB at some later point in time, they are more likely to delay in seeking medical care, present with advanced disease, require prolonged hospitalization, and be difficult to treat as outpatients, often requiring enforced, directly observed treatment. The cost of these measures can be used to offset the costs of the preventive treatment program.

Optimal Duration of Chemotherapy

The optimal duration of chemotherapy is controversial. As discussed in the section on Protection Provided by INH, 6 months of INH provides significant protection against TB, but this protection may not last more than 5 years.[18] Twelve months of INH has been shown to provide protection for at least 20 years.[19] However, the available data suggest that the chance of dying of hepatitis in persons who present with hepatitis in the last 6 months of therapy is at least equal to and perhaps higher than that for persons who present with hepatitis in the first 6 months (see "Deaths Associated with INH"). A careful cost-effectiveness analysis came to the conclusion that 6 months of INH was more cost effective than 12 months of INH.[30] I believe 6 months of INH is the optimal duration of preventive therapy for most reactors, except those with fibrotic pulmonary lesions and patients with concomitant HIV infection, who should receive 12 months of treatment. In addition, because children under the age of 3 years have a significant chance of developing TB meningitis with irreversible complications, I think they should receive 9 months of treatment.

Can Single Drug Preventive Treatment Cause Drug Resistance?

Multiple drugs are used when treating active disease to prevent the emergence of drug resistance. A single drug, usually INH, is preferred for preventive therapy because it is less expensive and less toxic. It is given on the assumption that we are treating a small population of organisms, making it highly unlikely that INH-resistant organisms will be selected, assuming that proper procedures for ruling out active disease are carried out before it is given.

Very little drug resistance following INH preventive treatment has been reported. This may change when preventive treatment is given to patients infected with both the tubercle bacillus and HIV. AIDS-TB patients tend to have radiographs that are not typical for TB, despite the presence of large numbers of bacilli. Occasionally, AIDS-TB patients with TB bacilli in their sputa have normal chest radiographs. If INH alone is given to these patients with large bacterial populations because active disease is not suspected and not ruled out, drug-resistant disease could readily develop. Therefore, proper bacteriologic sputum examinations are especially important for HIV-infected individuals for whom INH preventive treatment is being considered.

In addition, in poorly compliant HIV-infected persons, there is probably an increased chance that large bacterial populations and drug resistance could develop after starting INH. I saw a contact of an active case of TB who was given INH for preventive treatment, did not take it initially, developed active TB, took it at that time, and developed INH-resistant disease. This patient was not infected with HIV. If the same pattern of "off and on" medication usage occurs in HIV-infected persons, drug resistance is more likely to develop because the tubercle bacilli can multiply very rapidly during periods of noncompliance.

Alternative Drugs for Preventive Therapy

There are good theoretical reasons and one small study with silicotic patients to suggest that 3 months of rifampin (RMP) is at least as effective as 6 months of INH for preventive treatment.[31] Therefore, in persons who are contacts of patients with INH-resistant disease, RMP preventive treatment is reasonable. If the source case is resistant to both INH and RMP, the indications and drugs to use for preventive treatment are controversial. CDC has published suggestions for preventive treatment in this situation.[15]

Patients who experience toxicity or intolerance to INH can usually be given RMP preventive treatment. Furthermore, in situations where it is critical that the preventive therapy be given and one anticipates problems in delivering it, as in the case of a tuberculin-positive infant whom the family plans to take back to a developing country, it is reasonable to substitute RMP for INH, since RMP will probably provide equal protection against TB in a shorter period of time.

SPECIFIC RECOMMENDATIONS

Recently, the Advisory Committee for Elimination of Tuberculosis (ACET), which reports to CDC, has revised the 1986 ATS-CDC recommendations for the preventive treatment of TB,[32] and CDC has published a Core Curriculum on Tuberculosis,[33] which gives further suggestions. In my opinion, additional revisions are in order. In the following material, the ACET and CDC recommendations, with a few wording changes, are given in italics, with my statements presented in regular type.

In the following recommendations, the criterion for a positive reaction to a skin test (in millimeters of induration) for each group is given in parentheses and is based on the material cited in Chapter 5.

In routine health department operations, some patients may be given preventive treatment on the basis of a history of a positive tuberculin test result because of a standard policy not to repeat a tuberculin test if the result has ever been positive. If the "positive" test result was small or moderate in size, it may not meet current criteria for being positive. Therefore, if the induration of the last tuberculin test was not well-documented, the test should be repeated before giving INH, unless the induration was very large or the patient is HIV-positive, taking corticosteroids, or receiving immunosuppressive drugs, three conditions that reduce the size of the reaction.

For the most part, the recommendations listed below are concerned with achieving the proper balance of risk and benefit from giving INH. In my opinion, they do not consider cost effectiveness. Health departments with limited resources may have to restrict the use of INH to high-priority reactors.

Candidates for Preventive Therapy

Certain groups within the infected population are at greater risk than others and should receive high priority for preventive therapy. In the United States, persons with any of the following eight risk factors should be considered candidates for preventive therapy, regardless of age, if they have not previously been treated.

1. *Persons with HIV infection (tuberculin reaction ≥ 5 mm) and persons with risk factors for HIV infection whose HIV infection status is unknown but who are suspected of having HIV infection.* This recommendation should be extended to tuberculin-negative persons with known HIV infection who were known to be tuberculin positive in the past or who have been in contact with an infectious case of TB.
2. *Close contacts of persons with newly diagnosed infectious tuberculosis (tuberculin reaction ≥ 5 mm).* Judgment is needed in applying this recommendation to persons greater than 35 years of age. If the source case is smear-positive and/or most of the children in the family are tuberculin-positive, the source case is highly infectious and INH should be given. If the contact had prolonged exposure to the source case in enclosed spaces, it increases the chance for transmission and the need for using INH. However, if the contact had a known positive tuberculin test result in the past or is likely to have been a long-standing reactor because he or she came from a developing country, the indications for using INH are decreased.
3. *In addition, tuberculin-negative (tuberculin reaction < 5 mm) children and adolescents who have been close contacts of infectious persons within the past 3 months are candidates for preventive therapy until a tuberculin skin test is done 12 weeks after contact with the infectious source.* In situations where the source patient is not excreting large numbers of organisms and all family members are tuberculin-negative on initial testing, one might decide to withhold the use of INH, repeat the tuberculin test in 3 months, and give the INH only if the repeat test result is positive. This restricted use of INH is reasonable for all but children under 5 years of age, to whom INH should be given, because the risk of serious forms of TB in a small child far outweighs the risk of INH hepatitis.
4. Children under the age of 5 years (tuberculin reaction ≥ 5 mm). This recommendation is added to the high-priority list because small children have very high rates of developing fatal or permanently disabling forms of TB (e.g., TB meningitis).

5. *Recent convertors, as indicated by a tuberculin skin test (≥ 10 mm increase within a 2-year period for those < 35 years old; ≥ 15 mm increase for those ≥ 35 years of age).*

6. *Persons with abnormal chest radiographs that show fibrotic lesions likely to represent old healed TB (tuberculin reaction ≥ 5 mm).* Persons with fibrotic lesions or infiltrates on their radiograph have a significant increased risk of developing TB. Persons with calcifications, pleural thickening, but no other abnormalities have a minimal increased risk and should be managed the same as a reactor with a normal chest radiograph. If the radiologist reads the film with a general descriptive term, such as *old granulomatous disease*, the film should be examined to see if the abnormality is a calcification or a more extensive lesion.

7. *Intravenous drug users known to be HIV-seronegative (tuberculin reaction > 10 mm).*

8. *Persons with medical conditions that have been reported to increase the risk of TB (tuberculin reaction > 10 mm). These conditions are:*

   • *Silicosis.* If there is any suspicion of active TB, it is best to treat silicotic patients with multiple drugs.
   • *Gastrectomy.*
   • *Jejunoileal bypass.*
   • *Weight of 10 percent or more below ideal body weight.* In my opinion, this is not enough of a risk factor to justify giving INH to persons over the age of 35. The one study of the issue shows only a 50 percent increased risk of developing TB for reactors 10 percent or more below ideal body weight.[34] Instead, I think excessive weight should be used as a relative contraindication to giving INH because the same study showed that being 10 percent or more overweight reduced the chance of developing TB by 56 percent, which approaches the benefit from taking INH.[34]
   • *Chronic renal failure.*
   • *Diabetes mellitus.* I believe only type I or insulin-dependent diabetes should be considered as a risk factor for giving INH.
   • *Conditions requiring prolonged high-dose corticosteroid therapy and other immunosuppressive therapy.*
   • *Some hematologic disorders (e.g., leukemia and lymphomas).*

   In addition, in the absence of any of the above-mentioned risk factors, persons < 35 years of age in the following high-risk groups are appropriate candidates for preventive therapy if their reaction to a tuberculin skin test is ≥ 10 mm:

   • *Foreign-born persons from high-prevalence countries and medically underserved low-income populations, including high-risk racial or ethnic minority populations, especially blacks, Hispanics and Native Americans.* I would not give

INH to low-risk female reactors, including women in this group, who are pregnant, within 6 months postpartum, or above the age of 20.

• *Residents of facilities for long-term care, such as correctional institutions, nursing homes, and mental institutions.* To this I would add patients in residential drug and alcohol rehabilitation programs.

• *Infected persons < 35 years of age with no additional risk factors for TB should be evaluated for preventive therapy if their reaction to a tuberculin test is ≥ 15 mm. This group should be given a lower priority for preventive efforts than the groups listed above.* (This recommendation was taken from CDC's Core Curriculum on Tuberculosis[33] and Table 1 of the ACET recommendations.[32]) Once again, I would not give INH to low-risk female reactors who are pregnant, within 6 months postpartum, or above the age of 20. I would not give INH to low-risk reactors who received BCG after the first 2 years of life and within the past 20 years if they are from a country with a low prevalence of TB.

In addition to the groups listed above, public health officials should be alert for other high risk populations in their communities. For example, through a review of cases reported in the community over several years, health officials may use geographic or sociodemographic factors to identify groups that should be targeted for intervention. Screening and preventive therapy programs should be initiated and promoted within these populations based on an analysis of cases and infection in the community. To the extent possible, members of high-risk groups and their health care providers should be involved in the design, implementation, and evaluation of these programs. Staff of facilities in which an individual with disease would pose a risk to large numbers of susceptible persons (e.g., correctional institutions, nursing homes, mental institutions, other health care facilities, schools, and child care facilities) may also be considered for preventive therapy if their tuberculin reaction is ≥ 10 mm induration.

Details of Preventive Therapy: Drug, Dosage, Duration, and Method of Delivery

The usual preventive therapy regimen is INH (10 mg/kg daily for children, up to a maximum adult dose of 300 mg daily). The recommended duration of INH preventive treatment varies from 6 to 12 months of continuous therapy. Twelve months of therapy is recommended for persons with HIV infection and persons with stable, abnormal chest radiographs consistent with past TB. The other groups should receive a minimum of 6 months of continuous therapy. Since children under 3 years have a significant chance of developing serious forms of TB (e.g., TB meningitis) children under 3 years should be given a longer, 9-month, period of therapy.

To ensure that persons in high-risk groups comply with therapy, health care personnel should, if necessary, directly observe the therapy. INH can be given twice weekly in a dose of 15 mg/kg (up to 900 mg) when therapy must be directly observed and resources are inadequate for daily therapy. From a practical standpoint, directly observed therapy (DOT) can be delivered to patients in only a few limited settings, such as methadone maintenance programs and prisons and to household contacts of a patient with active TB, when a health worker is giving DOT to the source case. Close contacts of infectious TB patients excreting INH-resistant organisms should be given preventive therapy with RMP at the dose of 15 mg/kg up to 600 mg daily.

Patients should be thoroughly educated and should be monitored monthly, in person, by appropriately trained personnel. INH preventive therapy should not be prescribed if monthly monitoring cannot be done. Some data indicate that black and Hispanic women, especially postpartum, may be at greater risk of serious or fatal adverse reactions and therefore should be closely monitored. Reducing the risk of adverse reactions, even when this risk is low, is as important as providing the benefits of preventive therapy.

As previously mentioned, I would not give INH to women who are pregnant, within the first 6 months postpartum, or over the age of 20 unless they had risk factors that increased the rate of developing TB.

Procedures Prior to Giving Preventive Therapy

• *Before preventive therapy is started, it is important to exclude the possibility of active TB, which would require multiple-drug therapy.* These procedures are (1) taking a chest radiograph of all persons, (2) collecting sputa for smears and cultures if there is any significant abnormality on the radiograph other than calcifications and pleural thickening, and (3) waiting for culture results before giving the INH. Alternatively, the patient can be considered a TB suspect and given multiple drugs until the culture reports become available. If the sputum smear results are negative and the disease is small in extent and looks "inactive," I prefer using INH, RMP, and ethambutal for 3 months, together with a monthly serum transaminase test to monitor for liver toxicity, followed by a repeat radiograph. If the culture results are negative and the repeat radiograph is unchanged, I give one more month of INH and RMP, for a total of 4 months, a regimen that has been shown to be effective for such patients.[35]

For a tuberculin reactor age 3 years and under, it is best to start INH right away, even before a chest radiograph and physician's examination are carried out, if there is any chance that they will be delayed for a week or more. These examinations should be carried out as soon as possible and additional drugs introduced if the patient is found to have active disease.

This rapid initiation of preventive therapy is recommended to avoid the development of TB meningitis while waiting to exclude active TB. If this practice results in the occasional case of monotherapy for active disease, it is unlikely to lead to the selection of drug resistant organisms, since children rarely have cavitary disease with large bacterial populations.

- *Question for a history of previous completion of preventive therapy.*
- *Check for contraindications, including previous INH-associated hepatic injury; history of severe adverse reactions to INH, such as a drug fever or rash or active liver disease of any etiology.*
- *Identify patients who need special precautions, including age > 35 years, concurrent use of any other medication on a long-term basis (in view of possible drug interactions), daily use of alcohol (which is associated with a higher incidence of INH-associated hepatitis), history of previous discontinuation of INH because of side effects (e.g., headaches, dizziness, or nausea), possibility of chronic liver disease, existence of peripheral neuropathy or of a condition such as diabetes mellitus or alcoholism (which might predispose to the development of neuropathy), and pregnancy.*

Most of the conditions listed above, with the exception of diabetes, are relative contraindications to giving INH. When present, INH should be given only if the individual has a significantly higher risk of developing TB. The evidence for drug interactions is minimal, but acetaminophen, barbiturate anesthesia, and prolonged use of tetracycline may increase the chance of INH hepatotoxicity.[21] In addition, since INH alters the metabolism of phenytoin, a reduced dose of this drug must often be given.

Most important: Before giving preventive treatment, all patients should be advised of the side effects of INH that might indicate liver toxicity, stressing nausea, vomiting, yellow eyes, dark urine, unexplained fatigue, and/or abdominal pain and told to stop the drug and report to the clinic immediately if any of these signs or symptoms occurs.

This verbal warning can be supplemented by attaching a label to the INH bottle with this message written in the patient's language.

The patients should also be advised of other symptoms that can be caused by INH, such as skin rashes, joint pains, unexplained fever, and paresthesias of hands or feet. If the patient has an increased chance of developing peripheral neuritis (e.g., is malnourished or diabetic) it is probably wise to give 50 mg of pyridoxine along with the INH.

Monthly Monitoring Procedures

No more than 1 month's supply of medication should be given at any clinic visit to make sure the patients return for monthly counseling and to increase the chance that they will stop the medication if symptoms of liver toxicity occur. This is important, since continuing INH after symptoms appear is apparently a major factor leading to a fatal outcome of INH-associated hepatitis.[21]

At each visit, the patients should be questioned about their compliance with the regimen and urged to take the medications faithfully. They also should be asked about the occurrence of symptoms, especially the hepatotoxicity symptoms listed above, and instructed to stop the INH if they occur.

If too much emphasis is placed on taking the medication faithfully, the drugs may not be stopped when significant toxicity symptoms occur. If too much stress is placed on stopping the medication with symptoms, the drugs may not be taken faithfully. It is difficult to achieve the optimal message, but one should usually stress stopping the medication with symptoms.

If the patient presents with symptoms suggestive of hepatitis, the drugs should be stopped and a serum transaminase test (ALT or AST) performed, and the drug should not be restarted if the test results are over two to three times normal. If the patient has a normal ALT or AST test result but discontinued the drug for more than 1 week before the test was drawn, the test should be repeated 2 weeks after restarting the medication. If the patient has excessively elevated transaminase levels and preventive treatment is clearly needed, RMP can usually be given without a recurrence of hepatotoxicity but should be introduced with periodic transaminase tests to make sure no serious toxicity occurs.

Because of a higher risk of hepatotoxicity among persons over 35 years of age, such persons should have an ALT or AST test at the start of, and periodically during the course of, therapy. Routine transaminase tests are not recommended below the age of 35 because it is felt they are not cost effective. However, if INH must be given to a high-risk reactor under the age of 35 who also has an increased chance of hepatotoxicity (e.g., a postpartum woman who is a recent convertor), routine transaminase tests should be performed.

PREVENTIVE TREATMENT IN THE FUTURE: WILL INDICATIONS CHANGE?

If the recent resurgence of TB spreads to massive epidemic proportions, the factors entering into the decision to give INH will change. The relatively small amount of transmission of TB existing in the United States for the past 30 years could be replaced by extensive transmission. If this occurs, a greater proportion of the reactors will represent actual infection with the tubercle bacillus, and more of them will be recently infected. Both factors increase the chance that a reactor will develop TB and increase the justification for using preventive treatment. A careful watch on the epidemiologic data and a prompt response to changes in the epidemiology will be needed if we are to achieve and maintain an optimal usage of preventive treatment in this changing situation.

REFERENCES

1. American Thoracic Society and Centers for Disease Control (joint statement): Treatment of tuberculosis and tuberculosis infection in adults and children. *Am Rev Respir Dis* 134:355, 1986.
2. Rose DN, Schechter CB, Silver AL: The age threshold for isoniazid chemoprophylaxis: a decision analysis for low-risk tuberculin reactors. *JAMA* 256:2709, 1986.
3. Tsevat J, Taylor WC, Wong JB, Pauker SG: Isoniazid for the tuberculin reactor: take it or leave it. *Am Rev Respir Dis* 137:215, 1988.
4. Colice GL: Decision analysis, public health policy, and isoniazid chemoprophylaxis for young adult tuberculin skin reactors. *Arch Intern Med* 150:2517, 1990.
5. Jordan TJ, Lewit EM, Reichman LB: Isoniazid preventive therapy for tuberculosis: decision analysis considering ethnicity and gender. *Am Rev Respir Dis* 144:1357, 1991.
6. Rose DN, Schechter CB, Fahs MC, Silver AL: Tuberculosis prevention: cost-effectiveness analysis of isoniazid chemoprophylaxis. *Am J Prev Med* 4:102, 1988.
7. Fitzgerald JM, Gafni A: A cost-effectiveness analysis of the routine use of isoniazid prophylaxis in patients with a positive Mantoux skin test. *Am Rev Respir Dis* 142:848, 1990.
8. Comstock GW, Woolpert SF, Livesay VT: Tuberculosis studies in Muscogee County, Georgia: twenty-year evaluation of a community trial of BCG vaccination. *Public Health Rep* 91:276, 1976.
9. Chiba Y: Significance of endogenous reactivation: 30-year follow-up of tuberculin-positive converters. *Bull Int Union Tuberc* 49:321, 1974.
10. Rose DN, Silver AL, Schechter CB: Reply to reference 3, Tsevat et al (letter to editor) and reply by Tsevat J, Taylor WC, Wong JB, Pauker SG. *Am Rev Respir Dis* 138:489, 1988.
11. Stead WW, To T: The significance of the tuberculin skin test in elderly persons. *Ann Intern Med* 107:837, 1987.
12. Comstock GW, Edwards PQ: The competing risks of tuberculosis and hepatitis for adult tuberculin reactors. *Am Rev Respir Dis* 111:573, 1975.
13. Bass JB: The tuberculin test, in Reichman LB, Hershfield ES (eds), *Tuberculosis: A Comprehensive International Approach*. New York, Dekker, 1993, pp 139–146.
14. American Thoracic Society and Centers for Disease Control (joint statement): Diagnostic standards and classification of tuberculosis. *Am Rev Respir Dis* 142:725, 1990.
15. Division of TB Elimination, Centers for Disease Control: Preventive therapy considerations for persons likely to be infected with a multidrug-resistant strain of *Mycobacterium tuberculosis*. *MMWR* 11:66, 1992.
16. Division of TB Elimination, Centers for Disease Control: Purified protein derivative (PPD)-tuberculin anergy and HIV infection: guidelines for anergy testing and management of anergic persons at risk of tuberculosis. *MMWR* 5:27, 1991.
17. Comstock GW, Woolpert SF: Preventive therapy, in Kubica GP, Wayne LG (eds), *The Mycobacteria: A Sourcebook*. New York, Dekker, 1984, pp 1071–1082.
18. International Union against Tuberculosis Committee on Prophylaxis: Efficacy of various

durations of isoniazid preventive therapy for tuberculosis: five years of follow-up in the IUAT trial. *Bull WHO* 60:555, 1982.

19. Comstock GW, Baum C, Snider DE Jr: Isoniazid prophylaxis among Alaskan Eskimos: a final report of the bethel isoniazid studies. *Am Rev Respir Dis* 119:827, 1979.

20. Black M, Mitchell JR, Zimmerman HJ, Ishak KG, Epler GR: Isoniazid-associated hepatitis in 114 patients. *Gastroenterology* 69:289, 1975.

21. Moulding TS, Redeker AG, Kanel GC: Twenty isoniazid-associated deaths in one state. *Am Rev Respir Dis* 140:700, 1989.

22. Snider DE Jr, Caras GJ: Isoniazid-associated hepatitis deaths: a review of available information. *Am Rev Respir Dis* 145:494, 1992.

23. Murphy R, Swartz R, Watkins PB: Severe acetaminophen toxicity in a patient receiving isoniazid. *Ann Intern Med* 113:799, 1990.

24. Pessayre D, Bentata M, Degott C, Nouel O, Miguet JP, Rueff B, Benhamou JP: Isoniazid-rifampin fulminant hepatitis: a possible consequence of the enhancement of isoniazid hepatotoxicity by enzyme induction. *Gastroenterology* 72:284, 1977.

25. Riska N: Hepatitis cases in isoniazid-treated groups and in a control group. *Bull Int Union Tuberc* 51:203, 1976.

26. Boice JD, Fraumeni JF Jr: Late effects following isoniazid therapy. *Am J Public Health* 70:987, 1980.

27. Howe GR, Lindsay J, Coppock E, Miller AB: Isoniazid exposure in relation to cancer incidence and mortality in a cohort of tuberculosis patients. *Int J Epidemiol* 8:305, 1979.

28. Moulding TS, Barnes P: Reply to reference 3, Tsevat et al (letter to editor). *Am Rev Respir Dis* 138:489, 1988.

29. *A Report to the Surgeon General of the Public Health Service by a Task Force on Tuberculosis Control in the United States: The Future of Tuberculosis Control.* Washington, DC, US Department of Health, Education and Welfare, Public Health Service publication no. 1119, 1963.

30. Snider DE Jr, Caras CJ, Koplan JP: Preventive therapy with isoniazid: cost-effectiveness of different durations of therapy. *JAMA* 255:1579, 1986.

31. Hong Kong Chest Service/Tuberculosis Research Centre, Madras/British Medical Research Council: A double-blind placebo-controlled clinical trial of three antituberculosis chemoprophylaxis regimens in patients with silicosis in Hong Kong. *Am Rev Respir Dis* 145:36, 1992.

32. Advisory Committee for Elimination of TB: Use of preventive therapy for tuberculosis infection in the United States. *MMWR* 8:1, 1990.

33. Division of Tuberculosis Elimination, Centers for Disease Control: *Core Curriculum on Tuberculosis,* 2d ed. Atlanta, Centers for Disease Control, publication no. 00-5763, 1991, pp 17-20.

34. Edwards LB, Livesay VT, Acquaviva FA, Palmer CE: Height, weight, tuberculous infection and tuberculous disease. *Arch Environ Health* 22:106, 1971.

35. Dutt AK, Moers D, Stead WW: Smear and culture-negative pulmonary tuberculosis: four-month short-course chemotherapy. *Am Rev Respir Dis* 139:867, 1989.

Disease Manifestations

BCG Vaccination:
An Old Idea Revisited

H. GERARD TEN DAM

HISTORY

The possibility that immunity against tuberculosis (TB) could be acquired was first pointed out by Marfan,[1] who observed that persons with healed TB of the cervical glands apparently were protected against pulmonary TB. Koch[2] showed that guinea pigs infected experimentally with tubercle bacilli progressively developed TB but upon reinfection showed an accelerated reaction (the "Koch phenomenon") at the injection site that healed in a few weeks. Attempts to vaccinate animals with killed or attenuated bacilli gave disappointing results until 1921, when Calmette and Guérin introduced a live attenuated vaccine obtained by serial subculturing for 13 years (231 passages) of a bovine strain on glycerinated bile potato medium. The strain, bacille Calmette-Guérin (BCG), not only had lost its virulence for calves and guinea pigs but also both conferred protection against virulent challenge and induced a certain degree of tuberculin sensitivity.[3]

BCG vaccination started in France in 1924 on a modest scale, mostly in children in contact with cases of open TB, and the strain was distributed to many laboratories all over the world for investigation and vaccine production. An early criticism was that Calmette's method of oral vaccination induced only slight tuberculin sensitivity. Wallgren[4] therefore proposed intradermal vaccination as an alternative. The question of whether tuberculin sensitivity and immunity are related has been debated ever since (see Chapter 2).

In the early 1920s, it was generally held that TB infection was contracted during early childhood and that disease, predominately in adults, occurred through reactivation induced by some incidental extraneous event. It was therefore thought that the application of BCG vaccination should be limited to young children.

No convincing evidence was produced that BCG vaccination actually protected against TB, and its application in children remained limited, espe-

109

cially after a disaster in the German town of Lübeck, in which over 200 infants were vaccinated with vaccine contaminated with virulent bacilli and 73 died.

Heimbeck,[5] who was concerned about the high incidence of TB among student nurses at the Oslo municipal hospital, started tuberculin testing in 1924 and found that less than half of the students had positive results when they joined the service but that almost all did at the end of the 3-year training period. Among the students admitted in 1924–1926, 152 were tuberculin-positive and 185 tuberculin-negative. Three cases of TB occurred among the former and as many as 62 cases (with 8 deaths) among the latter. From these findings, Heimbeck concluded that tuberculin-positive students were far more resistant than tuberculin-negative students. He proposed that rendering the latter tuberculin-positive could protect them against TB. He found that parenteral vaccination with BCG (unlike oral administration) produced a high level of tuberculin sensitivity and so offered BCG to all new students from 1927. His findings are summarized in Table 7-1. Although the vaccinated group was self-selected, it appears that BCG vaccination provided significant protection in a situation where the risk of infection was very high.

Hyge[6] carried out a retrospective study of an epidemic in a state school for girls in the spring of 1943. The girls became exposed to infection at school 1–3 months after routine tuberculin testing and radiographic examination. One year previously, BCG vaccination had been offered at the school, but 46 of the tuberculin-negative girls (12–18 years of age) had refused, and another 59 had entered the school afterward. Among the 105 unvaccinated tuberculin-negative girls, 41 developed primary TB (bacteriologically confirmed in 37), and 14 subsequently developed progressive disease. Among 133 BCG-vaccinated girls, no primary TB was observed, but two girls developed cavitary pulmonary disease. BCG vaccination apparently protected both against primary TB and against progressive disease for at least 12 years.

It is mainly on the basis of these results that mass BCG vaccination campaigns were started after World War II as an "emergency" measure under the auspices of the Scandinavian Red Cross Societies in many European countries and with assistance from UNICEF in many developing countries.

VACCINES

Field assessment showed that the quality of the vaccines and of the vaccinations was often alarmingly poor. Not only did the vaccines differ widely in viability (in the number of culturable particles), but the strains of BCG also appeared to have widely different characteristics. The original strain of BCG had been distributed to a large number of laboratories, and propagation from

TABLE 7-1. Tuberculosis among Student Nurses, Oslo, Municipal Hospital

Year Admitted	Tuberculin-Positive		Tuberculin-Negative			
			Not Vaccinated		Vaccinated	
	Total	No. of Cases	Total	No. of Cases	Total	No. of Cases
1924	58	1	51	18		
1925	42	1	72	26		
1926	52	1	62	18		
1927	64	4	12	6	45	3
1928	65	4	19	11	40	4
1929	61	4	4	0	52	4
1930	58	4	7	4	43	12
1931	54	4	26	10	27	6
1932	42	2	13	5	53	3
1933	47	3	8	3	52	3
1934	45	2	6	3	56	2
Total	588	30	280	104	368	37
Risk		5%		37%		10%

111

culture to culture, through mutation and selection of mutants, mostly accidentally but sometimes deliberately, had given rise to a variety of daughter strains.

By 1960, freeze-drying of BCG vaccine was introduced, and since then freeze-dried vaccine has replaced liquid vaccine. The advantages of freeze-dried vaccine are that it can be stored much longer than liquid vaccine and that it is less sensitive to higher temperatures, which greatly facilitates transport. Further advantages are that quality control examinations can be completed before the vaccine is released, which was not possible for liquid vaccine, and that a reference vaccine can be used in the examinations. Freeze-drying also made it possible to replace propagation from culture to culture simply by keeping the BCG strain in dried form ("seed lot") and thus to prevent further genetic changes.

The availability of the most commonly used strains in the form of seed lots made it interesting to carry out comparisons with a view to identifying those strains that would have the highest immunogenic effect in humans. Evidence that the strains used in trials that showed disappointing results may have had poor immunogenic properties was produced, a posteriori, by Willis and Vandiviere[7] and Jespersen.[8]

Vallishayee et al.[9] showed that vaccines produced from 11 strains differed in terms of tuberculin sensitivity and lesion sizes induced in children. Ladefoged et al.[10] demonstrated that 12 strains could be ranked according to the minimum sensitizing dose needed to produce tuberculin sensitivity in guinea pigs. Strains can also be ranked according to the rate immunity develops in guinea pigs and in bank voles[11] and according to the virulence for hamsters.[12] The rankings obtained in terms of tuberculin reactions in children and in the various animal models were not identical but were concordant in many respects. High-ranking strains included the ones from Rio de Janeiro, Paris, Copenhagen, and Moscow.

EFFECTIVENESS IN ADOLESCENTS AND ADULTS

In the mass vaccination campaigns, it soon became clear that covering all age groups, first with a tuberculin test and 3 days later with vaccination of those whose test results were negative, was not only very difficult in practice but also inefficient, since the large majority of adults were infected already. Emphasis was therefore shifted to vaccinating children before adolescence, by the "direct" method (without a tuberculin test) and in combination with other vaccinations. This approach would be the most efficient TB control measure, provided, of course, that BCG vaccination of school-age children conferred a substantial level of protection.

TABLE 7-2. Mortality after 20 Years in a BCG Trial Among American Indians

Groups	BCG Vaccinated	Controls
No. of persons	1547	1448
No. of deaths from:		
Violence	45	40
Nontuberculosis diseases	46	42
Tuberculosis	13	68
Total no. of deaths	104	150

Unfortunately, on this point, experience varied widely. A controlled trial among American Indians started in 1936 among subjects aged 1 to 20 years whose results were negative on a high-dose tuberculin test produced particularly impressive results in terms of reduction in mortality after 18–20 years.[13] The mortality from all causes was reduced by 35 percent, that from any disease by 50 percent, and that from TB by over 80 percent (see Table 7-2). Other trials in the United States, started in the late 1940s in Georgia and Alabama and in Puerto Rico, showed protection from 0 to 31 percent, whereas a trial in England showed protection of 78 percent after 15 years of follow-up.

These results, together with those of some minor studies, have been reviewed several times[14-16] in attempts to find an explanation for their disparity. The main hypotheses put forward were that the vaccines differed in immunogenic potency (strains and viability); that in some trials the method of administration (dosage) was inadequate; and that in the trials where protection was low, the existence of immunity from infection with environmental mycobacteria, as evidenced by the prevalence of low-grade tuberculin sensitivity (small tuberculin reactions), forestalled protection being observed (i.e., that BCG did not add to the "natural immunity"). The background of the latter hypothesis is of particular interest, since low-grade sensitivity is highly prevalent in most subtropical and tropical countries.

By using concomitant tests with the international standard for purified protein derivative of tuberculin (PPD-S) and the new antigens PPD-B (prepared from a nonphotochromogen isolated at the Battey State Hospital, Rome, GA, now referred to as *Mycobacterium intracellulare*) and PPD-Y (prepared from the "yellow" bacillus, a photochromogen *Mycobacterium kansasii*), Edwards and Palmer[17] demonstrated that different sensitizing agents occurred in the United States. Evidence that low-grade sensitivity could be associated with immunity against TB was obtained in longitudinal studies in Navy recruits[18] and in English children.[19] That environmental mycobacteria can induce both skin sensitivity and protection against challenge with tubercle bacilli was demonstrated by Palmer and Long[20] in guinea pigs. The degree of protection correlated with the degree of sensitivity to PPD-S, although protection was at best not more than 50 percent of that induced by BCG. Moreover, additional BCG vaccination raised protection to the level induced by BCG alone. Thus, immunity associated with sensitization by environmental mycobacteria indeed could have reduced the observable protective effect of BCG vaccination in some trials but alone would have been unlikely to mask it altogether if a potent BCG product had been used. In the trial in Puerto Rico, where subjects with low-grade sensitivity had been included among the vaccinated and the control subjects, the protection among them was of the same (low) level as that among the tuberculin-negative.[21]

Because differences in vaccine quality appeared to be a likely explanation for at least part of the disparity of the results obtained in the controlled trials, it was felt that the more modern vaccines, produced with recent technology and knowledge acquired from experimental models, should show a high protective effect. This prompted the start of a new controlled trial. To verify the possible effect of "natural" protection, it was decided to undertake the trial in an area where low-grade tuberculin sensitivity was highly prevalent.

The trial was organized in South India by the Indian Council of Medical Research in cooperation with the World Health Organization (WHO) and the Centers for Disease Control (CDC) of the U.S. Public Health Services. The intake started in 1968 and was completed in 1971. By then, about 260,000 participants had been included out of a population of 360,000. The entire population (of all ages) was eligible, and, in contrast with previous trials, tuberculin reactors were not excluded, although, of course, the initial tuberculin reactions were carefully recorded so that the results could be analyzed accordingly.

Two vaccines were included, prepared from the Paris strain (seed lot 1173 P2) and the Copenhagen strain (seed lot 1331). They were used in two strengths to study the effect of dosage. The strains were selected because of their high ranking in experimental models and because the Paris seed lot was being used in 20 and the Copenhagen seed lot in 7 national production centers.

The follow-up was both passive and active in $2\frac{1}{2}$-year survey rounds. Case finding aimed at obtaining bacteriological evidence (by microscopy and culture) of pulmonary TB. The first results, after $7\frac{1}{2}$ years,[22] showed that there had been no protective effect at all, and after $10-12\frac{1}{2}$ years there were about equal numbers of cases in all groups.[23]

EXPLANATIONS FOR LACK OF PROTECTION

The results of the trial in India made it clear that the field of application of BCG vaccine is limited. Possible explanations for the lack of protection include the following:

1. *Persons with reactions of 0-7 mm to the initial tuberculin test (3 IU) were considered noninfected.* Since the prevalence of infection was high, some infected people may have been included, and, since the incidence of disease in the infected was some 20 times higher than among the noninfected, a proportion of the cases observed among those with reactions of 0-7 mm may have stemmed from the infected. This may have masked the effectiveness of BCG to some extent but certainly not completely.

2. *The South Indian variant of* Mycobacterium tuberculosis *has low virulence for guinea pigs.*[24] It was suggested that BCG may not protect against infection with this strain. This question was studied by Smith and coworkers.[25] They challenged guinea pigs, vaccinated with a weak or a strong vaccine, with strains of low-virulence, high-virulence, or H37Rv. The weak vaccine protected only against challenge with the low-virulence strain, the strong vaccine against all strains.[26]

3. *BCG vaccination may be followed by a period of increased susceptibility.* This old idea was brought up again in connection with the observed excess incidence in the control subjects. Smith and coworkers[25] addressed this question by varying the challenge interval in their guinea pig studies. Protection was observed after any interval except after 1 week.[27] The fact remained that increased initial susceptibility was observed in the trial and still required an explanation.

4. *The duration of protection from BCG may be very short.* In the trial in India, only very few cases occurred shortly after vaccination, and the risk of infection remained high throughout the follow-up period. Short-lived immunity, therefore, could scarcely have been observed.

5. *Environmental mycobacteria.* In the trial in India, lack of protection coincided again with a high prevalence of low-grade sensitivity. Sensitization was massive indeed: by the age of 10 years, practically all children were sensitized. If sensitization were associated with the same immunogenic effect as BCG, it is likely that protection would not be observed, at least in adults. It also was suggested that previous sensitization with certain environmental bacteria could adversely influence the immunogenic effect of BCG.[28] These questions were investigated by Smith and coworkers[25] in their guinea pig model. Infection with mycobacteria of the *M. avium - M. intracellulare* complex (isolated in the trial area) provided the same level of protection as BCG but only against challenge with a low-virulence strain. The response after BCG vaccination was the same as after subsequent BCG vaccination alone.[29] The latter observation confirms that sensitization with environmental mycobacteria does not interfere with the effect of BCG, as had been demonstrated before by Palmer and Long.[20] The fact that the incidence of TB in the trial area was high indicates that

protection associated with sensitization by environmental mycobacteria cannot be very effective.

6. *Exogenous reinfection.* BCG vaccination cannot be expected to show protection against TB if disease is the result of exogenous reinfection: the primary infection would determine the level of protection whether BCG vaccination were given or not. BCG vaccination does not prevent infection with TB, as is clear from animal experiments and was shown in autopsy studies.[30] From an analysis of the incidence patterns in different protection studies, ten Dam and Pio[31] found that, in studies showing high protection, TB had been predominantly of the primary and evolutive types. In these studies, most cases had been observed early after the intake. They therefore proposed that protection was not observed in the trial in India because the type of TB diagnosed had been the result of exogenous infection.

This hypothesis would also explain the initial excess of TB among the vaccinated. Among the control subjects, a first infection would not lead (according to the hypothesis) to primary or evolutive pulmonary TB, but among the vaccinated it might resemble reinfection and lead to the often cavitary "adult" type of TB, which would have readily been diagnosed in the trial.

The question of whether the "adult" type of TB is caused by endogenous reactivation or reinfection has been debated for a long time, since it was generally impossible to identify the origin of the causative organisms. With the large decreases in the risk of infection in various populations, however, it becomes apparent that the role of endogenous reactivation has been grossly overestimated. Certain special risk groups apart (notably the HIV-infected and persons on immunosuppressive treatment), the annual risk of late reactivation is not higher than about 12–15 per 100,000.[32] During the first 5 years of the trial in England, the average annual incidence among tuberculin reactors was 149 per 100,000. In 1978, among the reactors of the same age group, it was 14.1 per 100,000.[33] A large decrease in the risk of reinfection seems the most likely explanation for this more than 10-fold reduction in incidence.

In summary, three observations that together are indicative of disease from exogenous reinfection in the study population in India are the low incidence in the uninfected, the high incidence in the infected, and the high risk of infection. The low virulence of the infecting bacilli and the protection associated with low-grade sensitivity could explain the low incidence of primary and evolutive TB.

STUDIES IN CHILDREN

Tuberculosis control programs, especially in developing countries, rely mainly on case finding and domiciliary chemotherapy. Case finding followed by adequate treatment reduces not only human suffering but also transmission of TB in the community. However, case finding is often limited to examination of sputum from persons presenting with symptoms of pulmonary TB, and treatment is often not completed.

Young children scarcely benefit from these programs, either directly or indirectly. If they develop TB, they rarely produce sputum, and even if a sample can be obtained, it seldom tests positive on bacteriological examination. Children are prone to developing serious acute forms, such as meningitis and miliary disease, which are often fatal, even when treated. Transmission to young children is almost always intrafamilial and frequently takes place before the source of infection is detected. The control of childhood TB therefore rests mainly on BCG vaccination, especially when systematic examination of child contacts is not feasible. Since it was thought that childhood TB was very hard to detect in a prospective trial, no particular efforts were made to study this aspect in the trial in India. Because childhood TB was not observed, the trial gave no information in this respect. Nevertheless, it cast doubt on the current practice of providing BCG vaccination for children worldwide within the WHO's Expanded Program of Immunization. Some optimism seemed justified, since the main hypotheses that explained lack of protection — natural protection associated with low-grade sensitivity or TB from late exogenous reinfection — would not seem to apply in childhood tuberculosis. Given the uncertainty, it was clearly necessary to evaluate the effectiveness of BCG vaccination of the newborn in an expedient way.

The methods proposed were case control and contact studies. Moreover, a prospective study, which already had started before results of the trial in India were known, had been designed to compare the effects of two vaccines prepared from strains that had ranked quite differently in the experimental models.

CASE CONTROL STUDIES

In case control studies, the protective effect of BCG vaccination is calculated from the vaccination coverages among cases and comparable controls. In

TABLE 7-3. Case Control Studies on the Efficacy of BCG Vaccination of the Newborn

Country (Vaccine)	Age Group Observed	No. of Cases	No. of Controls	Efficacy, %
Brazil[42] (Rio de Janeiro strain)*	0–12	45	90	82
Brazil[43] (Rio de Janeiro strain)*	0–5	73	604	82–84
Burma[44] (Japan BCG Laboratory)	0–5	311	1536	38
Canada[45] (Connaught Laboratories)†	0–18	71	213	60
England[46] (Glaxo Laboratories)	0–1	111	555	49
England[47] (Glaxo Laboratories)	1–12	108	432	64
India[48] (Copenhagen strain)	0–12	61	183	85
Indonesia[25] (Japan BCG Laboratory)	0–5	103	412	40

*Fundação Ataulpho de Paiva, Rio de Janeiro, Brazil.
†Toronto Connaught Medical Research Laboratories.

Table 7-3, the results are shown of a number of case control studies for which it was known which BCG product had been used. The results vary considerably. The highest protection was observed in the studies in Brazil and India. In these studies, the cases were children with tuberculous meningitis. The other studies also included other forms of TB, for which overdiagnosis may have been more frequent. Overdiagnosis would have resulted in an underestimate of the efficacy. Nevertheless, more detailed analysis, by type of disease, confirmed that the highest levels of protection were against the types depending on hematogenous spread, especially meningitis and miliary TB. Protection was lowest against primary complex. Where the age group observed is wide, the observed protection is an average of the level occurring at various times after vaccination, since case control studies show the level at the time of observation, not for the period since vaccination. It also must be noted that, since the quality of the vaccinations (storage, handling, dosage, and administration) may have varied from country to country, it is difficult to draw any firm conclusion regarding the relative efficacy of the various vaccines used.

CONTACT STUDIES

Young children in contact with an infectious case of TB in the family run a high risk of developing TB within only a few months from the time the infectious case is detected. Examination of child contacts of newly detected infectious cases therefore makes it possible to investigate the protective effect of BCG vaccination in an efficient manner. When a vaccination program has been operative for several years, this case finding method ensures comparability of vaccinated and control groups among the cases by stratification (in the analysis) for variables that could influence the risk of TB or the chance of receiving BCG, such as age, sex, relationship to index case, place of birth, and socioeconomic status of the family. A disadvantage of active case finding is that the type of TB cannot be studied precisely because treatment must be provided as soon as TB is suspected. Overdiagnosis is therefore difficult to exclude, and underestimation of the protective effect may occur. The results of the contact studies are shown in Table 7-4. Children up to the age of 5 years were included. Protection varied but was significant in all studies and thus for all vaccines. In the study in Togo, it was clearly higher for disseminated forms of disease than for paratracheal and hilar adenopathy and infiltration without cavity.

A PROSPECTIVE COMPARATIVE STUDY

In order to study possible differences between vaccines, the Chest Service Central Office, Department of Health, Hong Kong, initiated a comparative study.[34] In terms of BCG vaccination, Hong Kong enjoys a particular situation, in that coverage of the newborn is virtually 100 percent. Childhood TB became rare as vaccination coverage increased in spite of the fact that the risk of infection — as judged from the numbers of infectious cases detected — remained considerable. In half of the children, the usual Glaxo vaccine was replaced by a vaccine prepared from the Paris strain by the Japan BCG Laboratory. Intradermal and percutaneous vaccinations were used, since these different techniques are routinely employed in Hong Kong. All children born between 1978 and 1982 were included.

Since vaccines of the Paris seed lot were known to produce suppurative lymphadenitis relatively often, a preliminary calibration study was carried out to find an intradermal dose sufficiently low to minimize complaints. The intradermal dose of the vaccine of the Paris strain applied was 0.05 ml of a

TABLE 7-4. Contact Studies on the Efficacy of BCG Vaccination against Childhood TB

Country (Vaccine)	No. of Contacts		No. of Cases		Efficacy, % (95% Confidence Interval)
	Vaccinated	Unvaccinated	Vaccinated	Unvaccinated	
Thailand[49] (Mérieux)	1253	253	218	66	53 (38–64)
Togo[50] (Glaxo Laboratories)	875	546	62	113	62 (50–70)
Korea[51] (Paris seed lot)	806	417	45	84	74 (62–82)
Colombia* (Paris seed lot)†	330	88	32	23	64 (36–80)

*Calculated from data supplied by Dr. C. E. Salgado.
†Institut Pasteur, Paris.

vaccine containing 0.1 mg/ml, which is one-tenth of the usual strength. This dose had been found to induce a level of tuberculin sensitivity comparable to that induced by the routine Glaxo vaccine. Percutaneous vaccination was by triangular needle (20 punctures). The concentration of the percutaneous vaccine prepared from the Paris seed lot was 16 mg/ml, which is one-tenth of a concentration found adequate in previous studies of percutaneous vaccination. The Glaxo vaccines were of the usual strengths.

By 1982, over 160,000 infants had received intradermal and over 140,000 percutaneous vaccination. For both techniques, the random allocation to the Glaxo or Paris strain vaccine had produced similar group sizes. By 1986, the total number of cases detected was 129: 79 among those given Glaxo vaccine and 50 among those given vaccine of the Paris strain.[34] The difference calculated after stratified analysis was statistically significant and the relative risk for those having received the vaccine of the Paris strain 63 percent. The advantage of the vaccine from the Paris strain was most apparent from the disseminated serious types of TB, as may be seen from Table 7-5. The practical significance of the difference observed, therefore, may be greater than suggested by the total figures.

By the end of 1991, 14 additional cases had been recorded (Chan SL 1992, personal communication), 13 among those given Glaxo vaccine and only 1 among those given vaccine from the Paris strain. The long-term effects may therefore differ substantially, and it will be interesting to continue observations at least well into adolescence, when the risk of TB is expected to be increased.

The significant difference observed so far clearly indicates that qualitative differences between vaccines can be of practical importance and should be studied further.

TABLE 7-5. **Hong Kong BCG Study 1978–1986: Disease Incidence by Type**

Type	Vaccine	
	Glaxo	*Paris Strain*
Primary TB and effusion	32	29
Glandular	7	8
Pulmonary	16	7
Meningeal alone or combined	11	4
Bone and joint	8	1
Multiple sites	5	1

REGULAR RESPONSES AND ADVERSE REACTIONS

The immediate response to a correctly administered intradermal injection of the usual "adult" dose (0.1 ml) is an anemic wheal with an orange peel aspect and a diameter of about 7 mm. Failure to observe this means that either the volume actually injected was inadequate (e.g., because of leakage of the syringe) or that the injection was too deep. Deep injection should be avoided because it will produce a subcutaneous abscess that heals only slowly and often produces an ugly, retracted scar. The wheal disappears within an hour.

Correct intradermal vaccination causes induration at the site of injection, followed by a superficial ulcer, usually covered with a crust, which heals in 2 to 3 months, leaving a slightly excavated round scar. The diameter of the tissue destruction varies according to the bacillary contents of the vaccine. Vaccine assessment in groups of schoolchildren has shown that for the usual vaccines the mean diameter is 5–7 mm, with a standard deviation of not more than 2 mm. In infants (or other people given half the adult dose), the diameter of the lesion will be about 1 mm smaller. If no or only a pinhead-sized lesion is observed during the months following vaccination, it may be concluded fairly firmly that BCG was not given (properly). Variations in the number of culturable particles in the vaccine only slightly influence the size of the local lesion. The lesion size, therefore, gives an indication of the quality of the vaccination rather than of the quality of the vaccine.

Of particular interest is the response to BCG vaccination in terms of sensitivity to a low-dose tuberculin test (usually equivalent to 5 IU of PPD). Unlike the qualitative outcome of the test when used to detect TB infection ("positive" or "negative"), the response to BCG vaccination is quantitative. For a group of children, the distribution of postvaccination tuberculin reactions will not show a dichotomy but will be normal in the statistical sense or at least unimodal. For a particular vaccine, the response is dose-dependent not only in terms of the bacillary content but especially in terms of the proportion of live bacilli in the vaccine. The dose dependence, however, is not very pronounced. If the concentration of a vaccine is reduced to one-tenth or if 99 percent of the bacilli are killed, the mean group reaction size will be reduced by only about 3 mm. Individual variations in response are fairly wide: for a mean reaction size of, say, 17 mm, the standard deviation will generally be about 5 mm. Retesting will produce about the same group results but will show considerable variation in the same subjects. For these reasons, postvaccination tuberculin testing can be used in vaccine assessment by comparing the responses in various groups (usually of some 100 children) but provides little information if applied in an individual subject.

It is not known which dose of BCG should be administered to achieve optimal protection, and the policy therefore has been to give the maximum dose that can be reasonably tolerated, considering lesion size and risk of complications. The best results are therefore obtained with a vaccine of high viability. Whether a high viability and the resulting high level of induced tuberculin sensitivity are relevant for protection in humans is not well known. In a trial in American Indians, a vaccine batch accidentally produced on a poor medium resulted in a low conversion rate as well as in reduced protection,[35] and a tendency for protection to be correlated with viability and tuberculin sensitivity was also seen in a trial in England.[36] BCG-induced tuberculin sensitivity tends to wane in the course of time at a rate that differs according to the population vaccinated and the vaccine used.

In certain tropical areas and especially when the initial level of sensitivity is relatively low, waning appears to occur much faster than, for instance, in European schoolchildren. Waning is prevented, or waned sensitivity restored, if vaccination is followed by a tuberculin test. This occurs to an equal degree for various vaccines but is more pronounced for Danish PPD [of the rinsed tuberculin (RT) batches] than for other tuberculins, including PPD-S. If a BCG-vaccinated person is tuberculin-tested at regular intervals, it will be possible to determine his or her level of acquired sensitivity, or reaction "profile." If this level is <15 mm of induration, an increase in reaction of 5 mm or more is likely to reflect recent infection with *M. tuberculosis.*

The immediate objective of BCG vaccination is to produce benign primary complex: a local lesion with involvement of the draining lymph nodes. The extent to which lymph node involvement occurs depends on the age of the subject, the dose given, and the vaccine strain. Whereas limited lymph node swelling in a large proportion of vaccinated children could be interpreted as a good "take" of the vaccinations, excessive reactions, often resulting in suppurative axillary or cervical lymphadenitis, should of course be avoided. The risk of such reactions is in practice limited to vaccination of the newborn and young infants, in whom it is much higher for vaccines of the Paris or the Copenhagen strain than, for instance, the London and Tokyo strains. The incidence of suppurative lymphadenitis caused by a particular vaccine can be reduced by reducing the dosage: there is a linear relationship.

Lymphadenitis eventually will heal spontaneously, and it is best not to treat the lesion if it remains unadherent to the skin. An adherent or fistulated lymph gland, however, may be drained, and an antituberculous drug may be instilled locally. Experience in WHO-assisted programs has shown that systemic treatment with isoniazid is ineffective. In a comparative study, no difference was observed in the healing process whether erythromycin, isoniazid, isoniazid plus rifampicin, or no drug was administered.[37]

A rare complication of BCG vaccination is disseminated BCG-itis, invariably associated with severe immunodeficiency. It has become a matter of concern in view of the rapidly increasing number of infants infected with HIV, particularly in African countries. By 1990, four cases had been reported.[38] Three of these patients had been treated and improved rapidly upon treatment with isoniazid and rifampicin or ethambutol. Disseminated BCG disease was not observed in two prospective studies, in Congo[39] and Rwanda.[40] These observations support the continued practice of vaccinating asymptomatic infants in Africa as early in life as possible. Children born to HIV-infected mothers most often are not infected with HIV and would benefit from the vaccinations, especially since the mothers are at a greatly increased risk of developing TB. In areas where the risk of TB is low, however, BCG vaccination may be withheld from children known or suspected to be infected with HIV. BCG should be withheld from symptomatic HIV-infected individuals.

Other rare complications include erythema nodosum, iritis, lupus vulgaris, and osteomyelitis. The latter complication was observed mainly in Sweden and Finland and seemed to be associated with the use of the Gothenburg strain of BCG. These complications should be treated with regimens including isoniazid and rifampicin.

FIELDS OF APPLICATION

BCG can only protect the still uninfected from progressive primary TB and endogenous reactivation later in life; it cannot protect those already infected or those that develop TB as a result of reinfection. About one-third of the world's population is infected with *M. tuberculosis*, and disease from reinfection is far more common than thought in the past. Since the infection prevalence and the risk of reinfection obviously increase with age, BCG is a priori indicated for young children. Although in case control and contact studies the results varied, BCG provided substantial protection, especially against serious disseminated forms of TB such as meningitis and miliary disease. BCG vaccination is indicated as early in life as possible in any situation where the risk of TB infection is high or where it is rapidly declining. Prevention of childhood TB has no indirect effect—it does not help to diminish transmission of infection in the community because childhood TB generally is not infectious. However, this should not be taken to imply that vaccination during childhood has no such effect. By preventing hematogenous spread of a subsequent infection, it may prevent not only the serious forms of childhood TB but also endogenous reactivation of residual foci later in life and thus future sources of infection. The potential benefit of BCG obviously diminishes as the risk of TB infection decreases. Eventually, a stage may be reached where the medium-term benefits no longer outweigh the costs and the harm from adverse reactions. At that stage, systematic vaccination of the newborn may be replaced by vaccination of high-risk groups.

BCG vaccination of adolescents has been practiced in many European countries and has been demonstrated to be effective in preventing TB in young adulthood.[41] It thus reduces the risk of infection in the community and contributes to the control of TB. However, again, if the risk of adult TB becomes low, detection and treatment may be more economical than vaccination. BCG vaccination of high-risk groups, such as medical personnel, used to be practiced widely but in several industrialized countries has been abandoned in favor of regular screening by means of the tuberculin test followed by preventive chemotherapy if conversion is observed. Tuberculin-negative individuals in contact with TB patients are at a far greater risk of contracting TB than tuberculin reactors. A screening and preventive treatment program may reduce this risk considerably but may not be effective in individuals who become infected with multidrug-resistant (MDR) bacilli. Such individuals are very difficult to cure if they develop TB. BCG could provide substantial protection and does not preclude other measures. Thus, its use may be helpful in a health care setting in which transmission of MDR strains is a significant danger.

In summary, BCG vaccination is mainly indicated in the newborn in all countries in the Third World as well as in other areas and population groups where the risk of TB infection remains substantial (>0.1 percent per year), which may include health care workers. Health care workers who are tuberculin-negative are at a highly increased risk of contracting TB if exposed to TB patients. If MDR TB is prevalent among patients, BCG vaccination for those workers may be considered if their contact with such patients cannot be excluded. However, it should be borne in mind that BCG should not be given to persons known to be or suspected of being infected with HIV.

REFERENCES

1. Marfan A: De l'immunité conférée par la guérison d'une tuberculose locale pour le phthisie pulmonaire. *Arch Gen Med* 1:423, 575, 1886.
2. Koch R: Weitere Mitteilungen über ein Heilmittel gegen Tuberculose. *Dtsch Med Wschr* 16:1029, 1890.
3. Guérin C: Early history, in Rosenthal SR, *BCG Vaccine: Tuberculosis-Cancer.* Littleton PSG, 1980, pp 35–41.

4. Wallgren A: Intradermal vaccinations with BCG virus. *JAMA* 91:1876, 1928.
5. Heimbeck J: Tuberkoloseschutzmittel BCG: Prinzipien und Resultate. *Schweiz Z Tuberk* 6:209, 1949.
6. Hyge TV: The efficacy of BCG vaccination. *Acta Tuberc Scand* 32:89, 1956.
7. Willis S, Vandiviere M: The heterogeneity of BCG. *Am Rev Respir Dis* 84:288, 1961.
8. Jespersen A: *The Potency of BCG Determined on Animals*. Copenhagen, Statens Seruminstitut, 1971.
9. Vallishayee RS, Shashidhara AN, Bunch-Christensen K, Guld J: Tuberculin sensitivity and skin lesions in children after vaccination with 11 different BCG strains. *Bull WHO* 51:489, 1974.
10. Ladefoged A, Bunch-Christensen K, Guld J: Tuberculin sensitivity in guinea pigs after vaccination with varying doses of BCG of 12 different strains. *Bull WHO* 53:435, 1976.
11. Ladefoged A, Bunch-Christensen K, Guld J: The protective effect in bankvoles of some strains of BCG. *Bull WHO* 43:71, 1970.
12. Bunch-Christensen K, Ladefoged A, Guld J: The virulence of some strains of BCG for golden hamsters. *Bull WHO* 39:821, 1968.
13. Aronson JD, Aronson DF, Taylor HC: A 20 year appraisal of BCG vaccination in the control of tuberculosis. *Arch Intern Med* 101:881, 1958.
14. Hart PD: Efficiency and applicability of mass BCG vaccination in tuberculosis control. *Br Med J* 1:587, 1967.
15. Sutherland I: State of the art in immunoprophylaxis in tuberculosis, in Fogarty International Centre Proceedings no. 14, *Immunization in Tuberculosis*. Washington, DC, US Department of Health, Education and Welfare, publication no (NIH) 72-68, 1972, pp 113–125.
16. ten Dam HG, Toman K, Hitze KL, Guld J: Present knowledge of immunization against tuberculosis. *Bull WHO* 54:255, 1976.
17. Edwards LB, Palmer CE: Epidemiological studies of tuberculin sensitivity: Part 1. Preliminary results with purified protein derivatives prepared from atypical acid fast organisms. *Am J Hyg* 68:213, 1958.
18. Edwards LB, Palmer CE: Identification of the tuberculous-infected by skin tests. *Ann N Y Acad Sci* 154:140, 1968.
19. Hart PD, Sutherland I: BCG and vole bacillus vaccines in the prevention of tuberculosis in adolescence and early adult life. *Br Med J* 2:293, 1977.
20. Palmer CE, Long MW: Effects of infection with atypical mycobacteria on BCG vaccination and tuberculosis. *Am Rev Respir Dis* 94:553, 1966.
21. Comstock GW, Edward PQ: An American view of BCG vaccination, illustrated by results of a controlled trial in Puerto Rico. *Scand J Respir Dis* 53:207, 1972.
22. Tuberculosis Prevention Trial: Trial of BCG vaccines in South India for tuberculosis prevention: first report. *Bull WHO* 57:819, 1979.
23. Tripathy SP: The case for BCG. *Ann Nat Acad Med Sci (India)* 19:12, 1983.
24. Mitchison DA: The virulence of tubercle bacilli from patients with pulmonary tuberculosis in India and other countries. *Bull Int Union Tuberc* 35:287, 1964.
25. Smith PG: Case control studies of the efficacy of BCG against tuberculosis, in *Tuberculosis and Respiratory Diseases: Papers Presented at the Plenary Sessions of the 26th World Conference of the IUAT*. Tokyo, Professional Postgraduate Services, 1987.
26. Hank JA, Chan JK, Edwards ML, Muller D, Smith DW: Influence of the virulence of *Mycobacterium tuberculosis* on protection induced by bacille Calmette-Guérin in guinea pigs. *J Infect Dis* 143:734, 1981.
27. Edwards ML, Muller D, Smith DW: Influence of vaccination-challenge interval on the

protective efficacy of bacille Calmette-Guérin against low-virulence *Mycobacterium tuberculosis. J Infect Dis* 143:739, 1981.

28. Rook GAW, Bahr GM, Stanford JL: The effects of two distinct forms of cell-mediated response to mycobacteria on the protective efficacy of BCG. *Tubercle* 62:63, 1981.
29. Edwards ML, Goodrich JM, Muller D, Pollack A, Ziegler JE, Smith DW: Infection with *Mycobacterium avium intracellulare* and the protective effects of bacille Calmette-Guérin. *J Infect Dis* 145:733, 1982.
30. Sutherland I, Lindgren I: The protective effect of BCG vaccination as indicated by autopsy studies. *Tubercle* 60:225, 1979.
31. ten Dam HG, Pio A: Pathogenesis of tuberculosis and effectiveness of BCG vaccination. *Tubercle* 63:225, 1982.
32. Styblo K: The elimination of tuberculosis in the Netherlands. *Bull Int Union Tuberc Lung Dis* 65:49, 1990.
33. British Thoracic Association: Effectiveness of BCG vaccination in Great Britain in 1978. *Br J Dis Chest* 74:215, 1980.
34. Chan SL, Allen G, Pio A, ten Dam HG, Sutherland I, Kerr I: Comparison of the efficacy of two strains of BCG vaccine for the prevention of tuberculosis among newborn children in Hong Kong. *Bull Int Union Tuberc* 61:36, 1986.
35. Aronson JD, Palmer CE: Experience with BCG vaccine in the control of tuberculosis among North American Indians. *Public Health Rep* 61:802, 1946.
36. Hart PD, Sutherland I, Thomas J: The immunity conferred by effective BCG and vole bacillus vaccines, in relation to individual variations in induced tuberculin sensitivity and to technical variations in the vaccines. *Tubercle (London)* 40:201, 1967.
37. Caglayan S, Yegin O, Kayran K, Timocin N, Kasirga E, Gun M: Is medical therapy effective for regional lymphadenitis following BCG vaccination? *Am J Dis Child* 141:1213, 1987.
38. ten Dam HG: BCG vaccination and HIV infection. *Bull Int Union Tuberc Lung Dis* 65:38, 1990.
39. Lallemant-LeCoeur S, Lallemant M, Cheynier D, Nzingoula S, Drucker J, Larouze B: Bacillus Calmette-Guérin immunization in infants born to HIV-1-seropositive mothers. *AIDS* 5:195, 1991.
40. Msellati P, Dabis F, Lepage P, Hitima DG, Van Goethem L, Vande Perre P: BCG vaccination and pediatric HIV infection, Rwanda, 1988–90. *MMWR* 40:833, 1991.
41. Sutherland I, Springett VH: The effects of the scheme for BCG vaccination of school children in England and Wales and the consequences of discontinuing the scheme at various dates. *J Epidemiol Community Health* 43:15, 1989.
42. Camargos PAM, Guimareas MDC, Antunes CMF: Risk assessment for acquiring meningitis tuberculosis among children not vaccinated with BCG: a case control study. *Int J Epidemiol* 17:193, 1988.
43. Wünsch Filho V, de Castilho EA, Rodrigues LC, Huttly SRA: Effectiveness of BCG vaccination against tuberculous meningitis: a case control study in Sao Paulo, Brazil. *Bull WHO* 68:69, 1990.
44. Myint TT, Win H, Aye OHH, Kyaw-Mint TO: Case control study on evaluation of BCG vaccination of newborn in Rangoon, Burma. *Ann Trop Paediatr* 7:159, 1987.
45. Young TK, Hershfield ES: A case control study to evaluate the effectiveness of mass neonatal BCG vaccination among Canadian Indians. *Am J Public Health* 76:783, 1981.
46. Rodrigues LC, Smith PG: Tuberculosis in developing countries and methods for its control. *Trans R Soc Trop Med* 84:739, 1990.
47. Packe GE, Innes JA: Protective effect of BCG vaccination in infant Asians: a case control study. *Arch Dis Child* 63:277, 1988.

48. Thilothammal N, Prabhakar R, Krishnamurthy PV, Runyan D: Does BCG vaccine prevent tuberculous meningitis in children? Tenth Annual Meeting of the International Clinical Epidemiology Network, Bali, Indonesia, abstract 125, 1992.
49. Padungchan S, Konjanart S, Kasiratta S, ten Dam HG: The effectiveness of BCG vaccination of the newborn against childhood tuberculosis in Bangkok. *Bull WHO* 64:247, 1986.
50. Tidjani O, Amedome A, ten Dam HG: The protective effect of BCG vaccination of the newborn against childhood tuberculosis in an African community. *Tubercle* 67:269, 1986.
51. Jin BW, Hong YP, Kim SJ: A contact study to evaluate the BCG vaccination program in Seoul. *Tubercle* 70:241, 1989.

CHAPTER 8

Pediatric Tuberculosis

RICHARD F. JACOBS

Mycobacterium tuberculosis remains a major infectious disease pathogen causing a significant amount of chronic disease and death throughout the world (Chapter 1). Every year, 8–10 million new cases and 3–5 million deaths are attributed to tuberculosis (TB).[1] Children <15 years of age in developing countries represent 1.3 million cases and 450,000 deaths annually from TB.[2] After decades of consistently declining incidence, a remarkable resurgence of TB is occurring in the world. Between 1987 and 1990, the number of TB cases among children <5 years of age increased 30 percent in the United States. Many experts cite three major factors contributing to the current increase in reported cases in the United States:

1. Coinfection with the human immunodeficiency virus (HIV) is the strongest risk factor. The current epidemic of acquired immunodeficiency syndrome (AIDS) undoubtedly has contributed to the increase in TB, especially among young urban adults.
2. There is a general decline in public health services and access to health care in many communities.[3]
3. The increase in immigration of people from countries with a high prevalence of TB has enlarged the pool of infected individuals in the United States.

   Current estimates indicate that approximately 10 million persons in the United States have asymptomatic tuberculous infection.[4] With no specific treatment, tuberculous disease will develop in 5–10 percent of immunologically normal adults with tuberculous infection at some time during their lives. The risk for children is greater. Estimates indicate that up to 43 percent of children <1 year of age with untreated tuberculous infection will have radiographic evidence of tuberculous diseases, versus 24 percent of children aged 1–5 years and 15 percent of adolescents aged 11–15 years.[5] Therefore, the two major factors that determine the chance that TB will develop in children are (1) environmental, or the likelihood of exposure to a person with infectious TB, and (2) host-related, or the ability of the child's immune system to control the infection.

EPIDEMIOLOGY

Pediatric tuberculous infection and disease rates are highest among children in contact with adults at high risk for TB. From 1953–1984, the incidence of tuberculous disease in the United States declined an average of about 5 percent per year.[4] In 1986, this decline ceased, with an increase in the reported number of cases.[6] In 1990, a total of 25,701 cases were reported, an increase of 9 percent from 1989. It is probable that the true incidence of TB is higher than indicated by these reported cases. Currently, TB is recognized to occur most frequently in fairly well-defined groups of high-risk persons (Table 8-1). Larger cities, with populations of >250,000, account for 18 percent of the nation's population but >42 percent of its reported TB cases. The disease is geographically focal, with 40 percent of the nation's counties reporting no cases and 11 percent of counties reporting 83 percent of the nation's TB cases.

From 1985–1990, the median age for reported TB cases dropped from 49 to 43 years, reversing a longstanding trend that previously was considered to be an indication that the older, more widely infected cohorts were being replaced by younger cohorts with fewer infected persons.[4,7] Among young adults in the United States, TB is predominantly a disease of racial and ethnic minorities. There is some epidemiological and immunological evidence that suggests that African-Americans may be slightly more susceptible to tuberculous infection and disease than are non-Hispanic white persons.[8-10] However,

TABLE 8-1. Groups at High Risk for TB in the United States

Increased risk of exposure to an infectious adult
  Foreign-born persons from high-prevalence countries
  Residents of correctional institutions
  Residents of nursing homes
  Homeless persons
  Users of intravenous and other street drugs
  Poor and medically indigent city dwellers
  Health care workers
  Children living with adults in categories listed above
Increased likelihood that disease will develop once infection occurs
  HIV coinfection
  Certain medical risk factors (e.g., silicosis, diabetes mellitus, or carcinoma)
  Immunosuppressive therapies
  Malnutrition and body weight at 10% less than ideal
  Infants

the extrinsic differences in socioeconomic status, nutrition, access to health care, and living conditions undoubtedly contribute heavily to the increased TB rates among racial minorities.

From 1986–1989, foreign-born persons accounted for 22 percent of the TB in the United States.[11] In 1989, the estimated TB case rate for foreign-born persons arriving in the United States was 13 times greater than the overall U.S. rate.[11] Similar data suggest that tuberculous infection and disease are common among foreign-born adoptee children.[12,13] The three major factors contributing to TB among foreign-born persons are (1) undocumented immigration; (2) lack of tuberculin skin test screening, and (3) poor compliance with preventive therapy among those known to be infected.[14]

For the period 1962–1987, childhood TB rates in the United States declined an average of 6 percent per year.[15] This trend was reversed in 1988. In 1990, a total of 1596 cases of tuberculous infection and disease were reported in children <15 years of age, a 36 percent increase over 1987 and a 21 percent increase over 1989. As expected, 59 percent of these cases occurred in infants and children <5 years of age, the group traditionally at the highest risk for infection and disease. The gender ratio for pediatric TB was 1:1. Tuberculosis is geographically focal. Seven states (California, Florida, Georgia, Illinois, New York, South Carolina, and Texas) account for 63 percent of reported cases among children <5 years of age. As expected, disease rates in children are highest in larger cities, with populations >250,000. The majority of children with TB were born in the United States, but the proportion of foreign-born children has been increasing during this period. Between 1986 and 1990, the proportion of foreign-born cases rose from 13 to 16 percent for children less than 5 years of age, and from 40 to 49 percent among adolescents aged 15–19 years.

The medical literature contains very few cases of children with coexisting TB and HIV infection.[16] Although each infection is relatively uncommon, children with HIV infection are more likely to be in contact with HIV-infected adults, a high-risk population for TB. The clinical presentations of TB in HIV-infected children is poorly described, but diagnosis may be hampered by cutaneous anergy, an extensive differential diagnosis, and difficulty in obtaining adequate samples for culture. All children with tuberculous disease should have HIV serotesting (with informed consent), because the two infections are linked epidemiologically in adults and recommended treatment for TB is prolonged for HIV-infected patients. Each case of TB in a child is a sentinel health event representing recent transmission of TB within the community and a failure of our ability to control TB. The challenge of the 1990s is to recognize new cases of TB in children, treat these cases effectively, and implement control and eradication programs.

CLINICAL MANIFESTATIONS

Most children infected with *M. tuberculosis* are asymptomatic. The characteristic radiographic changes found in an infant or child with primary pulmonary TB may not be present on the initial chest roentgenogram. The most common radiographic presentations in children include hilar lymphadenopathy, mediastinal lymphadenopathy, pulmonary involvement with segmental or lobar infiltrate, consolidated pneumonia, atelectasis, pleural effusion, or miliary TB. The clinical presentations of extrapulmonary TB include cervical lymphadenopathy, bone and joint involvement, and tuberculous meningitis. Although the classic triad of fever, weight loss, and night sweats can be seen in older children, presentation in children <5 years of age may vary from miliary TB and tuberculous meningitis to an unresponsive pneumonia to the finding of hilar adenopathy upon contact investigation in asymptomatic children.[5]

Extrapulmonary tuberculous disease occurs in approximately 20 percent of infants and children with TB. Early disease is characterized by lymphadenopathy or miliary, meningeal, bone, joint, or renal involvement. Later clinical presentations include chronic draining otorrhea, chronic mastoiditis, or fever of unknown origin. Progressive primary pulmonary TB, a rare but potentially fatal complication, is characterized by fever, cough, weight loss, and moist crackles heard over the involved segment of lung. The chest roentgenogram shows consolidation and often a cavity. Miliary disease follows the rupture of a small caseous focus into the bloodstream and is characterized by fever and weight loss without pulmonary symptoms. Results of the chest examination are normal, but the spleen is nearly always enlarged. Within 1–3 weeks of the onset of fever, multiple small nodules of a uniform size appear on the chest roentgenogram.

Tuberculous meningitis often is a complication of miliary disease and may be heralded by personality changes, irritability, anorexia, and listlessness. Within a few weeks, headache, stiff neck, vomiting, drowsiness, and cranial nerve palsies develop. The final stage is coma. The cerebrospinal fluid is clear, with 50–500 white blood cells. Polymorphonuclear leukocytes may predominate early, but the number of lymphocytes increases progressively, the glucose level decreases, and the protein content increases.

Generalized pleuritis with effusion occurs in the tuberculin-sensitive host after the rupture of a small subpleural caseous focus into the pleural space. Symptoms begin abruptly with fever, chest pain, and dyspnea. Physical examination of the chest reveals dullness to percussion and diminished breath sounds. The roentgenographic appearance is typical of a pleural effusion.[17]

Cervical lymphadenitis is the most common form of extrapulmonary TB in childhood. A reaction of greater than 10 mm of induration to a Mantoux tuberculin skin test and a nontender cervical or supraclavicular lymph node unresponsive to antibiotics in children is most likely mycobacterial lymphadenitis.

DIAGNOSIS

Tuberculin Skin Tests

In most children, tuberculin reactivity first appears in about 3–6 weeks but occasionally may take up to 3 months after initial infection. When tuberculin reactivity is due to infection by *M. tuberculosis*, it usually remains for the individual's lifetime, even after preventive chemotherapy is given.[18,19] Two major techniques are currently used for tuberculin skin testing: multiple-puncture tests (MPTs) and the Mantoux test. The MPTs are used widely because of the speed and ease with which they can be administered, even by unskilled personnel.

Several problems with MPTs severely limit their usefulness. First, since the dose of tuberculin antigen introduced into the skin cannot be precisely controlled, interpretation of reaction size cannot be standardized. As a result, MPTs are not intended to be used as diagnostic tests (with the exception of persons sustaining a vesicular reaction, interpreted as a positive result), and those with any other reaction must have a Mantoux test placed for diagnostic evaluation.[20] The need for a subsequent Mantoux test leads to the second problem. The booster phenomenon represents an increase in the reaction size to a skin test in a person already sensitized to mycobacterial antigens caused by repetitive tests. The incidence of the booster phenomenon increases with age, in geographic areas where exposure to nontuberculous mycobacteria (NTM) is common, and in children previously vaccinated with bacille Calmette-Guérin (BCG).[21,22] The booster phenomenon may occur for tuberculin tests done 10 days to 12 or more months apart. Thus, a false-positive result may be created.

The MPTs have extremely variable (and in many populations very high) rates of false-positive and false-negative results compared with the Mantoux test. Although some studies have demonstrated sensitivities of 95–99 percent and specificities of 98–99 percent for various MPTs compared with a simultaneous Mantoux test,[23,24] other studies have yielded false-positive rates of 10–15 percent and false-negative rates greater than 10 percent.[25-27] The widespread use of MPTs has also led to the practice of allowing parents to interpret the test results and report them to the physician's office or clinic by telephone or mail. Physicians often assume that nonreporting of results is equivalent to a negative result. MPTs are not adequate diagnostic tests, and their use should be severely restricted if not eliminated. They should never be used on children who have had BCG immunization or who are known contacts of persons with infectious TB or for screening of children who are in groups at high risk for TB (especially in areas where TB is prevalent).

The Mantoux tuberculin skin test using 5 tuberculin units (TU) of purified protein derivative (PPD) is the "gold standard" test. Testing technique must be precise and consistent. A negative Mantoux tuberculin skin test result never rules out tuberculous infection or disease in a child. A variety of host-related factors, such as young age (especially <3 months of age), poor nutrition, immunosuppression by disease or drugs, viral infections (especially measles, varicella, and influenza), and overwhelming TB can lower tuberculin reactivity in an infant or child.[20] Corticosteroid therapy may depress the reaction to tuberculin, but the effect is variable and may be limited to the first several months of steroid administration.[28] Approximately 10 percent of immunocompetent children with culture-documented TB do not react initially to 5 TU of PPD;[29,30] most become reactive after several months of therapy, suggesting that the disease, not factors intrinsic to the host, caused the anergy.

During the past decade, the recommendations for interpretation of the Mantoux tuberculin test reaction has changed and remain open to debate (Chapter 6). The interpretation of the reaction should be influenced by the purpose for which the test was given and by the consequences of false classification.[20] The appropriate cutoff size of induration indicating a positive reaction varies with the person being tested and related epidemiologic factors (Table 8-2).[31] For instance, in areas of the United States where NTMs are common, only 5 percent of children in the general population who have a 5–9 mm area of reaction to a Mantoux tuberculin skin test are infected with *M. tuberculosis*. However, a child with the same reaction who is in contact with an adult with infectious TB has an almost 50 percent chance of

TABLE 8-2. Probability of Tuberculous Infection

Size of Mantoux Test Reaction, mm	Noncontacts of Adult Case, %	Contacts of Adult Case, %
0–4	1	10
5–9	5	45
10–13	25	85
14–21	50–80	96–100
21+	100	100

Note: Values are estimated and may vary with geographic locale.

Source: Data from Reichman.[31]

TABLE 8-3. Cutoff Size of Reactive Diameter for Positive Mantoux Tuberculin Reaction

≥5 mm	≥10 mm	≥15 mm
Contacts to infectious cases	Foreign-born persons from	No risk factors
Abnormal chest radiograph	high-prevalence countries	
HIV-infected and other	Residents of prisons, nursing	
immunosuppressed	homes, or institutions	
patients	Low-income populations	
	Users of intravenous street drugs	
	Other medical risk factors	
	Health care workers	
	Locally identified high-risk	
	populations	
	Infants*	

*Not listed as a high-risk group under ATS and CDC guidelines but should be included in this category.

being infected.[31] The diameter of induration should always be exactly recorded.

As a result of the contribution of epidemiology to skin testing, the American Thoracic Society (ATS) and the Centers for Disease Control (CDC) recommend varying cutoff points for a positive reaction among various groups (Table 8-3).[20] For adults and children at the highest risk for TB — those who are contacts of adults with infectious TB, who have abnormalities on a chest roentgenograph or clinical evidence of TB, or who are HIV-seropositive — a reaction area ≥5 mm is classified as a positive result. For other high-risk groups, including all infants and children <4 years of age, and for children living with adults in high-risk groups, a reaction of ≥10 mm is a positive result. For all other persons who are at low risk for TB, a reactive area ≥15 mm is considered a positive result.

The recommendations for considering a Mantoux tuberculin skin test reaction as positive do not take into account prior BCG vaccination. There is no reliable method of distinguishing tuberculin reactions caused by BCG immunization from those caused by natural mycobacterial infections.[20] When there is a reaction due to BCG, the size of induration is often <10 mm and wanes after 3–5 years.[32,33] Prior BCG immunization is never a contraindication to tuberculin skin testing. In general, a reaction of ≥10 mm in a BCG-immunized child — especially one from a country with a high prevalence of TB — probably indicates infection with *M. tuberculosis*.

Contact Investigation

The most efficient method of finding children infected with *M. tuberculosis* is through contact investigations of adults with infectious pulmonary TB.[34] On average, 30–50 percent of household contacts of adults with infectious pulmonary TB will have positive Mantoux skin test results. An "associate investigation" is the examination of all adults and children in contact with a child infected with *M. tuberculosis* to find the source case and other infected contacts. An individual clinician whose pediatric patient of any age has a positive Mantoux skin test reaction should examine all household members with a Mantoux skin test. Only a properly placed Mantoux skin test should be used for all contact or associate investigations.

New Diagnostic Techniques

The most conclusive laboratory test for the diagnosis and management of TB is the mycobacterial culture. Unfortunately, the yield from cultures of early-morning gastric aspirates from children with pulmonary TB is approximately 40 percent.[30] Therapy usually is guided by the results of epidemiologic contact and associate investigations and culture with drug-susceptibility testing from the adult source case. Cultures should be attempted and susceptibility tests performed on all specimens from a child with suspected TB when the source case is unknown or when the source case is drug-resistant. Two recent studies have evaluated the role of bronchoscopy in managing pulmonary TB in children.[35,36] The culture yield from bronchoscopy varied from 13–62 percent. In the only study that compared the two sources of specimens used for culture, the yield from gastric aspirates was superior to that from specimens obtained by bronchoscopy.[36] More invasive approaches for culture and histopathological examination may be required in some cases.

The technique of polymerase chain reaction (PCR) may increase the sensitivity of nucleic acid probes (Chapter 16). No studies using PCR specimens from children have been reported. It is possible that PCR techniques will be too sensitive for use in children. Most children with either asymptomatic infection or disease have been recently infected, and it may be possible to detect mycobacterial DNA in either situation. If so, detection of DNA would not distinguish infection from disease, which has implications for appropriate therapy. Studies with good controls will be necessary to delineate the role of PCR DNA analysis in the diagnosis of tuberculosis in children. *M. tuberculosis* PCR probes are likely to be available commercially within several years, and caution will be needed when applying them to children. Another new approach has been to detect structural components of the cell wall of *M. tuberculosis* directly in samples from patients. Studies using samples from children have not yet been reported.

The serodiagnosis of TB has been investigated since 1898, when Arloing developed the first agglutination test. One study of a small number of children with pulmonary TB in Argentina, using a specific mycobacterial antigen, yielded a sensitivity of 86 percent and specificity of 100 percent.[37] However, a more recent study using whole mycobacterial sonicates had a sensitivity of 26 percent and a specificity of 40 percent.[38] It is unlikely that serodiagnosis will make a substantial contribution to the diagnosis of TB in children until further investigations have been completed.

TREATMENT OF PULMONARY TB

In the early 1980s, recommended treatment durations for pulmonary TB in children were 12–18 months. Failure rates were high because of poor compliance. Extensive studies of both children and adults have shown that treatment durations as short as 6 months with specific regimens are successful for most forms of TB. A major microbiological determinant of the success of antituberculous chemotherapy is the size of the bacillary population within the host (Chapter 12). Adults with pulmonary cavities and children with extensive pulmonary infiltrates have large bacterial populations. Many single-drug–resistant bacilli will be present, and adequate treatment requires the use of at least two antituberculosis drugs. Conversely, for children with infection (positive Mantoux skin test reaction only) but no radiographic or clinical evidence of disease, the bacterial population is small, drug-resistant organisms are rare or absent, and a single drug can be used for what is commonly called preventive therapy.

In contrast, many multiple-drug therapeutic trials for tuberculous disease in children have been reported in the past decade. In 1983, Abernathy et al.[39] reported successful treatment of 50 children with tuberculous disease using isoniazid (10–15 mg/kg) and rifampin (10–20 mg/kg) daily for 1 month, followed by isoniazid (20–40 mg/kg per dose) and rifampin (10–20 mg/kg per dose) twice weekly for 8 months, a total treatment course of two drugs for 9 months. Some patients with only hilar adenopathy were successfully treated with the two drugs given for 6 months.[40] However, the incidence of primary drug resistance is considerably lower in Arkansas than in many other regions in the United States. A subsequent study from Brazil reported successful treatment of 117 children with pulmonary TB using isoniazid and rifampin daily for 6 months.[41] Although these results are impressive, the two-drug, 6-month regimen has not been adopted for general use in the United States because of limited data and problems with drug resistance.

There have been several studies of a 6-month duration of antituberculous chemotherapy using at least three drugs for drug-susceptible pulmonary TB in children.[42-49] Although the regimens used in these various trials have differed slightly, the most common regimen has consisted of a 6-month period of isoniazid and rifampin administration supplemented during the first 2 months with the use of pyrazinamide. The success of these regimens was independent of the use of streptomycin. Most trials used daily therapy for the first 2 months followed by daily or twice-weekly therapy for the last 4 months. Regimens using twice-weekly therapy were as safe and effective as those using daily therapy. In all of these trials, the overall success rate was greater than 95 percent for complete cure and 99 percent for significant improvement during a 2-year follow-up. The incidence of clinically significant adverse drug reactions—usually gastrointestinal upset or skin rash—was less than 2 percent.

Among all clinical trials, more than 1000 children with pulmonary TB have been treated with a 6-month regimen using isoniazid, rifampin, and pyrazinamide as the initial treatment.[50] On the basis of these trials, the American Academy of Pediatrics (AAP) has endorsed as standard therapy for pulmonary TB in children a regimen of 6 months of isoniazid and rifampin supplemented during the first 2 months by pyrazinamide.[51] For patients in whom social issues or other constraints prevent reliable daily self-administration of drugs, even in the initial phase, drugs have been given under direct observation two or three times per week from the beginning.[47,49] Direct observation means that a health care worker is physically present when the medications are administered to the patient. The usual doses of antituberculosis medications are listed in Table 8-4.

The optimal treatment of TB in children with HIV infection has not been established. Data for children are limited to isolated case reports. It may be difficult to determine whether a pulmonary infiltrate in an HIV-infected child who has a positive tuberculin skin test reaction or a history of exposure to an adult with infectious tuberculosis is due to *M. tuberculosis.* Treatment usually is presumptive and is based on epidemiological and radiographic information, and it should be considered when TB cannot be excluded. Most experts believe that HIV-seropositive children with drug-susceptible tuberculous disease should receive isoniazid, rifampin, and pyrazinamide for 2 months, followed by isoniazid and rifampin to complete a total treatment duration of 9–12 months. Preventive therapy for HIV-seropositive children who have tuberculous infection without disease should be 12 months of isoniazid.

TREATMENT OF EXTRAPULMONARY TB

Controlled clinical trials for treatment of various forms of extrapulmonary TB are virtually nonexistent. Several of the 6-month, three-drug treatment trials in

TABLE 8-4. Antituberculosis Drugs in Children

Drugs	Dosage Forms	Daily Dose, mg/kg/day	Twice-Weekly Dose, mg/kg/dose	Maximum Dose
Isoniazid*	Scored tablets 100 mg 300 mg Syrup: 10 mg/ml†	10–15	20–40	Daily: 300 mg Twice weekly: 900 mg
Rifampin*	Capsules 150 mg 300 mg Syrup: formulated in syrup from capsules**	10–20	10–20	600 mg
Pyrazinamide	Scored tablets: 500 mg	20–40	50–70	2 gr
Streptomycin	Vials: 1 gr, 4 gr	20–40 (IM)	20–40 (IM)	1 gr
Ethambutol	Scored tablets 100 mg 400 mg	15–25	50	2.5 gr
Ethionamide	Tablets: 250 mg	10–20	—	1 gr
Kanamycin	Vials: 1 gr	15 (IM)	15–25 (IM)	1 gr
Cycloserine	Capsules: 250 mg	10–20	—	1 gr

*Rifamate is a capsule containing 150 mg of isoniazid and 300 mg of rifampin. Two capsules provide the usual adult (>50 kg) daily dose of each drug.

†Many experts recommend not using isoniazid syrup, since it is unstable and is associated with frequent gastrointestinal complaints, especially diarrhea.

**Merrell Dow Pharmaceuticals (Cincinnati, Ohio) issues directions for preparation of this "extemporaneous" syrup.

Note: IM = intramuscularly.

children included cases of lymph node and disseminated TB, and both responded favorably.[43,48,49] In general, the optimal treatment for most forms of extrapulmonary TB is the same as that for pulmonary TB. One exception may be bone and joint TB, which has been associated with a higher failure rate when 6-month regimens are used, especially if surgical intervention has not been undertaken.[52] For bone and joint TB, many experts recommend 9–12 months of chemotherapy.

Cases of tuberculous meningitis usually have not been included in trials of extrapulmonary TB because of their serious nature and fairly low incidence. For drug-susceptible disease, treatment with isoniazid and rifampin for 12 months is generally effective.[53] A recent study from Thailand has shown that the survival and morbidity rates are improved significantly if pyrazinamide, which crosses the blood-brain barrier well, is added to the initial 2 months of treatment.[54] Adding pyrazinamide may allow shortening the duration of successful therapy to 6 months. The recommendation of the AAP is 12 months of therapy, including at least isoniazid and rifampin, but many experts believe that a treatment duration of 6–9 months is adequate if pyrazinamide is included in the initial phase of treatment.

DRUG-RESISTANT TUBERCULOSIS

There are two major types of drug resistance (Chapter 18). Primary resistance occurs when a person is infected with *M. tuberculosis* already resistant to a drug. Secondary resistance occurs when drug-resistant organisms emerge as the dominant population during therapy. The major causes of secondary drug resistance are poor compliance by the patient or poor management by the physician. Patterns of primary drug resistance among children tend to mirror those found in their adult contacts. Epidemiological factors, such as disease in an Asian or Hispanic immigrant, homelessness, and a history of prior anti-TB treatment, correlate with drug resistance in adults and their contacts.[55,56] Therapy for drug-resistant TB is successful only when at least two bactericidal drugs to which the infecting strain of *M. tuberculosis* is susceptible are given. Among HIV-infected patients, the mortality rate associated with these strains of multiple drug-resistant *M. tuberculosis* has been up to 89 percent.

A recent change in the ATS-CDC recommendations for treatment of adults with tuberculous disease may affect therapy for the children who are contacts or reside in these select areas. A general recommendation for initial four-drug therapy (with the addition of ethambutol or streptomycin) is an attempt to prevent the development of secondary multiple-drug resistant TB isolates (MDR TB). This regimen would not be appropriate for many of the current cases of MDR TB. Therapeutic decisions for children in preventive and therapeutic regimens must be based on susceptibility data and recommendations in the adult contact cases. In a recent survey, CDC found that primary resistance to isoniazid had doubled to greater than 8 percent nationwide (unpublished data). Although primary resistance was highest in a few large cities that have the worst problems with MDR TB, there was an increase in primary isoniazid resistance in many areas of the United States. Current recommendations from the ATS-CDC and the AAP allow for two- or three-drug regimens to continue in areas where primary isoniazid resistance is low. It is imperative that this information be known and communicated to practicing physicians. Alternative regimens when MDR TB is suspected or confirmed should be used after consultation with a local TB expert.

CORTICOSTEROIDS

Corticosteroids are beneficial in the management of TB in children when the host inflammatory reaction is contributing significantly to tissue damage or impairment of function. There is convincing evidence that corticosteroids decrease mortality rates and long-term neurologic sequelae in patients with tuberculous meningitis by reducing vasculitis, inflammation, and intracranial pressure.[57] Children with enlarged hilar and mediastinal lymph nodes that compromise the tracheobronchial tree, causing respiratory distress, localized emphysema, or collapse-consolidation lesions, frequently benefit from corticosteroid therapy.[58] There is no convincing evidence that one corticosteroid is better than another. Most commonly used is prednisone, 1–2 mg/kg per day for 4–6 weeks.

PREVENTIVE THERAPY

The treatment of persons with asymptomatic tuberculous infection to prevent development of tuberculous disease is an established practice (Chapter 6). Placebo-controlled trials of 1 year of isoniazid preventive therapy involving more than 125,000 subjects have demonstrated a 90 percent reduction in the incidence of subsequent tuberculous disease among subjects with good compliance.[59] In children, the effectiveness has approached 100 percent, and the effect has lasted for at least 30 years.[60]

The AAP recommends a 9-month period of isoniazid preventive therapy in children, although a high level of protection probably is achieved with a 6-month course.[51] Rifampin given for 9 months is recommended for children with suspected isoniazid-resistant infection. Although controlled trials are lacking, either drug can be given twice weekly under direct observation when compliance with daily self-administered therapy cannot be ensured. In cases of suspect or proved MDR TB in contacts of Mantoux skin test positive children, a local TB expert should be consulted for recommendations on preventive therapy.

SUMMARY

There has been a remarkable resurgence of tuberculous infection and disease in children in the United States. It is increasingly likely that children with tuberculous infection and disease will be seen by a variety of clinicians, many of whom have not had to deal with tuberculosis in years. A working knowledge of pediatric TB will again be necessary in many locales, especially in urban practices, and represents the challenge of the 1990s in child health care.

REFERENCES

1. Styblo K, Rouillon A: Estimated global incidence of smear-positive pulmonary tuberculosis: unreliability of officially reported figures on tuberculosis. *Bull Int Union Tuberc* 56:118, 1981.
2. Childhood Tuberculosis and BCG Vaccine. Epidemiology Update (supplement). Geneva, World Health Organization, 1989.
3. Starke JR, Taylor-Watts KT: Preventable childhood tuberculosis in Houston, Texas (abstract). *Am Rev Respir Dis* 141:A336, 1990.
4. Bloch AB, Rieder HL, Kelly GD, Cauthen GM, Hayden CH, Snider DE Jr: The epidemiology of tuberculosis in the United States. *Clin Chest Med* 10:297, 1989.
5. Jacobs RF, Abernathy RS: Tuberculosis in children. *Semin Respir Med* 9:474, 1988.
6. Tuberculosis in the United States: 1987. HHS publication no (CDC) 89-8322. Atlanta, Centers for Disease Control, 1989.
7. Powell KE, Farer LS: The rising age of the tuberculosis patient: a sign of success and failure. *J Infect Dis* 142:946, 1980.
8. Stead WW, Senner JW, Reddick WT, Lofgren JP: Racial differences in susceptibility to infection by *Mycobacterium tuberculosis*. *N Engl J Med* 322:422, 1990.
9. Crowle AJ, Elkins N: Relative permissiveness of macrophages from black and white people for virulent tubercle bacilli. *Infect Immun* 58:632, 1990.
10. Rook GAW: The role of vitamin D in tuberculosis. *Am Rev Respir Dis* 138:768, 1988.
11. Centers for Disease Control: Tuberculosis among foreign-born persons entering the United States. *MMWR* 39:1, 1990.
12. Lange WR, Warnock-Eckhart E, Bean ME: *Mycobacterium tuberculosis* infection in foreign-born adoptees. *Pediatr Infect Dis J* 8:625, 1989.
13. Hostetter M, Iverson S, Thomas W, McKenzie D, Doyle K, Johnson DE: Medical evaluation of internationally adopted children. *N Engl J Med* 325:479, 1991.
14. Nolan CM, Aitken ML, Elarth AM, Anderson KM, Miller WT: Active tuberculosis after isoniazid chemoprophylaxis of Southeast Asian refugees. *Am Rev Respir Dis* 133:431, 1986.
15. Snider DE, Rieder HL, Combs D, Bloch AB, Hayden CH, Smith MHD: Tuberculosis in children. *Pediatr Infect Dis J* 7:271, 1988.
16. Vartersian-Karanfil L, Josephson A, Fikrig S, Kauffman S, Steiner P: Pulmonary infection and cavity formation caused by *Mycobacterium tuberculosis* in a child with AIDS. *N Engl J Med* 319:1018, 1988.
17. Smith MHD, Marquis JR: Tuberculosis and other mycobacterial infections, in Feigin RD, Cherry JD (eds), *Textbook of Pediatric Infectious Disease*. Philadelphia, Saunders, 1981, 1016.
18. Hsu KHK: Tuberculin reaction in children treated with isoniazid. *Am J Dis Child* 137: 1090, 1983.
19. Hardy JB: Persistence of hypersensitivity to old tuberculin following primary tuberculosis in childhood: a longterm study. *Am J Public Health* 36:1417, 1946.
20. American Thoracic Society: Diagnostic standards and classification of tuberculosis. *Am Rev Respir Dis* 142:725, 1990.

21. Seibert AF, Bass JB Jr: Tuberculin skin testing: guidelines for the 1990s. *J Respir Dis* 11:225, 1990.
22. Sepulveda RL, Burr C, Ferrer X, Sorensen RU: Booster effect of tuberculin testing in healthy six-year-old school children vaccinated with bacille Calmette-Guérin at birth in Santiago, Chile. *Pediatr Infect Dis J* 7:578, 1988.
23. Maha GE: Comparative study of tuberculin tine and Mantoux tests in 676 college students. *JAMA* 182:304, 1962.
24. Affronti L, Parlette RC, Pierson F, Arello C: An epidemiologic comparative study in Delaware of the tine and Mantoux tests. *Am Rev Respir Dis* 95:81, 1967.
25. Badger TL, Breitwieser ER, Muench H: Tuberculin tine test: multiple-puncture intradermal technique compared with PPD-S, intermediate strength (5 TU). *Am Rev Respir Dis* 87:338, 1963.
26. Furculow ML, Watson KA, Charron T, Lowe J: A comparison of the tine and Mono-Vacc tests with the intradermal tuberculin test. *Am Rev Respir Dis* 96:1009, 1967.
27. French JG, Fulmer HS: A comparison of the tuberculin tine test with the intermediate PPD (Mantoux) test in selected segments of the Kentucky population. *Am Rev Respir Dis* 88:802, 1963.
28. Saloman H, Angel JH: Corticotropin-induced changes in the tuberculin skin test. *Am Rev Respir Dis* 83:235, 1961.
29. Steiner P, Rao M, Victoria MS, et al: Persistently negative tuberculin reactions: their presence among children culture positive for *Mycobacterium tuberculosis*. *Am J Dis Child* 134:747, 1980.
30. Starke JR, Taylor-Watts KT: Tuberculosis in the pediatric population of Houston, Texas. *Pediatrics* 84:28, 1989.
31. Reichman LB: Tuberculin skin testing: the state of the art. *Chest* 76:764, 1979.
32. Nemir RL, Teichner A: Management of tuberculin reactions in children and adolescents previously vaccinated with BCG. *Pediatr Infect Dis J* 2:446, 1983.
33. Fox AS, Lepow ML: Tuberculin skin testing in Vietnamese refugees with a history of BCG vaccination. *Am J Dis Child* 137:1093, 1983.
34. Hsu KHK: Contact investigation: a practical approach to tuberculous eradication. *Am J Public Health* 53:1761, 1963.
35. Toppet M, Malfroot A, Derde MP, Toppet V, Spehl M, Dab I: Corticosteroids in primary tuberculosis with bronchial obstruction. *Arch Dis Child* 65:1222, 1990.
36. deBlic J, Azevedo I, Burren CP, LeBourgeois M, Lallemand D, Scheinmann P: The value of flexible bronchoscopy in childhood pulmonary tuberculosis. *Chest* 100:688, 1991.
37. Alde SLM, Pinasco HM, Pelosi FR, Budani HF, Palma-Beltran OH, Gonzalez-Montaner LJ: Evaluation of an enzyme-linked immunosorbent assay using an IgG antibody to *Mycobacterium tuberculosis* antigens in the diagnosis of active tuberculosis in children. *Am Rev Respir Dis* 139:748, 1989.
38. Rosen EU: The diagnostic value of an enzyme-linked immune sorbent assay using adsorbed mycobacterial sonicates in children. *Tubercle* 71:127, 1990.
39. Abernathy RS, Dutt AK, Stead WW, Moers DJ: Short-course chemotherapy for tuberculosis in children. *Pediatrics* 72:801, 1983.
40. Jacobs RF, Abernathy RS: The treatment of tuberculosis in children. *Pediatr Infect Dis J* 4:513, 1985.
41. Reis FJC, Bedran MBM, Moura JAR, et al: Six-month isoniazid-rifampin treatment for pulmonary tuberculosis in children. *Am Rev Respir Dis* 142:996, 1990.
42. Ibanez S, Ross G: Quimioterapia abreviada de 6 meses en tuberculosis pulmonar infantil. *Rev Chil Pediatr* 51:249, 1980.
43. Anane T, Cernay J, Bensenovci A. Resultats compares des regimens et des regimens long

dans la chimiotherapie de la tuberculose de l'enfant en Algerie. Presentation at the African Regional Meeting of the International Union Against Tuberculosis, Tunis, Tunisia, October 1984.

44. Pelosi F, Budani H, Rubenstein C, et al: Isoniazid, rifampin and pyrazinamide in the treatment of childhood tuberculosis with duration adjusted to the clincal status (abstract). *Am Rev Respir Dis* 131(suppl):A229, 1985.
45. Khubchandani RP, Kumta NB, Bharucha NB, Ramakantan R: Short-course chemotherapy in childhood pulmonary tuberculosis (abstract). *Am Rev Respir Dis* 141(suppl):A338, 1990.
46. Starke JR, Taylor-Watts K: Six-month chemotherapy of intrathoracic tuberculosis in children (abstract). *Am Rev Respir Dis* 139(suppl):A314, 1989.
47. Varudkar BL: Short-course chemotherapy for tuberculosis in children. *Indian J Pediatr* 52:593, 1985.
48. Biddulph J: Short-course chemotherapy for childhood tuberculosis. *Pediatr Infect Dis J* 9:794, 1990.
49. Kumar L, Dhand R, Singhi PD, Rao KLN, Katariya S: A randomized trial of fully intermittent and daily followed by intermittent short-course chemotherapy for childhood tuberculosis. *Pediatr Infect Dis J* 9:802, 1990.
50. Starke JR: Multidrug therapy for tuberculosis in children. *Pediatr Infect Dis J* 9:785, 1990.
51. *Report of the Committee on Infectious Diseases.* 22d ed. Elk Grove, Ill, American Academy of Pediatrics, 1991, pp 487.
52. Dutt AK, Moers D, Stead WW: Short-course chemotherapy for extrapulmonary tuberculosis. *Ann Intern Med* 107:7, 1986.
53. Visudhiphan P, Chiemchanya S: Tuberculous meningitis in children: treatment with isoniazid and rifampin for twelve months. *J Pediatr* 114:875, 1989.
54. Jacobs RF, Sunakorn P, Chotpitayasunonah T, Pope S, Kelleher K: Intensive short course chemotherapy for tuberculous meningitis. *Pediatr Infect Dis J* 11:194, 1992.
55. Aitlen ML, Sparks R, Anderson K, Albert RK: Predictors of drug-resistant *Mycobacterium tuberculosis. Am Rev Respir Dis* 130:831, 1984.
56. Barnes PF: The influence of epidemiologic factors on drug resistance rates in tuberculosis. *Am Rev Respir Dis* 136:325, 1987.
57. Girgis NI, Farid Z, Kilpatrick ME, Sultan Y, Mikhail IA: Dexamethasone as an adjunct to treatment of tuberculous meningitis. *Pediatr Infect Dis J* 10:179, 1991.
58. Nemir RL, Cordova J, Vaziri F, Toledo F: Prednisone as an adjunct in the chemotherapy of lymph node-bronchial tuberculosis in childhood, a double-blinded study: Part 2. Further term observation. *Am Rev Respir Dis* 95:402, 1967.
59. Ferebee SH: Controlled chemoprophylaxis trials in tuberculosis: a general review. *Adv Tuberc Res* 17:28, 1970.
60. Hsu KHK: Thirty years after isoniazid: its impact on tuberculosis in children and adolescents. *JAMA* 251:1283, 1984.

CHAPTER 9

Pulmonary Tuberculosis

MILTON D. ROSSMAN / ROBERT L. MAYOCK

Tuberculosis (TB) is spread by infectious droplet nuclei (Chapter 4) and thus the lung is the portal of entry in most cases.[1,2] Initial contact with *Mycobacterium tuberculosis* occurs in the periphery of the lung where it has been deposited by inhalation. The tubercle bacillus sets up a localized infestation that initially results in few or no clinical symptoms or signs. Inflammatory reactions appear to have little effect on the organism until the onset of tuberculin hypersensitivity (4–6 weeks). At this time, mild fever and malaise develop, and occasionally other hypersensitivity manifestations are noted.

Local spread to the hilar lymph nodes is a common occurrence, and from there the organisms drain into the bloodstream and spread to other areas of the body. It is this dissemination of the organism that results in the pulmonary and extrapulmonary foci that are responsible for the major clinical manifestations of TB. Initially, one observes the radiographic (Chapter 17) enlargement of the lymph nodes, and later occasionally calcification of both the lymph nodes and the parenchymal lesion. This is the classic Ghon's complex and is suggestive not only of an old tuberculous infection but also of diseases such as histoplasmosis. At the time of the initial bacteremia, no additional evidence of TB develops in the majority of patients because local and systemic defenses contain the infection. Progressive (reactivation) TB usually develops after a period of dormancy and arises from the sites of hematogenous dissemination.[3]

Thus, the initial infection with TB frequently is clinically insignificant and unrecognized. In the majority of patients, the disease stays dormant either indefinitely or for many years, and when a breakdown occurs, it may be secondary to a decrease in body immunity (Table 9-1).

CLINICAL PRESENTATION

Symptoms and Signs

Pulmonary TB frequently develops insidiously without any striking clinical evidence of disease. However, since the disease has a wide spectrum of manifestations ranging from skin positivity with negative radiographic evi-

145

TABLE 9-1. Increased Susceptibility to TB

Nonspecific decrease in resistance
  Adolescence
  Senescence
  Malnutrition
  Postgastrectomy state
  Uremia
  Diabetes mellitus
Decrease in resistance due to hormonal effects
  Pregnancy
  Therapy with adrenocortical steroids
Decrease in local resistance
  Silicosis
Decrease in specific immunity
  Lymphomas
  Immunosuppressive therapy
  Sarcoidosis
  Live virus vaccination
  AIDS

dence to far advanced TB, a variety of clinical presentations also occur. Until pulmonary disease is moderately or far advanced, as shown by changes on the roentgenogram, symptoms are usually minimal and often attributable to other causes, such as excessive smoking, hard work, pregnancy, or other conditions.

Symptoms may be divided into two categories: systemic and pulmonary. The systemic symptom most frequently observed is a low-grade fever. As the disease progresses, fevers can be quite marked. Characteristically, the fever develops in the late afternoon and may not be accompanied by pronounced symptoms. With defervescence, usually during sleep, sweating occurs — the classic "night sweats." Other systemic signs of toxemia, such as malaise, irritability, weakness, unusual fatigue, headache, and weight loss, may be present. In some reviews, the symptoms of cough, anorexia, and weight loss were the most common.[16] With the development of caseation necrosis and concomitant liquefaction of the caseation, the patient will usually notice cough and sputum, often associated with mild hemoptysis. Chest pain is often localized and pleuritic. Shortness of breath usually indicates extensive disease with widespread involvement of the lung and parenchyma or some form of tracheobronchial obstruction and therefore usually occurs late in the disease.

Physical examination of the chest is ordinarily of minimal help early in the disease, and frequently the findings are completely normal. The principal finding over areas of infiltration is one of fine rales detected on deep inspiration followed by full expiration and a hard, terminal cough — the so-called posttussive rales. They are usually detected in the apexes of the lungs, where reactivation disease is most common. As the disease progresses, more extensive findings are observed, corresponding to the areas of involvement and type of pathologic condition. Allergic manifestations may occur, usually developing at the time of onset of infection, including erythema nodosum and phlyctenular conjunctivitis. Erythema induratum, involvement of the lower leg and foot with redness, swelling, and necrosis, probably represents a combination of local subcutaneous bacterial infection with an allergic response and should not be confused with erythema nodosum. The latter is due to circulating immune complexes, with resultant localized vascular damage. Initially, erythema nodosum occurs in the dependent portion of the body and, if the reaction is severe, may be followed by a more disseminated process.

Laboratory Examination

Routine laboratory examinations are rarely helpful in establishing or suggesting the diagnosis.[4] A mild normochromic normocytic anemia may be present in chronic TB. The white blood cell (WBC) count is often normal, and counts over $20,000/\mu l$ would suggest another infectious process; however, a leukemoid reaction may occasionally occur in miliary TB but not in TB confined to the chest. Although a "left shift" in the differential WBC count can occur in advanced disease, these changes are neither specific nor useful. Other nonspecific test results that may be elevated in active TB include the sedimentation rate, α_2-globulins, and γ-globulin. The finding of pyuria without bacteria by Gram's stain suggests renal involvement. Liver enzymes (transaminases and alkaline phosphatase) may occasionally be elevated before treatment. However, this finding is usually due to concomitant liver disease secondary to other problems, such as alcoholism, rather than to tuberculous involvement. Since the drugs used in the treatment of TB may be associated with hepatotoxicity, it is important to quantify any hepatic abnormalities before treatment.[5] Rarely, the serum sodium level is low owing to inappropriate secretion of antidiuretic hormone. This only occurs in advanced pulmonary TB.

A positive delayed hypersensitivity reaction to tuberculin (as discussed in Chapters 2, 5, and 6) indicates the occurrence only of a prior primary infection and not of clinically active disease.[6]

CHEST RADIOGRAPHY

The chest radiograph is the single most useful study for suggesting the diagnosis of tuberculosis. The appearance of the radiograph differs in primary and reactivation TB[7] and is discussed in Chapter 17.

Primary TB

The most common radiographic appearance of primary TB is normal. As opposed to reactivation TB, which usually involves the superior and dorsal segments, in primary TB parenchymal involvement can happen in any segment of the lung.[8] In the primary infection there is only a slight predilection for the upper lobes; also, anterior as well as posterior segments can be involved. The air space consolidation appears as a homogeneous density with ill-defined borders, and cavitation is rare except in malnourished or other immunocompromised patients. Miliary involvement at the onset is seen in fewer than 3 percent of cases, most commonly in children <2 – 3 years of age. An isolated pleural effusion of mild-to-moderate degree may be the only manifestation of primary TB.

Hilar or paratracheal lymph node enlargement is a characteristic finding in primary TB. In 15 percent of the cases, bilateral hilar adenopathy may be present. More commonly, the adenopathy is unilateral. Unilateral hilar adenopathy and unilateral hilar and paratracheal adenopathy are equally common. Massive hilar adenopathy may herald a complicated course. Atelectasis with an obstructive pneumonia may result from bronchial compression by inflamed lymph nodes or from a caseous lymph node that ruptures into a bronchus.

Reactivation TB

Although reactivation TB may involve any lung segment, the characteristic distribution usually suggests the disease. In 95 percent of localized pulmonary TB, lesions are present in the apical or posterior segment of the upper lobes or the superior segment of the lower lobes. The anterior segment of the upper lobe is almost never the only manifest area of involvement.[9] Although a radiologist may attempt to describe the activity of a lesion based on its radiographic appearance, the documentation of activity is determined by bacteriologic and clinical evaluation (Table 9-2). Too often, a lesion reported as inactive or stable by radiographic findings progresses to symptomatic TB.

The typical parenchymal pattern of reactivation TB is air space consolidation of a patchy or confluent nature. Frequently, linear densities connect to the ipsilateral hilum. Cavitation is not uncommon, and lymph node enlargement is rare. As the lesions become more chronic, they become more sharply circumscribed and irregular in contour. Fibrosis will lead to volume loss in the involved lung. The combination of patchy pneumonitis, fibrosis, and calcification suggests chronic granulomatous disease, usually TB.

The cavities that develop in TB usually have a moderately thick wall, smooth inner surface, and no air-fluid level. Cavitation is frequently associated with endobronchial spread of disease. Radiographically, endobronchial spread appears as multiple, small acinar shadows.

TABLE 9-2. Criteria for Activity in Pulmonary TB

Symptoms
Change in chest radiograph
Evidence of cavitation on chest radiograph
Positive sputum smear or culture result
Response to therapeutic trial

DIAGNOSIS

The diagnosis of TB can often be very difficult (Table 9-3). A firm diagnosis of TB requires bacteriologic confirmation. It is important to remember that a positive acid-fast smear result is not specific for *M. tuberculosis*. Other mycobacteria, both saprophytes and potential pathogens, can be acid-fast. In addition, a negative acid-fast smear result should not perplex the clinician, since 50 percent of patients whose culture results are positive will have a negative acid-fast smear result. Thus, culture of *M. tuberculosis* is the only absolute way of confirming the diagnosis.

Freshly expectorated sputum is the best sample to stain and culture for *M. tuberculosis*. Sputum samples 24 h old are frequently overgrown with mouth flora and are much less useful. If a patient is not spontaneously producing sputum, induced sputum is the next best specimen for study. It can be obtained by having the patient breathe an aerosol of isotonic or hypertonic saline solution for 5–15 minutes. If the patient cannot cooperate to give a spontaneous sputum sample, a gastric aspirate to obtain swallowed sputum may be useful. This sample must be obtained in the morning before the patient arises or eats.

In the majority of patients, the procedures outlined above will be successful in obtaining material that will yield positive culture results. Smears of gastric contents for acid-fast bacilli are of limited value and are not recommended because of the presence of nontuberculous, ingested acid-fast bacilli.

TABLE 9-3. Diagnostic Difficulties

Lack of organisms for culture
Slow growth of TB culture
Chest radiograph findings absent or misinterpreted
Biopsy material may not be specific
Decreased tuberculin sensitivity
Symptoms and signs of TB easily attributed to a preexisting disease

In a few cases, one may have to resort to bronchoscopy. In 41 patients proven to have TB, results of cultures of specimens taken during fiberoptic bronchoscopy were positive in 39 cases.[10] Stainable mycobacteria were seen in 14 of the cases, and in 8 cases granuloma were seen on biopsy. Similar results have been obtained in another study of 22 patients with proven mycobacterial disease and negative smear results before bronchoscopy.[11] Since the local anesthetics used during fiberoptic bronchoscopy may be lethal to *M. tuberculosis*, specimens for culture should be obtained using a minimal amount of anesthesia. However, irritation of the bronchial tree during the fiberoptic bronchoscopy procedure frequently leaves the patient with a productive cough. Thus, collection of the postbronchoscopy sputum can be another valuable source of diagnostic material. In 9 (13 percent) of the above-mentioned cases, the postbronchoscopy sputum was the only source of material to test positive.

In 1990, 86.7 percent of pulmonary TB reported to the Centers for Disease Control (CDC) had the diagnosis confirmed by positive culture results. In an additional 3.9 percent of the cases, only the smear result was positive. In 9.4 percent of reported cases, both smear and culture results were negative. Thus, in a significant number of cases, the diagnosis of TB had been made in the absence of bacteriologic confirmation. In these cases, the diagnosis was made by a combination of a positive skin test result, a compatible chest radiograph, and a therapeutic trial.

Differential Diagnosis

Today, TB is a disease most frequently present in individuals >25 years of age. In adults, primary TB is becoming more common and may appear as a lower lobe pneumonia. Common bacterial pneumonias are usually easily differentiated from TB. The localized alveolar infiltrate on the chest radiograph and the prompt response to antibiotic therapy usually differentiate bacterial pneumonia from TB. When in doubt, treatment for a bacterial pneumonia should be given first and TB therapy withheld until adequate sputum samples have been obtained and the response to antibiotics determined. Lung abscesses can usually be differentiated from tuberculous cavities by (1) prominent air-fluid level, (2) more common lower-lobe distribution, and (3) clinical findings (i.e., associated with seizures, alcoholism, dental caries, etc.)

In the elderly, the major differential diagnosis is usually between TB and carcinoma of the lung. An important concept to remember is that carcinoma may cause a focus of TB to spread; thus, carcinoma of the lung and TB may be present simultaneously. In patients with the simultaneous presentation of carcinoma and TB, the diagnosis of TB frequently is made first, and the diagnosis of carcinoma is delayed for several months. Thus, if radiographic and clinical findings suggest carcinoma but the sputum has acid-fast bacilli, further procedures to diagnose carcinoma may still be indicated. Isolated involvement of the anterior segment of the upper lobe, isolated lower-lobe involvement, or the presence of irregular cavities suggest carcinoma, and further diagnostic workup may be indicated despite the presence of acid-fast bacilli in the sputum smear.

Any type of infectious or granulomatous disease may be radiologically identical to TB. Three broad categories must be distinguished: fungi (histoplasmosis, coccidioidomycosis, and blastomycosis), bacteria (*Pseudomonas pseudomallei*), and atypical mycobacteria (mainly *Mycobacterium kansasii* and *Mycobacterium avium* complex). Culture of the organism from the patient's sputum is the best way to differentiate these diseases, although serum antibody titers to fungi are also valuable.

TUBERCULOSIS AND ACQUIRED IMMUNE DEFICIENCY SYNDROME

A consensus has emerged that human immunodeficiency virus (HIV) infection is in part (Chapters 1, 14, and 15) the explanation for the resurgence of TB in the United States since 1984.[12]

Patients with HIV infection and TB can be divided into two groups.[13] In the first group, the acquisition and diagnosis of TB antedates the HIV infection. These patients are less immunosuppressed and are more likely to present with typical TB (upper-lobe infiltrates with cavities). However, mediastinal adenopathy and pleural effusions may occur in 10–20 percent of these patients. In the second group, TB infection occurs after the patient has already been infected with the HIV virus. These patients are more immunosuppressed and have fewer circulating CD4+ cells. In these individuals, cavitation is rare, and mediastinal adenopathy and pleural effusions are more common. Thus, TB needs to be considered in every HIV-infected patient with abnormal chest radiograph findings.

In patients with HIV infection but who have not reached the stage of acquired immune deficiency syndrome (AIDS), the tuberculin skin test will be positive in 50–80 percent of patients with TB. Once an individual has developed AIDS, the tuberculin skin test reaction will be less likely to be positive, but reactivity may be seen in as many as 30–50 percent of patients. Active TB should be considered in any HIV-infected patient with a tuberculin skin test reaction with >5 mm of induration.

The diagnosis of TB in patients with HIV infection is made by collecting respiratory secretions or other clinically relevant specimens. The proportion of positive sputum smear and culture results is similar for both HIV-infected and noninfected patients. If results from spontaneous or induced sputa are negative, then bronchoscopy with lavage and biopsy may be necessary to obtain material for histologic study and culture. Whenever an acid-fast organism is identified, the assumption must be that the organism is *M. tuberculosis*, and treatment should be initiated until definitive identification of the organism occurs.

COMPLICATIONS

Pneumothorax

Although a relatively uncommon complication of tuberculous infection, the development of a pneumothorax requires rapid attention. One of the postulated theories of etiology is the rupture of a cavity, which then connects the tracheobronchial tree with the pleural space, creating a bronchopleural fistula. In this occurrence, contamination of the pleural space with caseous material results in spread of the infection to the pleura and should be corrected immediately because of the tendency to produce pleural fibrosis with expansion failure.

A second possible mechanism is the development of a submucosal bronchiolar lesion with air trapping in an acinus or subsegment, which causes the development of a bleb. Rupture of this bleb allows air to enter the pleural space but often without tuberculous infection of the pleura. However, both occurrences should be treated with rapid expansion of the lungs by tube suction to avoid the possibility of further infection and fibrosis of the pleura with trapping of the lung. A bronchopleural fistula may persist after these episodes of pneumothorax and, especially if untreated, often results in major problems owing to the tuberculous infection complicated by secondary invaders ("mixed" empyema).

Endobronchial Stenosis

Minor endobronchial disease is a common occurrence in TB and usually involves the distal bronchi. Resected lung specimens frequently show either ulceration or stenosis of the draining bronchioles or bronchi. Stenosis of significance may rarely occur in the major bronchi. At times, it results from involvement of the central lymph nodes draining into the lobar bronchi with caseation, ulceration, and fibrosis. Since fibrosis due to TB tends to contract and aggravate the stenosis, resection of the involved lung segment may be required after chemotherapy has produced inactivity of the acute inflammatory reaction.

Bronchiectasis

The same endobronchial processes may result in bronchiectasis due to destruction of the bronchial wall. This usually is distal and frequently is in the upper lobes. The so-called "dry" bronchiectasis (without sputum) often is the result of prior pulmonary TB and may manifest itself chiefly as low-grade hemoptysis.

Empyema

Empyema due to TB may result uncommonly from a primary infection with an associated tuberculous pleural effusion. However, the latter usually clears; empyema is more common later in the disease associated with debility and loss of resistance to infection. It is usually a part of a progressive, extensive parenchymal infection with caseation and cavitation, the presumed sources for pleural contamination.

Late Secondary Infections

After treatment of extensive TB, the patient is often left with open, healed cavities as well as with areas of bronchiectasis. Colonization of these areas may occur with a variety of infectious agents. Usually ororespiratory flora may produce the syndrome of "wet" bronchiectasis (i.e., with sputum production). Other mycobacteria may be recovered during the development of inactivity and were at one time considered a sign of healing. The presence of other pathogenic mycobacteria brings up the possibility of a dual infection, especially when found early in the disease.

Mycetoma

Aspergillus species are common in badly damaged lung areas, especially those that are cavitary. In England, a prospective study[14] revealed that 25 percent of clinically healed TB patients who had residual cavities developed positive precipitins to *Aspergillus* species, and 11 percent had demonstrable cavitary "balls," presumed to be aspergillomas or "fungus balls." Three years later, these numbers had risen to 34 and 17 percent, respectively. This high incidence may be due in part to the increased incidence of *Aspergillus* noted in the United Kingdom, both in the environment and as an infective agent, probably as a result of the more humid environment.

Hemorrhage

Mild hemoptysis is very common in acute infection and not infrequently calls the attention of an otherwise unconcerned patient to the presence of serious disease. Massive hemorrhage, a dramatic event occurring in advanced cases of

TB, is frequently terminal. Rupture of a mycotic aneurysm of a branch of the pulmonary artery (Rasmussen's aneurysm) has been well-publicized as a cause of death; an aspergilloma may be associated with severe and fatal hemorrhage. However, less well-defined major hemorrhages may also occur.

Resection of the involved area has been the most widely used method of control; unfortunately, many patients die before this can be accomplished, and often (as in the case of aspergillomas) the areas are multiple, thus not lending themselves to excisional therapy. The extensive disease found in these patients often contraindicates surgery, since functional lung tissue necessary for survival must often be removed along with the diseased area at the time of surgery.

Hyponatremia

During the acute infectious phase of the disease, two interesting complications have been reported: the syndrome of inappropriate antidiuretic hormone excretion (SIADH) and a reset osmostat.[15] Both manifest themselves by abnormally low sodium. However, the former is associated with all of the clinical and renal abnormalities associated with SIADH. A reset osmostat is characterized by decreased serum osmolality without clinical symptoms and the obligatory renal salt wasting found in SIADH. Both conditions disappear with control of the infection; however, they should be differentiated from each other, since SIADH requires metabolic control.

REFERENCES

1. Glassroth J, Robbins AG, Snider DE: Tuberculosis in the 1980s. *N Engl J Med* 302:1441, 1980.
2. Mayock RL, MacGregor RR: Diagnosis, prevention and early therapy of tuberculosis. *Dis Mon* 22:1, 1976.
3. Comstock GW, Livesay VT, Woolpert SF: The prognosis of a positive tuberculin reaction in childhood and adolescence. *Am J Epidemiol* 99:131, 1974.
4. MacGregor RR: A year's experience with tuberculosis in a private urban teaching hospital in the post-sanatorium era. *Am J Med* 58:221, 1975.
5. Garibaldi RA, Drusin RE, Ferebee SH, et al: Isoniazid-associated hepatitis: report of an outbreak. *Am Rev Respir Dis* 106:357, 1972.
6. Holden M, Dubin MR, Diamond PH: Frequency of negative intermediate-strength tuberculin sensitivity in patients with active tuberculosis. *N Engl J Med* 285:1506, 1971.
7. Fraser RG, Pare JAP, Genereux GP: Infectious diseases of the lung, in Fraser RG, Pare JAP, Pare PD, Fraser RS, Genereux GP (eds), *Diagnosis of Diseases of the Chest*. Philadelphia, Saunders, 1989, pp 883.
8. Weber AL, Bird KT, Janower WL: Primary tuberculosis in childhood with particular emphasis on changes affecting the tracheobronchial tree. *Am J Roentgenol* 103:123, 1968.

9. Jackson HC, Shapiro JH: Pulmonary tuberculosis. *Radiol Clin North Am* 1:411, 1963.
10. Wallace JM, Deutsch AL, Harrell JH, et al: Bronchoscopy and transbronchial biopsy in evaluation of patients with suspected active tuberculosis. *Am J Med* 70:1189, 1981.
11. Danek SJ, Bower JS: Diagnosis of pulmonary tuberculosis by flexible fiberoptic bronchoscopy. *Am Rev Respir Dis* 119:677, 1979.
12. Barnes PF, Bloch AB, Davidson PT, Snider DE Jr: Tuberculosis in patients with human immunodeficiency virus infection. *N Engl J Med* 324:1644, 1991.
13. Pitchenik AE, Rubinson HA: The radiographic appearance of tuberculosis in patients with the acquired immune deficiency syndrome (AIDS) and pre-AIDS. *Am Rev Respir Dis* 131:393, 1985.
14. British Thoracic and Tuberculosis Association, Research Committee: *Aspergilloma* and residual tuberculous cavities: the results of a survey. *Tubercle* 51:227, 1970.
15. Mayock RL, Goldberg M: Metabolic considerations in disease of the respiratory system, in Duncan GG (ed), *Diseases of Metabolism*. Philadelphia, Saunders, 1964, pp 1395.
16. Miller WT, MacGregor RR: Tuberculosis: frequency of unusual radiographic findings. *Am J Roentgenol* 130:867, 1978.

Central Nervous System Tuberculosis

ANNE H. NORRIS / R. MICHAEL BUCKLEY

EPIDEMIOLOGY

Central nervous system (CNS) infection, particularly meningitis, is the most lethal manifestation of tuberculosis (TB). Tuberculous meningitis is uniformly fatal if untreated and has increasingly high morbidity and mortality rates as treatment is delayed. Mortality rates as high as 78 percent are still being reported for patients who present in late stages.[1] The recent increase in the incidence of pulmonary TB in the United States is closely matched by a rise in CNS TB, a trend that is attributed to the increasing prevalence of poverty and homelessness, the influx of immigrants from Asia and Africa, and the spread of the human immunodeficiency virus (HIV).[2] In the United States in 1991, 26,283 cases of TB were reported to the Centers for Disease Control (CDC). Extrapulmonary TB accounted for 4868 (18.5 percent) of these cases, and 241 (5 percent) of these were CNS TB (personal communication, CDC). Overall, about 1 percent of all clinical TB in the United States involves the CNS. In underdeveloped countries where TB is widespread, neurotuberculosis has not been as precisely measured but is thought to be far more common.

PATHOGENESIS

CNS TB occurs as either a parenchymal infection (tuberculoma) or meningitis. It most commonly involves the intracranial central nervous system but may affect the spinal cord as well. CNS involvement originates mainly at the time of primary pulmonary infection, before the onset of hypersensitivity, while microbial growth is virtually uninhibited. At this stage of early bacillemia, one or more tuberculous lesions (Rich foci) are established in the meninges, the spinal cord, or the brain parenchyma itself.[3] Months or years later, presumably due to an immunologic or physical stimulus, this focus may either rupture into the subarachnoid space, producing meningitis, or enlarge and behave as an expanding space-occupying mass, with a presentation characterized by the site

157

and size of the lesion. Such tuberculomas may be intracerebral or intraspinal, single or multiple, and may present acutely or in a chronic fashion.[4] In addition to dissemination at the time of initial infection, it is also likely that these metastatic foci form in debilitated patients with smoldering chronic organ TB. Neurotuberculosis may also occur in the setting of progressive miliary TB, where incessant bacillemia greatly increases the likelihood of CNS seeding. For instance, young children and infants (who are especially susceptible to miliary disease) develop tuberculous meningitis soon after primary infection.[5] Finally, CNS infection may rarely occur in the setting of contiguous spread from tuberculous spondylitis (Pott's disease), otitis, or skull osteitis. In addition to these settings, a significant number of cases of neurotuberculosis occur in the absence of any evidence of TB outside the CNS, either acute or quiescent.[1,6-11]

The distribution of the various forms of CNS TB varies worldwide. For instance, in a report from India, 82 percent of 500 cases of neurotuberculosis took the form of meningitis.[12] In contrast, in a study from Saudi Arabia, tuberculous meningitis was present in only 28 percent, while intracranial tuberculoma and spinal TB each occurred in 36 percent of patients.[4]

Clearly, the risk of developing disseminated TB and CNS involvement is increased for HIV-infected individuals, especially IV drug users or those from areas endemic for tuberculosis. In two small studies of acquired immune deficiency syndrome (AIDS) patients with TB, >70 percent of patients had evidence of extrapulmonary infection. Most subjects were Haitian or intravenous drug users.[13,14] In a study of 52 AIDS patients with TB, Bishburg documented 10 cases of CNS involvement (19 percent); all were Haitian or intravenous drug users.[15] In Spain, Berenguer recently reported a 10 percent incidence of tuberculous meningitis in 455 HIV-positive patients with TB. This rate is 10 times higher than that of his non-AIDS patients with TB. *Mycobacterium tuberculosis* was the most common cause of meningeal infection among HIV-infected individuals, far exceeding *Cryptococcus neoformans*.[11] Most of the AIDS patients with tuberculous meningitis in this study had a severely depressed CD4 count at the time of presentation, a finding that has been reported elsewhere.[13,14,16] Finally, a recent study of 194 patients with AIDS and neurologic findings noted 35 cases (18 percent) of CNS TB.[16] This finding supports the concept that neurotuberculosis must be seriously considered in the evaluation of HIV-infected patients with CNS abnormalities, particularly in areas endemic for TB, including American inner cities.

PATHOPHYSIOLOGY

Tuberculous meningitis causes a dense gelatinous meningeal exudate that extends along the brain stem from the pons to the optic chiasm, surrounding and compromising cranial nerves, resulting in a so-called basilar meningitis.[17] The exudate may encroach on blood vessels, most commonly the middle cerebral and internal carotid arteries, causing ischemia and infarction. In time, noncommunicating hydrocephalus develops due to obstruction of the basilar cisterns and the ventricular foramina, with accompanying evidence of elevated intracranial pressure. Rarely, the same gelatinous material can encase the spinal cord, causing spinal block and symptoms of spinal nerve compression in the absence of intracranial findings. Parenchymal tuberculomas are encapsulated, solid, granulomatous masses or necrotic abscesses located intracerebrally or ocassionally intraspinally.[12,18] They behave as does any mass lesion, causing seizures, intracranial hypertension, and focal neurologic findings.

CLINICAL MANIFESTATIONS

Meningitis

Clinical Presentation

The spectrum of disease in tuberculous meningitis is broad; illness may last many weeks or months, or it may occur in a sudden and fulminant way. Most patients with tuberculous meningitis suffer a prodromal phase for 2–3 weeks, characterized by fatigue, anorexia, intermittent mild fever and headache, and, frequently, abnormal behavior. In children, apathy, irritability, and gastrointestinal complaints are common. With the onset of the meningitic phase of illness, headache becomes severe and is accompanied by vomiting, fever, meningismus, confusion, and cranial nerve palsies.[4,19,20] Vomiting is much more prominent than headache in children.[20] In adults, the presence of persistent headache in a patient with miliary TB is highly suggestive of meningeal infection.[21] Seizures occur at all stages of illness and are far more common in children; they suggest the presence of parenchymal disease, either a tuberculoma or an infarction. Arteritis causes paresis, paralysis, and involuntary movements. The clinical course accelerates at this time with deterioration to stupor or coma. Terminally, posturing, spasm, and signs of brain stem herniation or infarction ensue. Typically, death occurs 5–8 weeks after the onset of illness, although reports of both shorter and longer courses are common.[1,9,22-24] A variety of atypical presentations have been reported, including the onset of seizures, focal neurologic deficits, or encephalopathy, all in the absence of meningeal signs.[12,18]

Clinical staging based on neurologic condition correlates with prognosis. In stage I, patients are fully conscious and rational with meningismus but a normal neurologic exam. Stage II patients have confusion or a focal neurologic exam. Stage III subjects are in coma or delerium, or have a dense hemiplegia or paraplegia.[25] Most patients who present in stage I recover completely. The mortality rate is strikingly high in stage III patients, most studies showing death rates of greater than 45 percent.[1,7,9,23,26-28] Therefore, the diagnosis of tuberculous meningitis is best made early. To do so, the physician requires a high index of suspicion for appropriate patients with compatible CSF findings because laboratory evaluation is usually nonspecific. Focused historical questioning is crucial. In adults, the presence of an underlying condition such as pregnancy, alcoholism, malignancy, AIDS, diabetes, or the use of immunosuppressive therapy can be detected in as many as 64 percent of patients[1] and should prompt early consideration of this diagnosis. Among children, evidence of active TB in the family is a prominent epidemiologic finding. In two recent studies of childhood tuberculous meningitis, TB was present among family members in 69 and 70 percent of cases, respectively.[8,29] While such historical clues are important to seek, their absence does not render the diagnosis of tuberculous infection unlikely, since greater than 25 percent of cases of tuberculous meningitis lack any clinical or historical evidence of either active or dormant TB.[5]

The importance of early intervention, and therefore early diagnosis, cannot be emphasized enough. In one report of 21 cases of neurotuberculosis, antituberculous therapy was started on admission in only 3 patients. The mean time to the initiation of appropriate treatment (if at all) was 4 days.[9] Such delays can be costly; in Kennedy's study of 52 patients with tuberculous meningitis, 4 of 5 subjects whose treatment was delayed 7 days or more died.[23]

The differential diagnosis of tuberculous meningitis is summarized in Table 10-1. It includes other chronic infections, such as syphilis and cryptococcosis; bacterial processes, such as listeriosis and parameningeal disease;

TABLE 10-1. Differential Diagnosis of Tuberculous Meningitis

Early or partially treated bacterial meningitis
Focal parameningeal infection (sinusitis or endocarditis)
Pyogenic brain abscess
Listeria meningitis
Neurosyphilis
Fungal meningitis (cryptococcosis, histoplasmosis, blastomycosis, or
    coccidiomycosis)
CNS toxoplasmosis
Viral meningitis
Neoplastic meningitis
CNS sarcoidosis
Cerebrovascular accident

Source: Used with permission. Adapted from Leonard and Des Prez.[19]

parasitic infection; and noninfectious illnesses, such as neoplasm and sarcoidosis. Distinguishing tuberculous meningitis from the meningoencephalitis of herpes simplex or mumps virus may also be clinically difficult.[19,23]

Laboratory Findings

Routine laboratory findings of some frequency but little specificity in tuberculous meningitis include mild anemia, leukocytosis, an elevated sedimentation rate, and hyponatremia. The chest radiograph shows evidence of TB—either infiltrates, granulomas, cavitary lesions, or a miliary pattern—in 30–70 percent of patients. Results of tuberculin skin testing are positive (>10 mm induration) in 38–93 percent of patients. Using intermediate-strength purified protein derivative (PPD) of tuberculin, Waecker found that 13 percent of patients with tuberculous meningitis had reactions of only 5–10 mm of induration. He recommended that all PPD reactions >5 mm be regarded as positive and be used in the early decision-making process to initiate antituberculosis therapy.[8] HIV-infected patients with CNS tuberculosis have been reported to be PPD-positive in no more than 30 percent of cases.[11,15] The presence of anergy appears to correlate with the severity of CD4+ count depression. Table 10-2 summarizes the clinical and laboratory characteristics of seven recently published series of tuberculous meningitis.

Examination and culture of the cerebrospinal fluid (CSF) is the key to diagnosis in most patients. Characteristically, the CSF is clear and colorless with a weblike pellicle at the surface of the tube. There are moderate lymphocytic pleocytosis, hypoglycorrhachia, and elevated protein levels. Kennedy found CSF WBC >100 cells per ml in 86 percent of cases; the glucose level was less than 45 in 83 percent of patients, and the protein level exceeded 100 mg/dl in 75 percent of subjects.[23] Early-stage patients and those who present acutely may have a polymorphonuclear predominance and near-normal chemistries in the initial lumbar puncture. Subsequent samplings, however, will show progressive lymphocytosis and, if untreated, falling glucose and rising protein levels.[1,18,29] Completely normal CSF that subsequently cultured TB has been reported.[11] Advanced-stage patients with subarachnoid block demonstrate xanthochromia and protein levels in excess of 1000 mg/dl. Overall, laboratory and clinical manifestations of tuberculous meningitis among AIDS patients do not appear to differ significantly from those of non-AIDS subjects.[11]

Microscopic examination of CSF for acid-fast bacilli (AFB) is necessary for early diagnosis and treatment. The sensitivity of AFB smear inspection is directly related to the amount of time spent searching, the volume of CSF spun, and the number of specimens examined. Kennedy found his yield improved from 37 percent on the first lumbar puncture to 87 percent by the fourth sequential lumbar puncture.[23] Two other series using meticulous exam-

TABLE 10-2.   Clinical Features of Tuberculous Meningitis among Non–HIV-Infected Patients upon Admission

	Berenguer	Waecker	Ogawa	Kilpatrick	Klein	Kennedy	Idriss
Reference	11	8	1	7	9	23	26
Year	1992	1990	1987	1986	1984	1979	1976
Site	Madrid	San Diego	New York	Cairo	New York	Glasgow	Beirut
No. of patients	19	30	45	100	21	52	42
Age	3–73	0–5	0–87	0–50	0–77	0–68	0–15
Signs and Symptoms, %							
Fever	89	97	80		62	19	47
Headache	63		62		48	73	21
Lethargy	32	73	44		52	44	23
Meningismus	84	27	71	76	57	90	77
Vomiting	53	73	42			71	30
Cranial nerve palsy			24	44	14	19	33
Seizure	0	47					9
Chest radiograph, %*	47	40	31	61	50	44	72
PPD, %†	42	50	50		38	83	93
CSF	‡	§	‡	§	§		
WBC, per ml	250	200	162	531	206		
Protein, mg/dl	78	239	151	166	183		
Glucose, mg/dl	20	25	35	23	45		
Smear, %	26	3	10	2	20	87	12
Culture, %	100**	37	45	100**	81	83	12

*Any radiographic evidence of TB (see text).

†>10 mm induration with intermediate-strength tuberculin test.

‡Median value.

§Mean value.

**By definition, all patients entered into study were culture-positive.

ination methods and multiple samplings succeeded in demonstrating AFB in 85 and 92 percent of patients, respectively,[30,31] but most other studies report positive smears in <30 percent of cases. Culture positivity also increases with multiple lumbar punctures, in Kennedy's experience increasing from 52 percent initially to 83 percent by the fourth specimen. Few other modern authors report positive CSF culture results in >50 percent of cases. For unknown reasons, tubercle bacilli cannot be isolated from all patients. There exist cases of autopsy-proven tuberculous meningitis in which multiple sequential CSF samples yielded sterile culture.[32] Therapy need not be delayed until bacteriologic proof of infection has been established, since specimens yielding both positive smear and culture results have commonly been obtained after the patient has begun antituberculosis drugs.

Because of the insensitivity of smear examination, alternative methods of mycobacterial detection have received much attention in the last decade. Indirect measures, such as CSF adenosine deaminase and bromide partition, appear to lack a high degree of specificity. Antibody to mycobacterial CSF antigens, while present in many patients with tuberculous meningitis, is also detectable in individuals with previous mycobacterial infection and even in tuberculin-negative patients. Direct tests, such as mass spectroscopy and gas chromatography of mycobacterial products, have shown some promise. For instance, tuberculostearic acid detected in the CSF in this way has been shown to have a 95 percent sensitivity and a 91–99 percent specificity.[33,34] Such assays may prove valuable in areas of the world with widely available advanced clinical laboratories; however, they are prohibitively expensive and complex for developing countries, where most tuberculous meningitis occurs. Many small reports of successful detection of tuberculous antigens, by enzyme-linked immunosorbent assay (ELISA), latex particle agglutination, radioimmunoassay, and polymerase chain reaction have appeared recently.[35-40] Most tests appear to be rapid, simple, sensitive, and specific, but a large series in patients with culture-proven disease remains to be done.[41]

Neuroradiologic Procedures

In the diagnosis of CNS tuberculosis, neuroradiologic procedures such as angiography, radionuclide brain scan, and air-contrast ventriculography have been supplanted by computed tomography (CT), with which there is now substantial experience,[1,6,8,11,16,42-44] and magnetic resonance imaging (MRI), a promising, although less-tested, technique. CT findings correspond well with the pathologic features previously discussed and correlate somewhat with prognosis. Meningeal enhancement, representing exudative arachnoiditis, is present quite variably, ranging from 6–86 percent of cases, although some of this variation is technique-related, since not all patients receive intravenous contrast. While one study of 60 patients from India[44] noted that subjects with severe degrees of basilar exudate did quite poorly, other series have not borne this out.[42,43] Hydrocephalus occurs in 40–100 percent of cases and appears to increase with duration of illness[8,44] and in younger age groups.[42] In the Indian study, it was nearly always present in subjects who had been ill for more than 4–6 weeks and occurred in children far more commonly than adults. Obstructive hydrocephalus, when present, was presumed to be caused by either exudative brain stem compression or an intraluminal tuberculoma.[44] Parenchymal tuberculomas are detected in less than half of patients with tuberculous meningitis in nearly all studies. Jinkins found that the coexistence of both meningeal and parenchymal forms of infection portended high morbidity and mortality rates, presumably due to severely impaired host defenses or a more virulent organism.[6] Normal CT scans are variably reported in 0–50 percent of patients, and, not surprisingly, are associated with complete recovery.[44] It is interesting to note that, in a study of 64 Chinese subjects, the presence of a normal scan in a drowsy patient virtually ruled out the presence of tuberculous meningitis.[42]

Recently, MRI has proved to be a more sensitive imaging modality than CT for CNS tuberculosis.[16,45,46] Autopsy has shown that CT fails to detect tuberculomas of <1 cm in diameter,[44] whereas MRI with gadolinium enhancement has demonstrated small tuberculomas and abnormal meningeal enhancement not seen on CT performed in the same patient over the same time period.[16,45] In addition to a more detailed visualization of supratentorial pathologic conditions, MRI also demonstrates brain stem disease to a much greater extent than does CT. Brain stem encephalopathy, responsible for disturbances of consciousness in many patients, has recently been correlated with focal MRI signal abnormalities, either punctate or confluent, in the brain stem.[46]

Tuberculomas

Until recently, CNS tuberculomas were said to occur exceedingly rarely in the western hemisphere. They were seen mainly in developing countries, the incidence approaching 30 percent of intracranial masses in India.[47] However, tuberculomas are now a prominent manifestation of neurotuberculosis in AIDS patients worldwide, ranging from 37–80 percent of CNS TB.[11,15,16] Berenguer found tuberculomas in 44 percent of AIDS patients with neurotuberculosis, versus 6 percent in non-AIDS subjects.[11]

A recent report of 57 cases of CNS tuberculomas in Saudi Arabia carefully characterized their appearance on enhanced CT.[6] Ninety percent of lesions were granulomas: enhancing, round or lobulated masses with solid or hypodense centers, surrounded by edema and irregular walls of varying thickness. Ten percent of lesions appeared to be true abscesses and were proven to be at biopsy. On CT, they demonstrated smooth, thin walls with occasional loculation. Pathologically, tuberculomas and tuberculous abscesses differ markedly. Granulomas are composed almost entirely of solid caseation with a fibrous capsule and few, if any, tubercle bacilli. Abscesses contain semiliquid pus loaded with organisms. These two lesions may represent different stages of the same process[48] and may not much differ clinically from each other. As noted previously, tuberculomas commonly coexist with frank meningitis and may carry a grave prognosis.[6] Reports of the development of tuberculoma during treatment for tuberculous meningitis are not rare.[19,49] In AIDS patients, multiple CNS pathogens may coexist; for instance, *Toxoplasma gondii* has been cultured from tuberculous brain lesions.[15,16]

Tuberculomas present as space-occupying lesions, with headache, seizures, visual and/or gait disturbances and evidence of elevated intracranial pressure.[47] Evidence of concomitant TB outside the CNS is surprisingly sparse. The chest radiograph suggests TB in only 20–39 percent of cases,[6,15,47] and findings on CSF examination can be entirely normal.[4] While neuroradiologic techniques are helpful in defining the extent of disease and in following the response to therapy, there are no pathognomonic features of tuberculomas. They are difficult to differentiate from either primary or secondary malignancy as well as a host of other nonneoplastic conditions, including pyogenic abscess, other granulomatous infections, and hemorrhage.[6] Among HIV-infected patients, distinguishing tuberculoma from lymphoma or toxoplasmosis is a troublesome clinical problem.

TB of the Spinal Cord

Tuberculosis can cause spinal cord disease with or without evidence of intracranial involvement. Spinal cord TB is uncommon, accounting for only 2 percent of neurotuberculosis even in endemic areas.[12] It may take the form of an advanced spinal meningitis with cord encasement, an intramedullary tuberculoma, or an extradural mass. In most cases of spinal TB, CSF protein levels are markedly elevated (frequently >1000 mg/dl), causing subarachnoid block. Cell counts and glucose levels may be normal.[18,50]

The pathophysiology of tuberculous spinal meningitis is identical to that of intracranial meningitis, with a dense fibrous exudate surrounding the cord and spinal roots. The clinical picture is one of acute or gradual, single- or multiple-level, transverse or ascending radiculomyelopathy. Predominant neurologic features include root pain, paresthesias, paralysis, bladder dysfunction, and muscle atrophy. Fever, malaise, and anorexia are sometimes present. Patients may be mistakenly diagnosed with Guillain-Barré syndrome, amyotrophic lateral sclerosis, or transverse or ascending myelitis.[18,50] Rarely, vertebral artery thrombosis secondary to compressive exudate presents with sudden paraplegia.[18] Spinal tuberculomas, originating as Rich foci, may be intramedullary, producing mass-lesion symptoms without suggestion of meningeal irritation, or may be located in the epidural space or meninges. Back pain and/or radicular symptoms may at first suggest intervertebral disk herniation. Often, biopsy is necessary to distinguish spinal tuberculoma from neoplasm, multiple sclerosis, or pyogenic abscess. MRI will probably prove to be a superior imaging tool here, although CT is more commonly used for percutaneous biopsy.

TREATMENT OF NEUROTUBERCULOSIS

The optimal management of tuberculous meningitis has not yet been established. A large prospective comparison of regimens has not been done, and no general consensus exists regarding the exact choice of chemotherapy or duration of treatment. Recommendations have generally been made by analogy to pulmonary TB; unlike pulmonary disease, however, in neurotuberculosis the number of organisms is few, and the challenge of chemotherapy is to deliver drug to the site of infection promptly to prevent the damage caused by the host's inflammatory response.[19]

The CDC now recommends the use of four drugs for the initial treatment of extrapulmonary TB.[51] Isoniazid (5–10 mg/kg per day for adults) diffuses into all tissues, with CSF levels approaching that of serum in the presence of inflamed meninges. Rifampin (600 mg/day in adults), in the presence of inflamed meninges, also reaches CSF levels well above the minimum inhibitory concentration for sensitive tubercle bacilli. Pyrazinamide crosses the blood-brain barrier well and is cidal for intracellular organisms. The fourth agent may be ethambutol (15 mg/kg per day) or streptomycin (1 g per day intramuscularly).

Duration of therapy is controversial. The American Thoracic Society (ATS)-CDC recommendations for pulmonary TB depend on the clinical response, with the length of treatment lasting at least 6 months and in some cases extending to 9 or 12 months, depending on the time of culture conversion and the clinical course. The timing of this approach has proven successful for pulmonary TB,[52] and a few small trials of such short-course chemotherapy for tuberculous meningitis have shown no higher relapse rate than with extended courses.[27,53] However, one large prospective series from India employing a combination of all five above-mentioned drugs for a total of 2 years found short-course chemotherapy inadequate. Only 273 of 724 patients with tuberculous meningitis were available for follow-up at the end of 2 years. Of these, 236 were cured. Thirty-five of 37 subjects who discontinued therapy before 2 years developed recurrent tuberculous meningitis; 12 of the recurrences were in patients who received at least 10 months of treatment. Five patients presented with recurrent disease >4 years after therapy had been discontinued.[54]

For immunocompromised patients, such as those with AIDS, the recommended initial regimen includes four drugs. Duration of treatment is also dependent on the clinical course but extends at least 9–12 months and continues for at least 6 months beyond the establishment of negative culture results.[55,56] Some authors advocate lifelong suppressive therapy with isoniazid after initial multidrug treatment of acute infection.[56]

The use of corticosteroids in the treatment of tuberculous meningitis has been debated for years. Cerebrospinal fluid indexes return to normal faster in patients who have received adjunctive steroids than in those who have not.[57] While several small studies have demonstrated decreased morbidity and mortality rates with the use of steroids,[58] others have failed to reproduce this success.[57] A recent comparison of antituberculous therapy with and without adjunctive steroids in 160 Egyptian patients with tuberculous meningitis showed that the addition of dexamethasone to a regimen of antituberculosis drugs decreased mortality from 59 to 43 percent. The incidence of permanent neurologic sequelae among survivors was also significantly reduced.[28] The current prevailing policy is to employ steroids (1) in patients with evidence of increased intracranial pressure (in an attempt to prevent herniation) and (2) in those with impending spinal block due to increased CSF protein levels. Some authors extend the indications to include altered consciousness and focal neurologic abnormalities as well.[20] The excellent prognosis of stage I patients who have no neurologic compromise seems to preclude the use of adjuvant corticosteroids. In addition, the diagnosis of fungal meningitis should be ruled out before steroids are initiated without the addition of an antifungal agent.[19]

Placement of a ventricular shunt is indicated in the presence of continued increased intracranial pressure if conservative measures (antituberculosis drugs, corticosteroids, diuretics, and serial lumbar punctures) have failed to relieve hydrocephalus. While such shunts are prone to dysfunction and infection, probably due to abnormally high CSF protein contents, they appear to decrease the incidence of permanent neurologic damage and death.[19,20,59]

The optimal management of intracranial tuberculomas also remains unclear at this time. In areas endemic for TB or in patients with a suspicious clinical setting, biopsy may be deferred for a course of empiric antituberculosis medical therapy, as neurosurgical intervention can be hazardous.[6,24] For instance, Traub reported 2 patient deaths directly related to biopsy of intracranial tuberculomas.[24] Harder compared a conservative medical course of antituberculosis drugs, steroids, and anticonvulsants with the same regimen plus craniotomy and excision of the tuberculoma in 20 subjects from Saudi Arabia.[47] At 1 year, 6 medically managed patients versus 1 surgically treated patient had returned to normal neurologic functioning. Most of the severe neurologic sequelae occurred in the surgically treated patients. Optimal duration of therapy has not been established. In the above-mentioned study, at 28 months there was no evidence of recurrence among any of the 20 patients, all of whom had been treated for 1 year. Jinkins used CT to follow 60 patients with intracranial tuberculoma, noting that resolution took many months to years, depending mainly on the original size of the lesion. The time for final radiographic resolution (calcification and/or atrophy) of isolated parenchymal tuberculomas on medical therapy varied from 8 months to 2 years. Three subjects continued to have residual enhancement with calcification in the original area of abnormality at 2 years. They were maintained on medical therapy, since they were felt to be "radiologically active."[6]

There are no definitive data on the management of the rare, isolated spinal cord TB. The choice of antituberculosis agents is the same as that for intracranial infection; duration of therapy is untested, and it should be based on clinical course.

OUTCOME

Clinical outcome for tuberculous meningitis correlates most closely with stage at presentation; morbidity and mortality rates increase with the degree of neurologic impairment. In addition to late initiation of treatment, other poor prognostic indicators include extremes of age, an underlying medical condition, a miliary pattern on the chest radiograph,[1,9,23] and a low CD4+ count in HIV-positive patients.[13,14,16] Mortality rates range from 3–70 percent. Most series report mortality rates below 30 percent, with the higher figures coming from series where medical care was initiated late in the disease course.[7] The reported incidence of neurologic deficits after recovery from tuberculous meningitis varies from 30–70 percent. Commonly cited neurologic residua include paraplegia, hemiplegia, dysphagia, dementia, blindness, gait disorders, cranial nerve palsies, seizure, mental retardation, and a variety of endocrine disorders, such as diabetes insipidis.[1,7-9,26] The mortality rate for tuberculoma appears to be lower than that for tuberculous meningitis.

SUMMARY

The incidence of CNS TB in the United States has increased in the last decade and is likely to continue to do so while the inner-city TB epidemic continues.

Clinicians need to maintain a high index of suspicion for neurotuberculosis in susceptible individuals because early treatment is the single most important factor affecting outcome, especially in cases of tuberculous meningitis. In patients with a compatible history and no other definitive diagnosis, empiric therapy is often the prudent course of action. Repeated lumbar punctures may be required to make the diagnosis. Clearly, with the current epidemics of both AIDS and TB, clinicians will be called upon to diagnose and treat CNS TB more often.

REFERENCES

1. Ogawa SK, Smith MA, Brennessel DJ, et al: Tuberculous meningitis in an urban medical center. *Medicine* 66:317, 1987.
2. Jereb JA, Kelly GD, Dooley SW, et al: Tuberculosis mortality in the United States: final data, 1990. *MMWR* 40:23, 1991.
3. Rich AR, McCordock HA: Pathogenesis of tuberculous meningitis. *Bull Johns Hopkins Hosp* 52:5, 1933.
4. Al-Deeb SM, Yaqub BA, Sharif HS, et al: Neurotuberculosis: a review. *Clin Neuro Neurosurg* 94:S30, 1992.
5. Auerbach O: Tuberculous meningitis: correlation of therapeutic results with the pathogenesis and pathologic changes. *Am Rev Tuberc* 64:408, 1951.
6. Jinkins JR: Computed tomography of intracranial tuberculosis. *Neuroradiology* 33:126, 1991.
7. Kilpatrick ME, Girgis NI, Yassin MW, et al: Tuberculous meningitis: clinical and laboratory review of 100 patients. *J Hyg* 96:231, 1986.
8. Waecker NJ, Connor JD: Central nervous system tuberculosis in children: a review of 30 cases. *Pediatr Infect Dis J* 9:539, 1990.
9. Klein NC, Damske B, Hirschman SZ: Mycobacterial meningitis. *Am J Med* 79:29, 1985.
10. Hinman AR: Tuberculous meningitis at Cleveland Metropolitan Hospital 1959 to 1963. *Am Rev Respir Dis* 95:670, 1967.
11. Berenguer J, Moreno S, Laguna F, et al: Tuberculous meningitis in patients infected with the human immunodeficiency virus. *N Engl J Med* 326:668, 1992.
12. Udani PM, Parekh UC, Dastur DK: Neurologic and related syndromes in CNS tuberculosis: clinical features and pathogenesis. *J Neurol Sci* 14:341, 1971.
13. Sunderman G, McDonald RJ, Maniatis T, et al: Tuberculosis as a manifestation of the acquired immune deficiency syndrome (AIDS). *JAMA* 256:362, 1986.
14. Pitchenik AE, Cole C, Russell BR: Tuberculosis, atypical mycobacteriosis, and the acquired immune deficiency syndrome among Haitian and non-Haitian patients in South Florida. *Ann Intern Med* 101:641, 1984.
15. Bishburg E, Sunderman G, Reichman LB, et al: Central nervous system tuberculosis with the acquired immune deficiency syndrome and its related complex. *Ann Intern Med* 105:210, 1986.
16. Villoria MF, de la Torre J, Fortea F, et al: Intracranial tuberculosis in AIDS: CT and MRI findings. *Neuroradiology* 34:11, 1992.
17. Dastur DK, Lalitha VF: The many facets of neurotuberculosis: an epitome of neuropathology. *Prog Neuropathol* 2:351, 1973.

18. Kocen RS, Parsons M: Neurologic complications of tuberculosis: some unusual manifestations. *Q J Med* 153:17, 1970.
19. Leonard JM, Des Prez RM: Tuberculous meningitis. *Infect Dis Clin North Am* 4:769, 1990.
20. Molavi A, LeFrock JL: Tuberculous meningitis. *Med Clin North Am* 69:315, 1985.
21. Beihl JP: Miliary tuberculosis: a review of 68 patients admitted to a municipal general hospital. *Am Rev Respir Dis* 77:605, 1958.
22. Traub M, Leake J, Scholtz C, et al: Chronic untreated tuberculous meningitis. *J Neurol* 233:254, 1986.
23. Kennedy DH, Fallon RJ: Tuberculous meningitis. *JAMA* 241:264, 1979.
24. Traub M, Colchester AC, Kingsley DP: Tuberculosis of the central nervous system. *Q J Med* 209:81, 1984.
25. Medical Research Council Report: Streptomycin treatment of tuberculous meningitis. *Lancet* 1:582, 1958.
26. Idriss ZH, Sinno AA, Kronfol NM: Tuberculous meningitis in childhood. *Am J Dis Child* 130:364, 1976.
27. Alarcon F, Escalante L, Perez Y, et al: Tuberculous meningitis: short course of chemotherapy. *Arch Neurol* 47:1313, 1990.
28. Girgis NI, Farid Z, Kilpatrick ME, et al: Dexamethasone adjunctive treatment for tuberculous meningitis. *Pediatr Infect Dis J* 10:179, 1991.
29. Sumaya CV, Simek M, Smith MH, et al: Tuberculous meningitis in children in the isoniazid era. *J Pediatr* 87:43, 1975.
30. Stewart SM: The bacteriologic diagnosis of tuberculous meningitis. *J Clin Pathol* 6:241, 1953.
31. Illingsworth RS: Miliary and meningeal tuberculosis: difficulties in diagnosis. *Lancet* 2:646, 1956.
32. Taylor KB: Tuberculous meningitis of acute onset. *J Neurol Neurosurg Psychiatry* 18:165, 1955.
33. Brooks JB, Daneshvar MI, Haberberger RL, et al: Rapid diagnosis of tuberculous meningitis by frequency-pulsed electron-capture gas-liquid chromotography detection of carboxylic acids in cerebrospinal fluid. *J Clin Microbiol* 28:989, 1990.
34. French GL, Teoh R, Chan CY, et al: Diagnosis of tuberculous meningitis by detection of tuberculostearic acid in cerebrospinal fluid. *Lancet* 2:117, 1987.
35. Krambovitis E, McIllmurray MB, Lock PE: Rapid diagnosis of tuberculous meningitis by latex particle agglutination. *Lancet* 2:1229, 1984.
36. Watt G, Zaraspe G, Bautista S, et al: Rapid diagnosis of tuberculous meningitis by using an enzyme-linked immunosorbent assay to detect mycobacterial antigen and antibody in cerebrospinal fluid. *J Infect Dis* 158:681, 1988.
37. Sada E, Ruiz-Palacios GM, Lopez-Vidal Y, et al: Detection of mycobacterial antigens in CSF of patients with tuberculous meningitis by enzyme-linked immunosorbent assay. *Lancet* 2:651, 1983.
38. Kalish SB, Radin RC, Levitz D, et al: The enzyme-linked immunosorbent assay method for IgG antibody to purified protein derivative in CSF of patients with tuberculous meningitis. *Ann Intern Med* 99:630, 1983.
39. Shankar P, Manjunath N, Mohan KK, et al: Rapid diagnosis of tuberculous meningitis by polymerase chain reaction. *Lancet* 337:5, 1991.
40. Kaneko K, Onodero O, Miyatake T: Rapid diagnosis of tuberculous meningitis by polymerase chain reaction. *Neurology* 40:1617, 1990.
41. Daniel TM: New approaches to the rapid diagnosis of tuberculous meningitis. *J Infect Dis* 155:599, 1987.
42. Teoh R, Humphries MJ, Hoare RD, et al: Clinical correlation of CT changes in 64 Chinese patients with tuberculous meningitis. *J Neurol* 236:48, 1989.

43. Bullock MR, Welchman JM: Diagnostic and prognostic features of tuberculous meningitis on CT scanning. *J Neurol Neurosurg Psychiatry* 45:1098, 1982.
44. Bhargava S, Gata AK, Tandon PN: Tuberculous meningitis: a CT study. *Br J Radiol* 55:189, 1982.
45. Chang KH, Han MH, Roh JK: Gd-DTPA-Enhanced MR imaging of the brain in patients with meningitis: comparison with CT. *AJNR* 11:69, 1990.
46. Schoeman J, Hewlett R, Donald P: MR of childhood tuberculous meningitis. *Neuroradiology* 30:473, 1988.
47. Harder E, Al-Kawi MZ, Carney P: Intracranial tuberculoma: conservative management. *Am J Med* 74:570, 1983.
48. Sheller JR, Des Prez RM: CNS tuberculosis. *Neurol Clin* 4:14, 1986.
49. Malone JL, Paparello S, Rickman LS, et al: Intracranial tuberculoma developing during therapy for tuberculous meningitis. *West J Med* 152:188, 1990.
50. Wadia NH, Dastur DK: Spinal meningitides with radiculomyelopathy: Part 1. Clinical and radiologic features. *J Neurol Sci* 8:239, 1969.
51. Snider DE, Rieder HL, Combs D, et al: CDC: Initial therapy for tuberculosis in the era of multidrug resistance: recommendations of the Advisory Council for the Elimination of Tuberculosis. *MMWR* 42:1, 1993.
52. Hong Kong Chest Service/British Medical Research Council: Five-year follow-up of a controlled trial of five six-month regimens of chemotherapy for pulmonary tuberculosis. *Am Rev Respir Dis* 136:1339, 1987.
53. Jacobs RF, Sunakorn P, Chotpitayasunonah T, et al: Intensive short course chemotherapy for tuberculous meningitis. *Pediatr Infect Dis* 11:194, 1992.
54. Goel A, Pandya SK, Satoskar AR: Whither short-course chemotherapy for tuberculous meningitis? *Neurosurgery* 27:418, 1990.
55. Holdiness MR: Management of tuberculous meningitis. *Drugs* 39:224, 1990.
56. Chaisson RE, Slutkin G: Tuberculosis and human immunodeficiency virus infection. *J Infect Dis* 159:96, 1989.
57. O'Toole RD, Thornton GF, Mukherjee MK: Dexamethasone in tuberculous meningitis. *Ann Intern Med* 70:39, 1969.
58. Escober JA, Belsey MA, Dueñas A, et al: Mortality from tuberculous meningitis reduced by steroid therapy. *Pediatrics* 56:1050, 1975.
59. Schoeman J, Donald P, van Zyl L, et al: Tuberculous hydrocephalus: comparison of different treatments with regard to ICP, ventricular size and clinical outcome. *Dev Med Child Neurol* 33:396, 1991.

CHAPTER 11

Extrapulmonary Tuberculosis, Excluding the Central Nervous System

GEORGE F. THORNTON

Although tuberculosis (TB) is predominately an infection involving the lungs, it can involve virtually any organ system. The presentation of extrapulmonary TB is often protean. It may be indolent or present as an acute illness. Signs and symptoms also depend on the organ system involved. This chapter is devoted to extrapulmonary TB (excluding central nervous system infection, which is discussed in Chapter 10), with an emphasis on epidemiology, pathogenesis, clinical presentation, diagnosis, and treatment.

PATHOGENESIS

Tuberculosis can be acquired in three ways. The first is by direct inoculation. This is seldom seen in the United States, although early in this century it was occasionally encountered in pathologists and morticians. A second way in which TB can be acquired is by the ingestion of foods contaminated with the tubercle bacillus. This also is rarely seen in the United States but is quite common in parts of the world where unpasteurized milk and milk products are sold. The third, and by far the most common, way TB is acquired is by the inhalation of droplet nuclei.[1] Droplet nuclei tend to infect the lower lung fields because they are the best-ventilated parts of the lung. These droplet nuclei are sufficiently small to escape many of the host defense mechanisms, such as pulmonary mucociliary clearance. At the time of initial infection, tubercle bacilli are carried via lymphatics to regional lymph nodes. From the regional nodes, bacteria continue to spread to other nodes and may reach the bloodstream, where they may be carried to distant sites, resulting in scattered foci of infection throughout the body. This lymphohematogenous dissemination is usually self-limited but has the potential to develop into active disease.

Within 4-8 weeks, cell-mediated immunity develops, contributing to the healing of the initial primary focus as well as distant foci.[2,3]

Although, in theory, tubercle bacilli can be disseminated to virtually any part of the host, they tend to persist and multiply at sites of the greatest tissue oxygen tension. This is felt to explain why extrapulmonary TB is much more likely to involve certain organs, such as kidneys, liver, adrenal gland, vertebral bodies, and proximal ends of long bones. This is also felt to explain why reactivation TB is most likely to involve the apex of the lung.[4,5] The acquired immune deficiency syndrome (AIDS) impairs the normal host defense, which ordinarily controls sites seeded by the hematogenous dissemination of primary infection; as a result, extrapulmonary TB is more common in this group of patients.[6,7] Extrapulmonary TB in an HIV-infected patient has been classified as an AIDS-defining infection since 1987.[8] AIDS patients appear to have an increased frequency of lymph node, central nervous system, genitourinary system, and disseminated TB.[9]

EPIDEMIOLOGY

The number of reported TB cases in the United States has decreased from 84,304 in 1953 (the time national recording of TB was initiated) to 22,255 by 1984. Between 1950 and 1980, there was an annual decline of approximately 5 percent in the number of cases of TB reported each year. From 1981-1984, this decrease accelerated to around 6.5 percent.[10] Between 1985 and 1992, however, the annual number of cases of TB increased by 18 percent. The reason for this change in the epidemiology is complex. The most important factor appears to be AIDS; other factors, however, include increasing immigration from Southeast Asia and Central and South America, an increased number of homeless people, and a general deterioration in the public health infrastructure of the United States.

During the era of decline in reported cases, the frequency of extrapulmonary infections remained relatively constant. As a result, even though the absolute number of cases of extrapulmonary TB has not increased dramatically in the last 10 years, an ever-increasing proportion of cases of TB had extrapulmonary foci.[4] In 1980, 3947 cases of extrapulmonary TB were reported in the United States. By 1990, the total had increased to 4595,[11] which represents a 16 percent increase. In addition, there has been a change in sites of reported extrapulmonary involvement, with a decrease in the frequency of genitourinary infection and a slight increase in lymphatic TB. The disease sites reported to the Centers for Disease Control (CDC) for 1990 are shown in Fig. 11-1.[11]

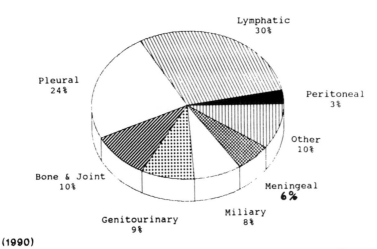

(1990)

FIGURE 11-1. Reported cases of TB by anatomic site, 1990.[11]

Since total cases of TB had been declining at a more rapid rate than intrapulmonary cases, a greater proportion of all cases of TB included extrapulmonary foci. In 1964, only 8 percent of the total number of cases represented extrapulmonary infection. By 1981, this had increased to 15 percent.[11] As seen in Table 11-1, the frequency of reported cases of extrapulmonary infection has continued to increase, from 16 percent in 1984 to 18 percent in 1990. The discordance of the epidemic curves for extrapulmonary TB and the overall TB infection rate has not been completely explained. While it has been suggested that there have been increases in recognition and reporting, or even overdiagnosis, to explain these observations, a more likely explanation is that extrapulmonary TB represents the emergence of disease developing in a reservoir of previously infected patients.[4] There is also not a good explanation of why the number of cases of genitourinary infection have decreased in the last decade despite increased genitourinary localization in AIDS patients.

TABLE 11-1. Tuberculous Infection in the United States

Year	Reported Cases	Extrapulmonary Infection	%
1984	22,255	3613	16.2
1990	25,701	4595	17.9

Source: From Jereb et al.[10] and CDC.[11]

TUBERCULOUS LYMPHADENITIS

The most common site of extrapulmonary infection in the United States in 1990 was the lymphatic system, comprising approximately 30 percent of all reported cases (Fig. 11-1). Infection of lymph nodes can occur either as a result of primary infection with direct extension or by reactivation of previous infection.[4,12,13] Although tuberculous lymphadenitis can involve patients of any age, it is more commonly seen in younger patients. In the United States, the peak age is between 20 and 40 years.[4,13]

Historically, TB of the cervical lymph nodes (scrofula), has been recognized for thousands of years. During the Middle Ages, it was known as the "King's evil" and was felt to be cured by the royal touch. It was most commonly caused by *Mycobacterium bovis*.[13]

The adenopathy is almost always palpable but is usually painless.[4] Anterior cervical nodes are involved more frequently than posterior, and right-sided node involvement is more common than left.[13] Intrathoracic tuberculous lymphadenitis usually involves the paratracheal and hilar lymph nodes.[4,13] It is more commonly seen with initial tuberculous infection. Lymph node TB has a striking female preponderance (2 : 1) and is more common in the dark-skinned races and in Asians.[13]

Symptoms depend predominantly on location.[4] Fever is usually absent, and the lymph node enlargement is usually painless.[4,12,13] Eventually the nodes may break down if untreated, with development of a chronic draining sinus.[13] Intrathoracic adenopathy can result in narrowing of the bronchial lumen in small children, but in adults it is more likely to present with fever, night sweats, and weight loss.[4,13] Tuberculous adenitis should always be considered in the differential diagnosis of hilar or cervical adenopathy. Diagnosis is best made by node biopsy. Acid-fast bacilli can be seen on smear in 25–50 percent of lymph node specimens, and approximately 70 percent of lymph nodes cultured for TB will yield positive results.[4,12,13,14] Recently, it has been suggested that gallium scanning and leukocyte scanning plus computed tomography may be valuable in establishing the diagnosis.[15] Although *M. bovis* historically accounted for most cases of lymph node TB, most cases in the United States are now due to *Mycobacterium tuberculosis*. About one-third of patients will have evidence of TB elsewhere.[13] The tuberculin test is almost always reactive, except in patients with impaired cell-mediated immunity.[6]

TUBERCULOUS PLEURISY

Involvement of the pleural surface is the second most common form of extrapulmonary TB reported in the United States. In 1990, it accounted for 24 percent of cases (Fig. 11-1). It most frequently occurs with primary pulmonary infection and is usually thought to result from the rupture of a subpleural, infected node.[4,16,17] Pleural TB can also develop secondary to hematogenous spread.[4,16]

The onset of illness may be insidious or abrupt. One can see fever, constitutional complaints, shortness of breath, and chest pain.[4,16,17] A chest radiograph usually reveals only a pleural effusion, but in one-third of the cases one can identify an underlying pulmonary infiltrate.[4]

Thoracentesis combined with pleural biopsy often provides bacteriologic confirmation. Culture of pleural fluid alone yields positive rates of 30 percent or less.[18] However, if one combines pleural biopsy with culture and histologic evaluation, accuracy can increase.[4,16,18] Although granulomatous pleuritis can be seen in 60 percent of biopsy specimens, there is often only chronic inflammation on histologic examination.[4] Pleural fluid is exudative, with a predominance of lymphocytes. The protein content usually is more than 4 g/dl, with cell counts ranging from $1000-6000/\mu l$.[18] Glucose level determination in pleural fluid is variable and of little help in establishing the diagnosis. Mesothelial cells account for <5 percent of total cells in tuberculous pleurisy.[15] The absence of mesothelial cells on careful examination of the pleural fluid can be suggestive of tuberculous pleural infection.[4,15] Although the tuberculin skin test reaction may be negative early in the disease, by 2 months virtually all patients have reactive skin tests, except for some AIDS patients. Adenosine deaminase has been reported to be of help in diagnosis, but it has been found to have poor sensitivity and specificity.[19] Most cases of tuberculous pleurisy will resolve even if untreated, but there is a significant risk of reactivation of pulmonary TB within the next few years if the pleurisy is not treated with antibiotics.

BONE AND JOINT TB

Bone and joint TB accounted for 10 percent of the extrapulmonary foci reported in 1990 (Fig. 11-1). In contrast to tuberculous lymphadenitis, skeletal TB is seen more commonly in the older population.[4] Bone and joint involvement is usually secondary to hematogenous dissemination but can occur by lymphatic spread or by local extension.[20] In one large study by Farer, the spine was involved in 41 percent, the hip in 13 percent, and the knee in 10 percent.[22] When long bones are infected, it is most commonly the proximal end that is involved;[4] most cases of vertebral TB involve the thoracic and lumbar spine.[20] Joint infection can be secondary either to hematogenous dissemination or to infection of the adjacent epiphysis.[4,20.]

There is often a long delay in establishing the diagnosis of skeletal TB because of failure to consider TB in the differential diagnosis.[4] Pain with or without change in range of motion, fever, and constitutional symptoms are frequent.[4,20,21] Joint infection is most often monarticular.[20] Occasionally, patients will have a chronic draining sinus that does not improve with empiric antibiotic therapy.[21] In skeletal TB, the tuberculin test reaction is almost always positive;[4] about 50 percent of cases will also have abnormal findings on a chest radiograph, suggesting previous pulmonary TB.[20]

Although there are no pathognomic radiographic findings, TB should always be considered in any destructive arthritis.[4] The diagnosis is best made by combining the radiographic findings, skin test results, and biopsy results.[4] Reduction in the intervertebral disk space combined with erosion of the adjoining vertebral body is rarely seen with metastatic tumor but is common in vertebral osteomyelitis.[20] A paravertebral soft-tissue mass can be seen in infection, in tumor, and even in compression fracture.[20] Tuberculous infection cannot be differentiated from pyogenic infection by radiograph alone.[4]

Culture of synovial fluid will yield positive results for tubercle bacilli in about 80 percent of cases; acid-fast bacilli can be seen by direct examination about 20 percent of the time. Synovial biopsy may be required if cultures of joint fluid yield negative results.[4,20]

The protein level of synovial fluid is characteristically elevated to 4–6 g/dl.[20] Joint fluid glucose content is of limited value in making the diagnosis but is often low.[4] The total white blood cell (WBC) count can vary from a low of 40 cells/μl to a high of 136,000 cells/μl; most commonly it is between 50,000 and 100,000 cells/μl.[20] Polymorphonuclear leukocytes predominate.

Early effective chemotherapy will prevent spinal deformity or ankylosis of a joint. The role of surgery as an adjunct to chemotherapy is controversial: in most cases, radical surgery, debridement, or immobilization is not needed.[20] The most dreaded complication of vertebral body TB is paraplegia. If it occurs with active disease, surgical decompression, combined with chemotherapy, gives good results; in healed disease, however, it is more difficult and appears to be related to mechanical factors rather than active infection.[20]

GENITOURINARY TB

Genitourinary TB accounts for 9 percent of the extrapulmonary sites reported in the United States in 1990 (Fig. 11-1). There was a reduction of approximately one-third in genitourinary TB between 1980 and 1990.[11] The reason for this impressive change is not clear. Genitourinary TB commonly presents only after a long latent period.[4] It is usually the result of hematogenous dissemination and, as a result, is almost always bilateral, although it may be asymmetric. The initial urinary tract involvement is felt to be the kidney, with secondary spread to the bladder and, in males, to the prostate, seminal vesicle, and epididymis.[4] In this form of extrapulmonary TB, evidence of tuberculous infection elsewhere is often absent.[4] Presenting symptoms are often nonspecific and can include urinary frequency, dysuria, back pain, and hematuria.[4,23] Renal TB is often present for years before it becomes clinically apparent.[4] As many as half of all patients with positive urinary culture will have no urinary tract symptoms.[4]

Although the combination of sterile pyuria, proteinuria, hematuria, and an acid pH suggests tuberculous infection of the urinary tract, almost half of patients with positive urine culture will have a negative urinalysis result.[4] The tuberculin skin test reaction is usually positive, except in AIDS patients,[20,21] when the diagnosis is best made by culturing the urine for acid-fast bacilli.[4] Three to six first-voided urine specimens should be obtained for culture. Early-morning urine specimens are as reliable as 24 h urine collections.[23]

Radiologic findings include calcification of the kidney and, in males, calcification of the prostate, seminal vesicles, or vas deferens. Early TB of the kidney involves the renal cortex, with no abnormality by intravenous pyelogram. Later, the infection may progress to papillary necrosis, usually associated with ureteral strictures.[4]

Tuberculosis of the female genital tract is also thought to arise via hematogenous spread.[4] Rarely, it can be secondary to urinary tract or gastrointestinal TB.[23] The distal end of the fallopian tube is most commonly involved.[4] About half the patients will also have a granulomatous endometritis.[4] The ovary may be involved in about 30 percent of cases.[23] Common complaints include vague abdominal pain, menstrual abnormalities, and infertility.[4,23] Constitutional symptoms are usually lacking. Infection of the vagina and external genitalia is unusual.[23]

Diagnosis can often be made by cervical or endometrial biopsy.[4] Biopsy of the endometrium should be done just before menstruation, as tubercle formation seems most frequent at that time.[23] The tuberculin test reaction is usually positive, except in AIDS patients.[4,9] Microbiological confirmation may be difficult, but the characteristic histopathology, combined with a positive skin test reaction, is highly suggestive.[4]

MILIARY TB

Miliary TB refers to tuberculous infection involving many different organ systems, including the lungs. The name is related to the small size of lesions, which are usually <2 mm in diameter, resembling millet seeds. Eight percent of extrapulmonary TB reported in 1990 was miliary (Fig. 11-1), and it was more common in older age groups and in AIDS patients.[4,9] The clinical symptoms and findings are nonspecific, including fever, weakness, malaise, and anorexia.[4,9,24] Duration of symptoms can vary from days to years.[4] The average duration between onset of symptoms and final diagnosis is often months because of the protean manifestations of the disease.[4] The physical findings are also very nonspecific. They include fever, lymphadenopathy, and enlargement of the liver and spleen.[4,9,24] On occasion, the lesions may not involve the lung, the pulmonary lesions may be too small to be picked up on a standard chest radiograph, or the miliary pattern on the chest radiograph may be misdiagnosed.[4] One-third to one-half will have an apparently normal chest radiograph.[4] Approximately 20 percent of patients with miliary TB will have negative skin test reactions;[4] this is even more common in AIDS patients.[9] The most common laboratory abnormality is anemia, occurring in approximately two-thirds of patients.[4] The mean corpuscular volume (MCV) and red blood cell size distribution width (RDW) are in the normal range. Leukemoid reactions, pancytopenia, and monocytosis have also been described.[4,24] Disseminated intravascular coagulation is a rare complication.[4] Hyponatremia is common.[4] The diagnosis is usually made on the basis of the clinical presentation plus demonstration of necrotizing granuloma in bone marrow or liver biopsy specimens.[4,24] Unfortunately, granulomas in liver and bone marrow are not specific for TB. Positive acid-fast smear results are rarely seen.[24] Other body sites may yield positive microbiologic culture results even when not symptomatically involved.[24] Blood culture results may be positive in AIDS patients.[9] Transbronchial biopsy of the lung can sometimes be diagnostic.[24]

MENINGEAL TB

Meningeal TB comprises only about 6 percent of all cases of extrapulmonary TB (Figure 11-1). Although this is a small percentage, it is potentially the most lethal and is covered in Chapter 9.

PERITONEAL TB

Peritoneal TB is responsible for 3 percent of cases of extrapulmonary TB seen in the United States (Fig. 11-1). Peritonitis is most commonly secondary to infection of mesenteric nodes infected via the hematogenous route.[4,24] Symptoms of peritoneal TB are often quite subtle, with complaints of fever, abdominal pain, and swelling of the abdomen.[4,24] Duration of symptoms can vary from days to years. Although ascites is usually found to be present on physical examination, the effusion is rarely large,[24] and there is often a palpable mass secondary to enlarged mesenteric lymph nodes.[4] Computed tomographic (CT) scanning of the abdomen can show high-density ascites, adenopathy, and inflammatory masses.[4] Sonographic studies may be of use in collecting peritoneal fluid.[24] Examination of the peritoneal fluid is often suggestive if there is a preponderance of lymphocytes and a protein concentration of 4 g/dl or more. Cell count ranges from 200 to 2000 cells/μl. Smears of peritoneal fluid usually yield negative results for acid-fast bacilli.[4] It has been suggested that if large volumes of fluid are cultured, culture results will be positive in up to 90 percent.[25] Multiple blind biopsies of the peritoneum may be helpful in establishing the diagnosis as well; however, the use of biopsy under direct visualization at either laparoscopy or laparotomy increases the yield.[26] Tuberculin skin tests are often reactive, and usually there is evidence of coexisting TB elsewhere.[4]

MISCELLANEOUS EXTRAPULMONARY TB

Approximately 10 percent of reported cases of extrapulmonary TB in the United States in 1990 involved sites other than those listed above (Fig. 11-1). Perhaps the most common and worthy of mention is gastrointestinal TB other than tuberculous peritonitis. It is important to remember that TB can involve any part of the gastrointestinal system,[4] although the most common is that involving the ilium.[27]

In the United States, TB of the gastrointestinal tract is usually a complication of widespread TB and is secondary to swallowing infected sputum.[4] However, in countries where milk and dairy products are not pasteurized, gastrointestinal infection may be primary.[27] Enteric infection may be indolent and even asymptomatic. When it is symptomatic, patients may complain of abdominal pain, constipation, diarrhea, and nausea in addition to constitutional complaints of fever, weight loss, and night sweats.[27] Fistula formation may be a late complication. Diagnosis is usually made by biopsy with characteristic histologic findings.[27]

Pericardial TB is uncommon and is often difficult to diagnose.[4] It may present either in an insidious fashion or as an acute illness. Symptoms include chest pain, shortness of breath, ankle edema, fever, malaise, and weight loss.[28-30] Physical examination is remarkable for signs of pericardial disease.[28-30] Pleural effusions are commonly seen, and they are often bilateral.[4]

Sonographic studies are sensitive in establishing the presence of fluid in the pericardial space.[4] Tubercle bacilli are hard to culture from pericardial fluid.[28,30] Early subxyphoid biopsy of the pericardium for culture and histologic examination can help to establish the diagnosis; however, limited pericardial biopsy may miss characteristic histologic findings.[4] The tuberculin test reaction is usually positive.

Upper respiratory tract involvement may be seen, including TB otitis media, laryngeal TB, and infection of the tonsils.[31] It has been suggested that laryngeal TB may enhance infectiousness because of aerosolization of large numbers of tubercle bacilli.[4] Tuberculosis of the larynx is often confused with malignancy. However, lymphadenopathy is uncommon with TB laryngitis but is very common in malignancies of the larynx.[31]

Tuberculous otitis media may be primary but is most commonly hematogenous. The signs and symptoms are nonspecific. Tuberculosis should be considered in the diagnosis of chronic otitis media, particularly if there are draining sinus tracts. Facial nerve involvement is seen in 16–30 percent of cases and should be a clue to a tuberculous etiology.[31]

Tuberculous infection of the adrenal gland was once an important cause of Addison's disease but is now rarely seen.[4] Involvement in tissues such as skin and breasts is also uncommon and usually represents involvement secondary to contiguous infection.[4]

TREATMENT

The therapy for extrapulmonary TB has changed with concerns about multiple-drug resistance. In theory, since most cases of extrapulmonary TB have a relatively small bacillary load, standard therapy for pulmonary TB should be sufficient as long as there is not a major defect in the host's defense.[32] If the organisms are susceptible to all the primary drugs, then short-course combination therapy with isoniazid, rifampin, and pyrazinamide for 2 months, followed by isoniazid and rifampin for 4 months more, should be adequate for most cases of extrapulmonary TB.[32] Since extrapulmonary TB is a relatively uncommon disease, there are few controlled studies establishing the efficacy of short-course therapy.[32] Many authors feel that tuberculous meningitis, TB of bones and joints, and miliary TB should be treated longer (9 months to 1 year). Most pediatricians favor longer therapy in the pediatric patient with extrapulmonary infection. In settings in which there is reason to suggest multiple-drug resistance, such as previous poor compliance or infection acquired in an area known to have a high frequency of primary drug resistance, then therapy should include at least four antituberculous agents. Duration of therapy has not been established in people who are profoundly immunocompromised, such as patients with AIDS. Some authors suggest life-long antituberculous therapy.[33] Although compliance is the most important factor in the development of multiple-drug resistance, the AIDS patient, because of increased susceptibility and exposure to patients infected with drug-resistant organisms, may acquire exogenous infection with a multiply drug-resistant strain.[34] It is important, therefore, that in all patients there be continuous microbiologic monitoring and directly observed therapy.

The use of corticosteroids as an adjunct to antituberculous chemotherapy may be of value in some forms of extrapulmonary TB when the inflammatory response of the host may be detrimental, such as tuberculous meningitis, pericarditis, and possibly pleuritis.[35] Experience has shown that steroid therapy can be used safely as long as the patient is receiving concurrent effective antituberculous chemotherapy.[35]

REFERENCES

1. Stead WS, Kerby GR, Schlueter DP, et al: The clinical spectrum of primary tuberculosis in adults: confusion with reinfection in the pathogenesis of chronic tuberculosis. *Ann Intern Med* 68:731, 1968.
2. Riley RL: Airborne infection. *Am J Med* 57:466, 1974.
3. Enarson DA, Ashley MJ, Grzybowski S, et al: Non-respiratory tuberculosis in Canada: epidemiologic and bacteriologic features. *Am J Epidemiol* 112:341, 1980.
4. Weir MR, Thornton GF: Extrapulmonary tuberculosis: experience of a community hospital and review of the literature. *Am J Med* 79:467, 1985.
5. Myers JA: The natural history of tuberculosis in the human body. *JAMA* 194:1086, 1965.
6. Braun MM, Byers RH, Heyward WL, et al: Acquired immunodeficiency syndrome and extrapulmonary tuberculosis in the United States. *Medicine* 150:1913, 1990.
7. Chaisson RE, Schecter GF, Theuer CP, et al: Tuberculosis in patients with the acquired immunodeficiency syndrome. *Am Rev Respir Dis* 136:570, 1987.
8. Centers for Disease Control: Revision of the CDC surveillance case definition for acquired immunodeficiency syndrome. *MMWR* 36:1S, 1987.
9. Shafer RW, Kim DS, Weiss JP, et al: Extrapulmonary tuberculosis in patients with human immunodeficiency virus infection. *Medicine* 70:384, 1991.
10. Jereb JA, Kelly GP, Dedey SW, et al: Tuberculosis morbidity in the United States: final data, 1990, in CDC surveillance summaries. *MMWR* 40:23, 1991.
11. Personal communication. Division of Tuberculosis Elimination, Centers for Disease Control, Atlanta.
12. Kent DC: Tuberculous lymphadenitis: not a localized disease process. *Am J Med Sci* 254:866, 1967.
13. Powell DA: Tuberculosis lymphadenitis, in Schlossberg D (ed), *Tuberculosis*, 2d ed. New York, Springer-Verlag, 1983, pp 99–107.
14. Huhti E, Brander E, Ploheimo S: Tuberculosis of the cervical lymph nodes: a clinical, pathological, and bacteriological study. *Tubercle* 56:27, 1975.

15. Prat L, Bajen MD, Ricart Y, et al: Ga-67 citrate and Tc-99m HMPAO leukocyte scanning in extrapulmonary tuberculosis. *Clin Nucl Med* 16:865, 1991.

16. Rossman MD, Mayock RL: Pulmonary tuberculosis, in Schlossberg D (ed), *Tuberculosis*, 2d ed. New York, Springer-Verlag, 1983, pp 61–70.

17. Stead WW, Eicheholz A, Strauss HK: Operative and pathologic findings in 24 patients with the syndrome of idiopathic pleurisy with effusion presumably tuberculosis. *Am Rev Tuberc Pul Dis* 71:473, 1955.

18. Berger HW, Mejia E: Tuberculous pleurisy. *Chest* 63:88, 1973.

19. Berenguer J, Moreno S, Lagure F, et al: Tuberculous meningitis in patients infected with the human immunodeficiency virus. *New Engl J Med* 326:668, 1992.

20. Davidson PT, Fernandez E: Bone and joint tuberculosis, in Schlossberg D (ed), *Tuberculosis*, 2d ed. New York, Springer-Verlag, 1983, pp 119–132.

21. Enarson DA, Fujii M, Nakielna EN, et al: Bone and joint tuberculosis: a continuing problem. *Can Med Assoc J* 120:139, 1979.

22. Farer S, Lowell AM: Extrapulmonary tuberculosis in the United States. *Am J Epidemiol* 109:205, 1979.

23. Weinstein AJ: Genitourinary tuberculosis, in Schlossberg D (ed), *Tuberculosis*, 2d ed. New York, Springer-Verlag, 1983, pp 179–190.

24. Israel HL: Tuberculous peritonitis, in Schlossberg D (ed), *Tuberculosis*, 2d ed. New York, Springer-Verlag, 1983, pp 143–148.

25. Singh MM, Bhargava AN, Jain KP: Tuberculous peritonitis: an evaluation of the pathogenic mechanisms, diagnostic procedures, and therapeutic measures. *N Engl J Med* 281:1091, 1969.

26. Wolfe JHN, Behn AR, Jackson BT: Tuberculous peritonitis and role of diagnostic laparoscopy. *Lancet* 1:852, 1979.

27. Paustian FF, Sahl MG: Tuberculosis enteritis, in Schlossberg D (ed), *Tuberculosis*, 2d ed. New York, Springer-Verlag, 1983, pp 139–142.

28. Ortbals DW, Avioliv LV: Tuberculous pericarditis. *Arch Intern Med* 139:231, 1979.

29. Fowler NO, Nanitsas GT: Infectious pericarditis. *Prog Cardiovasc Dis* 16:323, 1973.

30. Rooney JJ, Crocco JA, Lyons MA: Tuberculous pericarditis. *Ann Intern Med* 72:73, 1970.

31. Rohwedder JJ: Upper respiratory tract tuberculosis in a general hospital. *Ann Intern Med* 80:708, 1974.

32. Dutt AK, Moers D, Stead WW: Short-course chemotherapy for extrapulmonary tuberculosis: nine years' experience. *Ann Intern Med* 104:7, 1986.

33. Pitchenik AE, Ferkel D: Tuberculosis and non-tuberculosis mycobacterial disease. *Med Clin North Am* 76:121, 1992.

34. Small PM, Shafer RW, Hopewell PC, et al: Exogenous reinfection with multidrug-resistant *Mycobacterium tuberculosis* in patients with advanced HIV infection. *New Engl J Med* 328:117, 1993.

35. Thornton GF: The role of corticosteroids in the management of tuberculous infections, in Johnson JE (ed), *Rational Therapy and Control of Tuberculosis*. Gainesville, University of Florida Press, 1970, pp 113–125.

PART IV

Treatment

CHAPTER 12

Current Treatment and Management

DAVID W. HAAS / ROGER M. DES PREZ

Before the availability of effective drug therapy, approximately half of patients with active pulmonary tuberculosis (TB) died within 2 years, a quarter recovered, and a quarter survived with chronically active disease.[1] Sanatorium treatment was fairly effective for noncavitary disease but much less so for more advanced cases. The lifelong risk of relapse following disease arrest was about 25 percent among patients discharged from sanatoria.

In the 1950s and 1960s it became clear that prolonged chemotherapy could cure almost all patients, making such traditional measures as protracted bed rest and collapse therapy unnecessary. Lengthy isolation was also abandoned, since chemotherapy promptly rendered patients noninfectious. Although treatment failure should theoretically be a rare occurrence with effective drug therapy, results often fall far short of this ideal. Occasionally, failures may be due to unrecognized drug resistance or selection of an inappropriate regimen; a greater number are due to noncompliance, often carefully concealed by the patient, as health returns and motivation to continue medication decreases. Accordingly, education of the patient is essential to success. Frequent visits to the health care provider not only make it possible to monitor compliance, clinical response, and drug toxicity but serve to reinforce the seriousness of the treatment enterprise.

TREATMENT STRATEGIES BASED ON EFFECTS OF INDIVIDUAL DRUGS ON VARIOUS BACTERIAL SUBPOPULATIONS

The bacillary population in TB consists of organisms with various levels of metabolism. Knowledge of the effects of various drugs on these bacterial subpopulations is considered important in the design of treatment regimens. Chemotherapy is thought to involve an early *bactericidal phase*, during which the vast majority of organisms are rapidly killed, and a slower *sterilizing phase*, during which residual susceptible, slowly or intermittently metabolizing organisms are inhibited or killed (Table 12-1). Rapidly multiplying extracellular

187

188 • PART IV TREATMENT

TABLE 12-1. Actions of First-Line Antituberculous Agents

Agent	Activity
Isoniazid (INH)	Bactericidal against both intracellular and extracellular bacilli
Rifampin (RMP)	Bactericidal against both intracellular and extracellular bacilli; sterilizing against slowly metabolizing organisms
Pyrazinamide (PZA)	Poor bactericidal activity alone; good sterilizing activity acting synergistically with INH and perhaps other drugs; active at acid pH; greatest activity during first few months of therapy
Streptomycin (STM)	Bactericidal against extracellular bacilli only
Ethambutol (EMB)	Bactericidal, probably against both intracellular and extracellular organisms, at 25 mg/kg; bacteriostatic at 15 mg/kg

organisms in the hyperoxic, neutral pH environment of the pulmonary cavity are highly susceptible to bactericidal drugs. Other organisms are less or only intermittently metabolically active in the hypoxic and acidic environment within solid caseous material, the acid environment of acutely inflamed tissues, or the highly suppressive and acidic environment within activated macrophages. These organisms are not susceptible to the rapid bactericidal action of chemotherapeutic agents. It should be emphasized that in solid caseous tissue (unabsorbed solid necrosis), some trapped organisms become completely dormant and are unaffected by both antimicrobials and cellular immune mechanisms. Such persisting organisms can be securely contained only by healing with fibrosis and encapsulation.

ANTIMICROBIAL RESISTANCE

Populations of *Mycobacterium tuberculosis* never exposed to drugs contain mutants resistant to any single chemotherapeutic agent at a rate of $10^{-5}-10^{-8}$ organisms. This factor is relatively unimportant in noncavitary pulmonary or extrapulmonary lesions, where bacillary populations are relatively small ($<10^4$ in hard caseous foci). However, due to the great number of organisms present (10^7-10^9), cavitary lesions contain many organisms (10^4 or greater) resistant to any single drug, which under the selective pressure of single-drug therapy may multiply and repopulate the lesion. The importance of multiple-drug therapy was clear from very early studies demonstrating that para-aminosalicylic acid (PAS), a weak drug, effectively prevented emergence of resistance to streptomycin (STM), which otherwise rapidly developed in a large percentage of patients.[2] The ability to prevent the emergence of resistance to other components of a multiple-drug regimen is one important asset of an antituberculous drug. Isoniazid (INH) and rifampin (RMP) are highly effective, ethambutol (EMB) is next, and STM is less so; pyrazinamide (PZA) is least effective in this regard.[3]

Resistance to antituberculous drugs in the individual patient may be either primary or secondary. *Primary resistance* connotes the presence of predominantly drug-resistant organisms in a previously untreated patient; *secondary resistance* is resistance that develops during the course of treatment of an initially drug-sensitive infection or after relapse of an infection for which therapy was inappropriate.

Primary Resistance

During the 1970s, the prevalence of primary drug resistance in the United States was less than 3 percent. However, even then there were populations in which this figure was much greater. For example, approximately 50 percent of TB in the Asian wives of servicemen returning from Southeast Asia demonstrated primary resistance,[4] levels characteristic of countries where antituberculous drugs can be obtained without medical supervision.

A summary of the data between 1982 and 1986 indicates that primary resistance rose to approximately 9 percent in those 4 years and was mostly to INH or STM (Table 12-2). A that time, RMP resistance was rare,[5] although

TABLE 12-2. Patients Resistant to Antituberculous Drugs, 1982–1986

Drug	% Resistant	
	Never Treated	*Previously Treated*
Isoniazid (INH)	5.3	19.4
Streptomycin (STM)	4.8	10.3
Rifampin (RMP)	0.6	3.2
Ethambutol (EMB)	0.6	2.2
Pyrazinamide (PZA)*	0.5	1.5
Ethionamide (ETH)	1.5	3.7
Para-aminosalicylic acid (PAS)	1.0	3.5
Kanamycin	0.03	0.4
Capreomycin	0.08	0.2
Cycloserine	0.00	0.03
Any drug	9.0	22.8

*Excludes isolates with unknown PZA results.

Source: Adapted with permission from Snider.[5]

there were areas where it was more common. A report from south Texas in 1983 recorded primary resistance to at least one drug in 20 percent of patients and to RMP in approximately 10 percent.[6] Increased primary resistance to RMP was also noted in a longitudinal study of Brooklyn children. A more recent study (1988–1989) of adults from the same institution and area demonstrated resistance, either primary or secondary, to at least one drug in 31 percent and to RMP in 15 percent, and primary resistance to RMP in 4 percent of the population.[7]

Resistance to RMP compromises results of RMP-containing multiple-drug regimens more than resistance to other major drugs. As discussed below, it is surprising to note that the major studies of four-drug, 6-month chemotherapy demonstrated that initial INH or STM resistance did not compromise outcome. However, results were very poor (>50 percent lack of conversion or relapse) when patients demonstrated RMP resistance prior to therapy, contraindicating short-course (6- or 9-month) therapy in such patients.[8]

Secondary Resistance

Secondary resistance is usually due to poor compliance, insufficient supervision, or selection of an inappropriate drug regimen. As discussed below, when relapse occurs following an apparently successful response to an uninterrupted course of a proper drug regimen, the organisms almost always demonstrate the antimicrobial sensitivity pattern that had been present at the outset of treatment.

Historical clues that suggest drug resistance include prior chemotherapy (including INH prophylaxis), infection acquired in parts of the world where INH resistance is prevalent (including Asia, Latin America, and Africa), and contact with a patient with drug-resistant TB. A study from southern California recorded resistance in 71 percent of patients with prior treatment and cavitary disease.[9] Homelessness, drug abuse, and AIDS all favor acquisition or development of drug-resistant infections. Over 60 percent of homeless persons diagnosed with TB while living in a Boston hostel had resistant infections.[10] A retrospective study of serial positive culture results between 1982 and 1987 in one Manhattan hospital correlated drug resistance with living circumstances. Resistance was present in 8 percent of patients with homes, 21 percent of those without homes, and in 42 percent of homeless African-Americans, illustrating that compliance with drug treatment is unlikely in persons facing the much more pressing problems associated with homelessness. In a more recent study, resistance to at least one drug was demonstrated in 33 percent of *M. tuberculosis* isolates from 518 patients in New York City during 1 month in 1991; resistance to both INH and RMP occurred in 19 percent of those patients and in 30 percent of those who had been previously tested.

Resistance to RMP was only slightly less common than resistance to INH. The strongest predictor of drug resistance was a history of previous antituberculous therapy.[11] Microepidemics of multidrug-resistant (MDR) TB, affecting mostly acquired immunodeficiency syndrome (AIDS) patients in hospitals, prisons, and residential facilities, have occurred in New York, Miami, San Francisco, Michigan, and elsewhere and have been fatal in 80 percent of cases or more (see Chapter 18 for greater detail).[12] AIDS patients with TB may be highly contagious for others to contact, including health care workers.[13]

SPECIFIC ANTITUBERCULOUS DRUGS

The recommended dosages of the most commonly used antituberculous drugs are presented in Table 12-3. All are given by mouth except as indicated. First-line agents (see Table 12-1) are best administered as a single daily dose, since peak serum drug concentrations are more important than sustained levels. Clofazimine and thiacetazone are also administered once daily, while other second-line agents are given in divided doses.

Isoniazid

Isoniazid (INH) is the cornerstone of therapy and should be included in all regimens except when a high degree of INH resistance exists and the treatment regimen includes RMP. It is a nicotinic acid derivative that probably acts by inhibiting mycolic acid synthesis. INH rapidly kills both extracellular and intracellular organisms and is well-absorbed, reaching levels after ingestion equal to those following parenteral administration. Its small molecular size allows widespread distribution, providing levels far greater than the minimal bactericidal concentration in all tissues, including caseous foci, the interior of phagocytic cells, and the subarachnoid space. It undergoes hepatic metabolism by both acetylation and oxidation via the cytochrome p-450 system.

The major toxicities of INH are peripheral neuritis and hepatitis. Neuritis occurs in 40 percent of patients at daily doses of 20 mg/kg, 20 percent at 10 mg/kg, and 1–2 percent at 5 mg/kg and is due to INH-induced depletion of pyridoxine stores.[14] When baseline pyroxidine deficiency is anticipated, as in alcoholics, pregnant women, malnourished persons, cancer patients, uremics, and perhaps students with irregular eating habits, pyroxidine supplementation (10–50 mg daily) is indicated. When it occurs, INH-induced peripheral neuritis can be reversed by temporarily stopping INH and administering pyroxidine (100–200 mg daily). Hepatitis is discussed at length in Chapter 13.

TABLE 12-3. Dosage Recommendation for Initial Treatment of TB among Children* and Adults

Drugs	Daily Children	Daily Adults	2 Times/Week Children	2 Times/Week Adults	3 Times/Week Children	3 Times/Week Adults
Isoniazid (INH)	10–20 mg/kg max 300 mg	5 mg/kg max 300 mg	20–40 mg/kg max 900 mg	15 mg/kg max 900 mg	20–40 mg/kg max 900 mg	15 mg/kg max 900 mg
Rifampin (RMP)	10–20 mg/kg max 600 mg	10 mg/kg max 600 mg	10–20 mg/kg max 600 mg	10 mg/kg max 600 mg	10–20 mg/kg max 600 mg	10 mg/kg max 600 mg
Pyrazinamide (PZA)	15–30 mg/kg max 2 g	15–30 mg/kg max 2 g	50–70 mg/kg max 4 g	50–70 mg/kg max 4 g	50–70 mg/kg max 3 g	50–70 mg/kg max 3 g
Ethambutol† (EMB)	15–25 mg/kg max 2.5 g	15–25 mg/kg max 2.5 g	50 mg/kg max 2.5 g	50 mg/kg max 2.5 g	25–30 mg/kg max 2.5 g	25–30 mg/kg max 2.5 g
Streptomycin (STM)	20–30 mg/kg max 1 g	15 mg/kg max 1 g	25–30 mg/kg max 1.5 g	25–30 mg/kg max 1.5 g	25–30 mg/kg max 1 g	25–30 mg/kg max 1 g
Capreomycin, kanamycin	20–30 mg/kg max 1 g	15 mg/kg max 1 g	NI	NI	NI	NI
Cycloserine	10–20 mg/kg max 500 mg	10 mg/kg max 1 g	NI	NI	NI	NI
Ethionamide (ETH), prothionamide	10–15 mg/kg max 750 mg	10–15 mg/kg max 1 g	NI	NI	NI	NI
Para-aminosalicylic acid (PAS)	300 mg/kg	250 mg/kg at least 12 g				
Thiocetazone	NI	150 mg	NI	NI	NI	NI
Ciprofloxacin	NI	1–1.5 g	NI	NI	NI	NI
Ofloxacin	NI	600 mg	NI	NI	NI	NI
Clofazimine	NI	100–200 mg	NI	NI	NI	NI

Note: max = maximum; NI = not indicated. Source: Adapted with permission from Davidson and Le[30] and Centers for Disease Control.[46]

*Children ≤ 12 years of age.

Briefly, it occurs in 1–2 percent of treatment cases, more often in older persons and in slow acetylators, and may be fatal in up to 10 percent of cases if unrecognized. INH may also cause a clinically significant increase in the concentration of phenytoin, has been implicated in cases of aplastic anemia, and may decrease the threshold for acetaminophen hepatoxicity.[15] Rarely, it may cause seizures, usually when ingested in huge doses with suicidal intent. In this setting, intravenous pyridoxine (1 g per gram of INH ingested or 10 g if the amount ingested is not known) may be beneficial.

INH should be given after dialysis, but no dosage adjustment is required in the presence of renal or hepatic disease. While INH is generally given by nasogastric tube to unconscious patients, a solution for intramuscular injection is available. This preparation has also been successfully used for prolonged intravenous therapy.[16]

Rifampin

Rifampin (RMP) is the second major antituberculous agent. Like INH, it reaches therapeutic concentrations in caseous foci, within leukocytes, and in the central nervous system in the presence of inflamed meninges. For reasons probably related to its mechanism of action (inhibition of DNA-dependent RNA polymerase), it is more effective than INH in "sterilizing" relatively protected environments (e.g., solid caseous foci and inside phagocytic cells) containing slowly or intermittently metabolizing bacilli.[3] Side effects include gastrointestinal intolerance and, when given on a less than daily schedule at doses >600 mg/day, reactions that appear to be immunologically mediated, including hemolytic anemia, acute renal failure, and thrombocytopenia. The latter are rare with currently recommended dosages and schedules, but when they do occur RMP should not be administered again.

The potent inducing effect of RMP on the hepatic microsomal p-450 system may increase the metabolism of a number of drugs with clinically serious consequences. These drugs include corticosteroids (adrenal insufficiency and worsening of steroid-dependent asthma), estrogens (breakthrough bleeding and unplanned pregnancy), cyclosporine (transplant rejection), vitamin D (osteomalacia), coumadin (thrombotic events), oral hypoglycemic agents (hyperglycemia), phenytoin (seizures), digoxin, quinidine, β-blockers, and other compounds. RMP may critically decrease the concentration of ketoconazole, and, conversely, ketoconazole may inhibit the absorption of RMP when both drugs are given together. RMP also induces its own catabolism, although the significance of this is not clear.[17]

As with INH, the most important complication of RMP is hepatitis. Although a meta-analysis has indicated that the incidence of hepatitis in regimens containing both INH and RMP is approximately twice that of INH alone,[18] selected studies in which direct comparison is possible indicate that it may actually be 4 times more frequent. Hepatitis complicating INH and RMP given in combination is distinctive in important ways. Although biochemical evidence of hepatic toxicity may occur promptly after administration of INH alone, clinical evidence of hepatitis is rarely seen in the first month and often is delayed for 2 months or more.[19] In contrast, jaundice complicating INH and RMP may occur within the first 2 weeks of therapy and may be fulminant. It has been proposed, although not established, that INH-RMP hepatotoxicity is due to accelerated production of a toxic product of INH oxidation due to the inducing effect of RMP on the hepatic microsomal p-450 system.[18] This hypothesis is supported by the observation that phenobarbital and phenytoin, also inducers of the microsomal p-450 system, have been associated with fulminant hepatic failure in persons receiving INH and RMP. INH hepatotoxicity is rare in children. In contrast, as many as 25 percent of children taking INH and RMP develop jaundice, although this may not be the same phenomena as hepatitis in adults.[18]

The dosage of RMP need not be adjusted for renal or hepatic dysfunction. It is not eliminated by dialysis, due to extensive (>80 percent) protein binding. As with INH, RMP can be given to unconscious patients by nasogastric tube, but an intravenous preparation may be obtained from the manufacturer for compassionate use.

Pyrazinamide

Pyrazinamide (PZA) has emerged as an essential component of 6-month regimens, as discussed below. Like INH, PZA is a nicotinic acid derivative but has a distinct mechanism of action and no cross-resistance with INH. Early studies of INH plus PZA recorded such serious hepatotoxicity that the latter was largely abandoned as first-line treatment and relegated to use as "coverage" for surgical resection in drug-resistant cases. However, the doses used in these early studies were greater and the duration longer than now recommended. As currently used, PZA does not add to the hepatotoxicity of INH and RMP.[20] It has been hypothesized that its activity at acid pH makes PZA particularly effective against slowly metabolizing intracellular bacilli. However, recent studies suggest that PZA is active against extracellular organisms as well, presumably those in an acidic inflammatory milieu. Further, studies in ex vivo infected macrophages indicate that PZA has little bactericidal activity in that experimental system.[21] Although the details of how it acts remain unknown, it is one of the two effective "sterilizing" agents, the other being RMP. Several large clinical studies have established that PZA is critical in so-called short-course chemotherapy, making it possible, when administered with INH and RMP, to obtain in 6 months results that would otherwise require at least 9 months.[22] PZA is not thought to effectively prevent the emergence of resistance to companion drugs. Its beneficial effect is for the most part limited to the first 2–3 months of treatment, after which it is usually discontinued.[3]

Side effects due to PZA are relatively uncommon. It commonly causes hyperuricemia, occasionally mild nongouty polyarthralgias that respond to nonsteroidal anti-inflammatory agents, and rarely frank clinical gout. Unless overt gout develops, elevated serum urate levels need not be treated. The incidence of nongouty arthralgias is decreased when RMP is a part of the treatment regimen.[20] Because of its pH optimum, standard sensitivity studies cannot be used. Specialized methods have been developed but are not widely available.

Ethambutol

Ethambutol (EMB) is a component of most multiple-drug regimens. We recommend its use at a daily dosage of 25 mg/kg during the first 2 months of well-supervised therapy and at least 15 mg/kg for longer, often less well-supervised, periods. It is rapidly bactericidal at 25 mg/kg but bacteriostatic at 15 mg/kg[23] and is active against both intracellular and extracellular bacilli.[24] EMB prevents emergence of resistance to other drugs in multiple-drug regimens, which may be the major role of low-dose EMB, especially when given with INH as part of a two-drug regimen. Its only important toxicity is dose-dependent optic neuritis, manifested by central scotomata, decreased red-green color vision, decreased visual acuity, and, rarely, concentric contraction of visual fields, leading to gun barrel vision. Optic neuritis occurs in as many as 3 percent of patients at 25 mg/kg but rarely at 15 mg/kg.[25] It usually develops slowly and resolves when the drug is discontinued, but fulminant cases have been reported. Patients should be questioned concerning visual symptoms, and a simple test of visual acuity and color vision should be performed monthly, if possible. Ophthalmological monitoring is not required. The need to monitor visual symptoms argues against the use of EMB in very young children. Like PZA, EMB may also cause hyperuricemia and, rarely, gout. Accurately adjusting the dose during renal failure is difficult (see below), and some authorities advise against its use in this situation.[26]

Streptomycin

Streptomycin (STM), the first major antituberculous drug, was promptly replaced by INH as the cornerstone of therapy. The facts that STM is excluded from the interior of cells and is active at neutral pH and that PZA penetrates cells and is active at acid pH led to the now arguable hypothesis that STM and PZA together constitute "one strong drug."[3,20] This was the rationale for exploring 6-month courses of chemotherapy with INH, RMP, STM, and PZA. Subsequently, STM has been largely (and successfully) replaced by EMB in 6-month regimens, casting doubt on the "one strong drug" hypothesis. STM does not achieve very effective concentrations in the central nervous system. Although it was marginally effective as a single agent in the early studies of meningitis, its low cerebrospinal fluid concentrations led to its use via the intrathecal route in some cases, with enormous ototoxicity. Its major toxicity is eighth nerve damage, leading to vestibular dysfunction and, less frequently, deafness. This is more of a problem in those >50 years of age, to whom STM should be administered very cautiously, if at all. Patients should be questioned regarding balance and asked to perform simple tests of vestibular function, such as rapidly reversing direction while walking.

Second-Line Agents

The use of second-line agents is limited by less efficacy and/or greater toxicity than first-line drugs. Ethionamide and prothionamide are equivalent oral agents with prominent gastrointestinal toxicity thought to be centrally mediated. When given with INH for prolonged periods, ethionamide may cause a distinct rheumatologic syndrome characterized by distal polyarthritis, shoulder contractures, and fasciitis of the palms and sole.[27] Cycloserine frequently causes central nervous system toxicity, including mood change, psychosis, and seizures. Kanamycin and capreomycin are antibiotics with toxicities similar to but somewhat more severe than those of STM. They are probably less effective than STM but do not demonstrate cross-microbial resistance. Because of additive toxicity, only one of these three drugs should be given at a time, although in desperate situations kanamycin and capreomycin have been used together with some success.[28] PAS, once frequently used with INH but now largely replaced by EMB, is very difficult to tolerate, causing gastrointestinal upset in most patients as well as frequent hypersensitivity, hepatotoxicity, and, when given as the sodium salt, fluid overload. Thiacetazone is a commonly used companion drug to INH in developing countries, where its low cost is a major advantage. Its toxicities include gastrointestinal distress, bone marrow suppression, liver damage, and severe dermatitis in such patients. The quinolones, including ciprofloxacin and ofloxacin, have definite antimycobacterial activity and are being increasingly used, with some success, for patients who cannot be effectively treated with first-line agents. Clofazimine, rifabutin, clarithromycin, and ampicillin/clavulinic acid have also been used in multidrug-resistant cases.

SELECTING A DRUG REGIMEN FOR INITIAL TREATMENT

Overview of Chemotherapeutic Regimens

Before the availability of RMP, excellent results in drug-sensitive infections were obtained with INH plus either PAS or EMB given for 18–24 months, "reinforced" in extensive disease by STM for the first 6–12 weeks of treatment. Shorter courses were associated with unacceptable rates of relapse. For several years after RMP became available, in 1966, it was used mostly for treating INH-resistant cases, which it did spectacularly well. However, the desirability of shorter treatment regimens was clear, and attention was focused on accomplishing this by using INH and RMP together. Definitive studies in Great Britain, the United States, and elsewhere established that drug-sensitive infections were treated as effectively, with cure rates of approximately 97 percent, with 9 months of INH and RMP as with 18–24-month regimens not containing RMP.[26,29-31] Subsequently it was demonstrated that 6-month regimens based on an initial 2-month "bactericidal phase" consisting of INH, RMP, PZA, and either STM or EMB and a "continuation phase" of INH and RMP for 4 more months performed as well as longer regimens.[22] It was also established that during the "continuation phase" drugs could be administered twice or thrice weekly, providing the opportunity for directly observed therapy, an advantage that cannot be overemphasized when dealing with homeless or drug-addicted persons. It is surprising to note that initial resistance to either INH or STM did not compromise the results of 6-month regimens, although initial RMP resistance rendered them substantially ineffective.[8] Next it was demonstrated that results with INH, RMP, and PZA for 2 months followed by INH and RMP for 4 months were not improved by adding either STM or EMB *in drug-susceptible infections.*[22]

This 6-month regimen of three drugs is an acceptable alternative to 9 months of INH plus RMP in populations in which drug resistance is very unlikely. Older regimens lacking RMP should be used very infrequently. However, since the only advantage of the shorter regimens in drug-sensitive infection is shortening of therapy, a word of caution is in order. Development of drug resistance in an initially sensitive infection is almost always due to noncompliance by the patient. When the patient continues one drug but omits another, emergence of resistance to the omitted drug is likely. Further, hepatotoxicity is greater when giving INH and RMP together than with regimens containing INH but not RMP.[18] Although the incremental risk is not great, the justification of any increased risk needs to be scrutinized when treating disease of limited extent due to drug-sensitive bacilli and when compliance can be assured. In this admittedly unusual situation, 18–24 months of INH plus EMB is a reasonable alternative to shorter regimens. Several regimens have been suggested by the Centers for Disease Control (CDC) and are presented in Table 12-4.

6-Month Regimens

The American Thoracic Society (ATS) and CDC currently recommend an initial 2-month period of INH, RMP, and PZA (plus EMB at 15 – 25 mg/kg if INH resistance is suspected) followed by INH plus RMP daily or twice weekly for 4 months as an acceptable alternative to 9 months of INH plus RMP.[32] The impact of INH resistance on the success of this three-drug regimen has not been documented. However, in view of the increasing incidence of drug resistance, as discussed above, and the safety of EMB at a dose of 25 mg/kg under proper supervision and cooperation, it is our opinion (as well as that of others) that much is to be gained by including EMB in the initial 2 months of treatment.[33] It is important to note that results of 6-month treatment regimens in patients with initial resistance to RMP are unacceptable in nearly 50 percent of cases.[8] Clinical experience from the era before RMP became available suggests that RMP-resistant cases should be treated for 18 – 24 months.

When hepatitis occurs in patients receiving both INH and RMP, both drugs should be discontinued until the liver function tests return to normal. INH may then be cautiously (but usually successfully) reintroduced in graduated doses while transaminases are monitored, and a more prolonged (18 – 24-month) regimen based on INH and at least one companion drug other than RMP can be continued. Similarly, when patients developing drug-related hepatitis on INH and RMP have demonstrated microbial resistance to INH but not RMP, RMP can usually be gradually reintroduced, and a more prolonged (18 – 24-month) regimen based on RMP and, preferably, two new companion drugs other than INH can be continued. When both INH and RMP must be reintroduced (which is generally not the case), this can usually be done sequentially with close clinical and biochemical supervision after a period of time in many patients.[18]

Directly Observed Therapy in Noncompliant Patients

Persons whose lives are complicated by alcoholism, other drug addiction, or homelessness do not or cannot assume responsibility for complying with unsupervised treatment. The advantages of directly observed therapy are clear from the contrast between the successful control of TB in Nicaragua, where resources are meager and directly observed therapy is routine, and the failure in New York City, where directly observed therapy is less commonly used.[34]

TABLE 12-4. Regimen Options for Initial Treatment of TB among Children and Adults

	TB without HIV Infection		TB with HIV Infection
Option 1	Option 2	Option 3	
Administer daily INH, RMP, and PZA for 8 weeks, followed by 16 weeks of INH and RMP daily or 2–3 times/week* in areas where the INH resistance rate is not documented to be <4%. EMB or STM should be added to the initial regimen until susceptibility to INH and RMP is demonstrated. Continue treatment for at least 6 months and 3 months beyond culture conversion. Consult a TB medical expert if the patient is symptomatic or smear- or culture-positive after 3 months.	Administer daily INH, RMP, PZA, and STM for 2 weeks followed by 2 times/week* administration of the same drugs for 6 weeks (by DOT) and, subsequently, with 2 times/week administration of INH and RMP for 16 weeks (by DOT). Consult a TB medical expert if the patient is symptomatic or smear- or culture-positive after 3 months.	Treat by DOT, 3 times/week* with INH, RMP, PZA, and EMB or STM for 6 months. Consult a TB medical expert if the patient is symptomatic or smear- or culture-positive after 3 months.	Options 1, 2, or 3 can be used, but treatment regimens should continue for a total of 9 months and at least 6 months beyond culture conversion.

Note: DOT = directly observed therapy.

*All regimens administered 2 times/week or 3 times/week should be monitored by DOT for the duration of therapy.

Source: Adapted with permission from Centers for Disease Control.[46]

199

The failure of conventional treatment programs to cure socially disadvantaged persons, together with the fact that most of a 6-month regimen can be given on a less than daily basis, has led to regimens based on the direct observation of the administration of a minimal number of drug doses.[26,31] One such regimen, in use for several years by the Denver Department of Health, is presented in Table 12-4.[35] The total cost of this regimen, including supervision, differs little from that of unsupervised regimens using daily therapy: approximately $400 per patient. Since all doses are observed, compliance problems are eliminated, as is the likelihood of emergence of resistance. Health care and legal workers cooperate to quarantine or place in detention recalcitrant patients for completion of therapy. When the astronomical costs generated by single patients with multidrug-resistant TB and those they infect are considered, it is difficult to argue against directly observed therapy when compliance is at all suspect. (See Chapter 18 for more detail on this subject.)

Experience with Regimens of Less Than 6 Months in Less-Than-Extensive Disease

The extent of disease can be quantified by the mycobacterial content of sputum, with smear and culture positivity representing the greatest extent, smear negativity and culture positivity intermediate, and both smear and culture negativity the least. Good results have on occasion been obtained with as little as 2–4 months of 4-drug therapy in patients with less than extensive TB defined in this way.[36] While such short periods of chemotherapy are *not* recommended, the fact that even brief courses of intense, reliably taken therapy can cure many patients further supports the use of direct observation when completion of therapy is uncertain.

9-Month Regimens Based on INH and RMP

The combination of INH (300 mg) plus RMP (600 mg) daily by mouth on an empty stomach for 9 months has been advised by many for all forms of drug-sensitive TB, both pulmonary and extrapulmonary.[32] PZA (15–30 mg/kg) plus either STM (1 g) or EMB (15–25 mg/kg) is often added, initially pending sensitivity results, especially when epidemiological factors suggest that primary drug resistance is a possibility (see above).

An intermittent 9-month regimen consisting largely of twice-weekly doses of INH and RMP is an acceptable alternative based on a large series of cases studied by one group of investigators.[37] INH and RMP are administered daily as described above for 1–2 months and twice weekly thereafter with the same dose of RMP but a larger (900 mg) dose of INH. Emergence of drug resistance on this regimen has not been a major problem, and toxicity has been minimal. Its use is not advised in areas or situations with any substantial prevalence of antimicrobial resistance, however.

Use of Antimicrobial Tablets

A commercial preparation containing 300 mg of INH and 600 mg of RMP (Rifamate) is available. A major advantage of this combination pill is that it prevents the patient from neglecting or omitting one of the drugs at the risk of inducing resistance to the other. A preparation containing appropriate amounts of INH, RMP, and PZA (Rifater) is available abroad but not in the United States. The combined preparations appear to provide plasma concentrations similar to those obtained when the components are given individually.

Course of Treatment and Duration of Observation

The diagnosis of TB is often well-established via clinical, radiographic, and acid-fast bacilli smear data before therapy is initiated. In smear-negative cases, five or six sputum samples and, if possible, specimens obtained at bronchoscopy should be submitted before beginning treatment. In severely ill patients with presumed TB, treatment should be initiated immediately; a few days of antituberculous treatment will not interfere with bacteriologic diagnosis. In other patients in whom treatment is initiated before a microbiologic diagnosis is established, the roentgenographic and clinical response to treatment often provide a firm diagnosis. Monthly chest roentgenograms during therapy are helpful but not essential; changes occur slowly and usually lag behind clinical improvement. Beginning 1 month after initiation of therapy, and ideally at 2-week intervals thereafter, an early-morning sputum culture should be obtained to monitor conversion or, if sputum positivity persists, to detect the emergence of drug resistance. It is more practical, however, to obtain several sputum specimens for culture at 2, 4, and 6 months of therapy. Sputa should convert to negative within 2 months with regimens containing both INH and RMP and not much longer with INH plus EMB. In a minority of patients (20 percent in one study), smear results may remain positive after culture results revert to negative, and sporadic positive smear results can be seen for long periods, presumably representing inactive bacilli released from caseous foci. In the uncommon case in which sputum culture results remain positive beyond 4 months of treatment, emerging drug resistance should be a major concern. This circumstance almost never occurs when both INH and RMP are reliably taken as initial therapy for drug-sensitive TB and suggests initial drug resistance and/or noncompliance. At this point, repeat sensitivity testing should be performed from a current sputum isolate, and at least two new drugs to which the organism was sensitive at the outset of treatment should be added until the repeat sensitivities are known. *Addition of only one drug in this setting is highly improper, since it risks the rapid development of resistance to the added drug.* Patients receiving INH should be instructed about symptoms suggestive of hepatitis, and, when possible, serum transaminase levels should be monitored every 1 or 2 months. This is more important in patients receiving both INH and RMP. Patients receiving EMB should be regularly questioned regarding visual symptoms, and their visual acuity measured (Snellen chart). Testing of red-green color discrimination is desirable when the 25 mg/kg dosage is given. Patients receiving STM should be examined for balance and high-frequency hearing loss if they are over 50 years old.

Relapse after adequate treatment of drug-sensitive infections is very infrequent. Prolonged follow-up of patients who have complied with what should be appropriate therapy is no longer considered necessary, except in the case of unusually extensive disease, slow bacteriologic response to treatment, suspicion of poor compliance by the patient, or high-risk patients with intercurrent disease. Although many authorities recommend that observation can be discontinued upon completion of 6- or 9-month regimens containing both INH and RMP, it is our preference to continue observation for a total of 2 years when practical.

Treatment of Extrapulmonary TB

The bacilli-laden pulmonary cavity remains the most severe test of chemotherapy. The bacillary load in extrapulmonary foci in normal individuals is always much less, and the threat to the patient more due to involvement of such critical anatomic structures as the meninges, pericardium, or spine than to failure of the drug regimen. With the exception of skeletal TB, for which longer therapy is advised, regimens given for 6-9 months are adequate for extrapulmonary TB.[26]

RETREATMENT OF PATIENTS WHO HAVE RELAPSED

Most patients requiring retreatment due to relapse should be managed by physicians with expertise in this area. Clinical judgment based on experience is critical when the number of active drugs available is limited. Susceptibility testing of the organism to all potentially useful drugs is essential.

Although each case must be individualized, some generalizations concerning retreatment can be made:

1. A relapse after prompt sputum conversion indicates that drugs were stopped too soon, usually by the patient. If drugs were taken reliably

but stopped prematurely, the infection usually retains the drug-susceptibility pattern present at the outset and will respond again to the initial regimen.

2. If relapse occurs with organisms resistant to INH when initial treatment was with INH and EMB or with INH, EMB, and STM, retreatment with RMP plus two other drugs to which the organism is susceptible, with assured compliance for at least 24 months, is highly effective. A 9-month regimen that utilizes RMP, STM, PZA, and EMB for 2 months followed by RMP and EMB for 7 months has demonstrated good results in infections resistant to INH but sensitive to RMP and EMB.[38]

3. If compliance has been irregular, resistant organisms will probably be present.

4. A patient with positive sputum culture results beyond 4–6 months of treatment probably has drug-resistant TB.

5. When drug resistance is suspected or presumed, a two- or three-drug combination including at least one "new" strong drug (INH, RMP, STM, or EMB at 25 mg/kg or PZA) and a "new" weak drug (ethionamide, PAS, or cycloserine) may be added to drugs previously given pending susceptibility results.

6. Capreomycin can replace STM. Kanamycin is less effective and more toxic and is used as a last resort. As mentioned above, only one of these three drugs should ordinarily be used at a time.

7. In infections resistant to INH, RMP, STM, and PZA, three or four weak drugs (ethionamide, cycloserine, PAS, and capreomycin) may be used together with high-dose INH (15 mg/kg), since INH retains some suppressive effect even when in vitro resistance is demonstrated.

8. When drugs to which the organisms are sensitive are critically limited, newer agents, including fluoroquinolones, rifabutin, and amoxicillin/clavulanic acid may be used, although experience with these drugs is limited.[39] However, even in specialized centers for treatment of drug-resistant TB, sputum conversion may be achieved in only half of patients (see Chapter 18).

OTHER FORMS OF TREATMENT

Moderate amounts of bed rest may be welcome during symptomatic disease but do not influence outcome when effective chemotherapy is given. In treatment failures resistant to all drugs, strict bed rest with continued INH may salvage some otherwise hopeless cases and may also be of benefit during retreatment of patients resistant to all but the weakest drugs.

Surgical Therapy

In the 1950s, surgical resection of residual cavities was commonly performed but is now rarely used. It still has a role in the salvage of patients who fail treatment; who have localized, resectable disease; and whose organisms are resistant to all but the weakest drugs.

Use of Corticosteroids

In severely debilitated patients or those with unusually marked constitutional symptoms, moderate doses of prednisone (20–30 mg daily) will effect prompt symptomatic improvement, abolish fever, and improve serious anemia and hypoalbuminemia. The dosage can usually be tapered by 2–5 mg decrements every 3–5 days. When life-threatening hypoxemia complicates extensive and diffuse pulmonary inflammation in advanced miliary TB or extensive bronchogenic spread of cavitary tuberculosis, prednisone in higher doses (60–80 mg daily) may promptly improve oxygenation. Disseminated drug-sensitive TB associated with high fever and clinical deterioration in AIDS patients has been treated successfully with corticosteroids.[40] Most authorities advise adjunctive corticosteroids for all but completely uncomplicated cases of tuberculous meningitis (i.e., those with normal sensoria and without neurological signs). Prednisone should be begun at 60–80 mg daily and gradually be tapered after 1–2 weeks, using the patient's symptoms to guide how rapidly to taper. Corticosteroid therapy has been advised by some for established tuberculous pericarditis to prevent constriction. Although probably effective, this should be considered only when the diagnosis is secure and surgery is not contemplated.

SPECIAL TREATMENT CIRCUMSTANCES

Pregnancy

Treatment of TB should not be deferred during pregnancy. Usually, INH plus EMB has traditionally been the regimen of choice. RMP also appears to be safe and may be used in advanced disease or when a 9-month regimen is highly desirable. STM should not be used at any time during pregnancy because of eighth nerve toxicity in the fetus. Experience with PZA is too limited to recommend its routine use in pregnancy. Since INH chemoprophylaxis in pregnancy may be associated with a very slightly increased risk of fatal maternal hepatitis, added caution with respect to INH-induced hepatotoxicity is indicated.[42]

Uremia and End-Stage Renal Disease

Dosage of RMP need not be adjusted for renal failure, but the drug should be administered after dialysis. Most authorities recommend the same approach for INH, although there is some debate.[43,44] The dosage of EMB should be reduced to 8-10 mg/kg in anepheric patients. Recommendations concerning PZA are variable, but it should probably be used at 15-20 mg/kg, the lower end of the usual recommended dosage. STM should only be used in very unusual circumstances, and its blood level should be closely monitored. Pyridoxine supplementation is necessary in uremic patients. Biochemical monitoring of hepatotoxicity in patients with renal failure may be complicated by the fact that transaminase levels are abnormally low in this population.

Liver Disease

The selection and dosage of antituberculous agents probably does not need to be modified in the presence of alcoholism or liver disease. However, preexisting liver disease complicates the detection of drug-related liver dysfunction when it does occur; accordingly, clinical and biochemical supervision should be assiduous. In patients with overt liver failure, therapy with INH and EMB may be initiated until liver function improves, at which time RMP may be added.

Patients Receiving Immunosuppressive Drugs

Tuberculosis that develops during the course of immunosuppressive treatment for an intercurrent disease should be treated with the same regimens used to treat immunocompetent hosts. Immunosuppressive therapy should be continued as indicated for treatment of the underlying process.[43,45]

REFERENCES

1. Styblo K: Recent advances in epidemiological research in tuberculosis. *Adv Tuberc Res* 20:1, 1980.
2. D'Esopo ND: Clinical trials in pulmonary tuberculosis. *Am Rev Respir Dis* 125:85, 1982.
3. Girling DJ: The chemotherapy of tuberculosis. *Biol Mycobacteria* 3:285, 1989.
4. Byrd RB, Fisk DE, Roethe RA, et al: Tuberculosis in Oriental immigrants: a study in military dependents. *Chest* 76:136, 1979.
5. Snider DE, Cauthen GM, Farer LS, et al: Drug-resistant tuberculosis. *Am Rev Respir Dis* 144:732, 1991.
6. Carpenter JL, Obnibene AJ, Gorby EW, et al: Antituberculosis drug resistance in south Texas. *Am Rev Respir Dis* 128:1055, 1983.

7. Chawla PH, Klapper PJ, Kamholz SL, et al: Drug-resistant tuberculosis in an urban population including patients at risk for human immunodeficiency virus infection. *Am Rev Respir Dis* 146:280, 1992.

8. Mitchison DA, Nunn AJ: Influence of initial drug resistance on the response to short-course chemotherapy of pulmonary tuberculosis. *Am Rev Respir Dis* 133:423, 1986.

9. Ben-Dov I, Mason GR: Drug-resistant tuberculosis in a southern California hospital: trends from 1969 to 1984. *Am Rev Respir Dis* 135:1307, 1987.

10. Nardell E, McInnis B, Thomas B, et al: Exogenous reinfection with tuberculosis in a shelter for the homeless. *N Engl J Med* 315:1570, 1986.

11. Frieden TR, Sterling T, Pablos-Mendez A, et al: The emergence of drug resistant tuberculosis in New York City. *N Engl J Med* 328:521, 1993.

12. Fischl MA, Daikos GL, Uttamchandani RB, et al: Clinical presentation and outcome of patients with HIV infection and tuberculosis caused by multiple-drug-resistant bacilli. *Ann Intern Med* 117:184, 1992.

13. Di Perri G, Cadeo GP, Castelli F, et al: Transmission of HIV-associated tuberculosis to healthcare workers. *Infect Control Hosp Epidemiol* 14:67, 1993.

14. Snider DE: Pyridoxine supplementation during isoniazid therapy. *Tubercle* 61:191, 1980.

15. Murphy R, Swartz R, Watkins PB: Severe acetaminophen toxicity in a patient receiving isoniazid. *Ann Intern Med* 113:799, 1990.

16. Koestner JA, Jones LK, Polk WH, Sawyers JL: Prolonged use of intravenous isoniazid and rifampin. *DICP* 23:48, 1989.

17. Venkatesan K: Pharmacokinetic drug interactions with rifampicin. *Clin Pharmakokinet* 22:47, 1992.

18. Steele MA, Burk RF, Des Prez RM: Toxic hepatitis with isoniazid and rifampin: a meta-analysis. *Chest* 99:465, 1991.

19. Kopanoff DE, Snider DE, Caras GJ: Isoniazid-related hepatitis. *Am Rev Respir Dis* 117:991, 1978.

20. Steele MA, Des Prez RM: The role of pyrazinamide in tuberculosis chemotherapy. *Chest* 94:842, 1988.

21. Crowle AJ, Sbarbaro JA, Judson FN, et al: Inhibition by pyrazinamide of tubercle bacilli within cultured macrophages. *Am Rev Respir Dis* 134:1052, 1986.

22. Snider DE Jr, Zierski M, Graczyk J, et al: Short-course tuberculosis chemotherapy studies conducted in Poland during the past decade. *Eur J Respir Dis* 68:12, 1986.

23. Jindani A, Aber VR, Edwards EA, Mitchison DA: The early bactericidal activity of drugs in patients with pulmonary tuberculosis. *Am Rev Respir Dis* 121:939, 1980.

24. Crowle AJ, Sbarbaro JA, Judson FN, et al: The effect of ethambutol on tubercle bacilli within cultured human macrophages. *Am Rev Respir Dis* 132:742, 1985.

25. Citron KM: Ethambutol: a review with special reference to ocular toxicity. *Tubercle* 50(S):32, 1969.

26. Pérez-Stable EJ, Hopewell PC: Current tuberculosis treatment regimens: choosing the right one for your patient. *Clin Chest Med* 10:323, 1989.

27. Seaman JM, Goble M, Madsen L, et al: Fasciitis and polyarthritis during antituberculous therapy. *Arthritis Rheum* 28:1179, 1985.

28. Goble M, Iseman MD, Madsen LA, et al: Treatment of 171 patients with pulmonary tuberculosis resistant to isoniazid and rifampin. *N Engl J Med* 328:527, 1993.

29. Mitchison DA: Understanding the chemotherapy of tuberculosis: current problems. *J Antimicrob Chemother* 29:477, 1992.

30. Davidson PT, Le HQ: Drug treatment of tuberculosis: 1992. *Drugs* 43:651, 1992.

31. Ormerod LP et al: Chemotherapy and management of tuberculosis in the United Kingdom: recommendations of the Joint Tuberculosis Committee of the British Thoracic Society. *Thorax* 45:403, 1990.

32. American Thoracic Society/Centers for Disease Control: Treatment of tuberculosis and tuberculosis infection in adults and children. *Am Rev Respir Dis* 134:355, 1986.
33. Davidson PT: Drug resistance and the selection of therapy for tuberculosis. *Am Rev Respir Dis* 136:255, 1987.
34. Brudney K, Dobkin J: A tale of two cities: tuberculosis in Nicaragua and New York City. *Semin Respir Infect* 6:261, 1991.
35. Cohn DL, Catlin BJ, Peterson KL, et al: A 62-dose, 6-month therapy for pulmonary and extrapulmonary tuberculosis: a twice-weekly, directly observed, and cost-effective regimen. *Ann Intern Med* 112:407, 1990.
36. Hong Kong Chest Service/Tuberculosis Research Center, Madras/British Medical Research Council: A controlled trial of 3-month, 4-month, and 6-month regimens of chemotherapy for sputum-smear negative pulmonary tuberculosis: results at 5 years. *Am Rev Respir Dis* 139:871, 1989.
37. Dutt AK, Moers D, Stead WW: Short-course chemotherapy for tuberculosis with mainly twice-weekly isoniazid and rifampin: community physician's seven-year experience with mainly outpatients. *Am J Med* 77:233, 1984.
38. Babu Swai O, Aluoch JA, Githui WA, et al: Controlled clinical trial of a regimen of two durations for the treatment of isoniazid resistant pulmonary tuberculosis. *Tubercle* 69:5, 1988.
39. Busillo CP, Lessnau KD, Sanjana V, et al: Multidrug resistant *Mycobacterium tuberculosis* in patients with human immunodeficiency virus infection. *Chest* 102:797, 1992.
40. Masud T, Kemp E: Corticosteroids in treatment of disseminated tuberculosis in patient with HIV infection. *Br Med J* 296:464, 1988.
41. Small PM, Schecter GF, Goodman PC, et al: Treatment of tuberculosis in patients with advanced human immunodeficiency virus infection. *N Engl J Med* 324:289, 1991.
42. Hamadeh MA, Glassroth J: Tuberculosis and pregnancy. *Chest* 101:1114, 1992.
43. Davidson PT, Le HQ: Drug treatment of tuberculosis: 1992. *Drugs* 43:651, 1992.
44. Isoniazid, in Kucers A, Bennett NM (eds), *The Use of Antibiotics*, 4th ed. Philadelphia, Lippincott, 1987, pp 1351–1393.
45. Dantzenberg B, Grosset J, Fechner J, et al: The management of thirty immunocompromised patients with tuberculosis. *Am Rev Respir Dis* 129:494, 1984.
46. Centers for Disease Control: Initial therapy for tuberculosis in the era of multidrug resistance: recommendations of the Advisory Council for the Elimination of Tuberculosis. *MMWR* 42:1, 1993.

CHAPTER 13

Complications of Treatment

HILLAS SMITH

Modern treatment of tuberculosis (TB) involves appropriate and skillful manipulation of drugs or groups of drugs. Other therapeutic measures, such as surgery or bed rest, have very limited application today, since most patients are treated or cured by chemotherapy alone. The complications of treatment of TB are therefore the complications of drug therapy.

These untoward responses in drug management fall into two major classes of problems: those clearly related to drug toxicity or hypersensitivity, which affect the individual patient, or changes with wider epidemiological implications, namely, the emergence of resistant bacilli. A third, less well-defined class of untoward reactions will be briefly mentioned, that is, those that have been called immunological rebound phenomena.

MECHANISMS OF TOXICITY

Toxicity is a broad term, involving at one extreme effects that are clearly dose-related (e.g., in aminoglycoside ototoxicity) or, at the other extreme, vague hypersensitivity-derived effects. The factors governing the likelihood of a toxic reaction are multifarious. Any drug may on occasion produce headache, pruritus, diarrhea, or rash, and this risk is increased when treating TB because drugs are not used singly (except perhaps in prophylactic treatment). Such "nonspecific" effects occur in perhaps up to 2.5 percent of individuals given placebo. However, major determinants of toxicity include the dose and mode of administration of the drug, the age and sex of patient, previous experience with the drug, genetic status, nutritional state, concomitant therapy, and, particularly, the state of hepatic and renal function. It is appropriate to examine briefly the common untoward responses of the major antituberculous agents and to assess the resultant implications for treatment.

ISONIAZID

Isoniazid, synthesized in 1912, was not introduced as an antituberculous agent until almost 40 years later. It is now well-established as a major component of most antituberculous regimens. Its popularity rests not only upon its undoubted effectiveness against *Mycobacterium tuberculosis* and *Mycobacterium bovis* but also upon its cheapness. However, it has a number of adverse effects that are for the most part dose-related, the incidence of which may be as high as 15 percent when doses of 10 mg/kg per day are administered.

The major toxic manifestation is peripheral neuritis. The drug is acetylated in the liver by acetyl-transferase. An autosomal recessive trait causes a relative deficiency of the enzyme, leading to a slow inactivation of the drug and an increased incidence of adverse effects. Neuropathy can be prevented by simultaneous administration of pyridoxine (25–50 mg per day). It is usual to prescribe pyridoxine for all patients receiving isoniazid rather than to determine which subjects are slow inactivators. Anesthesia, paresthesia, and burning pain along the distribution of sensory nerves in the extremities are the usual symptoms of neuritis. A variety of central nervous system effects may be encountered, such as restlessness, insomnia, and muscle twitching; fits occur, usually with large doses, and may be terminated by the use of pyridoxine.

Other unusual responses encountered with isoniazid are hypersensitivity phenomena and fever. A rare effect is anemia in patients susceptible to pyridoxine deficiency.

Hepatic Toxicity

Early experience of antituberculous regimens that included isoniazid as one of the drugs suggested that the drug was implicated in hepatotoxic reactions, but it was difficult to stigmatize a particular drug with certainty. This was true even when other liver conditions, such as cirrhosis, alcoholism, or infections, were excluded.

In the United States, where isoniazid is widely used as a single agent in prophylaxis against TB, there is now abundant evidence that isoniazid alone can be responsible for hepatotoxicity, which in some instances may be fatal.

In one series, Maddrey[1] reported on 14 patients observed for a 5-year period. Three patients died of fulminant hepatic failure, and 8 of 11 survivors had major abnormalities on liver biopsy. Garibaldi et al.[10] followed 2231 asymptomatic government workers with positive tuberculin skin test results. Within 6 months of starting isoniazid therapy, 19 subjects developed clinical signs of liver disease, 13 were jaundiced, and 2 died.

This direct hepatic injury is related to isoniazid metabolism. After acetylation, the drug is converted to hydrazine, which may be changed to a toxic acetylating agent by induced enzymes.[3] Thus, rifampin, an enzyme inducer, increases the risk of hepatic damage when used in combination with isoniazid. Para-aminosalicylate, now rarely used, is an enzyme retarder and may confer a protective effect on the combination.

Raised transaminase values are frequently encountered during the first 2 months of therapy, making their monitoring difficult to interpret. Nonetheless, many authorities recommend monthly serum liver enzyme measurement in patients over 35 years old taking isoniazid, with consideration of discontinuing the drug if values rise above three times the upper limit of normal. When the drug is stopped with the onset of symptoms or even at the stage when jaundice is first noted, resolution is the rule.[1,4,5] To continue isoniazid in the presence of toxic jaundice or in the presence of a progressive rise in transaminase risks fatality. Patients older than 35 years, especially those with preexisting liver disease, cirrhosis, or alcoholic liver disease and malnourished subjects, have an increased risk of isoniazid hepatotoxicity.

Patients with potentially fatal liver damage may be asymptomatic, although most develop symptoms of weakness, fatigue, and generalized malaise before the onset of clinical jaundice. Patients given isoniazid treatment should be warned that such symptoms should be brought promptly to the attention of their physician and that the drug should be suspended if the physician cannot be contacted.

RIFAMPIN

Of the rifamycin group of antibiotics isolated in 1957, rifampin (rifampicin in Europe), discovered in 1965, was found to be the most active compound after oral administration. It quickly established itself as a potent antituberculous agent and today is recommended for treatment of all forms of TB in combination with other first-line drugs. It has two disadvantages: high cost and some toxicity. An oral dose of 600 mg in an adult may be expected to produce serum concentrations of up to 10 μg/ml 2 h after administration,[6] with a half-life of 2–5 h. The drug is metabolized in the liver and excreted in bile. Renal insufficiency does not demand reduced doses.

Since rifampin is an expensive drug (e.g., 100 capsules, 300 mg, cost £38.22, United Kingdom price, 1993 and $211.00, US avg. wholesale price, 1993),[7] it is often excluded from drug regimens in developing countries. Cheaper but also effective regimens can be devised, but omitting a major antituberculous agent where it is most required is, to say the least, unfortunate. Relief agencies or charities operating in developing countries might consider antituberculous drug subsidies a suitable target for their funds.

Rifampin and the Liver

In the initial stages of treatment with rifampin, a rise in serum level of liver enzymes, if sought, will be found in 5–10 percent of patients, but a true hepatitis is much less common.[8] In the vast majority of patients, this reaction resolves spontaneously, and treatment does not need to be altered or interrupted. What is still not completely clear, however, is in what proportion of patients, if any, does the "transaminitis" represent the early state of a progressive but rarely fatal rifampin-induced hepatic necrosis.

Histologically, rifampin hepatitis is characterized by diffuse liver cell damage with the presence of acidophilic bodies and an infiltrate of both neutrophils and mononuclear cells.[9] Another as yet not fully understood phenomenon is the risk of rifampin in inducing or perhaps aggravating rare fatal isoniazid hepatic toxicity.

The practical implication of this predicament is that, in any patient being treated with a regimen that includes rifampin or rifampin/isoniazid, there should be regular assessment of serum hepatic enzyme levels, and any progressive rise should lead to cessation of administration of both agents.

In patients with established liver disease, in alcoholics, and in many patients with HIV infection, the presence of liver cell damage imposes the need for careful assessment of increasing hepatocellular dysfunction and for reduced doses of rifampin.

Rifampin is a potent inducer of microsomal liver enzymes and enhances the metabolism of many drugs. This effect produces more rapid elimination of some drugs metabolized in the liver, major manifestations of which include diminished anticoagulant effect with warfarin, possible breakthrough bleeding and unwanted pregnancy with oral contraceptives, and poor diabetic control in patients taking oral hypoglycemic agents. It may be necessary to adjust doses of anticonvulsants, such as phenytoin or corticosteroids, in patients with Addison's disease (Table 13-1).

Taken intermittently in large doses (e.g., 900 mg), rifampin can induce some effects that probably have an immunological basis. These syndromes include abdominal, respiratory, and influenzal symptoms, thrombocytopenic purpura, and acute renal failure.

Rifampin is a brick-red powder, and patients taking the drug should be warned that body fluids, such as tears and urine, may become red or pink; soft contact lenses may become permanently discolored.

ETHAMBUTOL

An effective oral antituberculous agent, ethambutol, is much used in intermittent and short-course regimens. Its major toxic effect is optic neuritis, which

TABLE 13-1. Drugs Showing Increased Metabolism When Used Simultaneously with Rifampin

Analgesics: accelerated methadone metabolism
Anticoagulants: warfarin
Antidiabetic compounds: chlorpropamide, tolbutamide (possibly other sulfonylureas)
Antiepileptics: phenytoin
Antifungals: fluconazole, itraconazole, retoconazole
Antipsychotics: haloperidol
β-blockers: bisoprolol, propranolol
Calcium channel blockers: verapamil, possibly isradipine
Cardiac glycosides: dititoxin
Corticosteroids
Cyclosporin
Sex hormones: contraceptive effect of both combined and progestogen-only oral contraceptives reduced
Theophylline
Thyroxine: accelerated thyroxine metabolism (may increase requirements in hypothyroidism)
Ulcer-healing drugs: accelerated cimetidine metabolism

Source: Adapted from British National Formulary (Appendix I), p. 461. *British Medical Association and Royal Pharmacology Society, Great Britain, 1991.*

appears to be dose-related. Since excretion of ethambutol is principally by the kidney, patients receiving the drug should have initial assessment of renal function to decide if reduced doses are indicated. If creatinine clearance is less than 50 ml/min, ethambutol is best avoided.

The most commonly used regimens include a relatively high initial dose of 25 mg/kg per day by mouth, followed after a maximum period of 2 months by a dose of 15 mg/kg per day. With this dosage, less than 1 percent of patients are likely to exhibit decreased visual acuity.

Ethambutol produces a unilateral or bilateral optic neuritis, which is usually reversible if the drug is withdrawn as soon as symptoms are noted, although it may take months before normal sight is restored. Blindness results if the drug is continued.[10] The initial complaint resulting from optic neuritis is loss of color vision, followed by reduction in visual acuity and constriction of visual fields.

Although an initial ophthalmological assessment may be useful for subsequent comparison, regular eye examination will not predict optic neuritis.

The drug should be stopped immediately in any patients with ophthalmic symptoms. Patients must be warned to report these complaints.

Although ethambutol is a most effective antituberculous agent, it must be used with a degree of caution. It is probably best avoided in patients with severe renal insufficiency, in those whose vision is already impaired, or in young children and others who cannot be relied upon to report any alteration in vision.

PYRAZINAMIDE

A synthetic analog of nicotinamide, pyrazinamide is well-absorbed by mouth, with activity confined to *M. tuberculosis*. The drug is most active in an acid environment such as is found in sites of acute inflammation and inside the phagolysosomes of macrophages.

It is used as a first-line antituberculous drug. Minor complaints of anorexia, gastrointestinal distress, and mild flushing are common. The main adverse effects are hepatitis and hyperuricemia. Jaundice, occasionally progressing to acute yellow atrophy, was reported in up to 15 percent of patients who received high dosage levels used in the past but now is seldom encountered with the current recommended daily dosage of 25–30 mg/kg.

Patients with gout should avoid pyrazinamide. Inhibition of urate excretion may, in nongouty subjects, lead to raised serum urate concentrations and occasionally cause arthritis, which responds to aspirin and may be prevented by administration of allopurinol.

STREPTOMYCIN

Ototoxicity

Discovered by Waxman and introduced for clinical use in 1944, streptomycin was the first effective antituberculous agent. Used singly, two major disadvantages soon became apparent: the development of resistance and ototoxicity. Today, streptomycin is not used on its own, and obligatory parenteral administration has reduced its popularity, but it is a highly effective antituberculous drug when used in combination (see Chapter 12). Ototoxicity remains a hazard, but largely a predictable one. The earliest symptom of vestibular disorder is usually giddiness. Deafness is less common than the vestibular upset and is often manifested as tinnitus, which is an indication for stopping the drug.

There is wide variation in the time of onset of toxic manifestations. Reactions have been reported as early as the seventh day or as late as 6 months. Most adults can tolerate a dose of 1 g daily for 4–6 weeks without clinical evidence of toxicity, but if the dose is increased to 2 g per day, depression of vestibular function may occur after 4 weeks. Vestibular disturbance is related to total dosage and to excessive blood levels consequent on impaired renal function. Serum levels exceeding 3 μg/ml 24 h after administration produce increased likelihood of toxicity.

Because of the restrictions imposed by renal function, the recommended 1 g dose of streptomycin must be reduced to 750 mg in patients weighing 50 kg or in subjects over 40 years of age. If both these criteria are fulfilled, the dose should be 500 mg.[11-13]

Hypersensitivity

A variety of rashes, eosinophilia, fever, and even anaphylactic shock may occur during streptomycin therapy. Rash may occur in up to 5 percent of patients, with onset in the majority of cases within 2 weeks of starting therapy. Skin eruptions due to streptomycin tend to be tenacious, and, although it is possible to undertake a tedious desensitization program, in most hypersensitive patients, streptomycin will have to be avoided.

THIACETAZONE

A thiosemicarbazone available in Germany in 1946, thiacetazone was not widely used as an antituberculous agent until the 1960s. It is well-absorbed after oral administration, is usually effective against *M. tuberculosis*, but has a high incidence of side effects, particularly skin eruptions. Because it is cheap and despite its toxicity, it has found fairly wide application in treatment regimens in developing countries, usually in conjunction with isoniazid.

Skin eruptions vary from simple rash to exfoliating dermatitis, toxic epidermal necrolysis, and Stevens-Johnson syndrome. There appears to be an increased incidence and severity of skin complications in patients with HIV infection.[14] Thiacetazone should be avoided in patients with renal insufficiency and in pregnant women.

SECOND-LINE AGENTS

Ethionamide

A synthetic derivative of isonicotinic acid, ethionamide, well-absorbed by mouth, has wide action against mycobacteria and achieves useful concentrations in the cerebrospinal fluid, even in the absence of inflammation. Adverse effects, particularly gastrointestinal upsets, are common. Neurotoxicity and hepatitis also occur. Ethionamide should not be given to pregnant women, since it has been reported to be teratogenic.[15]

Para-Aminosalicylic Acid

A white crystalline powder that has been used extensively in the past in conjunction with streptomycin and isoniazid, para-aminosalicylic acid has now been superseded by more effective drugs. Para-aminosalicylic acid is usually tuberculostatic, must be taken in large (12–20 g per day) oral doses, and is frequently associated with gastrointestinal upset. Nearly all patients have some discomfort if the drug is taken for prolonged periods.

Amikacin

A chemically modified kanamycin, amikacin is sometimes used in the treatment of infections due to highly resistant bacilli. All the qualifications that apply to the aminoglycoside group of drugs apply to amikacin. In very ill patients, particularly when HIV infection coexists, it may be worthwhile including a relatively effective but toxic compound such as amikacin in the initial phase of treatment. Once the disease is under control, a more tolerable substitute may be offered over a long period of time.

Capreomycin and Kanamycin

Both capreomycin and kanamycin are administered parenterally, the usual intramuscular dose being 1 g. Ototoxicity and obligatory reduction of dosage in renal insufficiency have greatly reduced the use of these drugs.

Cycloserine

A wide-spectrum antibiotic, cycloserine has antituberculous activity when administered to adults in the usual daily dose of 0.5 g. Renal insufficiency produces high blood levels, which may cause increased risk of toxic effects. Cycloserine diffuses well into the cerebrospinal fluid. Toxicity is principally neurological or psychiatric. Convulsions, depression, confusion, and hallucinations may occur; some patients have committed suicide.

OTHER DRUGS

In high dosage, a surprising number of commonly used antibacterial agents, such as tetracyclines, macrolides, and some cephalosporins, have transient antimycobacterial activity and in unusual circumstances might be used, on the basis of laboratory sensitivity testing, with an array of similar "third-line" drugs. This situation is particularly likely to be encountered with infections due to atypical mycobacteria.

SPECIAL CIRCUMSTANCES

Pregnancy

Many drugs, including antibacterial agents, cross the placenta and reach the developing fetus. Some are capable of causing untoward responses.[16] Long-term administration of streptomycin is capable of causing deafness in the fetus and therefore should be avoided during pregnancy. Ethionamide and the related prothionamide, known to be teratogenic, should be avoided.[15] Although there is limited information on the use of pyrazinamide in pregnancy and caution has been advised when it is used,[15] there is now wide agreement that standard drug regimens that include isoniazid, rifampin, and pyrazinamide are not likely to harm the fetus.[15,17]

Renal Insufficiency

Streptomycin and ethambutol are best avoided, but if these drugs are considered essential, dosage must be controlled by regular estimation of serum concentrations.

For patients with a creatinine clearance <10 ml/min, the daily dose of isoniazid should not exceed 200 mg.

Superinfections

With the exception of patients with simultaneous HIV infection, superinfection in TB is not very common. The usual problem is the development of a mycetoma or fungus ball due to aspergilli. This complication is a form of noninvasive pulmonary aspergillosis, growing slowly in healed or inert tuberculous cavities and manifested by cough and repeated hemoptysis. If symptoms persist, especially hemoptysis, the treatment of choice is surgical resection of the affected cavity.

Immunological Rebound Phenomena

Another type of complication, immunological rebound phenomena, often arises when the response to therapy is considered satisfactory. Lesions appear to regress, and sensitive bacilli may have been cultured. There is then, paradoxically, a rapid deterioration in lesions. Such paradoxical responses have been documented in lymph nodes, in cerebral TB, and in certain advanced chest lesions encountered in very ill, wasted subjects. For instance, in their series of more than 100 patients with lymph node TB, Campbell and Dyson found paradoxical enlargement during therapy in 30 percent of patients.[18] Expansion of cerebral tuberculomas during successful treatment of tuberculous meningitis, manifested as convulsions or "tumor-like" effect, has been reported by Chambers et al.,[19] and rapid expansion of pulmonary distress in advanced TB has been documented.[20] Whether the same mechanism is responsible for these untoward responses at different sites is conjectural. The return and recruitment of cell-mediated responses in patients with sensitive organisms receiving appropriate therapy is considered the likely mode of causation. The subject has been reviewed.[21,22] Corticosteroids are most useful in suppressing this type of reaction.

Practical Management of Hypersensitivity Reactions

When allergy or hypersensitivity is considered to be the basis of rash, fever, or joint swelling in patients receiving antituberculous agents, the best approach is to stop all antituberculous drugs. From the author's experience, if one of the drugs involved is streptomycin, attempting to reintroduce this drug, even with steroid cover, almost invariably leads to its abandonment. Occasionally, it may be prudent and practicable to continue treatment with a drug known to be allergenic, especially if it is a first-line drug, when symptoms can be at least partially controlled by corticosteroids. The husbanding of first-line tuberculocidal agents becomes crucial when multiple-drug resistance is a problem. It must be recognized that in some patients, particularly those with AIDS, the adoption of a limited objective may be forced upon the physician. Obtaining negative results from sputum samples and maintaining noninfectivity with relatively simple therapy may be preferred in a few situations to persisting with impossibly complex therapy with increasing toxicity in the hope of achieving a "cure."

REFERENCES

1. Maddrey WC, Boitnott JK: Isoniazid hepatitis. *Ann Intern Med* 79:1, 1973.
2. Lees AW, Allan GW, Smith J, Tyrell WF, Fallon RJ: Toxicity from rifampin plus isoniazid, and rifampin plus ethambutol therapy. *Tubercle* 52:182, 1971.
3. Mitchell JR. Isoniazid liver injury: clinical spectrum, pathology and probable pathogenesis. *Ann Intern Med* 84:181, 1976.
4. Maddrey WC: Isoniazid-induced liver disease. *Semin Liver Dis* 1:129, 1981.
5. Black M, Mitchell JR, Zimmerman HJ, Ishak KG, Epler GR: Isoniazid-associated hepatitis in 114 patients. *Gastroenterology* 69:289, 1975.
6. Kenny MT, Strates B: Metabolism and pharmacokinetics of the antibiotic rifampin. *Drug Metab Rev* 12:159, 1981.
7. *Monthly Index of Medical Specialities (MIMS)*. London, Haymarket Medical, February 1993, p 169.
8. Grosset J, Leventis S: Adverse effects of rifampin. *Rev Infect Dis 5* (suppl 3):S440, 1983.
9. Schener PJ, Summerfield JA, Lal S, Sherlock S: Rifampicin hepatitis. *Lancet* 1:421, 1974.
10. Garibaldi RA, Drusin RE, Ferebee SH, et al: Isoniazid-associated hepatitis: report of an outbreak. *Am Rev Respir Dis* 106:357, 1972.
11. Garod LP, Lambert HP, O'Grady F: *Antibiotic and Chemotherapy*, 5th ed. Edinburgh, Churchill Livingstone, 1981, pp 122–123.
12. Smith H: *Antibiotics in Clinical Practice*, 3d ed. London, Pitman Medical, 1977, pp 60–61.
13. Angel JH: Modern management of pulmonary tuberculosis. *Prescribers J* 32:144, 1992.
14. Harris AD: Tuberculosis and human immunodeficiency virus infection in developing countries. *Lancet* 335:387, 1990.
15. Wolinsky E: Antimycobacterial drugs, in Gorbach SL, Bartlett JG, Blacklow NR (eds): *Infectious Diseases*. Philadelphia, Saunders, 1992, pp 313–318.
16. Chow AW, Jewesson PJ: Pharmacokinetics and safety of antimicrobial agents during pregnancy. *Rev Infect Dis* 7:287, 1985.
17. Martindale J: Tuberculostatics and tuberculocides. *Extrapharmacopoea*, 28th ed. Reynolds JEF, Prasad AB (eds) London, Pharmaceutical Press, 1982, pp 1564–1585.
18. Campbell IA, Dyson AJ: Lymph node tuberculosis: a comparison of various methods of treatment. *Tubercle* 58:171, 1977.
19. Chambers ST, Hendricksse WA, Record C, Rudge P, Smith H: Paradoxical expansion of intracranial tuberculomas during chemotherapy. *Lancet* 2:181, 1984.
20. Onwubalili JK, Scott GM, Smith H: Acute respiratory distress related to chemotherapy of advanced pulmonary tuberculosis. *Q J Med* 59:599, 1986.
21. Smith H: Immunology of cerebral tuberculosis. *Prog Clin Neurosci* 1:99, 1985.
22. Smith H: Paradoxical responses during the chemotherapy of tuberculosis. *J Infect* 15:1, 1987.

PART V

Current Challenges in Tuberculosis

C H A P T E R   1 4

Tuberculosis and HIV Infection

RICHARD E. CHAISSON / CONSTANCE A. BENSON

Infection with human immunodeficiency virus (HIV) has a profound effect on host immune responses to *Mycobacterium tuberculosis*, resulting in a high probability that individuals coinfected with both pathogens will develop active tuberculosis (TB). As a result, the HIV pandemic has seriously undermined TB control efforts in developing countries and resulted in explosive increases in the numbers of TB cases in developed countries. The resurgence of TB as a consequence of HIV infection is accompanied by a host of new therapeutic challenges, including a high prevalence of adverse drug reactions, the unavailability of some second-line antituberculous drugs, and the emergence of strains of *M. tuberculosis* resistant to multiple drugs transmitted among patients and within health care institutions. The rapid emergence of *M. tuberculosis* as a major HIV-related pathogen has caught the clinical, public health, and biomedical research communities by surprise. The neglect that characterized the control of TB for more than two decades will have grave clinical and public health consequences in the 1990s. A concerted national and global effort is now required to combat this growing dilemma effectively. This chapter reviews the clinical and public health aspects of TB and HIV infection.

EPIDEMIOLOGY OF HIV-ASSOCIATED TB

The overlap of HIV and *M. tuberculosis* infections has resulted in an unprecedented increase in the numbers of TB cases recently recorded in the United States. From 1953–1983, TB cases in the United States decreased by approximately 5 percent per year, from 88,000 cases in 1953 to 22,000 cases in 1983. However, as Fig. 14-1 shows, beginning in 1984 the number of TB cases plateaued and then increased, with an unparalleled 9 percent rise in 1990. Based on projections from historical trends, it is now estimated that 51,700 "excess" cases of TB have occurred in the United States between 1985 and 1992, largely a result of the HIV epidemic.[1] Similar increases in TB morbidity rates are being seen globally, particularly in the countries of sub-Saharan

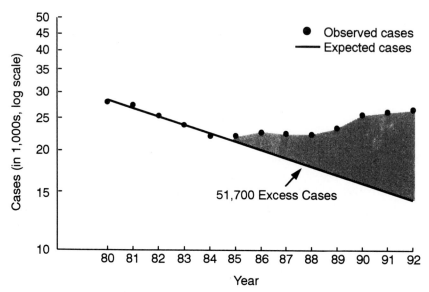

FIGURE 14-1. Incidence of TB in the United States, 1980–1992. The lower line shows projected case rates based on historical trends. The upper line shows actual case rates. The shaded area represents excess cases of TB, largely attributed to HIV infection. (*From Tuberculosis morbidity: United States, 1992.*[1])

Africa, where TB control has been limited by an inadequate health infrastructure and lack of funds.[2]

Worldwide it is likely that one-third to one-half of persons infected with HIV are also infected with *M. tuberculosis*. Tuberculous infection is of staggering proportions globally, with almost 2 billion people infected.[3] Approximately 10 million people are thought to be infected with HIV worldwide, half in developing countries. The overlap of HIV and TB is growing as HIV transmission continues in developing countries and, in the United States, among intravenous drug users and other impoverished, urban residents who have a high prevalence of *M. tuberculosis* infection.

As previously indicated, groups at risk of previous TB infection have a higher prevalence of TB disease when HIV is present. The earliest reports of AIDS-related TB from Pitchenik and colleagues noted that Haitian immigrants to south Florida who developed AIDS also were more likely to have TB than were non-Haitian AIDS patients.[4] The fact that *M. tuberculosis* infection is present in >50 percent of adults in Haiti and other developing countries suggested that reactivation of old TB infection after the acquisition of HIV was responsible for this common manifestation in those with advanced HIV disease. Other studies subsequently noted a high prevalence of TB in patients with AIDS whose HIV transmission risk also placed them at increased risk for previous TB infection, such as members of underrepresented ethnic groups, members of minority groups, and intravenous drug users.[5,6] These trends have now been widely reported, and, as HIV becomes more widely recognized in developing countries where TB is endemic, TB is emerging as the most common HIV-related opportunistic infection in the world.[7]

The prevalence of HIV infection in TB patients varies by clinical setting and geographic locale. Nonetheless, a growing proportion of patients with TB are coinfected with HIV. Onorato and colleagues reported that the prevalence of HIV infection in TB patients in 14 United States cities in 1989 and 1990 was 12 percent.[8] Among U.S.-born patients aged 30–39 years, 35 percent of men and 20 percent of women were infected with HIV. In many developing countries, 40–70 percent of TB patients are HIV-seropositive.[7]

Reactivation TB is most common in HIV-infected persons from populations or settings with a high prevalence of *M. tuberculosis* infection. This includes injected drug users, urban residents, members of racial and ethnic minorities, prisoners, contacts of TB patients, and residents of or immigrants from endemic areas.

As TB has increased in prevalence among AIDS patients, there is growing concern about patient-to-patient transmission of *M. tuberculosis* in health care facilities or residential settings. Reports of such outbreaks of TB have now been reported from Italy, Puerto Rico, Miami, San Francisco, and New York.[9-13] In both New York and Miami, outbreaks of multidrug-resistant (MDR) cases of TB have been documented (see Chapter 18). The common factor in all such outbreaks is the exposure of patients with advanced HIV disease to a patient with TB in hospital or residential facilities with inadequate ventilation and respiratory isolation procedures. Exposure to TB of susceptible HIV-infected persons results in an extraordinarily high rate of primary, progressive TB (see below). Previous hospitalization or incarceration are now important risk factors for TB in New York City.[14]

The growing awareness of the impact of HIV infection on TB has resulted in several revisions of the Centers for Disease Control and Prevention (CDC) AIDS case definition. In 1987, the CDC categorized extrapulmonary TB in HIV-seropositive persons as an AIDS indicator diagnosis.[15] In 1993, the AIDS case definition was further amended to include pulmonary TB in HIV-seropositive persons.[16] The impact of this change will be a large increase in AIDS cases with TB as the index diagnosis.

HIV AND THE PATHOPHYSIOLOGY OF TB

The natural history of *M. tuberculosis* infection is dramatically altered by the presence of HIV infection. When TB infection is first established, specific host cellular immune responses contain the organism and prevent development of disease in the majority of instances. In persons with intact cellular immunity, *M. tuberculosis* infection remains subclinical for years to decades after initial infection, and the majority of infected individuals never develop clinical illness. About 5 percent of otherwise healthy individuals will develop active disease, usually within the first 1–3 years following the acquisition of *M. tuberculosis* infection. An additional 5 percent will develop active disease years after acquiring infection. However, individuals with impaired cell-mediated immunity, such as persons with HIV infection, may more rapidly progress from primary infection to disease.

Several outbreaks of TB in confined settings have demonstrated the accelerated natural history of primary TB in HIV-infected individuals. Daley et al. studied an outbreak of TB in residents of a congregate housing facility for injection drug users with HIV.[10] Using restriction fragment length polymorphism (RFLP) analysis of DNA from patient isolates, they determined that, within a 12-week period, 37 percent of susceptible residents exposed to an index case of TB developed active pulmonary disease with a genetically identical organism. De Pierri et al. reported an outbreak of primary TB in HIV-infected patients exposed to an index case in a hospital.[9] This accelerated natural history of TB underlies community and institutional outbreaks of drug-susceptible and drug-resistant TB in this population.

Persons previously infected with *M. tuberculosis* who acquire HIV infection experience a very high rate of reactivation of tuberculous infection. In contrast to the 5–10 percent lifetime risk in immunologically intact persons, studies in the United States and Africa have documented that from 4–8 percent of persons coinfected with HIV and *M. tuberculosis* developed active TB each year. Selwyn et al. reported that the case rate of TB in HIV-infected injection drug users with a previous positive tuberculin skin test result was 7.9–9.9 cases per 100 person-years of follow-up.[17] Allen et al. reported an incidence of 2.4 cases per 100 person-years of follow-up in HIV-infected women in Rwanda, where 60–70 percent of adults are tuberculin skin test-positive.[18] Thus, HIV infection is among the most potent biologic factors associated with developing active TB.

The mechanisms by which an old nidus of TB infection becomes active are not well-studied. However, reactivation is strongly correlated with loss of CD4+ lymphocytes as HIV disease advances. T lymphocytes from patients with HIV infection have impaired proliferative responses when challenged with mycobacterial antigens such as purified protein derivative (PPD).[19] Cytolytic T-cell responses to cells bearing mycobacterial antigens are increasingly impaired as CD4+ cell levels decline.[20] In addition, lack of gamma-interferon synthesis and productive HIV infection in mononuclear cells of HIV-infected persons may cause macrophage dysfunction that permits the intracellular replication of mycobacteria, leading to reactivation of disease. While HIV infection does not appear to affect phagocytosis by macrophages, intracellular killing is impaired.[6] Genetic susceptibility to tuberculous infection and disease has been suggested by several studies, although the mechanism of this phenomenon is not apparent.[21] In the United States, both blacks and Hispanics with HIV infection or AIDS have a significantly higher prevalence of TB than do non-Hispanic whites. However, these same populations are more likely to be impoverished, live in crowded urban environments, and have repeated exposure to untreated persons with active TB. Consequently, a higher prevalence of tuberculous infection seen in minority populations could explain their higher prevalence of TB disease associated with concomitant HIV infection.

CLINICAL FEATURES OF HIV-ASSOCIATED TB

The clinical presentation of TB in patients with HIV ranges from the typical features of TB to atypical, disseminated disease. Because *M. tuberculosis* is a relatively virulent pathogen, reactivation of latent infection tends to occur earlier in the course of HIV-induced immunosuppression than for other opportunistic infections. Theuer et al. found that patients with HIV infection and TB had a median CD4+ lymphocyte count of 326 per cubic millimeter[22] compared to 928 per cubic millimeter in HIV-seronegative patients. In patients with higher CD4+ lymphocyte counts, the features of TB are often typical, including fever, night sweats, productive cough, and weight loss. Chest radiographic findings show focal infiltrates and cavities, although diffuse infiltrates and mediastinal adenopathy are not unusual. In patients with more advanced HIV infection and lower CD4+ lymphocyte counts, the clinical presentation may be more atypical, with a higher prevalence of diffuse pulmonary infiltrates, miliary disease, and extrapulmonary dissemination, including positive blood culture results. Because the differential diagnosis of febrile pulmonary or constitutional illness in a patient with HIV infection is so broad, a careful evaluation is required to diagnose or exclude TB.

A number of studies have documented the high prevalence of extrapulmonary disease in TB patients with HIV infection. Small et al. reported that among 132 patients with TB and AIDS, 38 percent had only pulmonary disease, 30 percent had only extrapulmonary disease, and 32 percent had both pulmonary and extrapulmonary tuberculosis (Table 14-1).[23] Berenguer et al. noted in a study of TB patients in a Spanish hospital that HIV-seropositive patients with TB were significantly more likely to have meningitis (10 percent) than were HIV-seronegative persons (2 percent).[24] Studies in developing

TABLE 14-1. Sites of Tuberculosis in Patients with AIDS by Time of AIDS Diagnosis

Sites	TB before AIDS	TB/AIDS	AIDS before TB	Total
Pulmonary	22 (28%)	10 (56%)	18 (50%)	50 (38%)
Extrapulmonary	30 (38%)	2 (11%)	8 (22%)	40 (30%)
Pulmonary and extrapulmonary	26 (33%)	6 (33%)	10 (28%)	42 (32%)
Total	78	18	36	132

Source: From Small et al.[23] Used with permission.

countries have also shown an increased prevalence of extrapulmonary disease.[25] Of clinical relevance is the fact that, in HIV-infected patients with known or suspected extrapulmonary TB, pulmonary involvement is also likely, and appropriate diagnostic and infection control measures should be instituted. Common extrapulmonary sites of TB in patients with HIV infec-

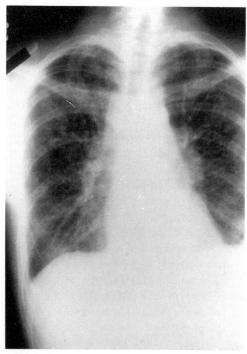

FIGURE 14-2. A. Admission chest radiograph of a 22-year-old man with HIV infection and progressive lower extremity weakness. No infiltrates are seen.

tion include lymph nodes, pleura, central nervous system, blood, bone marrow, and genitourinary tract.

The diagnosis of TB in a patient with HIV infection may be difficult, and the differential diagnosis is broad. Heightened clinical awareness of TB and careful attention to epidemiologic clues (e.g., recent incarceration or hospitalization, history of a positive PPD reaction, or immigration from an endemic area) are important to making a diagnosis. Because clinical features may be atypical, clinicians may not suspect TB and may not order appropriate tests to establish the diagnosis.[26] The yield of acid-fast smears of sputum and other respiratory secretions in patients with HIV and TB varies but is typically lower than that of other populations of patients with TB, particularly when nonfluorescent stains are used.[27] Because patients are less likely to have cavitary pulmonary lesions, the number of acid-fast organisms present in

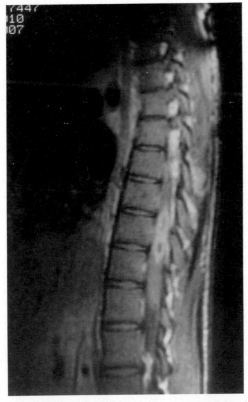

FIGURE 14-2 (*continued*). *B*. Magnetic resonance scan of the thoracic spinal cord reveals a ring-enhancing mass. Cultures of bronchoalveolar lavage fluid, a lymph node biopsy, and the spinal cord lesion yielded *M. tuberculosis*.

sputum may be low and the yield of acid-fast stains reduced. When sputum or other tissue stains do reveal acid-fast organisms, patients should be presumed to have TB and treated accordingly, with institution of empiric therapy and respiratory isolation. While *Mycobacterium avium* complex commonly colonizes the respiratory tract in patients with HIV, this organism is not usually associated with positive acid-fast smears.[28] Pulmonary TB in HIV-infected patients may present radiographically with focal infiltrates, diffuse infiltrates, cavities, effusions, or hilar and mediastinal adenopathy. Patients with normal chest radiographs but positive sputum culture results have been reported. Figure 14-2 shows radiographic findings in an HIV-infected man with a tuberculoma of the thoracic spinal cord. Despite having no respiratory symptoms and no infiltrates on a chest radiograph, sputum and bronchoalveolar lavage cultures grew *M. tuberculosis*.[29]

Patients with suspected TB and HIV infection should be placed in respiratory isolation while the diagnostic evaluation proceeds. Mycobacterial cultures and smears of sputum or bronchoalveolar lavage fluid and tissue from involved sites should be obtained before therapy is initiated. Mycobacterial blood cultures should also be performed.

Tuberculin skin tests remain an important clinical and epidemiologic tool for identifying persons infected with *M. tuberculosis*. In patients with HIV infection, ablation of cell-mediated immune responses to cutaneous antigens is an early hallmark of immunosuppression. Thus, response to PPD skin tests may be impaired in patients with HIV-associated TB. However, numerous studies of patients with TB and HIV have shown that the skin test is clinically useful, with 60–80 percent of TB patients who are HIV-seropositive but without AIDS having a PPD response of ≥10 mm induration. Among TB patients who have another AIDS-related opportunistic disease, response to tuberculin skin tests is more likely to be impaired, with only 20–40 percent of patients demonstrating ≥10 mm induration. Clinically, the presence of a positive tuberculin skin test reaction in a patient with suggestive clinical signs and symptoms is strongly predictive of TB. Because the sensitivity of PPD skin tests is reduced in HIV-infected persons, the Advisory Committee on the Elimination of Tuberculosis has changed the definition of a positive skin test to ≥5 mm induration in persons with HIV infection.[30]

A study by Johnson et al. in Haiti showed that in asymptomatic adults with HIV infection, the prevalence of a ≥5 mm response to PPD was the same as the prevalence of a ≥10 mm response in HIV-seronegative adults.[31] However, the prevalence of anergy (no response) was three times higher in HIV-seropositive persons than in HIV-seronegative persons. Thus, improved tests for identifying *M. tuberculosis* infection are urgently needed. The use of control antigens to determine whether anergy to multiple antigens is present has been recommended for screening populations with HIV infection at risk for tuberculous infection. It is interesting to note that the response to antigens such as *Candida*, mumps, and tetanus toxoid may be lost earlier in HIV-induced immunosuppression than is the response to PPD. Studies of injected drug users with and without HIV infection indicate that when the CD4+ lymphocyte count falls below 500 per cubic millimeter the prevalence of anergy to skin test antigens increases significantly.[32] Specific anergy to PPD has been reported in individuals infected with *M. tuberculosis* who are able to mount a response to other antigens. Thus, it is not clear whether use of control antigens is clinically helpful or whether knowledge of the CD4+ lymphocyte count would serve a similar function.

The definitive diagnosis of TB is made by culture, although results may not be available for several weeks to months. The use of radiometric culture techniques has considerably improved the diagnosis of TB. Regardless of the culture system used, the diagnosis is never confirmed immediately, and presumptive treatment for TB is required for patients with clinical findings suggestive of the disease. It is critically important that adequate clinical specimens be collected and cultured before initiating antituberculous therapy. While a clinical response to presumptive treatment may help confirm the diagnosis of TB, failure to respond may result from drug resistance or nonadherence to therapy on the part of the patient and cannot, therefore, reliably exclude the diagnosis.

TREATMENT OF TB IN HIV DISEASE

Patients with HIV infection and drug-susceptible TB have a gratifying response to standard therapy for TB. Even in patients with advanced HIV disease, clinical responses are prompt, and patients can be cured with short-course chemotherapy. Relapse rates for patients treated with short-course regimens containing isoniazid and rifampin do not appear to be greater than for HIV-seronegative patients, in the range of 3 percent per year.[23] Long-term follow-up studies have not been done yet, however, and it is not known whether patients with early HIV disease (CD4+ counts >500 per cubic millimeter) will experience relapses after short-course therapy.

Current treatment of TB in the United States combines isoniazid and rifampin, given for 6 months, with pyrazinamide and ethambutol or streptomycin, given for the first 2 months.[33] While the CDC recommends that therapy for patients with HIV infection and TB be prolonged to at least 9 months and at least 6 months following conversion of sputum culture results to negative, clinical experience suggests that shorter courses may be adequate. Small et al., from San Francisco, showed that 6 months of therapy was effective in curing TB in patients with advanced HIV disease. The authors evaluated outcomes in 125 patients with TB and AIDS who were treated with standard short-course regimens. Six percent of patients died early in treatment, with TB presumably contributing to mortality. The remainder were successfully treated, however, and the relapse rate for patients completing therapy was 3.5 cases per 100 person-years of follow-up. All relapses occurred in patients who had been poorly compliant with therapy. Only one patient was a treatment failure. This patient had isoniazid-resistant TB and was poorly compliant. He developed tuberculous meningitis during therapy. Thus, this study showed that TB could be successfully treated and cured with short-course therapy in patients with advanced HIV disease.

A prospective study in Haiti by Holt et al. showed that 6 months of thrice weekly therapy using isoniazid and rifampin, with pyrazinamide and ethambutol for the first 8 weeks, was highly effective in HIV-infected patients with TB.[34] Four hundred twenty-seven patients with TB, 42 percent of whom were HIV-seropositive, were enrolled. Response to therapy was similar in HIV-seropositive (81 percent with clinical cures) and -seronegative (87 percent with clinical cures) patients. The mortality rate was significantly higher, however, in seropositive patients.

A number of problems have emerged in the treatment of HIV-associated TB, underscoring the neglect that TB research has suffered in the past 20 years. No new drugs have been licensed for the treatment of TB since the approval of rifampin in 1972, and little research on TB drugs is currently under way. The need for newer agents is further highlighted by several treatment-related issues, including an increased rate of adverse reactions to first-line agents in patients with HIV infection; an upsurge in drug-resistant isolates, especially in patients with HIV; and the discontinuation of the manufacture of some key second-line drugs.

Treatment-limiting adverse reactions to antituberculous drugs occur with greater frequency in patients with HIV infection than in HIV-seronegative patients. Adverse reactions to rifampin, including rash, fever, hepatitis, and thrombocytopenia, may occur in 10 percent or more of patients with advanced HIV disease, while reactions to isoniazid, pyrazinamide, and ethambutol occur in 3 – 5 percent of patients. Patients with early HIV disease generally tolerate antituberculous drugs better than do patients with advanced HIV disease. Intermittent therapy (e.g., twice or thrice weekly) may be better-tolerated than daily therapy and appears to be as effective.

Management of adverse reactions may be difficult, particularly since patients may have underlying disease that mimics drug reactions and may also be taking other potentially toxic medications, such as zidovudine and trimetho-prim-sulfamethoxazole. As with other drugs that cause adverse reactions in patients with HIV, antituberculous drugs should be continued, if possible, when a drug reaction is suspected, and patients should be managed symptomatically and observed closely. When a drug is thought to be causing severe toxicity, it should be stopped and the patient observed for resolution of the reaction. If toxicity is not readily attributable to a single agent (e.g., severe hepatotoxicity), all drugs should be stopped and reintroduced individually, and the patient should be monitored for signs of toxicity. It is important to remember that TB itself is potentially more lethal than most drug reactions, and continuation of treatment is of the utmost importance. In addition, because resistance to antituberculous drugs can develop in patients receiving only a single agent, combination therapy is essential.

The growing prevalence of drug-resistant TB is particularly important for patients with HIV infection (Chapter 18). Recent outbreaks of multidrug-resistant (MDR) disease in New York and Miami have occurred almost exclusively in persons with HIV infection. Management of drug-resistant TB is increasingly difficult, since additional drugs for TB are in short supply. In patients with isoniazid-resistant isolates of *M. tuberculosis*, the most common form of antituberculous drug resistance, treatment with rifampin and ethambutol for 9–12 months, coupled with pyrazinamide for the first 2 months, is appropriate. For patients with MDR disease, treatment is more challenging. Use of second-line agents, such as para-aminosalicylic acid (PAS), ethionamide, cycloserine, and the aminoglycosides kanamycin, capreomycin, or amikacin, is necessary to treat suspected MDR TB. Initial presumptive treatment may be guided by the susceptibility pattern of isolates from source contacts or of known outbreak strains. Continued treatment should ultimately be guided by appropriate susceptibility testing of isolates recovered from patients. Additional agents with known antimycobacterial activity that may be useful in treating MDR TB include fluoroquinolones, clofazimine, and combinations of β-lactam drugs with β-lactamase inhibitors (e.g., amoxicillin/clavulanate). The fluoroquinolones have in vitro activity against *M. tuberculosis* and are generally well-tolerated by patients with HIV infection. Ciprofloxacin inhibits *M. tuberculosis* in concentrations of 0.5–5 μg/ml, while peak serum levels are in the 4–5 μg/ml range. Ofloxacin inhibits growth at concentrations of 0.5–2.0 μg/ml and has peak levels of about 5 μg/ml when given at doses of 400 mg twice a day. Both of these drugs are commercially available. The L-enantiomer of ofloxacin, levofloxacin, has potent antituberculous activity and is undergoing clinical evaluation. Other new drugs under investigation for TB include other quinolones, longer-acting rifamycin derivatives, nitroimidazoles, and a new class of antibiotics, the oxazolidinones. Most of these agents are unlikely to be available for several years or longer, and none has been studied in human clinical trials for TB.

It has recently been suggested that adjuvant immunotherapy may improve the response to antituberculous chemotherapy. Immunization with *Mycobacterium vaccae* vaccine at the initiation of therapy has been reported to improve treatment outcome in small, noncontrolled trials in Africa and the Middle East.[35] Larger, controlled trials of this approach are needed, including treatment of HIV-infected TB patients.

Perhaps the most important element for the successful treatment of TB is assuring compliance with therapy. Because therapy extends for a number of months, noncompliance is a major problem. This problem is compounded when patients lack the financial means for obtaining drugs or access to treatment or when drug or alcohol abuse interfere with health care. In one study of TB patients in New York, 89 percent of patients failed to continue therapy after discharge from the hospital and more than one-quarter developed recurrent TB within a year.[36] Referring patients to public health agencies is often an option for assuring continuation of care. Tuberculosis clinics adhere to strict treatment protocols and offer supervised or directly observed therapy as an option for patients at risk for not completing antituberculous treatment. Improved funding for TB control programs is urgently needed to ensure adequate treatment of an ever-increasing number of patients. A retrospective study in Baltimore revealed that HIV-infected patients given supervised intermittent therapy for TB were less likely to die of TB and more likely to complete 6 months of treatment than were patients whose treatment was unsupervised.[37]

PREVENTION OF TB IN PATIENTS WITH HIV

Identification of HIV-infected patients coinfected with *M. tuberculosis* and administration of chemoprophylaxis is perhaps the most important strategy for controlling TB in the context of the HIV pandemic. Because the risk of reactivation is so high, chemoprophylaxis is recommended for all HIV-seropositive persons with a positive tuberculin skin test reaction (≥ 5 mm). Screening of all HIV-infected persons with a PPD is an essential component of the initial HIV evaluation. Since the response to PPD corresponds to the absolute CD4+ count, skin tests should be applied as early in the HIV disease course as possible. As discussed above, the use of control antigens is recommended by the CDC. Repeat PPD testing is unnecessary for a patient with a documented previous positive test result. In some populations with ongoing exposure to TB in the community, annual testing may be appropriate.

The efficacy of isoniazid chemoprophylaxis in HIV-infected persons was recently established in a small controlled trial in Haiti. Investigators there showed that isoniazid (300 mg per day for 12 months) was associated with a TB incidence of 2.2 cases per 100 person-years, compared to 7.5 cases per 100 person-years in vitamin B_6 recipients,[38] after an average follow-up of 2.5 – 3.1 years. These investigators suggested that isoniazid also reduced the risk of progression to symptomatic HIV disease and death. Confirmation of these data in larger studies is necessary, however. The CDC recommends that isoniazid be administered at a dose of 300 mg per day for 12 months.

Alternative regimens for TB chemoprophylaxis are desirable for several reasons. First, compliance with prolonged courses of isoniazid is notoriously poor. Thus, shorter-duration therapy is likely to result in greater patient adherence. Second, as drug resistance increases, the use of agents unlikely to produce resistance is potentially important. Third, intracellular mycobacteria may persist with isoniazid therapy and result in reactivation of infection as immunocompetence wanes. Finally, because some patients with HIV and a positive PPD test result may have undiagnosed, active TB, a regimen that treats active disease is appealing. Studies done in the laboratory of Jacques Grosset in Paris have demonstrated that, in an animal model of chronic *M. tuberculosis* infection, 2-month courses of rifampin and pyrazinamide result in negative spleen culture results for 100 percent of test animals, versus 60 percent with 6 months of isoniazid.[39] Four months of rifampin alone results in 80 percent spleen culture conversion. Based on these animal data, the AIDS Clinical Trials Group (ACTG) and the Community Programs for Clinical Research on AIDS (CPCRA) have launched a multicenter trial of isoniazid for 12 months versus rifampin/pyrazinamide for 2 months in HIV-seropositive persons with a positive PPD test result. Similar studies are being conducted in Haiti and in drug treatment centers and public health departments in the United States. The results of these trials are eagerly anticipated. Currently, 12 months of isoniazid remains the therapy of choice for prophylaxis, but use of rifampin alone or rifampin and pyrazinamide may be considered as an alternative in patients unable to take isoniazid. Preventive therapy for patients exposed to MDR TB is discussed in Chapters 6 and 18.

Because anergy is common in advanced HIV infection, the CDC has recommended that prophylaxis be considered for HIV-seropositive persons who are anergic (to PPD and two control antigens) and have demographic characteristics placing them at more than 10 percent risk of tuberculous infection (e.g., injection drug users in New York or immigrants from endemic areas). A recent study using decision analysis concluded that such a strategy would result in prolongation of life if the prevalence of tuberculous infection exceeded 5 – 17 percent in a population of HIV-infected persons.[40] However, data from a controlled trial are preferred for directing clinical practice. These strategies are in part dependent on geographic influences. A recent retrospective study from Spain showed that, while the risk of TB was high in HIV-infected anergic patients, PPD-negative nonanergic patients also had an elevated risk of developing TB.[41]

SUMMARY

HIV infection has resulted in a major change in TB incidence in the past decade. As numbers of new cases of TB increase, clinicians and public health authorities are facing a host of new challenges in the control of TB. Drug intolerance, multidrug resistance, and the disappearance of second-line antituberculous drugs make the identification of newer and better agents for TB treatment more urgent. Ultimately, prevention of TB with chemoprophylaxis may be the best strategy for controlling this revitalized pathogen.

REFERENCES

1. Centers for Disease Control: Tuberculosis morbidity: United States, 1992. *MMWR* 42:696, 1993.
2. Murray CJL, Styblo K, Rouillon A: Tuberculosis in developing countries: burden, intervention and cost. *Bull Int Union Tuberc Lung Dis* 65:2, 1990.
3. Johnson MP, Chaisson RE: Tuberculosis and HIV disease, in Volberding PA, Jacobson MA (eds), *AIDS Clinical Review* 1993/1994. New York, Marcel Dekker, 1994, pp 73–93.
4. Pitchenik AE, Cole C, Russell BW, Fischl MA, et al: Tuberculosis, atypical mycobacteriosis, and the acquired immunodeficiency syndrome among Haitian and non-Haitian patients in south Florida. *Ann Intern Med* 101:641, 1984.
5. Chaisson RE, Schecter GF, Theuer CP, et al: Tuberculosis in patients with the acquired immunodeficiency syndrome: clinical features, response to therapy and outcome. *Am Rev Respir Dis* 136:570, 1987.
6. Fauci AS (moderator): NIH conference: immunopathogenic mechanisms in human immunodeficiency virus (HIV) infection. *Ann Intern Med* 114:678, 1991.
7. Harries AD: Tuberculosis and human immunodeficiency virus infection in developing countries. *Lancet* 335:387, 1990.
8. Onorato IM, McCray E, Field Services Branch: Prevalence of human immunodeficiency virus infection among patients attending tuberculosis clinics in the United States. *J Infect Dis* 165:87, 1992.
9. De Pierri G, Gruciani M, Danzi MC, et al: Nosocomial epidemic of active tuberculosis among HIV-infected patients. *Lancet* 2:1502, 1989.
10. Daley CL, Small PM, Schecter GF, et al: An outbreak of tuberculosis with accelerated progression among persons infected with the human immunodeficiency virus: an analysis using restriction-fragment-length polymorphisms. *N Engl J Med* 326:231, 1992.

11. Centers for Disease Control: Nosocomial transmission of multidrug-resistant tuberculosis among HIV-infected persons: Florida and New York, 1988–1991. *MMWR* 40:585, 1991.

12. Fischl MA, Uttamchandani RB, Daikos GL, Poblete RB, et al: An outbreak of tuberculosis caused by multiple-drug-resistant tubercle bacilli among patients with HIV infection. *Ann Intern Med* 117:177, 1992.

13. Dooley SW, Villarino ME, Lawrence M, et al: Nosocomial transmission of tuberculosis in a hospital unit for HIV-infected patients. *JAMA* 267:2632, 1992.

14. Bellin EY, Fletcher DD, Safyer SM: Association of tuberculosis infection with increased time in or admission to the New York City jail system. *JAMA* 269:2228, 1993.

15. Centers for Disease Control: Revision of the case definition of acquired immune deficiency syndrome. *MMWR* 36(suppl):1S, 1987.

16. Centers for Disease Control: 1993 revised classification system for HIV infection and expanded surveillance case definition for AIDS among adolescents and adults. *MMWR* 41:1, 1992.

17. Selwyn PA, Hartel D, Lewis VA, et al: A prospective study of the risk of tuberculosis among intravenous drug users with human immunodeficiency virus infection. *N Engl J Med* 320:545, 1989.

18. Allen S, Batungwanayo J, Kerlikowske K, et al: Two-year incidence of tuberculosis in cohorts of HIV-infected and uninfected urban Rwandan women. *Am Rev Respir Dis* 146:1439, 1992.

19. Wallis RS, Vjecha M, Amir-Tahmasseb M, et al: Influence of tuberculosis on human immunodeficiency virus (HIV-1): enhanced cytokine expression and elevated beta-2 microglobulin in HIV-associated tuberculosis. *J Infect Dis* 167:43, 1993.

20. Forte M, Maartens G, Rahelu M, et al: Cytolytic T-cell activity against mycobacterial agents in HIV. *AIDS* 6:407, 1992.

21. Stead WW, Senner JW, Reddick WT, Lofgren JP: Racial differences in susceptibility to infection by *Mycobacterium tuberculosis*. *N Engl J Med* 322:422, 1990.

22. Theuer CP, Hopewell PC, Elias D, Schecter GF, et al: Human immunodeficiency virus infection in tuberculosis patients. *J Infect Dis* 162:8, 1990.

23. Small PM, Schecter GF, Goodman PC, et al: Treatment of tuberculosis in patients with advanced human immunodeficiency virus infection. *N Engl J Med* 324:289, 1991.

24. Berenguer J, Moreneo S, Launa F, et al: Tuberculous meningitis in patients infected with human immunodeficiency virus. *N Engl J Med* 326:668, 1992.

25. DeCock KM, Soro B, Coulibaly AM, Lucas SB: Tuberculosis and HIV infection in sub-saharan Africa. *JAMA* 268:1581, 1992.

26. Kramer F, Modilevsky T, Waliany AR, Leedom JM, Barnes PF: Delayed diagnosis of tuberculosis in patients with human immunodeficiency virus infection. *Am J Med* 89:451, 1990.

27. Elliott AM, Luo N, Tembo G, et al: Impact of HIV on tuberculosis in Zambia: a cross section study. *Br Med J* 301:412, 1990.

28. Ng VL, Yajko DM, McPhaul LW, Gartner I, et al: Evaluation of an indirect fluorescent-antibody stain for detection of *Pneumocystis carinii* in respiratory specimens. *J Clin Microbiol* 5:975, 1990.

29. Gallant JE, Mueller PS, McArthur J, Chaisson RE: Intramedullary tuberculoma in a patient with HIV infection. *AIDS* 6:889, 1992.

30. Centers for Disease Control: Purified protein derivative (PPD)-tuberculin anergy and HIV: guidelines for anergy testing and management of anergic persons at risk of tuberculosis. *MMWR* 40:27, 1991.

31. Johnson MP, Coberly JS, Clermont HC, Chaisson RE, et al: Tuberculin skin test reactivity among adults infected with human immunodeficiency virus. *J Infect Dis* 166:194, 1992.

32. Graham NMH, Nelson KE, Solomon L, et al: Prevalence of tuberculin positivity and skin test

anergy in HIV-1-seropositive and -seronegative intravenous drug user. *JAMA* 267:369, 1992.

33. Advisory Council for the Elimination of Tuberculosis: Initial therapy for tuberculosis in the era of multidrug resistance. *MMWR* 42:RR-7, 1, 1993.

34. Holt E, Cantave M, Johnson M, Clermont HC, Atkinson J, Chaisson RE: Efficacy of supervised, intermittent, short course therapy of tuberculosis in HIV infection (Abstract No. WS-B09-4). In: Proceedings, IXth International Conference on AIDs, Berlin, June 7–11, 1993.

35. Stanford JL, Bahr GM, Rook GAW, et al: Immunotherapy with *Mycobacterium vaccae* as an adjunct to chemotherapy in the treatment of pulmonary tuberculosis. *Tubercle* 71:87, 1990.

36. Brudney K, Dobkin J: Resurgent tuberculosis in New York City: human immunodeficiency virus, homelessness, and the decline of tuberculosis control programs. *Am Rev Respir Dis* 144:745, 1991.

37. Alwood K, Moore-Rice K, Keruly J, et al: Effectiveness of supervised, intermittent therapy for tuberculosis in HIV infection. *Am Rev Respir Dis* 147:A489, 1993.

38. Pape JW, Jean SS, Ho JL, Hafner A, Johnson WD Jr: Effect of isoniazid prophylaxis on incidence of active tuberculosis and progression of HIV infection. *Lancet* 342:268, 1993.

39. Lacoeur HF, Truffot-Pernot C, Grosset JH: Experimental short-course preventive therapy of tuberculosis with rifampin and pyrazinamide. *Am Rev Respir Dis* 140:1189, 1989.

40. Jordan TJ, Lewit EM, Montgomery RL, et al: Isoniazid as preventive therapy in HIV-infected intravenous drug users. *JAMA* 265:2987, 1991.

41. Moreno S, Baraia-Etxaburu J, Bouza E, et al: Risk for developing tuberculosis among anergic patients infected with HIV. *Ann Intern Med* 119:194, 1993.

CHAPTER 15

Populations at Special Risk for Tuberculosis

WILLIAM W. STEAD / ASIM K. DUTT

In their book *The White Plague*, the famous tuberculosis (TB) bacteriologists Drs. Rene and Jean Dubos of the Rockefeller Institute called TB a social disease.[1] By this they meant that social factors are as important in its pathogenesis as the tubercle bacillus is. The truth of this concept has never been more clear than it is today, as we see the incidence of TB rising around the world and in this country, despite our great knowledge of the germ and its host and the availability of curative chemotherapy.

In 1983, TB was so well-controlled in the United States that many thought it was largely of historic interest. Public health funds for its control were cut to the bone, and most practicing physicians almost never saw a case. It was scarcely mentioned in most medical and nursing schools. However, in 1985 the steady 5 percent annual decrease in number of cases in the United States leveled off, and then the rate began to rise. Within 8 years, a total of 51,700 cases in excess of the expected number had been reported.[2] The purpose of this chapter is to show the importance of social factors in this resurgence. Although much of the country has not yet experienced this dramatic increase in TB, several large cities have. What social factors might Drs. Dubos cite for this?

THE POOR AND DISADVANTAGED

The Dubos might point to the social changes that have occurred in the past 10–15 years as reasons for the rise in TB. In this period, the western world has experienced great economic growth. Former President Reagan boasted about the longest uninterrupted period of economic growth in United States history. However, the benefits of the economic growth were felt mainly by the wealthy, as the stock market flourished because of increased profits due to cost savings through moving factories to developing countries, where wages are a fraction of those in the United States.[3] This meant that millions of people who

239

had been employed and self-sufficient all their lives were now out of work or employed only part time and at a lower wage. Many unskilled workers found themselves unable to provide for their families and forced to apply for welfare.

Such a state of affairs had a devastating effect on the breadwinners and their families. The situation became even worse as affordable housing was razed to make room for higher-cost high-rise apartments. Whatever lower-cost housing was spared jumped in price due to its scarcity. Meantime, there was a rise in the cost of everything the poor had to buy. Their situation was so marginal that any unexpected expense (e.g., an illness in the family, a further cut in pay, etc.) could completely destroy all hope of becoming self-sufficient again. Thousands lost their homes. In such circumstances, many people turned to alcohol, illegal drugs, and illicit methods of surviving. Then came the problem of homelessness and being crowded into shelter dormitories, where many people are at risk if one of the number happens to have TB.

For persons caught in the web of poverty, immediate concerns for short-term survival often overshadow normal human concerns for the long term. Such patients may not show up at a clinic for medication after symptoms subside, as occurs with chemotherapy for TB long before cure is achieved. We have found that attention to the problems underlying noncompliance can enable many patients to cooperate adequately to achieve a cure of the disease. Furnishing a homeless person with a low-cost hotel room near the clinic can work wonders. Furnishing transportation vouchers, helping with an application for food stamps, and attention to other pressing needs are also ways by which cooperation can be obtained. Such measures are easier to achieve in medium-sized cities than in large cities, where patients may live in areas where even public health nurses are afraid to go.

At the same time, President Reagan declared a "war on drugs," based on getting the pushers off the streets and into prison on mandatory minimum sentences.[4] In addition, a hard-line approach was taken on street crime in general, although an increase in "white collar" crime seemed to escape the administration's attention. This created some hard feelings and legitimate paranoia among those who were being crowded into prisons as never before.[4]

To this must be added the ethnic and racial tensions that arose as skilled and semiskilled workers displaced the disproportionately black and Hispanic minimum wage workers. The latter were thrown onto the welfare rolls in droves. African-Americans felt that the cutting of government social programs and of other efforts to right the wrongs of the past effectively ended the progress of the civil rights movement. Moreover, every apparent break an African-American might get was seen by some whites as reverse discrimination. The truth is that the number of jobs paying a living wage was shrinking as manufacturing was moved to developing countries and the demand for jobs exceeded the supply by such a large margin that competition often became ugly. Also, it was apparent to African-Americans that they still were treated unjustly by the police and the criminal justice system, which effectively created a large number of "angry young men" for whom escape into the oblivion of illegal drugs seemed the only answer.

The effect of this vastly widening gulf between the ever-richer rich and the ever-poorer poor and between minority groups and whites can be seen from the statistics of the criminal justice system. In the past decade, prison and jail populations have doubled, outpacing all attempts to increase the spaces available, so that prisons were 18–29 percent over their capacities.[4] On any day, more than 1.2 million Americans are behind bars, with a daily turnover of over 30,000. African-Americans, who comprise 12 percent of the population, constitute 47 percent of those incarcerated in jails and prisons. Arrests for drug violations rose 126 percent in the last decade, while arrests for all offenses rose only 28 percent. Moreover, state prison populations are projected to increase by 68 percent by 1994.[4] Furthermore, the disproportionate rate of incarceration of minorities will increase considerably, largely because of the war on drugs and the great lure of crack cocaine. In the meantime, the individuals who make the drug trade possible go largely untouched.

PERSONS INFECTED WITH HUMAN IMMUNODEFICIENCY VIRUS

Due largely to injected drug use and the sharing of needles, the incidence of human immunodeficiency virus (HIV) infection among prisoners is 14 times that in the general population.[2] The incidence of TB among prisoners is more than three times that in the general population.[5] *A major factor determining the course of TB in the United States will be the overlap of groups with a high prevalence of tuberculous infection (poor, African-American, and Hispanic) and groups with a high prevalence of HIV infection (injected drug users who share needles).* The Centers for Disease Control (CDC) estimates the risk of TB to be increased 113-fold by HIV infection and 170-fold among persons with AIDS.[2] This can only spell disaster when one considers the number of jail and prison inmates with a new tuberculous infection who will be released into the community each year as prison populations increase by 13 percent annually.[4]

Although economists did not recognize the recent recession until the middle of the Bush administration, the slide of the working class into poverty began shortly after President Reagan's policies took effect in 1981. There were a large tax reduction for the wealthy, the relaxation of regulations on business, and the financing of leveraged buy-outs of multibillion dollar companies (e.g, RJR/Nabisco) with debt and money speculated by savings and loan associations. Meanwhile self-sufficient middle class workers lost their jobs and slipped below the poverty level. Those whose jobs they took were forced onto the welfare rolls. So, the scenario outlined above had its beginning long before economists recognized the recession.

While the well-to-do were enjoying unprecedented prosperity at the expense of their less fortunate compatriots, developing countries were sinking deeper into poverty, overcrowding, and disease. In crowded cities of Africa, the HIV pandemic made its appearance and worsened rapidly. Tuberculosis, an epidemic that had begun in sub-Saharan African in about 1910 and appeared only recently to have passed its peak, took a sharp upturn. The already considerable susceptibility to TB in Africa was increased 113- to 170-fold among those infected with HIV.[2] A 1991 editorial in *The Lancet* seriously raised the question, "Is Africa Lost?"[6] The solutions offered by the authors all depend on widespread, intelligent use of TB chemotherapy, a dubious proposition at best.

POPULATIONS AT RISK FOR MULTIDRUG-RESISTANT *MYCOBACTERIUM TUBERCULOSIS*

Populations of tubercle bacilli change from drug-susceptible to drug-resistant by the same mechanism that populations of mosquitoes become resistant to DDT.[7] Individual tubercle bacilli do not gradually develop resistance. Instead, resistance is an all-or-none phenomenon due to a chance mutation that may occur in one organism in a million. Then, in the presence of a normally lethal dose of drug, the million ordinary organisms are killed, while the one with this mutation survives and passes the resistance gene to its progeny. When the mosquito population of an area becomes resistant to DDT, it does no good to double the intensity of spraying. Nor does it do any good to double the dose of medication against a resistant population of microorganisms.

As knowledge of population genetics developed, therapy for tuberculosis became more rational and effective. It was realized early on that even isoniazid (INH), the best bactericidal drug, could not kill *all* of a large population of bacilli before a chance mutation would endow a single bacillus with resistance to the drug. Increasing the dose of INH was ineffective because the resistant organisms had a genetically determined alternative metabolic pathway that was not affected by INH. The progeny of this single organism soon would multiply enough to cause the disease to progress in spite of the INH.

It had been known for many years that bacteriostatic drugs such as para-aminosalicylic acid or ethambutol (EMB) could give some protection from development of INH resistance in active TB. However, the mechanism by which this happens was not clear until the advent of rifampin (RMP). This drug is also lethal to tubercle bacilli but by a mechanism totally different from that of INH. A mutation conferring resistance to it also occurs in only one of a million organisms. Thus, when the two drugs are given to a patient infected by a strain of tubercle bacilli that has had no previous contact with either drug, a resistant mutant would occur much less frequently (i.e., in 1 out of 1 $\times$ 10^{12} organisms).[8] This assured success in treatment, but only if the drugs were taken regularly and in the proper dosage. This is where practice could not come up to the potential of the treatment for a very practical reason. Some patients failed to take the two drugs as directed, thus permitting resistant mutants to multiply.

If at this stage a physician were to add another drug (EMB, streptomycin, pyrazinamide, etc.) to which the organisms are still susceptible, it would not take long for additional mutations to occur, conferring resistance to the new drug if the patient continues to fail to comply with treatment.[8] The resistant mutant then multiplies without deterrence until the entire population of the lesion is replaced by resistant organisms. At this point we have a case of TB with organisms that will be very difficult to cure with drugs even in an immune-competent patient and often impossible in an HIV-infected patient. Compliance with second-line medications is much more difficult because of unpleasant side effects and toxicity.

Clearly, this situation is the beginning of a tragedy, particularly if it occurs where highly susceptible HIV-infected persons are exposed to such a patient. Essentially all the organisms shed by the patient will be resistant to three drugs. This is by far the greatest challenge that we face for the nineties, in large measure due to the situation described earlier in regard to crowding of persons with tuberculous infection into prisons with people with HIV infection.[9]

The possible effects of such a development are demonstrated by the figures from one prison in upper New York state. In an outbreak of multi-drug-resistant (MDR) TB, there were 14 deaths, all in immunocompromised persons, in 13 due to HIV infection and in 1 to cancer chemotherapy.[2,10] By contrast, where MDR TB has occurred in a few normal persons, most have recovered with prolonged therapy with some combination of four or five less-potent drugs.

Perhaps it is not as well known that the occurrence of TB, even if drug-susceptible, accelerates the course of HIV infection.[11] The release of cytokines and tumor necrosis factor by the cells in the tuberculous lesions probably accounts for this acceleration.

One more factor is associated with the combination of TB and HIV infection: the atypical clinical presentation of TB. Instead of the expected chronic pulmonary presentation, TB in HIV-infected persons is much more likely to be extrapulmonary in location.[12] When it does present in the lungs, it is likely to be more of a subacute disease with too little pulmonary infiltration to show up on a radiograph despite shedding enough tubercle bacilli to produce a positive sputum smear result. Any acid-fast bacilli seen on a sputum or tissue smear may be, not tubercle bacilli, but "atypical" organisms (usually, *Mycobacterium avium intracellulare*). This makes arriving at the correct diagnosis a great challenge. It very commonly will be missed unless one has a policy of obtaining material for culture for tubercle bacilli from every person with HIV infection. Fortunately, drug-susceptible TB in HIV-infected persons responds to treatment about as well as it does in normal persons.

Because of the likelihood of a large population of tubercle bacilli in persons with impaired resistance, persons who are coinfected with TB and HIV are likely to be more infectious than the average immune-competent patient. Also, admission of HIV-infected persons to specialized wards necessitates redoubling efforts to prevent spread of TB among these exquisitely susceptible individuals. For this, our preference is upper-air sterilization by irradiation with germicidal ultraviolet light in all patients' rooms and corridors (Chapter 4). When architectural design makes this impracticable, germicidal lights may be installed in the ducts of the ventilation system. Although this method has great appeal because it is out of sight, *it is not the best means of decontamination. It provides the equivalent of an open window, whereas upper-air irradiation can provide the equivalent of 15–20 air exchanges per hour.*[13]

The development of drug resistance is much more likely in TB patients who are coinfected with HIV because coinfected patients have large populations of bacilli and a greater likelihood of being mentally ill and hostile, homeless, former prison inmates, and/or drug and/or alcohol abusers. All of these problems bespeak a resistance to compliance with a therapeutic regimen long enough to achieve a cure.

IMMIGRANTS FROM COUNTRIES OF HIGH TB PREVALENCE

The prevalence of tuberculous infection is still several times greater in many countries than in Europe and the United States. A prevalence of 30–60 percent with dormant TB infection is not uncommon in developing countries. In some instances, the reduced sunlight in the United Kingdom appears to be a factor in recrudescence of dormant tuberculous infections in immigrants from India and Pakistan.[14]

Emigration from one's native country most often is brought on by such dissatisfaction with life that one feels compelled to take the many chances entailed in starting a new life in another country.[15] Statistics have shown that such persons are at great risk of developing TB within the first year or two after emigration. Initial living conditions in the new land are commonly such that even those who had never been infected with TB in the past may become infected by living in close quarters with a person whose old infection has reactivated and become infectious.

Many of these persons are highly motivated and may be ideal patients if they develop TB. Even in such cases, however, language and cultural barriers may make it difficult to convey to the patient the need for treatment to extend well beyond the time when symptoms have cleared.

Other immigrants, particularly if illegal, present enormous problems in treatment. Because of its prevalence in their native land, they may view TB as little more than an inconvenience and almost inevitable. Therefore, it may be low on their list of priorities, very subordinate to learning to communicate, fighting off the dangers of their neighborhood, avoiding arrest, finding and holding a job, and so on. Such stress greatly increases the risk of developing TB and also makes cooperation in its prolonged treatment difficult. Fear of detection and deportation may make attendance at government-operated clinics a frightening experience that they will avoid at almost any cost. For all these reasons, immigrants make up a group that is at great risk for TB, treatment failure, and development of drug resistance.

Tuberculosis control is especially difficult along our long and easily breached border with Mexico. The prevalence of TB in Mexico is several times that of this country, and many Mexican nationals are here illegally.

The language barrier is particularly great in such cities as New York, Boston, Miami, Seattle, San Francisco, and Los Angeles, where there are immigrants from hundreds of countries with a high prevalence of TB. The written material for them is extremely limited and, as with illegal Mexican immigrants, of little value because they are often functionally illiterate even in their native language. Explaining TB and giving instructions regarding its treatment through a nonmedical interpreter leaves a great deal to be desired.

Tuberculosis is the sole excludable disease currently under the Immigration and Nationalization Service, but this applies only to its active stage. However, persons with active disease who apply for an emigrant visa may be detained only until a multiple-drug regimen has been instituted, with the understanding that treatment will be continued after they arrive here. However, new immigrants are often so beset with the many problems associated with getting settled in a new environment that reporting to a clinic for medication is often not high on their agenda. Moreover, there may be a distrust of official agencies and grossly distorted views regarding TB, all of which make treatment for several months unlikely.

Because of little or no control over the sale of drugs in most developing countries, INH is commonly included in cough remedies sold over the counter in the immigrant's country of origin. This assures a very high prevalence of INH resistance in immigrants from such countries. Then, if INH and RMP are given to such a patient without the addition of another drug, the likelihood of development of MDR is also assured.

Vaccination of children at birth with bacille Calmette-Guérin (BCG) is common practice in many developing countries. This leads to a higher prevalence of reactivity to tuberculin than there would be from natural infection alone. For this reason, many physicians do not prescribe INH prophylaxis to children and young adults who are tuberculin-positive. Even if the physician follows the recommendation of the CDC to prescribe INH prophylaxis for such persons, the advice may be taken lightly in the belief that the vaccination afforded adequate protection from the disease.

NATIVE AMERICANS

Tuberculosis prevalence remains high among Native Americans, whether living on a reservation or not.[16] Failure to complete a prescribed course of therapy is also common, again because they may feel that once medication has cleared their symptoms, there is no need to continue the medicine. Native Americans may have so many immediately pressing problems that completion of therapy may not be high on their agenda. There may also be a considerable distrust of white physicians and nurses. When these factors are coupled with the poverty in which many Native Americans must live, the door is open for development of drug resistance and its spread to anyone living under the same roof.

HEALTH CARE WORKERS

With the rather rapid decline in incidence of TB over the past 40 years, the risk of the disease for doctors, nurses, and others with close contact with sick people decreased accordingly. However, this situation has changed in such places as New York City, where the increase in the number of cases and of MDR is alarming.[17] History teaches us that whatever happens in our largest city eventually reaches the rest of the country. Therefore, it is appropriate to sound the alarm that health care workers will be at increasing risk throughout the country.

Several authors have reported an increased incidence of TB among health care workers, including physicians, in comparison with the population at large. This makes sense when one considers that, in the course of our work, we are as closely exposed to sick people as anyone.

In 1992, a patient with INH- and RMP-resistant pulmonary TB, laryngitis, and a bronchopleural fistula with empyema was admitted to a private hospital in Little Rock, Arkansas, for surgical drainage of the empyema. The patient was assigned to a room equipped with upper-air irradiation by germicidal ultraviolet light. Before the procedure, similar fixtures were installed in the operating suite. Also, with this most infectious and dangerous combination possible, great care was taken to make certain that all members of the staff were current with their annual tuberculin tests, so that any new infection among them could be detected without delay.

The patient lived for about 6 weeks after surgery and was seen by many consulting physicians as well as ward staff, laboratory and radiology technicians, dietitians, and so on. Eight weeks after his death, the 141 persons who had been identified as having been in this patient's room were retested with 5 tuberculin units of PPD. Fortunately, there was only one skin test converter, a radiology technician who had taken daily chest radiographs at the bedside. However, *none of the physicians and surgeons was listed.* On inquiry, it was learned that the responsibility of the hospital infection control nurse does not extend to the professional medical staff, because technically they are not hospital employees. If this is not corrected, we can look forward to tragedies among physicians and surgeons in the future, with a steady increase in the number of TB cases, some of which will excrete drug-resistant organisms.

OTHER EMPLOYEES AT INCREASED RISK FOR TB

Employees in many other situations are at increased risk for tuberculosis, for example, prison and jail guards,[18] ambulance attendants, and the staff of nursing homes, shelters for the homeless, mental hospitals, renal dialysis units, alcohol and drug abuse treatment and rehabilitation units, shelters for battered women, veterans' domiciliary homes, and so on. It seems fair to say that many such facilities have given little thought to TB. This must change as we see more HIV infections and increasing numbers of cases of drug-resistant TB.

THE EVER-INCREASING NUMBER OF ELDERLY PERSONS

Tuberculosis first became a special problem for the elderly when significant numbers of people began to outlive their previously robust immune systems.[19]

Now, however, the elderly constitute the fastest-growing segment of the population in the United States and the one with the highest incidence of TB. The problem of TB in this group is not as obvious as in the other groups discussed, because the diagnosis of TB is delayed or missed when the condition is mistaken for pneumonia. Moreover, while death may not be expected in an octogenarian, it is fair to say it is never a great surprise, either. Thus, many cases of TB in the elderly go unrecognized for lack of aggressive investigation. Meanwhile, a few fellow patients, as well as hospital and nursing home personnel caring for them, may have been infected. As the number of HIV-infected persons increases, unrecognized cases will surely be point sources for many new infections and reinfections in this highly susceptible group.

For the elderly themselves, TB presents special problems. Because of their great longevity, tubercle bacilli often remain viable within a healthy host for many years, silently sequestered within macrophages and old caseous foci. A reaction of 10 mm or more to 5 units of purified protein derivative of tuberculin generally indicates that viable tubercle bacilli are still present. They remain capable of causing active TB if circumstances permit (e.g., failing health, insulin-dependent diabetes mellitus, prolonged corticosteroid therapy, or deterioration of the immune system with age). Thus, in the United States today, the TB case rate among persons over the age of 65 is higher than in any segment of the population except for persons with HIV infection.[2] In addition, many older persons have negative skin test results and thus have no immune protection against infection.[19] Thus, in a nursing home, where spread of TB is not uncommon, the TB cases comprise a mixture of new infections and recrudescence of old infections. The TB case rate in such circumstances is several times that in elderly persons living in private homes.[20]

It was shown by tuberculin skin test surveys 50–60 years ago, when most current nursing home residents were in the prime of life, that 80 percent of adults were infected by *M. tuberculosis*. About 90 percent of TB cases among elderly persons today arise from recrudescence of ancient infection among those who survived those years. Tuberculin nonreactors who are healthy and living at home are at almost no risk of spontaneously developing TB without exposure. However, in a nursing home they may pick up a new infection from a fellow resident with unsuspected TB.[21]

When a new infection is established in an elderly person, there is an 8–12 percent chance that this person will develop clinical TB if not treated preventively.[21] The presentation of the disease is then likely to be atypical, presenting as pneumonia or bronchitis or even masquerading as congestive heart failure with a pleural effusion. In contrast, recrudescent infection is more likely to present with apical infiltration and cavitation.

The TB case rate observed among the elderly is influenced by two factors. It varies directly with the prevalence of the infection in the same cohort in

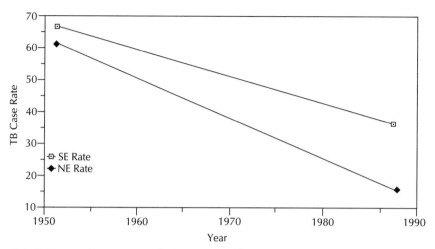

FIGURE 15-1. Comparison of TB case rates (cases per 100,000 persons) in individuals of 25–44 years of age in 1953 and 36 years later, when that cohort is over age 65. Although the starting rates are similar, the decline in the case rate in the northeastern (NE) states is much steeper than that in the southeastern (SE) states. (*Used with permission. From Stead and Dutt.*[23])

earlier years and with the diligence with which the nature of pulmonary infiltrates is sought.[23] Figure 15-1 illustrates the first point. In the early 1950s, the TB case rate in the 15–44-year-old age group in the northeastern United States was 60.0 per 100,000. Forty years later, now that members of that group are largely over age 65, their case rate averages 14.7 per 100,000. In 10 southeastern states where in the 1950s the case rate in the 25–44-year-old age group was 65.4, it has fallen to only 34.6 today. The great difference in the decline in the case rate in these two sections of the country suggests that different factors were operative in the two geographic sections in the ensuing 40 years.

With the decline in incidence of TB in western countries, many physicians see so little TB that they often fail to include it in their considerations. Table 15-1 shows that in 1987–1990 the TB case rate for adults under age 65 years was identical in Arkansas and in the six surrounding states (Missouri, Oklahoma, Texas, Louisiana, Mississippi, and Tennessee). However, the case rate among the elderly in Arkansas is nearly twice that in the surrounding states, which suggests differences in awareness of TB in this age group.

Our experience has shown that, although tuberculin reactors as a group survive longer than nonreactors, they also have a 150-fold greater chance of developing clinical TB than do nonreactors (Fig. 15-2).[21] Thus, when an

TABLE 15-1.   Annual TB Case Rates in Adults in Arkansas versus Six Surrounding States, 1987–1989

Age	Arkansas	Surrounding States*	x^2	p
20–64	909	10.0	0.1	NS
65+	50.8	28.5	160.0	.001

Note: x = chi squared; p = probability; NS = not significant.

*Louisiana, Mississippi, Missouri, Oklahoma, Tennessee, and Texas.

Source: Data from Centers for Disease Control.[24]

elderly person is being examined as a new patient or at the time of admission to a nursing home, it is a good practice to perform a tuberculin skin test to have it on record and to get a chest radiograph for reactors to make sure the disease has not already started. A positive skin test reaction identifies those in whom respiratory symptoms should trigger the submission of one or two sputum samples for tuberculosis culture.

Although the TB case rate is much higher among nursing home residents than among elderly persons as a whole, 80 percent of all TB cases in the

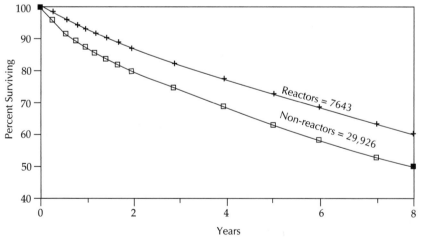

FIGURE 15-2. Survival of nonreactors to tuberculin in comparison with tuberculin-positive nursing home residents. Although nonreactors suffer rapid initial loss due to death, those surviving 6–12 months show their immunocompetence by surviving about as well as tuberculin reactors thereafter. (*Used with permission. From Stead and To.*[21])

elderly arise among the 95 percent living at home, largely due to recrudescence of old infection. The fact that 20 percent of the cases occur among the 5 percent who live in nursing homes as a mixture of old and recently acquired infection means that the case rate among nursing home residents is four times greater than among the elderly living elsewhere.

Only 5–10 percent of elderly persons who fail to react to tuberculin are truly anergic.[21,22] Tuberculin-negative nursing home residents show a high death rate (of 5–10 percent) in the first few months after admission. However, those who survive for 6–12 months in the home are clearly immunocompetent, as shown by the fact that then they survive about as well as those whose immunocompetence is shown by their reaction to tuberculin.[21]

A positive skin test reaction indicates that the individual still harbors viable tubercle bacilli from the past, which are still capable of producing clinical TB. If there is no evidence of TB, the positive skin test reading should be recorded in the medical chart (and posted on the chart cover). This practice should serve to remind the nursing and medical staff of the possibility of TB and to expedite study of sputum for acid-fast bacilli whenever the patient has bronchitis or pneumonia. We suggest that the nursing staff be directed to submit a sputum sample for tuberculosis culture from any tuberculin reactor who develops respiratory symptoms.

Whenever there is suspicion of the spread of TB in a nursing home, all previously nonreactive persons who may have been exposed should be retested with tuberculin. If proper testing of each resident had been recorded at the time of entry, it is easy to identify residents who are newly infected by finding an increase of 15 mm or more of induration over the negative test results obtained at entry.[21] However, without the previous test results, one is left to guess whether a newly found, large reaction signifies a new infection, for which the patient should be given preventive therapy with INH, or simply an old dormant infection, which usually does not need treatment.

Once all converters have been identified, all tuberculin reactors (whether old or conversions) should have chest radiographs to detect evidence of TB. In addition, in an outbreak, all persons with chronic cough should have a chest radiograph in order to detect any individuals with active TB who are too sick to mount a significant reaction to tuberculin.

Transmission of TB to staff members is not as likely as to residents because staff members spend only about one-fourth as much time in the same space as the residents do (40 versus 168 h per week). If members of the staff are tested at the time of employment and annually thereafter, new infections will be detected in ample time for preventive therapy with INH to prevent the development of TB.

The CDC now recommends giving pyrazinamide (PZA) and streptomycin or EMB along with RMP and INH as initial treatment for all persons with TB.

However, this need not be applied routinely to the elderly. Treatment of elderly persons with TB can generally be accomplished with RMP and INH without the addition of other drugs. The reason is that TB in the elderly is almost always the result of recrudescence of an infection acquired before the chemotherapy era. Thus, virtually all initial isolates in this age group are fully susceptible to both drugs. Additional drugs for this group add no advantage and may contribute significantly to undesirable drug interactions in people who are already receiving an average of 8–10 medications. On this point, we differ with the blanket recommendation of the CDC for starting four drugs in all patients with active TB.

REFERENCES

1. Dubos R, Dubos J: *The White Plague.* New Brunswick, NJ, Rutgers University Press, 1952.
2. Centers for Disease Control: National action plan to combat multidrug-resistant tuberculosis. *MMWR* 41:1, 1992.
3. Phillips K: *The Boiling Point: Republicans, Democrats and the Decline of the Middle Class.* New York, Random House, 1993, chapter 1, pp 1–31.
4. American College of Physicians, National Commission on Correctional Health Care, American Correctional Health Service Association: The crisis in correctional health care: the impact of the national drug control strategy on correctional health services. *Ann Intern Med* 117:71, 1992.
5. Centers for Disease Control: Prevention and control of tuberculosis in correctional institutions. *MMWR* 38:18, 1989.
6. Stanford JL, Grange JM, Pozniak A: Is Africa Lost? *Lancet* 2:557, 1991.
7. Stead WW: Genetics and resistance to tuberculosis: could resistance be enhanced by genetic engineering? *Ann Intern Med* 116:937, 1992.
8. Grosset J: Bacteriologic basis of short-course chemotherapy for tuberculosis. *Clin Chest Med* 1:231, 1980.
9. Barnes PF, Bloch AB, Davidson PT, Snider DE Jr: Tuberculosis in patients with human immunodeficiency virus. *N Engl J Med* 324:1644, 1991.
10. Daley CL, Small PM, Schecter GF, Schoolnik GK, McAdam RA, Jacobs WR Jr, et al: An outbreak of tuberculosis with accelerated progression among persons infected with the human immunodeficiency virus: an analysis using restriction-fragment-length polymorphisms. *N Engl J Med* 326:231, 1992.
11. Wallis RS, Vjecha M, Amir-Tahmasseb M, Okwera A, Byekwaso F, Nyole S, Kabengera W, Mugerwa RD, Ellner JJ: Influence of tuberculosis on human immunodeficiency virus (HIV-1)-associated tuberculosis. *J Infect Dis* 167:43, 1993.
12. Pitchenik AE, Burr J, Suarez M, Fertel D, et al: Human T-cell lymphotropic virus-III (HTLV-III) seropositivity and related disease among 71 consecutive patients in whom tuberculosis was diagnosed. *Am Rev Respir Dis* 135:875, 1987.
13. Stead WW: Control of tuberculosis in crowded public places in the HIV/AIDS era: the value and application of germicidal ultraviolet light. *J Prison Health* 12:13, 1993.
14. Davies PDO: A possible link between vitamin D deficiency and impaired host defence to *M. tuberculosis. Tubercle* 66:301, 1985.

15. Curtin PD: *Death by Migration*. Cambridge, Cambridge University Press, 1989, pp 93–94.
16. Ferguson RG: *Studies in Tuberculosis*. Toronto, University of Toronto Press, 1955, p 6.
17. Centers for Disease Control: Nosocomial transmission of multidrug-resistant tuberculosis among HIV-infected persons: Florida and New York, 1988–1991. *MMWR* 40:585, 1991.
18. Glaser JB, Greifinger RB: Correctional health care: a public health opportunity. *Ann Intern Med* 118:139, 1993.
19. Stead WW, Lofgren JP: Medical perspective: does the risk of tuberculosis increase in old age? *J Infect Dis* 147:951, 1983.
20. Stead WW: Why does tuberculosis remain so common among the elderly? *Hosp Pract* September(22):9, 1987.
21. Stead WW, To T: The significance of the tuberculin skin test in elderly persons. *Ann Intern Med* 107:837, 1987.
22. Creditor MC, Smith EC, Gallai JB, et al: Tuberculosis, tuberculin reactivity and delayed cutaneous reactivity in nursing home residents. *J Gerontol* 43:97, 1988.
23. Stead WW, Dutt AK: Tuberculosis in elderly persons. *Ann Rev Med* 42:267, 1991.
24. Dr. George Cauthen, Division of Tuberculosis Elimination, Centers for Disease Control (personal communication).

New Developments for the Diagnosis of Tuberculosis: The Impact of Molecular Biology

JACK T. CRAWFORD

Advances in molecular biology have provided new approaches for the detection and identification of microorganisms. The development of molecular cloning techniques allowed the characterization of DNA segments that could be used in hybridization assays to detect specific organisms, and rapid DNA sequencing methods have facilitated the design of specific probes. Nucleic acid amplification methods that provide the means, at least in theory, for detection of a single organism in a clinical sample represent an alternative to culture and identification of microorganisms. In addition to providing more rapid results, these newer methods are more specific than classical methods based on growth characteristics and biochemical tests. Molecular biology research has also provided cloned genes that can be used to produce antigens for serological assays and the production of monoclonal antibodies. In addition, molecular approaches have also revolutionized epidemiology. Highly specific markers for subtyping of *Mycobacterium tuberculosis* isolates are now available and are being applied to new questions such as the spread of tuberculosis (TB) in HIV-positive individuals and the spread of multidrug-resistant (MDR) strains. The use of probes has already changed the standard for identification of *M. tuberculosis* isolates, and newer methods will certainly be available in the mid- to late 1990s that will revolutionize laboratory diagnosis of TB.

NUCLEIC ACID PROBES

Nucleic acid probe hybridization assays provide rapid and highly specific identification of microorganisms. These assays are most useful for identification of organisms that are difficult or impossible to grow and, therefore, *M.*

255

tuberculosis and other slow-growing mycobacteria are prime candidates for its use. DNA probe assays consist of (1) release of the target nucleic acid from the microorganisms, (2) incubation of the target nucleic acid in the presence of the labeled probe nucleic acid to allow formation of hybrids, (3) elimination of the unhybridized probe, and (4) detection of the label attached to the hybridized probe. These assays require the identification of a target sequence specific for the organism of interest. A number of research laboratories have pursued the goal of identifying *M. tuberculosis*-specific DNA sequences for use in hybridization assays. The first practical application was the (Gen-Probe, Inc., San Diego, CA) culture identification system, which allowed identification of *M. tuberculosis* in a few hours, starting from colonies on solid media. The most distinctive feature of the Gen-Probe assay is the targeting of ribosomal RNA (rRNA) sequences. Most DNA sequences, including the genes that encode rRNA, are present in one or a few copies in the bacterial genome, whereas rRNA is present in high copy numbers (perhaps 1000–2000 ribosomes per *M. tuberculosis* bacterium). This high copy number greatly increases the sensitivity of the assay. In addition, rRNA is single-stranded, allowing in-solution hybridization. For most DNA probe assays, the target nucleic acid is immobilized on a membrane or other solid support and hybridized with a solution containing the labeled probe. Following hybridization, the membrane is washed under carefully controlled conditions to eliminate any free probe. In the Gen-Probe system, both the target rRNA and the labeled DNA probe are in solution. In the original system, the DNA-RNA hybrids were separated from free probe by binding of the hybrid to hydroxyapatite and washing of the hydroxyapatite by repeated centrifugation and resuspension. The probe was labeled with ^{125}I, and hybridization was detected using gamma counting. This method worked fairly well but was somewhat laborious. In addition, the radioactive label posed problems including a short shelf life. These shortcomings have been alleviated with the newer Gen-Probe Accuprobe system, which uses a chemiluminescent label. The probe is labeled with an acridinium ester that emits light in the presence of hydrogen peroxide at alkaline pH. The problem of eliminating unhybridized probe has been dealt with by the development of an elegant chemical selection method termed *hybridization protection.* Addition of a selection reagent and incubation for 5 min destroy the acridinium label in unhybridized single-stranded probe, whereas label in rRNA-probe hybrids is protected. In the final step, the alkali and peroxide are added, and the flash of light is detected in a luminometer with the quantity of light recorded as relative light units. This assay is simple to perform and requires only about 2 h. The application of this assay in the clinical laboratory is discussed in Chapter 3.

HIGH-PERFORMANCE LIQUID CHROMATOGRAPHY OF MYCOLIC ACIDS

An alternative to DNA probe assays for identification of mycobacterial isolates is the use of high-performance liquid chromatography (HPLC) analysis of mycolic acids.[1,2] Although this method is not based on molecular biology, it is a new method being adopted in many large laboratories. Mycolic acids are a major component of the cell wall of mycobacteria. Although mycolic acids are also present in nocardia and corynebacteria, the mycolic acids of mycobacteria are unique in having very long chain lengths (60–90 carbons). There is considerable diversity in the structure of mycolic acids, and the various mycolic acid species can be separated by HPLC to produce patterns that are useful for differentiating mycobacteria.

HPLC has been applied primarily to identification of isolates on solid media but can also be used with liquid cultures, including radiometric (BACTEC; Becton Dickinson, Towson, MD) cultures. The procedure consists of saponification of mycolic acids by heating in alkali, derivatization to bromophenacylesters, separation of mycolic acid species by reverse-phase HPLC, and ultraviolet (UV) detection. The pattern of mycolic acid peaks differs for the various species of mycobacteria. Initial processing of the cultures is performed in batches and requires about 2 h. HPLC analysis is performed sequentially and requires about 10–15 min per sample. *M. tuberculosis* can be recognized easily, but identification of the complete range of mycobacteria requires analysis of the patterns. Computerized pattern recognition software is now available to automate this analysis.

Identical patterns are obtained with *M. tuberculosis* and *Mycobacterium bovis*, and, as is the case with the DNA probe assay, these subspecies cannot be differentiated. However, *M. bovis* bacille Calmette-Guérin (BCG) can be identified. The specificity of identification of *M. tuberculosis* complex isolates is greater than 99.9 percent. The major advantage of using the HPLC method is the fact that a single procedure is used to identify all of the recognized pathogenic species of mycobacteria.

DIRECT SEQUENCING FOR IDENTIFICATION

An interesting alternative to hybridization assays is direct sequencing of polymerase chain reaction (PCR) products.[3] This method has been applied primarily to sequencing of 16S rRNA genes but could also be used with other common genes, such as the 65-kilodalton antigen gene, that are present in all mycobacteria but show species-specific sequence heterogeneity. The procedure consists of amplification with a set of common primers and direct sequencing of the product. This method has been used for identification of isolates but could be used to detect and identify mycobacteria in clinical material. Difficulty would arise if there was more than one species of mycobacteria in the sample. A mixture of PCR products would produce ambiguous results on sequencing, with the predominant product being recognized. As with HPLC, a single procedure is used for all samples, and a result is obtained regardless of the species present. Sequencing can be used to recognize previously unknown strains or species such as *Mycobacterium genavense*.[4] Sequences of 16S rRNA have been used as the basis of phylogenetic schemes. Data from mycobacteria have shown that the 16S sequence is highly conserved in any given species. A discussion of whether differences in 16S sequence alone are sufficient to define a new species is beyond the scope of this chapter, but it is clear that new strains can be recognized reliably. Direct sequencing is not a simple alternative to hybridization assays for rapid detection of *M. tuberculosis* or the more common nontuberculous mycobacteria but does provide a very specific means of identifying the wide range of mycobacteria that are isolated from clinical material.

NUCLEIC ACID AMPLIFICATION METHODS

Overview

DNA probe assays provide rapid identification of isolates, but the number of bacilli present in many clinical samples is below the level of detection. Because of the slow growth of *M. tuberculosis*, long periods of incubation may be required to yield sufficient organisms for detection. Using nucleic acid amplification, the amount of nucleic acid target is increased by in vitro enzymatic methods rather than by growth of the organisms. The first amplification method was PCR, and this method has been used most widely by researchers. Other amplification methods, including transcription-based amplification, strand displacement amplification, and ligase chain reaction, have been adapted for detection of mycobacteria. None of these assays is available at the present time in an approved kit form for routine use in clinical laboratories. However, considering the urgent need for more rapid diagnostic tests for TB and the sensitivity and specificity that amplification assays can provide, it is fairly certain than one or more of these assays will be widely used in the near future.

Polymerase Chain Reaction Assays

The PCR methodology allows detection of even single copies of specific DNA sequences. This fact has not been lost on researchers working with mycobacteria, as evidenced by the steady stream of papers that have appeared in the past several years. Development of a PCR assay can be divided into three parts: (1) identification of a DNA sequence specific for the target organism, design of primers based on that sequence, and determination of optimal conditions (annealing temperatures, extension times, etc.) for amplification; (2) adoption of an assay format for detection of the end product of amplification; and (3) development of a procedure for processing clinical samples to obtain target DNA suitable for amplification.

Targets for PCR

The availability of the λgt11 library of cloned *M. tuberculosis* DNA[5] allowed the isolation and sequencing of a number of specific genes encoding various antigens, and those sequences have provided targets for a number of PCR assays. Genes for rRNA have also been used as targets, relying on the same specificities that make the sequences useful for species-specific probes. Other targets have been identified by screening of recombinant DNA libraries by hybridization to detect segments that are specific for *M. tuberculosis*. Although *M. tuberculosis* is used throughout this discussion, all of the widely studied assays actually detect all members of the *M. tuberculosis* complex including *M. bovis*, *Mycobacterium africanum*, and *Mycobacterium microti*.

There have been two basic types of PCR assays for mycobacteria: assays that amplify only DNA from a particular species, such as *M. tuberculosis*, and assays that amplify a sequence common to most or all mycobacteria. In the latter case, specific probes are used to identify products from different species. These two approaches can be illustrated by assays targeting the gene encoding the 65-kilodalton heat shock protein. This gene has been demonstrated in all mycobacteria tested. The sequences of some segments of the gene are conserved among all mycobacteria, whereas other regions are variable. The first published PCR assay for mycobacteria[6] used primers for conserved regions to produce a 383-base pair (bp) product from all mycobacteria. A labeled oligonucleotide probe for a variable region within this segment was used to specifically identify the product from *M. tuberculosis*. Other probes can be used to identify the products from other species. A variation of this approach is PCR–restriction fragment length polymorphism (RFLP) analysis.[7] In this assay, primers for conserved sequences are used to amplify a large common fragment from all mycobacteria. Digestion of this product with restriction endonucleases yields fragments that provide a species-specific pattern. In contrast, Shinnick et al. used primers for variable regions to produce assays specific for *M. tuberculosis* and *Mycobacterium leprae*. The *M. tuberculosis* assay yields product with *M. tuberculosis* DNA and no product even with a gross excess of *M. leprae* DNA and vice versa.[8] At present there is no consensus as to which approach is best—the decision depends in part on the role that the assay is to play in the clinical laboratory. This topic is discussed below.

Assays targeting the genes encoding rRNA have also been described. Again, such assays allow the amplification of target DNA from any species of mycobacteria using primers for conserved regions followed by identification with specific probes. Such an assay has been described by Roche Molecular Systems (Branchburg, NJ) and is likely to be the basis of their anticipated PCR test for mycobacteria. It is also possible to target the rRNA itself, taking advantage of the high copy number, by using reverse transcriptase to generate the DNA target for the PCR.

Several assays have targeted randomly cloned sequences of unknown function. One such *M. tuberculosis*-specific fragment that has proven to be a useful target has been shown to be an insertion sequence and was designated IS6110.[9,10] One advantage of this target is the fact that it is repeated up to 20 times in most *M. tuberculosis* strains. This increases the sensitivity of detection in comparison to single-copy genes, such as the 65-kilodalton antigen gene. However, a few isolates have been found that lack IS6110.

Published results clearly show that a number of target sequences can be used to develop highly specific PCR assays for *M. tuberculosis* and other mycobacteria. These studies also show that it is possible to develop PCR amplification protocols that allow detection of DNA equivalent to that found in one organism (or less if the target is multicopy), that is, in the range of 1–10 fg.

Assay Format

The next requirement is the development of a simple assay format for detection of the PCR product. Most research work has relied on gel electrophoresis and visualization of PCR products by ethidium bromide staining. This provides an accurate assessment of the size of the product, but sensitivity is limited. To increase sensitivity and specificity, most researchers have blotted the gels and performed hybridization assays. Obviously, this is not the preferred method for a routine test in the clinical laboratory. Commercial kits will probably use a colorimetric or chemiluminescent assay to detect the amplification products in a dot blot or microtiter plate format. A reverse dot blot format, in which the specific oligonucleotides are immobilized in microtiter wells and the PCR product is in solution, will allow simultaneous hybridization against several specific probes (*M. tuberculosis, M. avium, M. kansasii,* etc.) providing detection of several species in a single assay.

Sample Preparation

The most challenging aspect of assay development has been specimen processing. It is generally agreed that the first step in processing of clinical samples for amplification assays will be a standard liquefaction/decontamination procedure. This step eliminates much of the material in the sample that could inhibit amplification and concentrates the bacilli into a small volume. It is also compatible with routine culture methods. Nucleic acid amplification assays require release of target DNA or RNA from the organisms, which in the case of mycobacteria is not a simple task. Published methods for lysis of mycobacteria include enzymatic digestion, treatment with alkali and/or detergents, freeze-thaw, sonication, mechanical lysis by shaking with glass beads, boiling, and various combinations of these techniques. Once the nucleic acid is released, it is desirable to partially purify and concentrate it. Phenol-chloroform extraction and ethanol precipitation, binding to powdered glass, or purification on commercially available minicolumns has been used for this purpose. The merits of various approaches have been debated, but there is no agreement on a method that is simple, rapid, and highly efficient. Simple methods, such as boiling in PCR buffer, work with specimens with large numbers of bacilli. More complex methods involving purification steps provide greater sensitivity but may not be practical as routine methods in clinical laboratories.

Evaluations of PCR

Although most publications describing PCR assays for *M. tuberculosis* have presented some data on clinical samples, only a few substantial studies have been published. Available data indicate that PCR assays have excellent specificity, but sensitivity is not as good as expected. Eisenach et al. reported results of a study using an *M. tuberculosis*-specific assay (based on detection of IS6110) for analysis of 178 sputum samples.[11] The results showed that, for TB patients, all smear-positive samples yielded positive results by PCR. Even strongly smear-positive samples from patients with nontuberculous mycobacterial infections yielded negative results, demonstrating the specificity of the assay. The test samples contained too few smear-negative or culture-positive samples to draw any firm conclusions about the overall sensitivity of the assay. Much larger studies performed in clinical laboratories have demonstrated the excellent specificity of such assays.[12-14] Again, good results were obtained with smear-positive samples with sensitivity relative to culture of >90 percent. Significantly lower sensitivity was obtained with smear-negative samples. Most significantly, these three studies demonstrated that amplification assays can be performed on a routine basis in clinical laboratories. No clinical trials involving commercially developed assays have been published, but one would anticipate that such assays will be more sensitive than those developed by small research laboratories.

Other Amplification Methods

A number of other approaches have been developed for increasing the sensitivity of nucleic acid–based assays.[15] All of the methods require a specific target sequence, and some of the same sequences used in published PCR assays are being adapted to alternative methods. The problems of specimen processing are common to all of the approaches. Only limited data on applications to mycobacteria have been published or presented. A transcription-based amplification assay is being evaluated by Gen-Probe. This assay targets the 16s rRNA and presumably has specificity similar to their current probes tests. The assay uses reverse transcriptase to generate a DNA copy from the rRNA. Amplification is accomplished by an RNA polymerase that produces RNA transcripts. Unlike PCR, this is an isothermal reaction (i.e., no thermal cycler is required). The final RNA product is detected with the well-proven chemiluminescent system currently used for the Accuprobe (Gen-Probe, San Diego, CA) assay.

Strand displacement amplification (SDA) has also been applied to detection of *M. tuberculosis*.[16] Preliminary data indicate that this assay also provides very sensitive detection. Other methods, including ligase chain reaction, cycling probe reaction, and Q*β* replicase amplification have been described. In addition, methods that use amplification of the signal, rather than amplification of the target, have been developed. Each of the various methods has advantages and limitations that affect the sensitivity and specificity of the assays. Many factors, including ease of use, cost, and the time of initial introduction into the market, will determine which of the assays become widely used.

Possible Role of Amplification Assays

It is fairly certain that refinements in methodology will yield amplification assays that are fairly simple and rapid to perform and are thus suitable for general use in the clinical laboratory. The role that such assays will play in the diagnosis of mycobacterial disease is still uncertain. Several types of mycobacterial assays have been proposed, including genus-specific assays for detection of all mycobacteria in the sample and specific assays for *M. tuberculosis*, *M. avium*, *M. kansasii*, and other nontuberculous mycobacterial species. These could be a series of specific assays performed in parallel or in a single tube using a multiplex primer approach, or a single amplification of a conserved fragment followed by differentiation by hybridization assays. Clearly, an assay to detect *M. tuberculosis* is urgently needed. Rapid detection of *M. tuberculosis* in clinical samples would not only assist in the management of patient's care but would have a significant impact on TB control. Because *M. tuberculosis* is not found in the environment and is not carried as a commensal organism, a positive culture result generally is considered diagnostic for TB. Similarly, detection of *M. tuberculosis* in clinical material by nucleic acid amplification would be diagnostic. In both cases, one assumes that there has been no laboratory error or cross-contamination and that the assay, either amplification or culture and identification, is highly specific. Not all clinical samples from patients with TB contain organisms, and therefore neither procedure can provide 100 percent sensitivity, even if multiple specimens are used. Patients who are shedding higher numbers of organisms are much more likely to transmit TB; thus, a rapid-detection assay that was very specific and only moderately sensitive could still have a major impact on control of transmission.

The usefulness of rapid assays for detection of *M. avium* and other nontuberculous mycobacteria is less certain. These infections generally do not progress rapidly and are not considered communicable. Nontuberculous mycobacteria are common in the environment and are sometimes detected repeatedly in respiratory samples from persons who have no evidence of disease. However, rapid detection of mycobacteria, especially *M. avium*, in normally sterile samples, such as blood from AIDS patients, would be advantageous. It is likely that such assays will be developed for the more common mycobacteria as part of a hybridization panel for analysis of common amplification products.

Genus-specific assays are intended to provide a screen for mycobacteria. Samples that are positive for mycobacteria would be tested further for *M. tuberculosis* and perhaps other mycobacterial species. Amplification-negative samples would be discarded; thus, any such assay would need to be at least as sensitive as culture. Because the majority of clinical samples do not contain mycobacteria, this approach would eliminate much of the culture work, helping to offset the expense and time required for performing amplifications. Samples that are positive in the genus-specific assay or in a species-specific assay would probably still be cultured. In the case of *M. tuberculosis*, the isolates are needed for drug susceptibility testing and probably for confirmation of the amplification result. They may also be needed for epidemiologic investigations.

DRUG SUSCEPTIBILITY TESTING

The increasing problem of drug resistance has spurred interest in more rapid methods of susceptibility testing. Two approaches based on recent advances in the molecular biology of mycobacteria have been touted: direct detection of drug resistance at the DNA sequence level and assessment of drug resistance using luciferase reporter mycobacteriophages.

Direct Detection

Detection of drug-resistant bacteria at the molecular level is not a new concept. However, most previous work has concentrated on detection of specific genes that encode enzymes that impart resistance, such as β-lactamases or aminoglycoside transferases. These genes are frequently carried on transposons and may be plasmid-borne. In theory, such genes are not present in sensitive strains, and therefore detection by hybridization assays should indicate a resistant strain. In the case of *M. tuberculosis*, drug resistance is thought to result primarily from modification of the targets of drug action rather than by introduction of genes encoding resistance. At the genetic level, resistance can be accomplished by single base changes that occur spontaneously. Thus, detection of drug resistance will require the identification of the genes involved and determination of the specific mutations that result in the resistance phenotype. Assays to detect these mutations will require determination of the sequence of a specific gene in the test strain, either by actual sequencing or by very specific hybridization reactions that can detect single base changes. The experimental basis for such assays is now being reported.

The clearest application of this approach is resistance to rifampin. It is well-established that rifampin binds to the β subunit of RNA polymerase, and resistance can be imparted by single base changes in the gene (*rpo*B). Analysis of rifampin-resistant mutants of *Escherichia coli* has identified a series of specific mutations that occur in several sites within this gene. The *rpo*B gene of *M. leprae* has been cloned and sequenced, and mutations occurring in rifampin-resistant strains have been determined. This work has been extended to *M. tuberculosis*.[17] The region in which the mutations occur can be amplified using PCR and sequenced to rapidly determine the mutation in any specific strain. Results to date show that many, but not all, rifampin-resistant mutations in *M. tuberculosis* are located in two codons. Development of a simple assay to detect these mutations will be challenging. Amplification and direct sequencing is possible, but this is not a practical method for clinical laboratories. Single base changes can be detected by PCR–single-strand conformation polymorphism (PCR-SSCP) analysis or by hybridization of PCR products from a test strain and a wild-type (rifampin-sensitive) strain and analysis of migration of hybrids in agarose gels (gel retardation assay). These assays demonstrate that a mutation has occurred but do not determine the nature of the change. Hybridization assays using oligonucleotide probes can reliably detect single base changes, and two probes could be used to detect the most common mutations. Regardless of the specific approach, mutations occurring at loci outside the amplified segment would be missed.

Detection of the *rpo*B gene was aided by the known sequence of the gene in other organisms. A similar approach was used to demonstrate that mutations to streptomycin resistance in *M. tuberculosis* reside in a single site in the gene encoding the S12 ribosomal protein. For drugs such as isoniazid, ethambutol, and ethionamide, which are specific for mycobacteria, a genetic approach is required to identify the relevant genes. The first success was achieved in identifying the gene encoding catalase/peroxidase.[18] It was demonstrated that deletion of this gene results in resistance to isoniazid. Presumably, single base substitutions could also result in loss of activity and isoniazid resistance. Because RNA polymerase is an essential enzyme, there is a limited number of possible mutations in *rpo*B that can impart rifampin resistance while retaining enzymatic activity. In contrast, many different mutations could inactivate a nonessential gene such as catalase/peroxidase, and it will be much more difficult to develop a hybridization assay for this gene. While catalase/peroxidase is involved in isoniazid activity, it is not the actual target of the drug, and loss of activity accounts for only a fraction of isoniazid-resistant isolates. The most likely target is an unknown enzyme that is involved in mycolic acid synthesis and thus would probably be essential. Recent evidence suggests that the gene for the target enzyme for isoniazid and ethionamide resistance may have been identified.

While this approach is possible, many problems remain. Clearly, separate assays will be needed for each drug, and it is likely that multiple assays will be required to detect various types of resistance mutations for even a single drug. It will also be necessary to develop new assays for any newly introduced drugs. For the near future, limited application only to isoniazid and rifampin resistance is most probable.

Luciferase Reporter Assay

The most promising approach for rapid drug susceptibility testing is the use of luciferase reporter mycobacteriophages.[19] The assay involves introduction of the firefly luciferase gene into *M. tuberculosis*. To obtain expression, a mycobacterial promoter was inserted upstream of the luciferase gene. Luciferase catalyzes the production of light from luciferin and adenosine triphosphate (ATP), and the light can be detected and quantitated with exquisite sensitivity using a luminometer. Luciferase can be stably cloned into *M. tuberculosis*, but to apply a luciferase assay to new isolates, it was necessary to develop a system for rapidly introducing the gene. Bacteriophages are perfectly suited to perform this function, and recombinant mycobacteriophages that carry the luciferase gene have been constructed. Infection of *M. tuberculosis* by these phages begins with injection of the phage genome carrying the luciferase gene into the cells and leads to expression of luciferase within a few hours. Addition of luciferin to the infected cells results in production of light. Light production requires both expression of the luciferase enzyme and sufficient intracellular ATP. Drugs that inhibit transcription or translation or that indirectly disrupt

Luciferase reporter mycobacteriophage assay

1. Prepare a suspension of the *Mycobacterium tuberculosis* isolate
2. Inoculate into tubes containing the test drugs
3. Incubate cultures 12–72 h
4. Add reporter mycobacteriophage
5. Incubate 2–3 h
6. Add luciferin, measure light production using a luminometer

Interpretation

No light production: susceptible isolate
Light production: drug-resistant isolate

FIGURE 16–1. A suspension of mycobacteria, either directly from a processed clinical sample or from a culture, is dispensed into a series of tubes with media containing the various test drugs. The cultures are incubated to allow the drug to act. Each culture is infected with a high titer suspension of the reporter mycobacteriophage carrying the luciferase gene. After 2–3 h incubation to allow expression of the luciferase gene, luciferase is assayed by addition of luciferin and measurement of light production. If the drug has inhibited or killed the mycobacteria, no light will be produced. If the strain is resistant to the drug, luciferase will be expressed and light will be produced.

metabolism or kill the cells will inhibit light production following phage infection. The proposed assay format is outlined in Fig. 16-1. This approach has two distinct advantages over the nucleic acid probe approach: the assay measures actual drug activity, and the same assay can be applied simultaneously to numerous drugs, including new drugs whose mechanism of action is not known. This assay could theoretically be applied directly to processed clinical samples. If the reporter mycobacteriophage were specific for *M. tuberculosis*, the assay could be used both to detect *M. tuberculosis* and perform drug susceptibility testing.

A modification of this assay can also be used for large-scale screening of new compounds for activity against test strains of mycobacteria. Such an assay using a strain that stably expresses luciferase from a recombinant plasmid rather than a reporter mycobacteriophage has been reported.[20]

SEROLOGICAL DIAGNOSIS, SKIN TESTING, AND RECOMBINANT ANTIGENS

In addition to providing the means for producing large quantities of specific nucleic acids, molecular cloning techniques allow the expression of foreign genes in *E. coli* or other systems and the production of specific proteins. Large-scale production of mycobacterial proteins using recombinant techniques should facilitate the development of assays to detect specific antibodies in the sera of patients and the production of specific antibodies, including monoclonals, to detect mycobacterial antigens in clinical material. The production of purified proteins could also assist in the development of more specific skin testing reagents.

Screening of the original λgt11 library of *M. tuberculosis* DNA using sera from patients with TB allowed the identification of a number of genes encoding antigens. Most of these antigens were produced as fusion proteins consisting of a portion of the mycobacterial protein fused to the *E. coli* β-galactosidase and expressed from the β-galactosidase promoter. Introduction of mycobacterial DNA into other vectors allows the expression of the complete mycobacterial proteins. However, these proteins may not have precisely the structure of the native protein present in the mycobacteria, in some cases because of lack of posttranslational modification. It is not possible to produce glycoproteins, lipoproteins, or the complex mycobacterial lipid and carbohydrate antigens by expression of mycobacterial genes in *E. coli*. Recent advances allow cloning and expression of mycobacterial genes in mycobacteria, which may permit the large-scale production of such material, but it is not clear that there is any advantage in this approach over simply preparing the proteins or antigens from the original mycobacteria. Despite considerable success in molecular characterization of mycobacterial products, no real breakthroughs in diagnosis are apparent.

DNA FINGERPRINTING

Fingerprinting Methods

Investigations of the epidemiology of TB have been hindered by the lack of a reliable method of subtyping isolates to identify the spread of specific strains. *M. tuberculosis* isolates cannot be distinguished by routine biochemical tests or serological methods. Drug resistance provides a reproducible marker in some outbreak situations, but fortunately this marker is not generally usable. Until recently, the only available typing method was phage typing.[21] Theoretically, the phage typing scheme provides a sufficient number of types to allow reasonable differentiation of isolates. In practice, many isolates fall into a few major types, and frequently the method does not provide the required specificity.

DNA fingerprinting methods have provided highly specific markers for typing isolates. These methods are based on the use of restriction endonucleases, which recognize specific sequences and cleave DNA into fragments of varying length. Sequence heterogeneity will yield variations in these fragments, giving rise to the term *restriction fragment length polymorphism* (RFLP). Hundreds of fragments are produced when mycobacterial DNA is digested with most restriction enzymes that recognize six base sequences, and these fragments do not produce clear patterns when electrophoresed on agarose gels. Good results have been obtained using enzymes that cut infrequently and produce smaller numbers of large fragments.[22] Mycobacterial DNA has a high guanine plus cytosine content (about 65 percent), and enzymes with recognition sequences containing adenine and thymine residues are suitable. Pulsed field or field inversion electrophoresis methods are used to resolve the large fragments (mostly >50 kilobases) produced by these enzymes. This method provides specific patterns but is technically challenging.

Standard RFLP analysis involves detection of specific restriction fragments by hybridization of southern blots using labeled DNA probes. Heterogeneity in the length of the restriction fragments usually results from point mutations that create or eliminate restriction sites, or from deletions or rearrangements in the chromosome. Analysis of the sequence of a number of genes from *M. tuberculosis* and *M. bovis* shows a high degree of conservation, and no single copy gene or random fragment has demonstrated the degree of polymorphism needed for a useful typing system. Probing restriction digests with insertion elements or other repetitive sequences has proven to be a very useful method of typing of isolates. The most widely used system is based on probing with the insertion element IS6110, which is present only in isolates of the *M. tuberculosis* complex.[23,24] The copy number of IS6110 is high, 7–20, in most isolates of *M. tuberculosis*; low, 1–4, in most isolates of *M. bovis* from animals, and 1 or 2 in the various strains of *M. bovis* bacille Calmette-Guérin (BCG). Recent studies indicate that occasionally isolates of *M. tuberculosis* do not contain IS6110.

Heterogeneity in the fingerprint patterns reflects the differences in copy number and sites of insertion in the chromosome due to duplication or movement of the element. Results to date indicate that the number of patterns is very large, and, because IS6110 is an active insertion element, the number is continuously increasing. Small sets of random isolates (<50) from a given community will probably all have unique fingerprint patterns; thus, outbreak-associated isolates can easily be identified (Fig. 16-2). However, there has not been a sufficiently large study to define the approximate number of patterns in any geographic region.

Analysis of isolates from outbreaks that have spanned several years indicates that the IS6110 fingerprint is quite stable, with changes only occasionally in one or two bands. This observation, combined with the diversity of patterns obtained with random isolates and the presence of IS6110 in isolates from around the world, indicates that the insertion element has been present in the

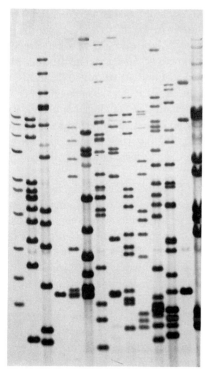

FIGURE 16-2. DNA fingerprint patterns for 13 random isolates of *M. tuberculosis*. These patterns reflect the vast diversity seen in epidemiologically unrelated isolates in contrast to the identity seen in isolates from outbreaks.

M. tuberculosis complex for a long period of time, apparently before divergence of the human and bovine subspecies.

Applications of Fingerprinting

The primary application of DNA fingerprinting of *M. tuberculosis* isolates has been the tracing of outbreaks. Hermans et al.[25] described an outbreak of TB resulting from injection of a contaminated drug preparation. This paper demonstrated the usefulness of fingerprinting for supporting an epidemiologic investigation and showed that fingerprinting could be used to identify epidemiologically related isolates in large sets of isolates.

Fingerprinting has proven valuable in tracing the spread of MDR strains. Several studies have described nosocomial transmission of MDR strains among HIV-positive individuals, with fingerprinting supporting the epidemiologic investigations.[26-28] In each of these studies, one or two outbreak strains was identified, and all control isolates were distinct. A larger and continuing outbreak involves a strain resistant to at least six drugs: isoniazid, rifampin, streptomycin, ethambutol, ethionamide, and kanamycin. To date, >150 isolates of this strain from patients in several institutions over an extended period of time have been fingerprinted. With few exceptions, all of the isolates gave an identical fingerprint pattern. The exceptions have one or two additional bands. The insertion element IS6110 does not encode drug resistance, and the fingerprint pattern has no direct relationship to drug resistance. However, in outbreaks such as these, the fingerprint type may serve as a marker for specific strains and predict the drug resistance pattern in new isolates with the same fingerprint.

In the outbreaks of MDR TB, the drug resistance patterns indicated an epidemiologic link among the outbreak strains; fingerprinting provided the final proof. The fingerprinting method is even more valuable in supporting investigations of drug-sensitive isolates where it is the only laboratory evidence for strain relatedness. This was illustrated in an outbreak involving transmission of TB in a communal living environment.[29] Another example was an investigation of apparent nosocomial transmission among renal transplant patients.[30] Initially, a simple chain of transmission was plotted based on known contact between the series of patients. Fingerprinting of the isolates showed that only some of the patients had a common strain. The source of the outbreak was shown to be a chance exposure of one of the renal transplant recipients to a patient with TB at a second hospital.

Larger-scale application of this method to all isolates in a given geographic area may reveal common strains and identify previously unsuspected sources of transmission. It has yet to be determined whether this approach is practical and could assist in control of community-acquired TB. It is certain that the laboratory analysis of isolates will be much easier than the investigation required to track all leads provided by fingerprinting.

Another application of fingerprinting is the confirmation of suspected cross-contamination of cultures and other laboratory errors. Culture of *M. tuberculosis* is considered definitive for a diagnosis of TB, but occasionally clinical findings indicate that the diagnosis is incorrect. If the suspect isolate has a fingerprint identical to that of another, apparently epidemiologically unrelated isolate processed in the laboratory at the same time, cross-contamination is a distinct possibility, as was demonstrated in a recent publication.[31]

PCR-Based Fingerprinting

One problem with the standard method of fingerprinting is the requirement for extraction of about 1 μg of DNA from each isolate. Two PCR-based methods of fingerprinting *M. tuberculosis* have been developed recently.[32,33]

One method, called ampliprinting, uses a primer specific for IS6110 in conjunction with a primer specific for a polymorphic tandem repeat that occurs numerous times in the genome. The second method, mixed-linker PCR, starts with restriction digestion and ligation of a linker to the ends of the fragments. The amplification reaction uses one primer specific for IS6110 and a second specific for the added linker sequence. This method generates a complete fingerprint compatible with the standard method. Only very small amounts of crude input DNA are required for these assays. Because of this, fingerprinting can be performed from single colonies and old nonviable cultures and probably with clinical specimens that are strongly smear-positive.

REFERENCES

1. Butler WR, Kilburn JO: Identification of major slowly growing pathogenic mycobacteria and *Mycobacterium gordonae* by high-performance liquid chromatography of their mycolic acids. *J Clin Microbiol* 26:50, 1988.
2. Butler WR, Jost KC, Kilburn JO: Identification of mycobacteria by high-performance liquid chromatography. *J Clin Microbiol* 29:2468, 1991.
3. Rogall T, Flohr T, Bottger EC: Differentiation of *Mycobacterium* species by direct sequencing of amplified DNA. *J Gen Microbiol* 136:1915, 1990.
4. Coyle MB, Carlson LDC, Wallis CK, Leonard RB, Raisys VA, Kilburn JO, Samadpour M, Bottger EC: Laboratory aspects of "*Mycobacterium genavense*," a proposed species isolated from AIDS patients. *J Clin Microbiol* 30:3206, 1992.
5. Young RA, Bloom BR, Grosskinsky CM, Ivanyi J, Thomas D, Davis RW: Dissection of *Mycobacterium tuberculosis* antigens using recombinant DNA. *Proc Natl Acad Sci U S A* 82:2583, 1985.
6. Hance AJ, Grandchamp B, Levy-Frebault V, Lecossier D, Rauzier J, Bocart D, Gicquel B: Detection of and identification of mycobacteria by amplification of mycobacterial DNA. *Mol Microbiol* 3:843, 1989.
7. Plikaytis BB, Plikaytis BD, Yakrus MA, Butler WR, Woodley CL, Silcox VA, Shinnick TM: Differentiation of slowly growing *Mycobacterium* species, including *Mycobacterium tuberculosis*, by gene amplification and restriction fragment length polymorphism analysis. *J Clin Microbiol* 30:1815, 1992.
8. Plikaytis BB, Gelber RH, Shinnick TM: Rapid and sensitive detection of *Mycobacterium leprae* using a nested-primer amplification assay. *J Clin Microbiol* 28:1913, 1990.
9. Eisenach KD, Cave MD, Bates JH, Crawford JT: Polymerase chain reaction amplification of a repetitive DNA sequence specific for *Mycobacterium tuberculosis*. *J Infect Dis* 161:977, 1990.
10. Thierry D, Cave MD, Eisenach KD, Crawford JT, Bates JH, Gicquel B, Guesdon JL: IS6110, an IS-like element of *Mycobacterium tuberculosis* complex. *Nucleic Acids Res* 18:188, 1990.
11. Eisenach KD, Sifford MD, Cave MD, Bates JH, Crawford JT: Detection of *Mycobacterium tuberculosis* in sputum samples using a polymerase chain reaction. *Am Rev Respir Dis* 144:1160, 1991.
12. Forbes BA, Hicks KES: Direct detection of *Mycobacterium tuberculosis* in respiratory specimens in a clinical laboratory by polymerase chain reaction. *J Clin Microbiol* 31:1688, 1993.

13. Nolte FS, Metchock B, McGowan JE Jr, Edwards A, Okwumabua O, Thurmond C, Mitchell PS, Plikaytis B, Shinnick T: Direct detection of *Mycobacterium tuberculosis* in sputum by polymerase chain reaction and DNA hybridization. *J Clin Microbiol* 31:1777, 1993.
14. Clarridge JE III, Shawar RM, Shinnick TM, Plikaytis BB: Large-scale use of polymerase chain reaction for detection of *Mycobacterium tuberculosis* in a routine mycobacteriology laboratory. *J Clin Microbiol* 31:2049, 1993.
15. Wolcott MJ: Advances in nucleic acid-based detection methods. *Clin Microbiol Rev* 5:370, 1992.
16. Walker GT, Frasier MS, Schram JL, Little MC, Nadeay JG, Malinowski DP: Strand displacement amplification: an isothermal, in vitro DNA amplification technique. *Nucleic Acids Res* 20:1691, 1992.
17. Telenti A, Imboden P, Marchesi F, Lowrie D, Cole S, Colston MJ, Matter L, Schopfer K, Bodmer T: Detection of rifampicin-resistance mutations in *Mycobacterium tuberculosis*. *Lancet* 341:647, 1993.
18. Zhang Y, Heym B, Allen B, Young D, Cole S: The catalase-peroxidase gene and isoniazid resistance of *Mycobacterium tuberculosis*. *Nature* 358:591, 1992.
19. Jacobs WR Jr, Barletta RG, Udani R, Chan J, Kalkut G, Sosne G, Kieser T, Sarkis G, Hatfull GF, Bloom BR: Rapid assessment of drug susceptibility of *Mycobacterium tuberculosis* by means of luciferase reporter phages. *Science* 260:819, 1993.
20. Cooksey RC, Crawford JT, Jacobs WR Jr, Shinnick TM: A rapid method for screening antimicrobial agents for activity against a strain of *Mycobacterium tuberculosis* expressing firefly luciferase. *Antimicrob Agents Chemother* 37:1348, 1993.
21. Crawford JT, Bates JH: Phage typing of mycobacteria, in Kubica GP, Wayne LW (eds), *The Mycobacteria: A Sourcebook*, part A. New York, Dekker, 1984, pp 123–132.
22. Zhang Y, Mazurek GH, Cave MD, Eisenach KD, Pang Y, Murphy DT, Wallace RJ: DNA polymorphisms in strains of *Mycobacterium tuberculosis* analyzed by pulse-field gel electrophoresis: a tool for epidemiology. *J Clin Microbiol* 30:1551, 1992.
23. Cave MD, Eisenach KD, McDermott PF, Bates JH, Crawford JT: IS6110: conservation of sequence in the *Mycobacterium tuberculosis* complex and its utilization in DNA fingerprinting. *Mol Cell Probes* 5:73, 1991.
24. van Embden JDA, Cave MD, Crawford JT, Dale JW, Eisenach KD, Gicquel B, Hermans P, McAdam R, Shinnick TM, Small PM: Strain identification of *Mycobacterium tuberculosis* by DNA fingerprinting: recommendations for a standardized methodology. *J Clin Microbiol* 31:406, 1993.
25. Hermans PWM, Van Soolingen D, Dale JW, Schuitema AR, McAdam RA, Catty D, van Embden JDA: Insertion element IS986 from *Mycobacterium tuberculosis*: a useful tool for diagnosis and epidemiology of tuberculosis. *J Clin Microbiol* 28:2051, 1990.
26. Edlin BR, Tokars JI, Grieco MH, Crawford JT, Williams J, Sordillo EM, Ong KR, Kilburn JO, Dooley SW, Castro KG, Jarvis WR, Holmberg SD: An outbreak of multidrug-resistant tuberculosis among hospitalized patients with the acquired immunodeficiency syndrome. *N Engl J Med* 326:1514, 1992.
27. Beck-Sague C, Dooley SW, Hutton MD, Otten J, Breeden A, Crawford JT, Pitchenik AE, Cleary T, Woodley C, Cauthen G, Jarvis WR: Hospital outbreak of multidrug-resistant *Mycobacterium tuberculosis* infections: factors in transmission to staff and HIV-infected patients. *J Am Med Assoc* 268:1280, 1992.
28. Pearson ML, Jereb JA, Frieden TR, Crawford JT, Davis BJ, Dooley SW, Jarvis WR: Nosocomial transmission of multidrug-resistant *Mycobacterium tuberculosis*: a risk to patients and healthcare workers. *Ann Intern Med* 117:191, 1992.
29. Daley CL, Small PM, Schecter GF, Schoolnik GK, McAdam RA, Jacobs WR Jr, Hopewell PC: An outbreak of tuberculosis with accelerated progression among persons infected with

the human immunodeficiency virus: an analysis using restricion fragment length polymorphisms. *N Engl J Med* 326:231, 1992.

30. Jereb JA, Berwin DR, Dooley SW, Haas WH, Crawford JT, Geiter LJ, Edmund MB, Dowling JN, Shapiro R, Pasculle AW, Shanahan S, Jarvis WR: Nosocomial outbreak of tuberculosis on a renal transplant unit: application of a new technique for restriction fragment length polymorphism analysis of *Mycobacterium tuberculosis* isolates. *J Infect Dis* 168:1219–1224, 1993.

31. Small PM, McClenny NB, Singh SP, Schoolnik GK, Tompkins LS, Mickelsen PA: Molecular strain typing of *Mycobacterium tuberculosis* to confirm cross-contamination in the mycobacteriology laboratory and modification of procedures to minimize occurrence of false-positive cultures. *J Clin Microbiol* 31:1677, 1993.

32. Plikaytis BB, Crawford JT, Woodley CL, Butler WR, Eisenach KD, Cave MD, Shinnick TM: Rapid, amplification-based fingerprinting of *Mycobacterium tuberculosis*. *J Gen Microbiol* 139:1537, 1993.

33. Haas WH, Butler WR, Woodley CL, Crawford JT: Mixed-linker PCR: a new method for rapid fingerprinting of *Mycobacterium tuberculosis* isolates. *J Clin Microbiol* 31:1293, 1993.

CHAPTER 17

Expanding Options for the Radiographic Evaluation of Tuberculosis

WALLACE T. MILLER

Following the discovery of x-rays by Roentgen in 1895, the radiographic image rapidly emerged as a primary tool in the diagnosis of tuberculosis (TB).[1] In particular, the chest radiograph became the major instrument for diagnosing pulmonary TB, a position it maintains to this day.[2] Recent decades have seen an explosion of alternative imaging methods in the investigation of various disease processes. In particular, computed tomography (CT) and magnetic resonance imaging (MRI) are widely used and invaluable modalities. Sonography and angiography have also proven to be major sources of diagnostic information in various diseases. In TB, the primary supplemental imaging modality beyond the plain film is CT,[3] although MRI plays a role in certain extrapulmonary manifestations of TB.[4,5]

THE CHEST RADIOGRAPH

The chest radiograph remains the most widely used and most valuable tool in the diagnosis of TB. Radiographic findings accurately reflect the pathologic process that occurs in the development of primary and reactivation TB.

Primary TB has traditionally been a disease of infants and children.[6,7] Since the patients are often asymptomatic or mildly symptomatic, they may never be investigated radiographically. However, if a chest radiograph is made, it will generally show lobar consolidation in a lower lobe, with or without associated hilar or mediastinal adenopathy.[2] In the presence of normal T-cell immunity, this process is arrested, and the pulmonary infiltrate regresses slowly, perhaps leaving a noncalcified nodule initially, which may subsequently become calcified, or perhaps disappearing completely.[8,9] The mediastinal nodes may regress completely or also may become calcified. In the

275

absence of a normal immunologic response, primary TB may be followed by hematogenous dissemination, and progressive primary TB or even miliary TB may develop in a patient with a very poor immune response.[12,13]

In most patients, if hematogenous dissemination occurs, the focal areas of disseminated organisms are walled off by the immune system and remain dormant at the site of dissemination (lung apexes, renal cortex, long bone metaphyses, or brain cortex).

The traditional appearance of reactivation TB in the chest is a focal infiltrate and/or cavity in the apical or posterior segment of an upper lobe or perhaps in the superior segment of a lower lobe (Figs. 17-1, 17-2, and 17-3).[2]

While these traditional concepts of TB are still valid, a significant change in the pattern of pulmonary TB has occurred in the past 30 years, with a much greater incidence of primary TB in adults. This change was first pointed out in 1977 and 1978 in two separate papers that noted a high incidence of nontraditional radiographic findings in adults with TB.[10,11] These nontraditional findings reflected primarily the increasing occurrence of primary TB in adults. This occurred due to a change in the demography of TB, with most patients in the United States not having been exposed to TB as children.[7] Subsequent

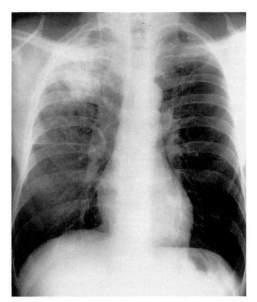

FIGURE 17-1. Right upper lobe TB. A patchy infiltrate can be seen in the right upper lobe of this 52-year-old man. The distribution is consistent with reactivation TB. However, the lack of cavitation suggests that this may be primary TB involving an upper lobe.

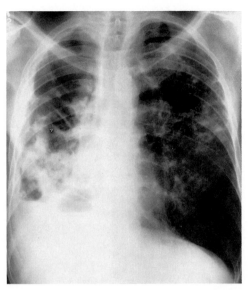

FIGURE 17-2. Tuberculosis and cancer. The right lung of this 46-year-old man is essentially destroyed by TB, with a very large cavity in the right upper lobe and multiple cavities in the right lower lobe. Typical bronchogenic spread can be seen to the left lung, with patchy nodules in the left mid-lung field with some cavitation. All of these findings are consistent with TB alone. However, bronchoscopy revealed a primary carcinoma of the lung in the right middle lobe bronchus. It is not unusual for TB and malignancy to coexist.

papers have confirmed these findings,[12,13] with one exception.[14] Table 17-1 shows the frequency of various findings in these radiographic series.

Primary TB in adults can occur in any lobe of the lung (Fig. 17-1). However, more commonly these infiltrates occur in the lower lobe. In a study of adult primary TB by Choyke et al.,[13] 85 percent of patients had pulmonary infiltrates, with 54 percent occurring in the lower lobes. This finding suggests that a chronic infiltrate in any area of the lung is potentially a manifestation of TB.

Pleural effusion is another common manifestation of primary TB,[10-13] although it can also occur as a manifestation of reactivation TB.[15] Pleural effusion is, of course, a nonspecific finding, but a chronic pleural effusion in an adult is potentially tuberculous. Mediastinal adenopathy is the final member of the triumvirate of common findings in primary TB in adults (Fig. 17-4).[10-13] Four to 13 percent of patients with TB have lymphadenopathy, and these patients probably all have primary TB. This may be associated with pulmonary consolidation but is frequently an isolated finding (mediastinal adenopathy is a particularly common finding in those patients with AIDS and TB).[2,16]

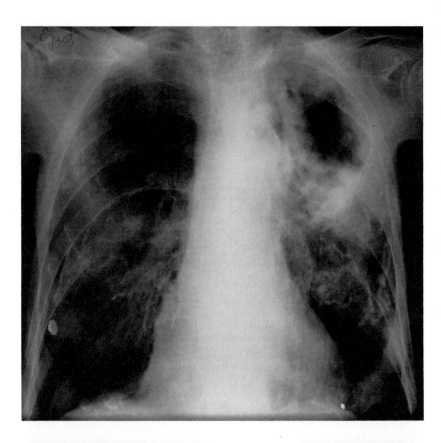

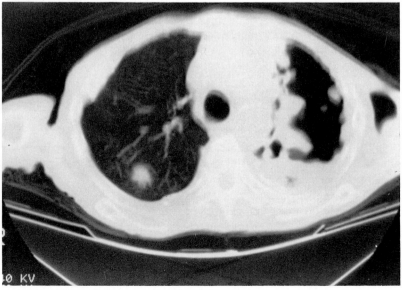

Miliary TB occurred in 1 – 7 percent of various reported series of patients with pulmonary TB. This is probably a manifestation of primary TB in most instances (Fig. 17-5).[2,13]

In most of the recent series on TB, 1 – 2 percent of patients demonstrated a normal finding on chest radiograph even in retrospect.[10-13] These patients all had positive sputum culture results for *Mycobacterium tuberculosis*. Thus, active pulmonary TB can occur with a normal-appearing chest radiograph.

Typical reactivation TB is still the most common manifestation of adult TB, although 20 – 35 percent of most recent series presented with radiographic findings more typical of primary TB.[10-14] Reactivation TB is usually manifested by a chronic infiltration in an upper lobe (Fig. 17-1).[10-14] Cavitation, the second most common manifestation of reactivation TB, occurs in approximately 40 percent of patients with reactivation TB (Figs. 17-2 and 17-3).[10-14] The diagnosis of TB can usually be strongly suspected in the presence of cavitary disease, particularly if it is associated with bronchogenic spread to other parts of the lung, a finding that occurred more than 15 percent of the time in several series (Fig. 17-3).[11,12,14] In a CT study from Japan,[3] bronchogenic spread was present in 98 percent of cases. Such tuberculous infiltrates and cavities may be very minimal or very extensive.

No particular characteristics of cavitary disease can be said to be typical of TB. Cavities can be thin-walled or thick-walled, with or without air fluid levels, and associated with little or extensive exudative reaction.[17,18]

Tuberculosis frequently heals, with a residual fibronodular scar. It is impossible to be certain that active TB is absent in the presence of what appears to be an old scar.[19] If a tuberculous infiltrate is stable for 6 months, it is much less likely to be shedding organisms, but even radiographically stable lesions can sometimes be associated with positive sputum culture results (Fig. 17-6).[11]

Several series have reported a pulmonary mass as an occasional manifestation of TB.[11,12] In two series, this occurred in 5 and 7 percent of all of the cases of TB, respectively. These masses often occur in an upper lobe but may also occur in the middle and lower lobes, where one is less likely to consider

FIGURE 17-3. Tuberculosis and asbestos exposure. *A.* This 77-year-old man has a cavitary mass in the left upper lobe and extensive pleural calcification from asbestos exposure. The left upper lobe mass was thought to be a primary carcinoma of the lung. *B.* A CT scan shows the large irregular cavity in the left upper lobe as well as a patchy nodular infiltrate in the right upper lobe, which was unsuspected on the plain radiograph. The multiplicity of areas of involvement suggests an infectious process. This proved to be TB.

TABLE 17-1. Incidence of Chest Radiographic Findings in Various Series

	Reactivation				Primary						
	Percent Total	Cavitation	Bronchogenic Spread	Mass	Percent Total	Normal	Consolidation Lower Lobe	Atelectasis	Pleural Effusion	Adenopathy	Miliary
Khan[10]	66				34	—	11/7	—	7	—	5
Miller[11]	70	30	16	7	30	3	94	2	7	4	7
Woodring[12]	77	35	16	5	23	3	12/7	4	6	13	1
Hadlock[14]	98	44	17		2	2/270	1	—	1	1	1
Choyke[13]	0				100	10	85/54	—	29	10	6

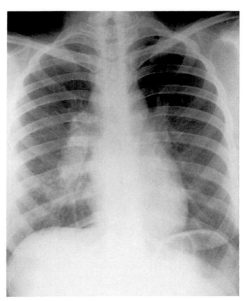

FIGURE 17-4. Primary TB presenting as adenopathy. A 31-year-old woman presented with right hilar and mediastinal adenopathy. Sarcoid was suspected, but primary TB was proven.

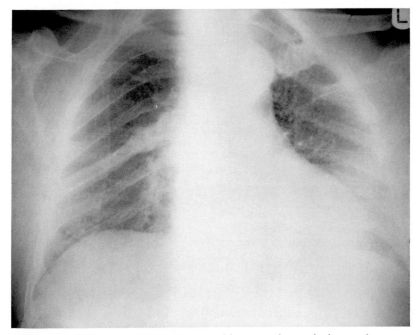

FIGURE 17-5. Miliary TB. In this 60-year-old man with weight loss, a fine nodular pattern can be seen throughout the lung. This proved to be miliary TB. Incidentally noted is Paget's disease of the right sixth rib.

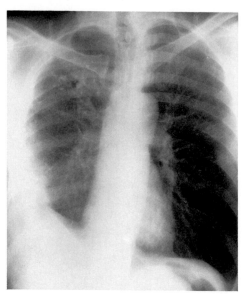

FIGURE 17-6. Active TB in the presence of radiographically stable disease. The chest radiograph of this 51-year-old man was completely unchanged from a study done 2 years previously. Tubercle bacilli were cultured from the lung (fibrocalcific right upper lung infiltrate) and from pleural fluid (loculated right pleural effusion). Thus, radiographic stability does not exclude activity.

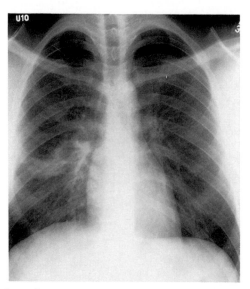

FIGURE 17-7. Tuberculosis as a cavitary right middle lobe mass. A 50-year-old alcoholic man presented with cough and weight loss. A cavitary masslike lesion is seen in the right middle lobe. Primary carcinoma of the lung was suspected, but the lesion proved to be TB.

the possibility of TB (Fig. 17-7). In the presence of such a mass, the usual diagnosis is (and should be) primary carcinoma of the lung. Nonetheless, one must be aware that TB can sometimes present in this fashion. It may be possible to save a patient from thoracotomy by identifying TB organisms in smear or biopsy.

In addition to mimicking lung cancer, TB is also associated with cancer. Because cancer impairs host T-cell response, reactivation TB may be induced by the presence of malignancies. Thus, one must be careful not to completely abandon the possibility of malignancy in the presence of a positive sputum culture result for TB (Fig. 17-2), particularly if the radiographic picture is not totally compatible with TB alone.

In those patients with AIDS and TB, TB may present in a typical fashion, with cavitary upper lobe disease, but frequently presents as a chronic, localized, very extensive pulmonary infiltration (Fig. 17-8) or as mediastinal adenopathy alone.[16] Miliary TB may also occur in the AIDS population.[16]

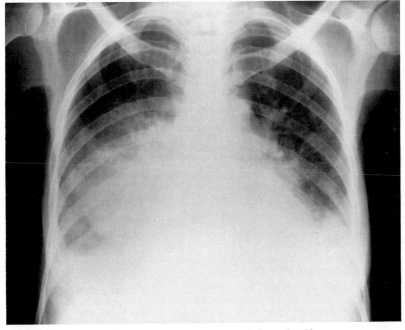

FIGURE 17-8. Tuberculosis and AIDS. Extensive bilateral infiltrates are present in this 35-year-old woman with AIDS. This pattern is relatively common for TB in the AIDS population.

CT IN PULMONARY TB

Computed tomography has a small but important role in the diagnosis of pulmonary TB.[3,20] It may show cavitary disease in the lung where a cavity was not suspected on plain film (Fig. 17-9). CT may also show multifocal disease in the lungs where only localized disease was identified by plain film

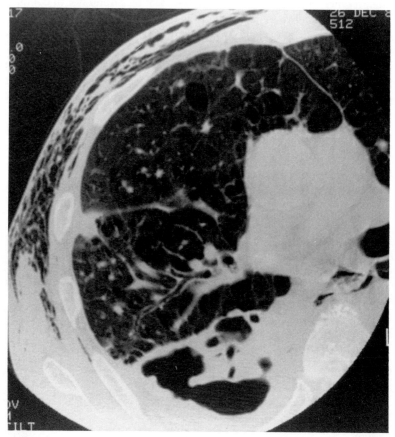

FIGURE 17-9. Pleural TB and bronchopleural fistula demonstrated by CT scan. This 60-year-old man had cough and fever. Pleural thickening was recognized on a plain radiograph of the right chest, but air in the pleural space was not appreciated. The CT scan shows a loculated collection of pleural fluid posteriorly in the right chest with air within it, indicating a bronchopleural fistula. There are also consolidation in the lung immediately anterior to the loculated pleural collection and some patchy nodules in the remainder of the lung, which probably represent tuberculous infection. *M. tuberculosis* was smeared from the lung and pleural fluid.

(Fig. 17-3*B*). This should change one's index of suspicion from tumor to inflammatory disease. CT will clearly document the extent of tuberculous involvement with greater accuracy than plain chest film. Identification of central lobular, branching, acinonodose findings on CT suggest activity in cases where plain radiographic findings will be labeled TB of indeterminate activity.[3] CT is also useful in distinguishing pleural thickening and loculated pleural effusion. Viable tuberculous organisms may be found in chronic loculated effusions (Fig. 17-6).[21]

Magnetic resonance imaging has little or no role in pulmonary TB. Computerized tomography has much better resolution than does MRI. The ability of MRI to characterize invasion of the mediastinal vessels and chest wall, which is important in imaging tumors, is not important in TB. Currently, MRI tissue characterization does not allow separation of tumor from TB or other infections.

EXTRAPULMONARY TB

The Skeleton

Skeletal TB represents approximately 3 percent of all cases of TB and about 30 percent of all cases of TB in extrapulmonary locations.[1] The most common site of skeletal involvement is the spine, with the hip and the knee the next most commonly involved areas. However skeletal TB can occur in any bone or joint.[22]

The plain film remains the primary source of identification of skeletal TB. However, CT and MRI can be extremely useful in identifying the extent of the disease, particularly of soft tissue extension of a bony focus (Fig. 17-10). Both CT and MRI may identify disease in a symptomatic patient where the plain film is normal.[5] This is particularly true in joint TB. Nuclear medicine imaging may also be useful in this regard.[22] The findings at CT and MRI are nonspecific, in that they do not specifically indicate TB as the causative organism. However, CT and MRI images will strongly suggest infection, rather than a tumor, as a cause for a destructive lesion, which is sometimes a consideration (Fig. 17-11).

Genitourinary TB

The primary organ involved in genitourinary TB is the kidney, which is infected by hematogenous dissemination from a primary source, usually in the lung.[23] Renal TB is also a manifestation of reactivation TB in most instances. Involvement of the ureters and bladder may occur secondary to renal involvement. The primary imaging technique in renal TB is the urogram, which may show calcification in the kidney and frequently shows atrophy of portions of

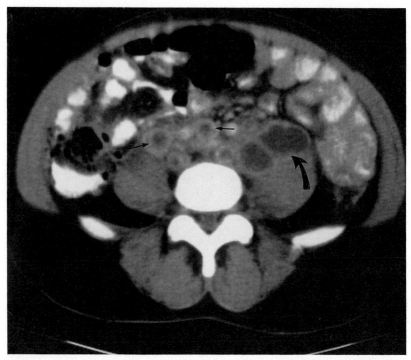

FIGURE 17-10. CT scan demonstrating paraspinal abscess in TB. A destructive lesion was identified in a vertebral body on plain radiographs, and tumor was suspected. CT examination of the abdomen shows a paraspinal abscess (large arrow) and multiple low-density nodes (small arrow), which are characteristic of TB.

the kidney, with associated strictures in the pelvocalyceal system or ureters. Involvement of the bladder usually results in a small, shrunken bladder.[23]

Sonography can be useful in the identification of renal TB by showing obstruction of all or part of a collecting system. CT is quite useful in characterizing the renal involvement of TB. The use of MRI in urinary tract TB is anecdotal.[23]

Central Nervous System TB

While the plain film is the major imaging technique for identifying TB throughout most of the body, it has no role in TB of the central nervous

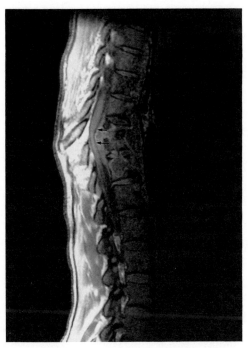

FIGURE 17-11. MRI of spinal TB. An MRI examination shows destruction of three adjacent vertebral bodies and their interspaces with a soft tissue mass extending posteriorly and compressing the cord (arrows). These findings strongly indicate infection involving the spine and are consistent with TB.

system. CT and MRI have revolutionized our ability to identify and characterize central nervous system disease.[4] Tuberculosis has a varied appearance in the central nervous system. It may involve the brain parenchyma, the ventricular system, or the leptomeninges. Meningeal TB, common in infants and small children, can be a manifestation of miliary TB but also may appear as the sole manifestation of hematogenously disseminated TB.[4] The meninges at the base of the brain are primarily involved, frequently leading to hydrocephalus (Fig. 17-12). Tuberculous abscesses may also occur in the brain and may be indistinguishable from pyogenic abscesses or from metastatic tumor.[4] Calcified granulomas or meningeal calcification and hydrocephalus may occur as late sequelae of TB.

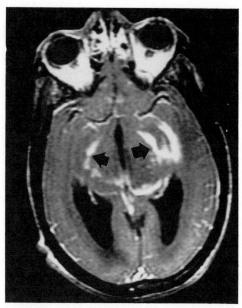

FIGURE 17-12. Meningeal TB. A proton-weighted gallium-enhanced image of the brain shows marked enhancement of the basilar cisterns (arrows) and dilatation of the occipital horns of the ventricular system. These findings are characteristic of meningeal TB.

REFERENCES

1. Williams FH: *The Roentgen Rays in Medicine and Surgery: Pulmonary Tuberculosis.* London, Macmillan, 1903, pp 111–163.
2. Miller WT, Miller WT Jr: Tuberculosis in the normal host. *Semin Roentgenol* 28:109, 1993.
3. Im JG, Itoh H, Shim US, et al: Pulmonary tuberculosis, CT findings: early active disease and 50 sequential changes with antituberculous therapy. *Radiology* 186:653, 1993.
4. Deeb SM, Yaqub BA, Sharif HS, Motaery KR: Neurotuberculosis: a review. *Clin Neurol Neurosurg Suppl* 94:530, 1992.
5. Thrush A, Enzmann D: MR imaging of infectious spondylitis. *Am J Neuroradiol* 11:1171, 1990.
6. Styblo K, Rouilon A: Tuberculosis in the world: Part 2. Estimated global incidence of smear positive pulmonary tuberculosis. *Bull Int Union Tuberc* 56:118, 1981.
7. Bloch AB, Reider HL, Kelly GD, et al: Epidemiology of tuberculosis in the United States. *Clin Chest Med* 10:297, 1989.
8. DesPrez RM, Goodwin RA Jr: *Mycobacterium tuberculosis* in principals and practices of infectious diseases, in Mandell GA, Douglas RG Jr, Bennett JE (eds), *Principles and Practices of Infectious Diseases.* New York, Churchill Livingstone, 1985, pp 1383–1406.
9. Dannenberg AM Jr: Pathogenesis of pulmonary tuberculosis. *Am Rev Respir Dis* 125:25, 1982.

10. Khan MA, Kovnat DM, Bachus B, et al: Clinical and roentgenographic spectrum of pulmonary tuberculosis in the adult. *Am J Med* 62:31, 1977.
11. Miller WT, MacGregor RR: Tuberculosis: the frequency of unusual radiographic findings. *Am J Roentgenol* 130:867, 1978.
12. Woodring JH, Vandiviere HM, Fried AM, et al: Update: radiographic features of pulmonary tuberculosis. *Am J Roentgenol* 146:497, 1986.
13. Choyke PL, Sostman HD, Curtis AM, et al: Adult onset of pulmonary tuberculosis. *Radiology* 148:357, 1983.
14. Hadlock FP, Park SK, Awe RJ, Rivera M: Unusual findings in adult pulmonary tuberculosis. *Am J Roentgenol* 134:1015, 1980.
15. Epstein DM, Kline LR, Albelda SM, Miller WT: Tuberculous pleural effusions. *Chest* 91:106, 1987.
16. Barnes PF, Bloch AB, Davidson PT, Snider DE: Tuberculosis in patients with human immunodeficiency virus infection. *N Engl J Med* 324:1644, 1991.
17. Cohen JP, Amorosa JH, Smith PR: The air-fluid level in cavitary pulmonary tuberculosis. *Radiology* 127:315, 1978.
18. Maranjuola D: Fluid levels in pulmonary tuberculosis cavities in a rural population of Nigeria. *Am J Roentgenol* 141:519, 1983.
19. *Diagnostic Standards and Classification of TB*. New York, National Tuberculosis and Respiratory Disease Association, 1969, p. 47.
20. Lea KS, Kim YH, Kim WS, et al: Endobronchial features: CT features. *J CAT* 15:424, 1991.
21. Hulnick DH, Naidich DP, McCauley DF: Pleural tuberculosis evaluated by computed tomography. *Radiology* 149:759, 1983.
22. Subbarao K: Tuberculosis, in Taveras J, Ferrucci J (eds), *Radiology: Diagnosis, Imaging, Intervention*, vol 5. Philadelphia, Lippincott, 1990, p. 1.
23. Premkuamer A: Genitourinary tuberculosis and schistosomiasis, in Taveras J, Ferrucci J (eds), *Radiology: Diagnosis, Imaging, Intervention*, vol 4. Philadelphia, Lippincott, 1990, p. 1.

CHAPTER 18

The Phenomenon of Multidrug-Resistant Tuberculosis

PATRICIA M. SIMONE / SAMUEL W. DOOLEY

PATHOGENESIS OF DRUG RESISTANCE

Bacteriologic Factors

Scientists first recognized drug resistance to antituberculous medications soon after these medications were introduced. Pyle described the emergence of drug resistance during treatment with streptomycin in 1947.[1] In the 1950s, researchers demonstrated that drug-resistant bacilli existed in wild strains of *Mycobacterium tuberculosis*, even before contact with any antituberculous medications.[2,3] Scientists found that some isoniazid-resistant strains had reduced catalase activity, but the molecular basis of resistance remained a mystery until recently.[4-6]

In 1970, David demonstrated that drug resistance in tubercle bacilli resulted from the spontaneous and random occurrence of mutations in the bacterial chromosome.[7] He was able to calculate the average mutation rates for isoniazid, rifampin, ethambutol, and streptomycin and the highest proportion of mutants expected in unselected populations of *M. tuberculosis* for each of the drugs. The average mutation rate in *M. tuberculosis* for resistance to isoniazid was 2.56×10^{-8} mutations per bacterium per generation; for rifampin, 2.25×10^{-10}; for ethambutol, 1.0×10^{-7}; and for streptomycin, 2.95×10^{-8}. The expected ratio of resistant bacilli to susceptible bacilli in an unselected population of *M. tuberculosis* was about $1:10^6$ each for isoniazid and streptomycin, $1:10^5$ for ethambutol, and $1:10^8$ for rifampin. The probability that random mutations will produce tubercle bacilli resistant to more than one drug is calculated by multiplying the rates for the individual drugs. Therefore, mutants resistant to both isoniazid and rifampin, for example, should occur less than once in an unselected population of 10^{14} bacilli. Since pulmonary cavities contain about 10^7 to 10^9 bacilli, they are likely to contain a small number of bacilli resistant to each of the antituberculous drugs but unlikely to contain bacilli resistant to two drugs simultaneously.[8]

Recently, scientists discovered the first clues to the molecular basis of drug resistance in some strains of *M. tuberculosis*. Zhang et al. reported that deletion of a single gene encoding both catalase and peroxidase was associated with isoniazid resistance in two clinical isolates of *M. tuberculosis*.[9] Furthermore, the gene restored sensitivity to a resistant mutant of *Mycobacterium smegmatis*.

Clinical Factors

Drug-resistant tuberculosis (TB) occurs when drug-resistant bacilli outgrow drug-susceptible bacilli due to selection and multiplication of the resistant mutants by inappropriate therapy.[8] This occurs most commonly early in therapy, when the population of bacilli is large and when a single drug is used.[10] During the initial phase of treatment with a single drug, the majority of the bacilli — which are susceptible to the drug — are destroyed, and the number of bacilli found in the sputum decreases sharply. However, the small number of resistant mutants continue to grow unhampered (Fig. 18-1). After 2 weeks to several months, the resistant bacilli outgrow the susceptible bacilli. The number of the bacilli in the sputum rises, and clinical drug resistance develops. This is known as the "fall and rise" phenomenon.[8] Furthermore, in a large population of resistant mutants, additional mutations can occur, resulting in doubly-resistant mutants (Fig. 18-2).

The two main causes of the development of clinical drug resistance are nonadherence to prescribed therapy and the use of inadequate treatment regimens.[11,12] When medications are not taken as prescribed, the infecting bacilli may be exposed to a single drug for long periods of time, which allows drug-resistant organisms to emerge (Fig. 18-3). In addition, some regimens may contain multiple drugs but only one drug to which the infecting bacilli are susceptible. This can happen when primary drug resistance is not suspected or when a single drug is added to a failing regimen (Fig. 18-4). These regimens are equivalent to single-drug therapy, and they can select multidrug-resistant organisms. Acquired multidrug resistance usually results from a combination of nonadherence and inappropriate therapy.

The emergence of drug-resistant bacilli can be avoided by treating TB with two or more drugs in combination.[8,10,11-13] Combination therapy is most important in the initial phase of treatment, when the bacillary population is the greatest. The antituberculous drugs vary in their ability to prevent the emergence of resistance to other drugs with isoniazid and rifampin appearing to be the most effective.[8,10] Triple-drug therapy may be necessary to prevent the emergence of resistance when other relatively weaker drugs are used. Later, in the continuation phase of treatment, combination therapy is less important because the bacillary population is much smaller.[10]

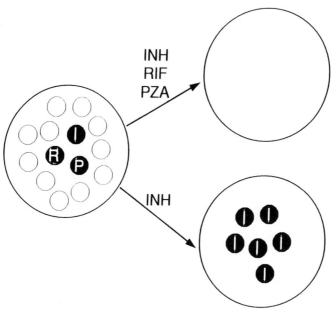

FIGURE 18-1. Pathogenesis of drug resistance I. A large population of tubercle bacilli is likely to contain a small number of resistant mutants. All of the bacilli are killed by multiple-drug therapy, whereas single-drug therapy results in the selection of resistant mutants. (Adapted with permission from © 1992 American Lung Association.) Empty circles represent tubercle bacilli that are susceptible to all the antituberculous drugs. Circles with letters in them represent tubercle bacilli resistant to one or more of the antituberculous drugs, as indicated by the letters. I, INH = isoniazid; R, RIF = rifampin; P, PZA = pyrazinamide.

The emergence of drug resistance is far less likely in most types of extrapulmonary TB, in which the bacillary population is much smaller.[8] Because the bacillary population is even smaller in latent TB infection, the chances that drug resistance will emerge during preventive therapy are negligible, even with monotherapy. A study by Nolan et al. illustrates this point. Patients with TB infection who took isoniazid preventive therapy for 3 months or fewer were at a six times greater risk for the development of active, isoniazid-susceptible TB but at no greater risk for isoniazid-resistant TB than those who completed 12 months of preventive therapy.[14]

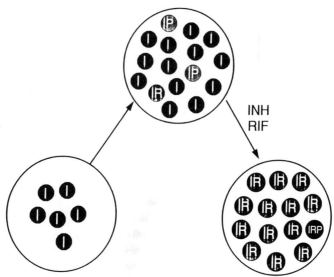

FIGURE 18-2. Pathogenesis of drug resistance II. Mutations in a population of isoniazid-resistant tubercle bacilli result in multidrug-resistant bacilli. Treatment with isoniazid and rifampin alone selects isoniazid- and rifampin-resistant mutants. (Adapted with permission from © 1992 American Lung Association.) Empty circles represent tubercle bacilli that are susceptible to all the antituberculous drugs. Circles with letters in them represent tubercle bacilli resistant to one or more of the antituberculous drugs, as indicated by the letters. I, INH = isoniazid; R, RIF = rifampin; P, PZA = pyrazinamide.

Definitions

Bacteriologically, a population of *M. tuberculosis* is considered resistant if 1 percent or more of the organisms are resistant to a designated concentration of a drug. Clinically, drug resistance is divided into two types: primary resistance and acquired (or secondary) resistance.[10,15] Primary resistance occurs in persons who have never been treated for TB; these persons are infected with resistant organisms. Acquired resistance develops during therapy for TB, either because the patient was treated with an inadequate regimen or because the patient did not take the prescribed regimen appropriately. Because it is difficult to verify whether a patient has received antituberculous therapy in the past, the term *initial resistance* is sometimes used instead of *primary resistance*.

Multidrug resistance is defined as in vitro resistance of a strain of *M. tuberculosis* to two or more of the antituberculous drugs. Clinically, the most important pattern of multidrug resistance is resistance to both isoniazid and

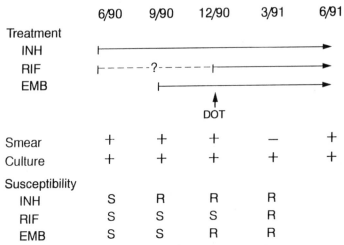

FIGURE 18-3. Emergence of resistance due to inappropriate treatment and nonadherence with therapy. A patient who has drug-susceptible TB is treated with isoniazid and rifampin but fails to take the rifampin, and isoniazid resistance develops. Further resistance develops when ethambutol is added alone and when rifampin is re-added when directly observed therapy (DOT) is started.

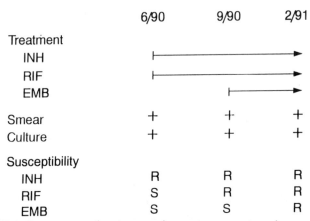

FIGURE 18-4. Emergence of resistance due to inappropriate therapy in a patient who has TB with unsuspected primary resistance to isoniazid. The patient is treated with isoniazid and rifampin, and resistance to rifampin emerges. Ethambutol resistance also develops when ethambutol is added alone to a failing regimen.

rifampin. This combination has been associated with a much lower cure rate than drug-susceptible TB. In one series of patients with TB resistant to a median of six drugs, including both isoniazid and rifampin, only 56 percent had a successful outcome despite very aggressive inpatient treatment.[16] This is similar to the rate of cure of TB before the discovery of antituberculous drugs.

TRANSMISSION

Drug-resistant and drug-susceptible TB are transmitted in the same way. For many years, drug-resistant bacilli were believed to be less infectious and less pathogenic than drug-susceptible bacilli.[4-6] Laboratory studies demonstrating reduced virulence of isoniazid-resistant bacilli supported this belief. However, epidemiologic evidence began to accumulate indicating that drug-resistant bacilli were not only infectious but also capable of causing severe disease.[17-19] In 1970, Steiner et al. described an outbreak of drug-resistant TB in which all of the household contacts were infected and two cases of severe TB developed.[18] In an outbreak of multidrug-resistant TB in Alcorn County, Mississippi, in 1976, 64 percent of close contacts and 35 percent of more distant contacts to the index case became infected. A total of 15 new cases of TB were linked to the index case.[19]

In 1985, Snider et al. compared the risk of infection among persons exposed to drug-resistant bacilli with the risk among persons exposed to drug-susceptible bacilli.[20] They found that contacts of previously untreated patients had a similar risk of infection, regardless of whether the bacilli were drug-resistant or drug-susceptible. However, they found an increased risk of infection in contacts of patients with drug-resistant TB who had been treated previously. They suggested that the increased risk resulted from prolonged exposure rather than increased infectiousness of the drug-resistant bacilli because patients with drug-resistant TB who have a history of prior treatment are more likely to have been nonadherent to therapy and infectious for longer periods of time than patients with drug-susceptible TB. Recent nosocomial outbreaks of multidrug-resistant TB support the concept that drug-resistant TB is no less infectious than drug-susceptible TB and that, in fact, prolonged periods of infectiousness may facilitate transmission.[21-29]

EPIDEMIOLOGY

Until recently, the national surveillance system for TB has not included the reporting of drug susceptibility. Therefore, recent information about trends in drug-resistant TB is limited. Several regional surveys and some larger national surveys provide some information, but methodological differences make comparing the surveys difficult. The Centers for Disease Control and Prevention (CDC) has conducted several surveys of primary drug resistance. The first survey examined drug susceptibility results among TB patients hospitalized between 1961 and 1968.[30] Resistance to at least one drug was found in 3.5 percent of the 9350 strains tested, and resistance to two or more drugs was found in 1 percent of the strains tested. In a second survey of city and state laboratories conducted between 1975 and 1982, 6.9 percent of the cases involved resistance to one or more drugs, and 2.3 percent of the cases involved resistance to two or more drugs.[31-33] The third survey, conducted between 1982 and 1986, found that 9 percent of strains isolated in 31 health department laboratories were resistant to one or more drugs.[34] The difference in primary resistance rates in the three surveys may be due to methodological differences; however, each survey showed a rate of primary drug resistance that was relatively low and that was stable or decreasing during the study period. Drug resistance did not appear to be an increasing problem, and the surveys were discontinued.

Prompted by nosocomial outbreaks of multidrug-resistant TB, CDC conducted an additional survey of drug resistance among TB cases reported from January through March 1991.[34a] Preliminary analysis of these data revealed that susceptibility test results were available for 82.7 percent of the 4051 culture-positive cases. Resistance to at least one drug was found in 13.0 percent of new cases, 26.2 percent of recurrent cases, and 13.9 percent of cases overall. Resistance to both isoniazid and rifampin was reported in 3.2 percent of new cases and 6.8 percent of recurrent cases.

The findings of this survey may not be comparable to the findings of the previous surveys because of significant methodological differences. In the previous surveys, susceptibility testing was performed at a single laboratory on isolates from only a sample of areas. In contrast, in the 1991 survey, susceptibility tests were performed at local laboratories, and researchers attempted to collect results from all areas for all of the cases reported during the study period. Furthermore, in the previous surveys, attempts were made to determine whether "new" cases had a history of previous treatment and if so, to exclude them from the study, whereas in the 1991 survey classification of cases as "new" or "recurrent" was not verified. Although the full effect of these methodological differences cannot be determined, the most recent CDC survey suggests that drug resistance has increased, at least in parts of the United States, after years of relative stability.

Some regional data suggest that the increases in drug-resistant TB may be concentrated in large urban areas. In the 1991 CDC survey, 67 percent of the cases of primary drug resistance were reported from only five areas: New York City, California, Texas, New Jersey, and Florida. Of the cases of multidrug-resistant TB, 61 percent were reported from New York City alone.

Frieden et al. conducted a survey in New York City of drug susceptibility results from all specimens that grew *M. tuberculosis* during April 1991.[35] Of patients who had been treated previously, 44 percent had isolates resistant to one or more drugs, and 30 percent had isolates resistant to both isoniazid and rifampin. Of patients who had never been treated for TB, 23 percent had organisms resistant to at least one drug, and 7 percent had organisms resistant to both isoniazid and rifampin. In comparison, in the CDC survey conducted from 1982 to 1986, only 9.7 percent of cases with no previous treatment from New York City had organisms resistant to at least one drug, and only 3 percent had organisms resistant to both isoniazid and rifampin.

Factors Associated with Drug Resistance

One important risk factor for drug resistance is previous treatment with antituberculous medications (Table 18-1). In the study conducted in New York City by Frieden et al., a history of previous treatment was the strongest predictor of the presence of drug-resistant organisms.[35] Other studies have found that rates of drug resistance increase as the duration of previous treatment increases.[36] In most instances, drug resistance associated with previous therapy develops because of inadequate or erratic therapy.

On the other hand, previous treatment has not been associated with drug resistance when treatment with short-course regimens is adequately supervised. Bacteriologic relapses after completion of supervised short-course chemotherapy with regimens containing both isoniazid and rifampin are usually due to drug-sensitive organisms. These patients respond well to repetition of the previous treatment.[10,13,15,37]

Another risk factor for drug-resistant TB is contact with a person who has infectious, drug-resistant TB.[17] Recent nosocomial outbreaks demonstrate a strong correlation between previous exposure to a patient who has infectious, multidrug-resistant TB and the subsequent development of multidrug-resistant TB in the contact.[17,21-29] In addition, it has been shown that persons previously treated for drug-susceptible TB can be reinfected with drug-resistant strains.[38-40]

TABLE 18-1. Groups at Increased Risk for Drug-Resistant TB

Persons who have a history of treatment with antituberculous medications
Contacts of persons who have TB known to be drug-resistant
Foreign-born persons from areas with high prevalence of drug-resistant TB
  (e.g., Latin America, Asia, and Africa)
Persons whose smear or culture results remain positive after 3 months of
  therapy with antituberculous medications

Drug resistance occurs more frequently in persons from areas of the world with a high prevalence of drug-resistant TB, such as Southeast Asia, Latin America, Haiti, and the Phillipines.[41-44] Several studies have found high rates of primary drug resistance in these persons, suggesting transmission of drug-resistant TB in the country of origin. However, because an accurate history of treatment may be difficult to obtain, some previously treated patients may be misclassified as having primary resistance. In the CDC survey conducted from 1982 to 1986, the rates of both primary and acquired drug resistance were two times higher among foreign-born persons than among persons born in the United States.[34]

OUTBREAKS

Drug-resistant TB was described soon after antituberculous drugs were introduced, but the first documented outbreak of drug-resistant TB was not reported until 1970.[45] Between 1970 and 1990, a few outbreaks of isoniazid-resistant TB and multidrug-resistant TB were reported.[18,19,38,39,46-49] In general, these outbreaks involved small numbers of cases among close contacts who had had prolonged or repeated exposure to source patients.

From 1990 through October 1992, in collaboration with state and local health departments, CDC investigated outbreaks of multidrug-resistant TB in eight hospitals in Florida, New York, and New Jersey and in the New York State correctional system (Table 18-2).[21-29] The recent outbreaks differ considerably from previous outbreaks of drug-resistant TB in several ways. First, the recent outbreaks involved large numbers of patients; at least 297 cases have been identified so far. In addition, in the recent outbreaks TB was transmitted not only from patient to patient but also from patient to health care worker. The epidemiologic evidence of nosocomial transmission was confirmed by DNA fingerprinting data: strains from epidemiologically linked cases were found to have identical patterns by restriction fragment length polymorphism (RFLP) analysis. RFLP analysis also suggested that several of the outbreaks in New York State were connected. Finally, the recent outbreaks involved a large percentage of highly susceptible patients who became infected with highly drug-resistant organisms, which are more difficult to treat. More than 80 percent of the cases occurred in persons infected with human immunodeficiency virus (HIV), and all but six of the patients had organisms resistant to both isoniazid and rifampin (Table 18-3). Mortality rates in these outbreaks were very high. In seven of the eight outbreaks, more than 70 percent of the patients died with the median interval between diagnosis and death ranging from 4-16 weeks.

TABLE 18-2. **Nosocomial HIV-Related Multidrug-Resistant TB Outbreaks as of October 1992**

Facility	Location	Time Period	Total Cases	Resistance Pattern
Hospital A	Miami	1988–1991	65	INH, RIF (EMB, ETA)†
Hospital B	New York City	1989–1991	51	INH, SM (RIF, EMB)
Hospital C	New York City	1989–1992	70	INH, RIF, SM (EMB, ETA, KM, RBT)
Hospital D	New York City	1990–1991	29	INH, RIF (EMB, ETA)
Hospital E	New York City	1990–1991	7	INH, RIF, SM (EMB, ETA, KM, RBT)
Hospital F	New York City	1990–1991	16	INH, RIF, SM (EMB, ETA, KM, RBT)
Hospital I	New Jersey	1990–1992	13	INH, RIF (EMB)
Hospital J	New York City	1991–1992	28	INH, RIF (SM, EMB, ETA, KM)
Prison system*	New York State	1990–1992	42	INF, RIF (SM, EMB, ETA, KM, RBT)
Total cases			297	

Note: INH = isoniazid; RIF = rifampin; SM = streptomycin; EMB = ethambutol; ETA = ethionamide; KM = kanamycin; RBT = rifabutin.

*Twenty-four prison cases are also counted with Hospital C.

† All isolates were resistant to drugs not in ( ); some of the isolates were also resistant to the drugs in ( ).

Most of the outbreaks were centered in wards or outpatient clinics where HIV-infected persons received care. There is no evidence that persons with HIV infection are more likely to be infected with TB if exposed. However, it is clear that, once infected with TB, persons who are infected with HIV have a much higher risk for the development of active disease than persons who are not infected with HIV. In addition, infection may progress rapidly to active disease.[50] In these outbreaks, active TB sometimes developed in patients within a few weeks of their exposure to the disease. These patients then became sources of transmission themselves, so that multiple generations of transmission occurred within a very short period of time.

TABLE 18-3. **HIV Prevalence and Mortality Rates of Multidrug-Resistant TB Patients as of October 1992**

Facility	HIV Infection, %	Mortality Rate, %	Median Interval TB Diagnosis to Death, Weeks
Hospital A	93	72	7
Hospital B*	100	89	16
Hospital C	95	77	4
Hospital D	91	83	4
Hospital E	14	43	4
Hospital F	82	82	4
Hospital I	100	85	4
Hospital J	96	93	4
Prison system†	98	79	4

Note: Includes only cases for which outcome information has been ascertained.
*HIV infection was part of case definition.
†Includes 24 cases also counted with Hospital C.

Prolonged infectiousness also promoted transmission. The diagnosis of TB in HIV-infected persons was delayed because of the unusual radiographic presentations of TB, coinfection with other pulmonary pathogens to which patients' symptoms were attributed, and the overgrowth of *M. tuberculosis* in the laboratory by other mycobacteria. Delays in diagnosis led to delays in the initiation of isolation and treatment. In addition, drug resistance was not recognized promptly because of lengthy laboratory delays, which postponed the initiation of effective treatment and prolonged infectiousness.

Inadequate infection control practices also facilitated transmission. Isolation rooms were found to be at positive pressure relative to other parts of the facility. Patients who had been assigned to isolation rooms were found in hallways, patients' lounges, or other common areas. Furthermore, isolation precautions were discontinued prematurely, after an arbitrary number of days, rather than when there was clinical or laboratory evidence of decreased infectiousness.

Finally, some patients who were given appropriate therapy in the hospital were lost to follow-up after discharge. Brudney and Dobkin studied 224 TB patients admitted to Harlem Hospital in 1988.[51] Of 178 patients discharged on TB treatment, 89 percent were lost to follow-up and did not complete therapy. Forty-eight patients were readmitted to the hospital with infectious TB within 1 year. A lack of consistent follow-up after discharge promotes lapses in therapy and heightens the potential for transmission both in the hospital and in the community.

Multidrug-resistant TB was also transmitted to health care workers in these outbreaks. At two hospitals, 33 percent and 39 percent of workers, respectively, had documented skin test conversions after exposure to patients with multidrug-resistant TB. At a third hospital, more than 50 health care workers had skin test conversions following exposure to hospitalized prison inmates with multidrug-resistant TB. Active, multidrug-resistant TB has developed in at least 16 health care workers and one correctional worker. Eight of the health care workers were known to be HIV-seropositive, and the correctional worker was immunocompromised because of a malignancy. At least six of these workers have died, including five health care workers (four of whom were known to be HIV seropositive) and the correctional worker.

TREATMENT

In response to the increasing prevalence of drug-resistant TB, CDC's Advisory Council for the Elimination of Tuberculosis has issued new recommendations for the initial therapy for TB to reduce the emergence of drug-resistant TB and the frequency of treatment failure.[52] First, drug susceptibility testing should be performed on the initial isolate from all persons with TB. Susceptibility test results provide important information not only for clinical therapeutic decisions but also for TB control efforts. Surveillance of drug susceptibility results is necessary to detect changes in local drug susceptibility patterns and monitor the appropriateness of initial regimens. Repeat susceptibility testing should be performed on isolates from patients whose culture results remain positive 3 months after starting treatment or who have clinical signs of failure or relapse.

Second, the initial phase of treatment in most areas of the country should include four drugs: isoniazid, rifampin, pyrazinamide, and either ethambutol or streptomycin. Selection of two drugs to which the patient's organism is likely to be susceptible can be difficult at the beginning of therapy before susceptibility test results are available. Improper selection of drugs for the treatment of drug-resistant TB may lead to the selection of further drug-resistant organisms. Unpublished CDC data indicate that 95 percent of patients would receive an adequate regimen if this initial four-drug regimen is used. The four-drug regimen has been shown to be highly effective even for isoniazid-resistant TB.[53,54]

Finally, the use of directly observed therapy (DOT) should be considered for all patients with tuberculosis. DOT means observation of the patient by a health-care provider or other responsible person as the patient swallows antituberculous medications. Ensuring adherence with the more widespread use of DOT is an important step in preventing treatment failure and the emergence of drug resistance.

Treatment of Drug-Resistant TB

The recommended treatment for isoniazid-resistant TB is rifampin and ethambutol alone for 12 months.[55] Alternatively, there is evidence that some 6-month regimens may be effective. Six-month regimens containing four or five drugs have been found to be effective even when primary isoniazid resistance was present.[53,54] In general, the successful regimens have contained isoniazid, rifampin, pyrazinamide, and either ethambutol or streptomycin for the first 2 months and isoniazid and rifampin alone for the remaining 4 months. The regimens have been very successful in isoniazid-resistant disease despite apparent monotherapy with rifampin in the continuation phase. Based on the principle of multiple-drug therapy, however, it is strongly recommended that the continuation phase include at least two drugs to which the organism is susceptible.[13]

The use of isoniazid in the treatment of isoniazid-resistant TB is controversial.[13,56] Large populations of isoniazid-resistant bacilli may contain some isoniazid-susceptible organisms, which may be more virulent than the resistant bacilli. For this reason, some clinicians continue isoniazid even when the organisms are resistant. However, if other effective medications are included in the regimen, the addition of isoniazid has not been shown to improve the effectiveness of the regimen.

In contrast, for rifampin-resistant TB, short-course regimens have been less successful.[54,57] Treatment with isoniazid and ethambutol for 18 months, supplemented by pyrazinamide for the first 2 months, has been recommended.[13]

Treatment of Multidrug-Resistant TB

The treatment of TB resistant to both isoniazid and rifampin, the two most potent antituberculous drugs, is frequently unsuccessful even in the best of circumstances.[11,12,16] The drugs available to treat multidrug-resistant TB are less effective than the first-line drugs, necessitating regimens that contain more drugs, which are administered for much longer periods of time. The ability to complete therapy is further complicated by the frequency of adverse reactions with these less commonly used agents.

Goble et al. reported a series of 171 patients with pulmonary TB resistant to both isoniazid and rifampin.[16] The patients had been treated previously with a median of six drugs and had organisms resistant to a median of six drugs. Despite intensive efforts, only 65 percent responded to therapy, and of those,

14 percent relapsed. Of those patients who failed to respond or relapsed, 46 percent died. The overall response rate was only 56 percent.

Although there have been no controlled trials for the treatment of multidrug-resistant TB, there are some basic principles of treatment to be followed.[11,12] The regimen should include at least three drugs to which the patient's organisms are susceptible, preferably drugs that the patient has not received before, including one injectable medication. The orally administered drugs should be continued for 24 months after the culture results have converted to negative. The injectable medication should be continued for at least 4 months after the culture results become negative. If the regimen must be adjusted because of drug toxicity or apparent treatment failure while the culture results are still positive, at least two drugs should be added simultaneously to avoid adding a single drug to a failing regimen and selecting bacilli resistant to more drugs. Treatment of patients with drug-resistant TB should be directly observed to ensure adherence. In addition, clinicians who are not familiar with the management of patients with multidrug-resistant TB should seek expert consultation.

Second-Line Drugs

The drugs available to treat multidrug-resistant TB include some older drugs that were used early in the treatment of TB but fell out of favor when more potent, less toxic medications became available: ethionamide, cycloserine, para-aminosalicylic acid (PAS), capreomycin, and kanamycin. In addition, some newer drugs, such as the fluoroquinolones and amikacin, have shown good in vitro activity against *M. tuberculosis*, but controlled clinical trials of their use in the treatment of TB have not been conducted. Finally, clofazimine, a drug used to treat leprosy, is sometimes used but has unproven efficacy.

The second-line drugs are associated with a variety of adverse reactions, ranging from minor and reversible to serious and permanent (Table 18-4).[11,12,58-60] Many minor adverse reactions can be overcome by symptomatic treatment, adjustment of the time of administration, and, most important, reassurance and persistence. The potential for more serious reactions can be diminished but not eliminated with careful clinical and laboratory monitoring.

Ethionamide frequently causes gastrointestinal side effects, including abdominal pain, nausea, and anorexia. Gastrointestinal intolerance may be reduced by starting with a low dose and increasing to a full dose over several days, using antiemetics and antacids, or bedtime dosing. Hypersensitivity reactions and hepatitis may also occur. Endocrine disturbances, such as hypothyroidism, menstrual irregularities, and impotence, have been associated with ethionamide administration.

Cycloserine commonly causes neurologic and psychiatric disturbances ranging from minor reactions, such as headache, tremor, memory problems,

TABLE 18-4. Second-Line Antituberculous Drugs

Drug	Daily Dose	Side Effects	Monitoring	Other
Ethionamide	500–1000 mg by mouth (in divided doses if necessary for tolerance)	Gastrointestinal intolerance, hepatitis, endocrine disturbances, hypersensitivity	SGOT	Consider antiemetics or bedtime dosing.
Cycloserine	250–750 mg by mouth (in divided doses; adjust for renal impairment)	Neurologic and psychiatric disturbances	Serum levels	Administer pyridoxine (vitamin B_6).
Capreomycin, amikacin, kanamycin	15 mg/kg intramuscularly 5 days a week (adjust for renal impairment)	Hearing loss, vestibular damage, renal toxicity, electrolyte disturbances	Audiogram, vestibular examination, BUN and creatinine levels	
Para-aminosalicylic acid (PAS)	10–20 g by mouth (in divided doses for tolerance)	Gastrointestinal intolerance, hepatitis, hypersensitivity	SGOT	Consider antacids or dosing at mealtime.
Ciprofloxacin, ofloxacin	500–1000 mg by mouth 400–800 mg by mouth	Gastrointestinal intolerance, headache, restlessness, hypersensitivity, drug interactions	Monitoring for drug interactions	Avoid antacids, iron, zinc, and sucralfate, which decrease absorption.
Clofazimine	100–300 mg by mouth	Abdominal pain, skin discoloration (both dose-related), photosensitivity		Consider dosing at mealtime; avoid sunlight. Efficacy is unproven.

and insomnia, to more serious reactions, such as psychosis and seizures. Most reactions are dose-related and disappear when the medication is discontinued. Concomitant use of pyridoxine and monitoring of serum drug levels may help prevent most serious reactions. The dosage of cycloserine must be adjusted for renal impairment.

Capreomycin, kanamycin, and amikacin must be given parenterally, usually by intramuscular injection. Even at the usual dosage of 15 mg/kg 5 days a week, these medications may cause ototoxicity, such as hearing loss, tinnitus, or vestibular disturbances, especially in elderly patients or patients with preexisting renal disease. Patients should have a baseline audiogram and be monitored with monthly audiograms and for vestibular problems during therapy. Because of potential renal toxicity, blood urea nitrogen (BUN) and creatinine levels should be monitored, and, if they are elevated, the dose should be adjusted accordingly.

PAS frequently causes gastrointestinal complaints. Symptoms may be diminished by beginning therapy with a low dose and gradually increasing to a full dose over 7 – 10 days, by taking the medication on a full stomach, or by using antacids. Patients frequently complain about the large number of pills (20 – 40) in the recommended daily dose when 500 mg tablets are used. Granular PAS may be more acceptable to some patients. Infrequently, PAS may cause hypersensitivity reactions, hypothyroidism, or hemolytic anemia.

Ciprofloxacin and ofloxacin are generally well-tolerated. The most frequently reported adverse reactions are nausea, diarrhea, abdominal discomfort, headache, restlessness, and rash. Significant drug interactions may occur with cimetidine, cyclosporin, nonsteroidal anti-inflammatory agents, warfarin, theophylline, and even caffeine.[61] Antacids and iron supplements reduce the absorption of these drugs and should be avoided within 2 h of the dose.

Clofazimine has been used for many years to treat leprosy. It has excellent in vitro activity against *M. tuberculosis* but has never been proven to be clinically effective for treatment of TB. It is occasionally included in the regimen when there are not three other drugs that the patient has not received before to which the organism is susceptible. The drug deposits in various tissues in the body, including the skin, producing an orange or brown discoloration. Gastrointestinal complaints are common. Clofazimine has a very long half-life. The usual starting dosage is 200 – 300 mg a day, decreasing to 100 mg a day once there is evidence of tissue saturation, such as skin discoloration.

Clinicians should always remember that, when a medication must be discontinued because of a serious reaction before the culture results have become negative, two new drugs should be substituted, to avoid selecting organisms resistant to more medications.

Monitoring Patients Being Treated for Multidrug-Resistant TB

Patients being treated for multidrug-resistant TB should be evaluated by a clinician at least once a month. The monthly evaluation should include a history, physical examination, laboratory tests, and any other diagnostic tests that are pertinent to the medications in the regimen (Table 18-4). Monthly monitoring of sputum smears and cultures is sufficient for outpatients. Sputum specimens from inpatients should be obtained more frequently to help monitor infectiousness. Tuberculosis isolation may be discontinued once the patient's sputum smears are free of acid-fast bacilli on three consecutive days. However, even after isolation is discontinued, the sputum smears should be closely monitored because of the high risk of relapse with multidrug-resistant TB.

Multidrug-resistant TB tends to respond to therapy more slowly than drug-susceptible TB. It frequently takes several weeks for an initial response (i.e., improvement in symptoms and decreasing number of acid-fast bacilli on sputum smear) to occur. The sputum culture results may not become negative for several months. In some patients, relapse occurs after an initial response. In other patients, the sputum culture results never become negative. Culture results that are persistently positive after 4–6 months of intensive therapy are likely to remain positive.

Surgery

Because of the high failure and relapse rates associated with multidrug-resistant TB, surgical resection has been used by some clinicians as a supplement to medical therapy. The surgical resection of a major pulmonary focus is best performed once aggressive medical therapy has achieved a clinical response. The administration of antituberculous medications should continue for 24 months after culture results convert to negative. Iseman et al. reported that, in a series of 99 patients being treated for multidrug-resistant TB, the combination of surgical resection and medical therapy produced lower rates of failure and relapse than among historical control subjects.[62]

PREVENTIVE THERAPY

The appropriate use of preventive therapy is critical to the control and elimination of TB. When the infecting strain of *M. tuberculosis* is susceptible to isoniazid and the medication is taken as prescribed, isoniazid therapy is very effective in preventing latent tuberculous infection from progressing to clinically active disease.[63-65] Rifampin is the recommended alternative when the infecting organism is resistant to isoniazid but susceptible to rifampin.[66] The effectiveness of preventive therapy for persons exposed to multidrug-resistant organisms, however, has not been studied.

In 1992, the CDC issued recommendations for the management of persons exposed to multidrug-resistant TB.[67] Management decisions should be based on an estimation of the likelihood that the contact is newly infected with *M. tuberculosis*, that the contact is infected with a multidrug-resistant strain of *M. tuberculosis*, and that the contact's infection will progress to active disease. Newly infected contacts who are thought to have a low likelihood of infection with multidrug-resistant TB should be managed according to standard recommendations.[55] Alternative preventive therapy regimens should be considered for persons likely to be infected with multidrug-resistant *M. tuberculosis* who have a high risk of their infection progressing to active disease. The regimens should include at least two drugs to which the isolate from the presumed source case is known to be susceptible. Two potential regimens are pyrazinamide and ethambutol or pyrazinamide and a fluoroquinolone (e.g., ciprofloxacin or ofloxacin). Because the efficacy of preventive therapy with drugs other than isoniazid or rifampin is unknown, persons placed on alternative preventive therapy regimens should have periodic medical and radiographic evaluation for the first 2 years after infection.

REFERENCES

1. Pyle MM: Relative numbers of resistant tubercle bacilli in sputum of patients before and during treatment with streptomycin. *Proc Mayo Clinic* 22:465, 1947.
2. Cavalli-Sforza LL, Lederberg J: Isolation of pre-adaptive mutants in bacteria by sub-selection. *Genetics* 41:367, 1955.
3. Lederberg J, Lederberg EM: Replica plating and indirect selection of bacterial mutants. *J Bacteriol* 63:399, 1952.
4. Middlebrook G, Cohn ML: Some observations on the pathogenicity of isoniazid-resistant variants of tubercle bacilli. *Science* 118:297, 1953.
5. Cohn ML, Davis CL: Infectivity and pathogenicity of drug-resistant strains of tubercle bacilli studied by aerogenic infection of guinea pigs. *Am Rev Respir Dis* 102:97, 1970.
6. Cohn ML, Kovitz C, Oda U, Middlebrook G: Studies on isoniazid and tubercle bacilli: the growth requirements, catalase activities, and pathogenic properties of isoniazid-resistant mutants. *Am Rev Tuberc* 70:641, 1954.
7. David HL: Probability distribution of drug-resistant mutants in unselected populations of *Mycobacterium tuberculosis*. *Appl Microbiol* 20:810, 1970.
8. Canetti G: The J. Burns Amberson Lecture: present aspects of bacterial resistance in tuberculosis. *Am Rev Respir Dis* 92:687, 1965.
9. Zhang Y, Heym B, Allen B, et al: The catalase-peroxidase gene and isoniazid resistance of *Mycobacterium tuberculosis*. *Nature* 358:591, 1992.
10. Mitchison DA: Drug resistance in mycobacteria. *Br Med Bull* 40:84, 1984.
11. Iseman MD, Madsen LA: Drug-resistant tuberculosis. *Clin Chest Med* 10:341, 1989.

12. Goble M: Drug-resistant tuberculosis. *Semin Respir Infect* 1:220, 1986.
13. Bass JB, Kirkpatrick MB: Drug-resistant tuberculosis. *Semin Respir Med* 9:470, 1988.
14. Nolan CM, Aitken ML, Elarth AM, et al: Active tuberculosis after isoniazid chemoprophylaxis of Southeast Asian refugees. *Am Rev Respir Dis* 133:431, 1986.
15. Grange JM: Drug resistance and tuberculosis elimination. *Bull Int Union Tuberc Lung Dis* 65:57, 1990.
16. Goble M, Iseman MD, Madsen LA, et al: Treatment of 171 patients with pulmonary tuberculosis resistant to isoniazid and rifampin. *N Engl J Med* 328:527, 1993.
17. Steiner M, Zimmerman R, Park BH, et al: Primary tuberculosis in children: correlation of susceptibility patterns from *M. tuberculosis* isolated from children with those isolated from source cases as an index of drug-resistant infection in a community. *Am Rev Respir Dis* 98:201, 1968.
18. Steiner M, Chaves AD, Lyons HA, et al: Primary drug-resistant tuberculosis: report of an outbreak. *N Engl J Med* 283:1353, 1970.
19. Reves R, Blakely D, Snider DE Jr, et al: Transmission of multiple drug-resistant tuberculosis: report of a school and community outbreak. *Am J Epidemiol* 113:423, 1981.
20. Snider DE, Kelly GD, Cauthen GM, et al: Infections and disease among contacts of tuberculosis cases with drug-resistant and drug-susceptible bacilli. *Am Rev Respir Dis* 132:125, 1985.
21. Centers for Disease Control: Nosocomial transmission of multidrug-resistant TB to health-care workers and HIV-infected patients in an urban hospital: Florida. *MMWR* 39:718, 1990.
22. Centers for Disease Control: Nosocomial transmission of multidrug-resistant tuberculosis among HIV-infected persons: Florida and New York, 1988–1991. *MMWR* 40:585, 1991.
23. Edlin BR, Tokars JI, Grieco MH, Crawford JT, Williams J, Sordillo EM, Ong KR, Kilburn JO, Dooley SW, Castro KG, Jarvis WR, Holmberg SD: An outbreak of multidrug-resistant tuberculosis among hospitalized patients with the acquired immunodeficiency syndrome. *N Engl J Med* 326:1514, 1992.
24. Pearson ML, Jereb JA, Frieden TR, Crawford JT, Davis BJ, Dooley SW, Jarvis WR: Nosocomial transmission of multidrug-resistant *Mycobacterium tuberculosis*: a risk to patients and health care workers. *Ann Intern Med* 117:191, 1992.
25. Beck-Sague C, Dooley SW, Hutton MD, Otten J, Breeden A, Crawford JT, Pitchenik AE, Woodley C, Cauthen G, Jarvis WR: Outbreak of multidrug-resistant *Mycobacterium tuberculosis* infections in a hospital: transmission to patients with HIV infection and staff. *JAMA* 268:1280, 1992.
26. Fischl MA, Uttamchandani RB, Daikos GL, Poblete RB, Morena JN, Reyes RR, Boota AM, Thompson LM, Cleary TJ, Lai S: An outbreak of tuberculosis caused by multiple-drug-resistant tubercle bacilli among patients with HIV infection. *Ann Intern Med* 117:177, 1992.
27. Fischl MA, Daikos GL, Uttamchandani RB, Poblete RB, Moreno JN, Reyes RR, Boota AM, Thompson LM, Cleary TJ, Oldham SA, Saldana MJ, Lai S: Clinical presentation and outcome of patients with HIV infection and tuberculosis caused by multiple-drug-resistant bacilli. *Ann Intern Med* 117:184, 1992.
28. Centers for Disease Control: Transmission of multidrug-resistant tuberculosis among immunocompromised persons in a correctional system: New York, 1991. *MMWR* 41:507, 1992.
29. Dooley SW, Jarvis WR, Martone WJ, Snider DE: Multidrug-resistant tuberculosis (editorial). *Ann Intern Med* 117:257, 1992.
30. Doster B, Caras GJ, Snider DE: A continuing survey of primary drug resistance in tuberculosis, 1961 to 1968: a U.S. Public Health Service cooperative study. *Am Rev Respir Dis* 113:419, 1976.

31. Kopanoff DE, Kilburn JO, Glassroth JL, Snider DE, Farer LS, Good RC: A continuing survey of tuberculosis primary drug resistance in the United States, March 1975 to November 1977: a United States Public Health Service cooperative study. *Am Rev Respir Dis* 118:835, 1978.
32. Centers for Disease Control: Primary resistance to antituberculosis drugs: United States. *MMWR* 29:345, 1980.
33. Centers for Disease Control: Primary resistance to antituberculosis drugs: United States. *MMWR* 32:521, 1983.
34. Snider DE, Cauthen GM, Farer LS, Kelly GD, Kilburn JO, Good RC, Dooley SW: Drug-resistant tuberculosis (letter). *Am Rev Respir Dis* 144:732, 1991.
34a. Bloch AB, Cauthen GM, Onorato IM, Dansbury KG, Kelly GD, Driver CR, Snider DE Jr: Nationwide survey of drug-resistant tuberculosis in the United States. *JAMA* 271:665, 1994.
35. Frieden TR, Sterling T, Pablos-Mendez A, et al: The emergence of drug-resistant tuberculosis in New York City. *N Engl J Med* 328:521, 1993.
36. Costello HD, Caras GJ, Snider DE: Drug resistance among previously treated tuberculosis patients: a brief report. *Am Rev Respir Dis* 121:313, 1980.
37. Hong Kong Tuberculosis Treatment Service and East African and British Medical Research Council: First-line chemotherapy in the retreatment of bacteriological relapses of pulmonary tuberculosis following a short-course regimen. *Lancet* 1:162, 1976.
38. Centers for Disease Control: Drug-resistant tuberculosis among the homeless: Boston. *MMWR* 34:429, 1985.
39. Nardell E, McInnis B, Thomas B, Weidhaas S: Exogenous reinfection with tuberculosis in a shelter for the homeless. *N Engl J Med* 315:1570, 1986.
40. Small PM, Shafer RW, Hopewell PC, et al: Exogenous reinfection with multidrug-resistant *Mycobacterium tuberculosis* in patients with advanced HIV infection. *N Engl J Med* 328:1137, 1993.
41. Barnes PF: The influence of epidemiologic factors on drug resistance rates in tuberculosis. *Am Rev Respir Dis* 136:325, 1987.
42. Riley LW, Arathoon E, Loverde VD: The epidemiologic patterns of drug-resistant *Mycobacterium tuberculosis*: a community-based study. *Am Rev Respir Dis* 139:1282, 1989.
43. Centers for Disease Control: Drug resistance among Indochinese refugees with tuberculosis. *MMWR* 30:273, 1981.
44. Pitchenik AE, Russell BW, Cleary T, Pejovic I, Cole C, Snider DE: The prevalence of tuberculosis and drug resistance among Haitians. *N Engl J Med* 307:162, 1982.
45. Lincoln EM: Epidemics of tuberculosis. *Adv Tuberc Res* 14:157, 1965.
46. Centers for Disease Control: INH-resistant tuberculosis in an urban high school: Oregon. *MMWR* 29:194, 1980.
47. Centers for Disease Control: Interstate outbreak of drug-resistant tuberculosis involving children: California, Montana, Nevada, Utah. *MMWR* 32:516, 1983.
48. Centers for Disease Control: Multidrug-resistant tuberculosis: North Carolina. *MMWR* 35:785, 1987.
49. Centers for Disease Control: Outbreak of multidrug-resistant tuberculosis: Texas, California, and Pennsylvania. *MMWR* 39:369, 1990.
50. Daley CL, Small PM, Schecter GF, Schoolnik GK, McAdam RA, Jacobs WR, Hopewell PC: An outbreak of tuberculosis with accelerated progression among persons infected with the human immunodeficiency virus: an analysis using restriction-fragment-length polymorphisms. *N Engl J Med* 326:231, 1992.
51. Brudney K, Dobkin J: Resurgent tuberculosis in New York City: human immunodeficiency virus, homelessness and the decline of tuberculosis control programs. *Am Rev Respir Dis* 144:745, 1991.

52. Centers for Disease Control: Initial therapy for tuberculosis in the era of multidrug resistance: recommendations of the Advisory Council for the Elimination of Tuberculosis. *MMWR* 42(RR-7):1, 1993.
53. Hong Kong Chest Service/British Medical Research Council: Controlled trial of 4 three-times-weekly regimens and a daily regimen all given for 6 months for pulmonary tuberculosis, second report: the results of final results up to 24 months. *Tubercle* 63:89, 1982.
54. Mitchison DA, Nunn AJ: Influence of initial drug resistance on the response to short-course chemotherapy of pulmonary tuberculosis. *Am Rev Respir Dis* 133:423, 1986.
55. American Thoracic Society/Centers for Disease Control: Treatment of tuberculosis and tuberculosis infection in adults and children. *Am Rev Respir Dis* 134:355, 1986.
56. Moulding TS: Should isoniazid be used in retreatment of tuberculosis despite acquired isoniazid resistance? *Am Rev Respir Dis* 123:262, 1981.
57. Manalo F, Tan F, Sbarbaro JA, Iseman MD: Community-based short-course treatment of pulmonary tuberculosis in a developing nation. *Am Rev Respir Dis* 142:1301, 1990.
58. Girling DJ: Adverse effects of antituberculosis drugs. *Drugs* 23:56, 1982.
59. Moulding T, Davidson PT: Tuberculosis: Part 2. Toxicity and intolerance to antituberculosis drugs. *Drug Therapy* February:39, 1974.
60. Lefkowitz MS: The antimycobacterial drugs. *Semin Respir Med* 2:196, 1981.
61. Stein GE: Drug interactions with fluoroquinolones. *Am J Med* 91(suppl):81S, 1991.
62. Iseman MD, Madsen L, Goble M, Pomerantz M: Surgical intervention in the treatment of pulmonary disease caused by drug-resistant *Mycobacterium tuberculosis*. *Am Rev Respir Dis* 141:623, 1990.
63. Stead WW, To T, Harrison RW, Abraham JH: Benefit-risk considerations in preventive treatment for tuberculosis in elderly persons. *Ann Intern Med* 107:843, 1987.
64. International Union against Tuberculosis Committee on Prophylaxis: Efficacy of various durations of isoniazid preventive therapy for tuberculosis: five-year follow-up in the IUAT trial. *Bull WHO* 60:555, 1982.
65. Ferebee SH: Controlled chemoprophylaxis trials in tuberculosis. *Adv Tuberc Res* 17:28, 1970.
66. Koplan JP, Farer LS: Choice of preventive treatment for isoniazid-resistant tuberculosis infection. *JAMA* 244:2736, 1980.
67. Centers for Disease Control: Management of persons exposed to multidrug-resistant tuberculosis. *MMWR* 41:61, 1992.

CHAPTER 19

Treatment of Recalcitrant Patients

JOHN A. SBARBARO / JAN B. SBARBARO

The word *recalcitrant* is defined in various dictionaries as "obstinately defiant of authority; refusing to obey authority, custom, or regulation; difficult to handle." When applied to a tuberculosis (TB) patient, *recalcitrant* implies *direct* refusal to follow an appropriate and curative course of treatment and blatant refusal to behave in a manner that would both cure the disease and render the patient noncontagious to others. Although the resulting danger to themselves and others is identical, more gentle terminology—*noncompliant* and *nonadherent*—is used to reflect such behavior when it occurs through forgetfulness, fear, mistrust, disbelief, or ignorance.

The resurgence of TB and the rising incidence of drug-resistant tuberculous organisms within the United States can be traced directly to human recalcitrance and noncompliance. This noncompliance is not only evident on the part of patients, it is also enacted through the noncompliant and even recalcitrant behavior of physicians, public health authorities, and politicians who have failed, and continue to fail, to meet their professional and legal obligations. Such behavior, if permitted to continue, can only result in our society's repeating its historical experience with this airborne, contagious disease that is again unresponsive to treatment with medication.

QUARANTINE

Shortly after Koch's 1882 identification of *Mycobacterium tuberculosis* as the etiological agent of "consumption," Hermann Biggs of New York recognized that only by physically removing the human source of contagion from society could those susceptible to infection and progressive disease be protected. In essence, the civil rights of the many to be free of disease were to take precedence over the civil rights of a contagious individual to move freely throughout the community. Communicable disease laws in each state codified *quarantine* as a legitimate and appropriate act of society to protect itself, and all states have exercised this police power to control the spread of TB.[1]

These laws, passed by the legislative branch of state governments, are to be enforced by the executive branch of government through the police powers of the health department. The legitimacy of each law and its application to an affected individual remain the province of the judicial branch of government: the courts.

Recognizing that the development of active pulmonary TB was often akin to a death sentence (65 percent of patients with untreated, smear-positive disease died within 5 years), both health departments and the courts took seriously their responsibility to protect the public, and physical quarantine was strictly enforced when voluntary cooperation from the patient could not be obtained.

The introduction of successful drug treatment in the 1950s markedly diminished society's concern over the disease. Studies by Jones et al.[2] and Yeager et al.[3] revealed that a progressive decline in the number of TB bacilli present in the sputum could be expected to begin within 2 weeks after the initiation of effective chemotherapy. The rate of disappearance of bacilli was directly related to the original extent of the disease process.

Moreover, well-controlled studies appeared to establish a direct relationship between the bacillary content of the sputum and the infectiousness of patients. For example, Shaw and Wynn Williams reported that patients who had smear-negative and culture-positive disease were only slightly more infectious for children than those whose specimens tested negative by both smear and culture.[4] A study by Riley et al.[5] of airborne infection of guinea pigs from the rooms of TB patients showed that untreated patients were generally more infectious than those who had recently been started on antituberculous drugs. (It should be noted that the effect of drug treatment was difficult to exactly evaluate because the researchers did not study the same patients before and after treatment.)

The sum of this information led to the conclusion that the risk of infection from patients on initial treatment who were receiving adequate chemotherapy and who were excreting small numbers of bacilli in their sputum was minimal.[6] Thus, "chemical isolation" could replace "physical isolation-quarantine" as a means of public protection.

During that same time period, society began to focus on the inequalities faced by members of minority groups and by women. As the rights of the individual rose in public interest, the focus of many governmental officials turned from law enforcement to the education of patients as the appropriate vehicle by which to ensure adherence to and/or compliance with effective antituberculous chemotherapy. This transformation occurred despite clear and growing evidence that 35 percent of patients would not adhere to their treatment regimen despite educational efforts,[7] others would select only certain drugs to take, and a few would openly reject any medication. Moreover, evidence was also rapidly accumulating to demonstrate that physicians and public health authorities were unable to predict which patients were destined to be nonadherent to treatment.[8] Nor were physicians able to identify which patients were being noncompliant during treatment![8]

Unfortunately, this combination of events established the environment for the emergence and spread of drug-resistant TB organisms in the 1990s. Many private physicians, believing they were protecting their patients, failed to report active disease cases to public health authorities. Compounding their error, treatment was often initiated with insufficient numbers of drugs, inadequate dosages, and outdated regimens. Treatment was prescribed with the belief that the patient would adhere to the regimen as prescribed and complete a full course of treatment. There was little recognition of the fact that patients often discontinued one or two of their antituberculous medications while erratically continuing others, thus selecting drug-resistant organisms for survival and further multiplication. Patients failing to appear for subsequent appointments with their physician were assumed to have gone elsewhere for care, and little concern was given to the potential for relapse and the spread to other members of society.

NONADHERENCE AND NONCOMPLIANCE: THE PHYSICIAN'S RESPONSIBILITY

Many investigators have tried to pinpoint characteristics or features that would allow the physician to identify patients who are likely to be noncompliant. The results of these studies have led to the recognition that demographic variables such as age, race, marital status, and religious choice are rarely predictive of compliant behavior. Similarly, socioeconomic status, occupation (including physicians), and level of income are not characteristics that predict noncompliance. Little association has been found between educational level and compliance.[8]

Although patients with serious illnesses are more likely to seek medical care, there is little evidence that the severity or duration of the illness, the degree of functional impairment, the number of concurrent diseases, or previous hospitalization influences medical compliance.[9]

Nonetheless, there are some testing techniques that can assist a physician to identify the noncompliant patient. Urine tests for the presence of medication, medication metabolites, or tracer substances added to the medication have all been employed. Spot measurements of drug serum levels have also been studied. Both urine and serum measurements suffer from the same weakness; they represent the patient's actions only during the previous

12-18 h. Multiple tests, preferably on specimens obtained during surprise visits at home, are required before a composite portrait of a patient's medication ingestion activity can be determined.[8]

Devices capable of measuring the patient's regularity in removing medication from the device have been used to identify the noncompliant patient, but evidence that the patient actually ingested the medication still requires spot sampling or urine or serum.

The elimination of long waiting times through individual patient appointment systems, appointment reminders by postcard or phone call, expansion of services into evening and weekend hours, relocation of treatment facilities into community neighborhoods, and personalized transportation services have all been effective in improving patient satisfaction and attendance. However, there is no evidence that such programmatic changes actually improve patient compliance with or adherence to medical regimens. Educational efforts can increase a patient's knowledge of the disease and its complications, but multiple studies confirm that they have little effect on patients' compliance.

It is now clear that physicians *can* improve patients' compliance by instituting changes in the therapeutic regimen that reduce the number of times each day that medications must be taken, shorten the total duration of therapy, and fit the regimen into the patient's personal daily habits and lifestyle. It is also important for the physician to identify whether the patient attributes any perceived adverse effects to the medications (not just the side effects usually associated with the drugs).

However, the most important factor in patient compliance is unquestionably the strength of the physician's relationship with the patient and its continued growth over the full duration of treatment. The assignment of a single professional or community worker to a patient over the entire duration of therapy provides a basis for the development of a strong interpersonal relationship and has been repeatedly shown to improve patient adherence to treatment.

Ensuring treatment becomes even more difficult when the patient is homeless or from an unstable environment. Drug dependency, alcoholism, and mental illness require additional social support systems and counseling, rehabilitation, housing, and employment programs. Ethnically and culturally distinct subpopulations often adhere to health beliefs and practices that can conflict with prescribed treatment, and treatment must be adapted to these beliefs.

A wide array of inducements and incentives have been developed to encourage patients' compliance with therapy. Food, clothing, books, baby-sitting services, bus tokens, and cash payments have been shown to be effective in maintaining patients' cooperation.

Medications combining two to four antituberculous drugs in a single tablet or capsule eliminate the opportunity for a patient to take only one or two drugs selectively and therefore can eliminate the potential for the emergence of drug-resistant disease. If available, such combinations are the medications of choice when a self-administered regimen is to be prescribed.

Because society as a whole is affected by the degree to which antituberculous therapy succeeds, a physician treating TB must be certain that adequate treatment is being taken by the patient. However, as a result of all the problems discussed above, confirmation of compliance with treatment can only be achieved through the direct administration of the medications by a second party who gives and observes the ingestion of *each* dose of medication (directly observed therapy, or DOT).

Fortunately, because of its slow metabolic growth rate (24 h doubling time), TB is ideally suited for low dosages, once-daily treatment, or high dosages of the same medications administered intermittently only twice or three times a week (all treatment medications given at the same time). Intermittent regimens, involving as few as 62 doses directly administered over a 6-month period, have cure rates equal to those for the best of the daily treatment regimens (180 doses; Table 19-1).[10] High rates of treatment completion are consistently achieved with directly administered regimens.

These directly administered regimens deny the patient an opportunity to take medications selectively, thereby avoiding the risk of developing resistant disease. Should the patient prematurely discontinue treatment, the physician is

---

TABLE 19-1. Effective High-Dose Intermittent Regimens

Initial Phase	Continuation Phase	
2 Months Daily Treatment Rifampin 600 mg Isoniazid 300 mg Pyrazinamide 30 mg/kg Ethambutol 15 mg/kg	**4 Months High-Dose Intermittent, Twice Weekly** Rifampin 600 mg Isoniazid 14 mg/kg Total 94 doses	
	5.5 Months High-Dose Intermittent	
2 Weeks Daily Treatment Rifampin 600 mg Isoniazid 300 mg Pyrazinamide 30 mg/kg Streptomycin 15 mg/kg	**6 Weeks, Twice Weekly** Rifampin 600 mg Isoniazid 14 mg/kg Pyrazinamide 45 mg/kg Streptomycin 27 mg/kg	**18 Weeks, Twice Weekly** Rifampin 600 mg Isoniazid 14 mg/kg Total 62 doses

Source: Modified from Iseman et al.[11]

immediately made aware of the situation and, of equal importance, should relapse subsequently occur, the disease organisms will usually be susceptible to the same medications. Savings in both the laboratory and radiological monitoring of treatment and in the cost of medications can offset the extra costs for personnel associated with DOT, making such regimens both effective and efficient.[11]

The establishment of a program of directly administered therapy requires the services of a core staff of three people — a clerk, a nurse, and a community worker — all supported by the medical expertise and license of a knowledgeable and committed physician. The primary provider of care is usually the nurse, acting under protocols preapproved by the physician or, if and where considered necessary, carrying out the direct order of the physician.

To maximize an opportunity for the establishment of a supportive relationship with a patient, the initial encounter between the nurse and the patient should be scheduled for 1 h. During this initial time, the nurse has an opportunity to gain insight into the patient's lifestyle: what the patient does during a usual day, where he or she goes, the patient's close friends and relatives, and the sources of the patient's money. This information becomes vital if the patient is to be effectively found after prematurely discontinuing therapy. During this initial encounter, a quarantine order (described below) should be given to the patient, along with an explanation of the program's substitution of "chemical quarantine" for "physical quarantine," the continuation of which is dependent on the patient's cooperation with the outpatient treatment program.

Subsequent twice weekly encounters usually involve less than 15–20 min, a 62-dose regimen thereby involving a total of 17–20 h of the nurse's time. When circumstances minimize the likelihood that the patient will actually appear for scheduled treatments or when a scheduled encounter is missed, the community worker is *immediately* assigned to find and transport the patient to the clinic or to deliver and observe medication ingestion by the patient. Failure of the patient to cooperate should *immediately* initiate appropriate public health enforcement action, ranging from assertive educational intervention by the physician to physical detention and confinement under public health quarantine restrictions (see below). Experience has demonstrated that forceful detention is seldom required (usually 2 or 3 per 100 patients). Knowledge of such action is quickly shared among other patients and appears to serve as a strong incentive for their continued cooperation.

The employment of community workers (without traditional educational requirements) who are familiar with the "street" provides the program with an effective mechanism for both outreach and community-based treatment and is integral to the success of any directly administered program.

There is no question that directly administered treatment is absolutely required for patients with a history of nonadherence with medical care or for those whose social situation suggests that they face daily challenges of subsistence and existence. Although some argument can be made that many patients will adhere to a self-administered regimen, it is impossible to guarantee which patients will cooperate, and health department programs that have utilized directly administered treatment for *all* patients have experienced dramatic reductions in failure and relapse rates compared to those that have not.

When appropriately presented, the potentially adverse political impact of untreated contagious TB within a community can be made clear to elected officials. Further support for the program's existence can be elicited from the criminal justice system once the alternative of the potential involvement in prolonged institutionalization is fully appreciated.

Recognizing these realities, many health departments are now instituting programs of directly administered therapy utilizing high doses of medications given two to three times a week. Whenever available, such programs clearly constitute the treatment regimen of choice. It should be noted that 38 states charge their public health departments with the duty to pay for or provide care to TB patients, especially those unable to pay for their own care.[1] Therefore, close cooperation between the patient's physician and health authorities is essential.

PHYSICIAN NONCOMPLIANCE

Unfortunately, noncompliance is not limited to patients. Physicians are equally noncompliant with authoritative treatment guidelines produced by professional societies and governmental agencies. The ever-widening arena of personal injury litigation becomes especially focused when a third party is injured by a predictable and avoidable event directly attributable to a physician's decision. When combined with failure to comply with public health laws and regulations, prescribing inadequate antituberculous regimens places physicians in significant legal jeopardy (see "Public Health Enforcement," below).

PUBLIC HEALTH ENFORCEMENT

Inevitably, a physician will encounter a truly recalcitrant patient, one who clearly is refusing to cooperate with therapy. Despite the establishment of a patient-physician relationship in which the physician is ethically expected to serve the wishes and needs of the patient, every physician is obligated to report the existence of contagious TB to the health department. Patients who fail to adhere to or comply with a regimen of TB treatment experience high rates of disease relapse. Therefore, the physician treating such a patient must assume that relapse has occurred (or soon will) and must so inform local or state public health authorities.

As an enforcement arm of the executive branch of government, public health authorities should issue an order of isolation and/or quarantine to every patient identified as having a sputum culture result that is positive for *M. tuberculosis*. Patients subsequently failing to follow a regimen that protects the public through "chemical isolation" also fail to meet the conditions of their quarantine order and therefore fall under the immediate jurisdiction of health officials, who can then move promptly to obtain the necessary court orders to physically confine the individual who has openly breached a legal order. In some states, failure to have issued an initial order of quarantine when the patient was first diagnosed can delay public health action until new cultures are obtained from the patient.

Courts have been most supportive of such public health intervention when efforts have clearly been made to treat the patient on a voluntary basis and to accommodate treatment to the patient's lifestyle and personal needs.[12] Documentation of a patient's failure to adhere to a reasonable regimen adds further strength to any legal action instituted against the patient by health officials. The involved physician is free of further responsibility for the patient once the report and appropriate documentation have been provided to health officials.

However, failure to fulfill these legal obligations can result in both *criminal action* against the physician by government and *civil action* against the physician by individuals who have become infected or diseased through contact with the TB patient while the patient was presumed to be under the care of the physician. (It is to be noted that malpractice policies encompass only civil suits relating to a breach of professional duty and do not cover the legal costs arising from criminal charges.)

Although 24 states and the District of Columbia specifically grant health departments the power to impose compulsory treatment,[1] indefinite confinement is the preferable alternative for the intransigent, recalcitrant patient who poses a direct threat to the community. Appropriate access to due process is obviously essential in all such circumstances.

REFERENCES

1. Gostin LO: Controlling the resurgent tuberculosis epidemic. *JAMA* 269:255, 1993.
2. Jones JM, McClement JH, Garfield JW: Serial counts of tubercle bacilli in the sputum of

patients under treatment for tuberculosis. Transactions of the Twenty-fifth Research Conference in Pulmonary Diseases, VA-Armed Forces, 1966, p 17.

3. Yeager H, Lacy J, Smith R, LeMaistre CA: Quantitative studies of mycobacterial populations in sputum and saliva. *Am Rev Respir Dis* 95:998, 1967.

4. Shaw JB, Wynn Williams N: Infectivity of pulmonary tuberculosis in relation to sputum status. *Am Rev Respir Dis* 93:998, 1967.

5. Riley RL, Mills L, O'Grady F, Sultan LU, Wittstadt F, Sivpuri DN: Infectiousness of air from a tuberculosis ward. *Am Rev Respir Dis* 85:511, 1962.

6. Cashman HH, D'Esopo ND, Dickinson W, Houk VN, Muchmore HG, Sbarbaro JA, Wolinsky E: Bacteriologic standards for the discharge of patients. *Am Rev Respir Dis* 102:470, 1970.

7. Davis MS: Variations in patient compliance with doctor's orders: analysis of congruence between survey responses and results of empirical investigations. *J Med Educ* 41:1037, 1966.

8. Sbarbaro JA: The patient-physician relationship: complicance revisited. *Ann Allerg* 64: 325, 1990.

9. Hulka BS, Cassel JC, Kupper LL, et al: Communication, compliance, and concordance between physicians and patients with prescribed medications. *Am J Public Health* 66: 847, 1976.

10. Cohn DL, Catlin BJ, Peterson KL, Judson FN, Sbarbaro JA: A 62-dose, six-month therapy for pulmonary and extrapulmonay tuberculosis: a twice-weekly, directly observed, and cost-effective regimen. *Ann Intern Med* 112:407, 1990.

11. Iseman MD, Cohn DL, Sbarbaro JA: Directly observed treatment of tuberculosis: we can't afford not to try it. *N Engl J Med* 328:576, 1993.

12. *In RC Halko* 246 CAL. App. 2D553, 54 CAL. Rptr 661 (CAL Court App. 1966).

CHAPTER 20

Inpatient Management Issues

P. J. BRENNAN / ROB ROY MacGREGOR

In recent decades, the declining incidence of pulmonary tuberculosis (TB) and the circulation of susceptible strains attracted little attention to the disease and created the impression that the elimination of TB was at hand.[1] As better antituberculous drugs were added to our armamentarium, the duration of therapy shortened and patients rarely died of the disease in the United States. Since 1985, decades-old trends have been reversed, and hospitals and other health care settings have become common meeting grounds for *Mycobacterium tuberculosis* and immunocompromised hosts. The extreme vulnerability of patients coinfected with human immunodeficiency virus (HIV) and *M. tuberculosis* has resulted in rapid progression from infection to clinical disease and death. Multidrug-resistant (MDR) strains of TB and high mortality rates among HIV-infected persons have increased our awareness of the importance of appropriate inpatient management of TB.[2-5]

The decline of TB in developed societies coincided with the architectural development of buildings with closed internal environments requiring recirculated heating, ventilation, and air-conditioning (HVAC) systems. As a result, many hospitals constructed in recent decades are ill-suited for the management of air contaminated by patients with active pulmonary TB. Ventilation systems can provide routes for the spread of airborne pathogens such as TB and viruses in hospitals and clinics, placing employees as well as compromised patients at risk.[6,7] A recent survey by the Centers for Disease Control and Prevention (CDC, unpublished) revealed that most clinicians do not recognize the signs and symptoms of TB. Recent reports have documented infection of health care workers after exposure to TB.[5,8,9] With these influences at work, the systems and practices of health care facilities must be examined to better protect their patients and workers from exposure to TB. In addition, a generation of health care personnel unaccustomed to the clinical manifestations of TB must be educated. The means of controlling the transmission of TB already exist. Early recognition, respiratory isolation using environmental control systems and personal protective equipment, and effective treatment will prevent the continued spread of TB.

All health care institutions will have to weigh the benefit of interventions to prevent the transmission of TB within the environment (e.g., environmental controls and personal protective equipment) against the cost. The multidisciplinary nature of the problem requires a coordinated response within hospitals. This chapter addresses the issues related to the respiratory isolation of patients with TB and the protection of health care workers in the inpatient setting.

COORDINATION OF TB CONTROL IN HOSPITALS: THE FUNCTIONS OF THE HOSPITAL TB WORKING GROUP

For the treatment of TB to be effective, the duration of treatment requires both an inpatient and outpatient phase. Admission to a hospital and the subsequent discharge of patients with chronic, infectious diseases encompasses a set of events that, if not executed smoothly and efficiently, may create obstacles to follow-up for the patient and poor compliance rates. Inpatient management of TB presents multiple problems of coordination, which require forethought and planning for their resolution. In reviewing the management of TB cases referred to their center, Mahmoudi and Iseman (Table 20-1) found that errors occurred in 80 percent of their cases.[10] On average, four management errors occurred per case. These errors not only resulted in ineffective therapy but also failed to identify risk factors for noncompliance. The problems identified in this case series are not unique. Brudney and Dobkin have reported an 89 percent noncompliance rate among a cohort of patients with active pulmonary TB discharged from one institution.[11] These obstacles to effective management of TB must be addressed if an institution is to manage appropriately a complex disease that is unfamiliar to many of its practitioners.

A working group of interested parties can bring together diverse elements of a hospital community, thereby pooling resources and serving as a conduit for information back to the community. A TB working group should include physician representatives, such as a local TB expert, and the hospital infection control officer as well as representatives of the nursing, radiology, emergency,

---

TABLE 20-1.   Common Errors in Management of Patients with TB

Addition of a single drug to a failing regimen
Failure to identify preexisting or acquired drug resistance
Initiation of inadequate primary therapy
Failure to identify noncompliance
Inappropriate preventive therapy

Source: Mahmoudi and Iseman.[10]

social services, pharmacy, and microbiology departments; the administration; the house staff; and the hospital attorney. The diverse membership represents the spectrum of individuals and departments involved in the management of patients with TB. Small institutions may find that one person can coordinate all these activities, particularly if the local TB prevalence is low.

The suggested activities of a TB working group are listed in Table 20-2. The development of a detailed hospital action plan for TB control can define objectives, assign responsibility for objectives, and be used to track progress toward effective TB control in-hospital, much as the CDC's National Action Plan to Combat MDR TB does at the national level.[12]

Education should play a prominent role in the activities of a TB working group. Group members should disseminate information to their constituencies, raise the institutional awareness of TB, and enhance understanding of the mechanisms of transmission, risk of acquisition, and signs and symptoms of disease. Educational activities should be both hospital-wide and directed to serve the needs of departments likely to care for patients with active TB. Concurrent review of active in-house cases of TB by clinician members of the group can provide expert oversight into management and reduce deviations in practice. The surveillance of secular trends in case load, drug susceptibility patterns, and skin test conversions among hospital personnel will provide useful information for the development of practice guidelines and assessment of the efficacy of institutional infection control measures. The knowledge of local secular trends in case load and susceptibility may be used by a working group to create local practice guidelines regarding appropriate initial antituberculous therapy and duration of isolation following the initiation of treatment.

Credible guidelines based on local data may avoid the sort of management errors identified by Mahmoudi and Iseman and prevent the unnecessary exposure of patients and hospital personnel to contagious individuals. Suggested areas for guideline development are outlined in Table 20-3. Diagnostic ser-

---

TABLE 20-2.   Activities of a Hospital TB Working Group

Development of hospital action plan
Education of hospital staff regarding TB transmission and prevention
Surveillance of secular trends
    Case rates
    Rate of coinfection with HIV
    Drug susceptibility patterns
    Skin test conversion rates among workers
Oversight of employee screening program
Practice guideline development

TABLE 20-3. Areas for TB Practice Guideline Development

Local guidelines for initial therapy
Reporting of suspicious radiographs by radiology department
Isolation of suspected patients
Criteria for discontinuation of isolation
Daily and after-hours availability of sputum AFB screening
Triage of patients in outpatient areas to screen for TB

vices, such as those provided by the radiology and clinical microbiology departments, can play a critical role in isolation management by providing timely information needed to make judgments regarding the need for isolation: reporting of radiographs suspicious for TB and results of AFB smears should occur on a priority basis. AFB smears should be available 7 days a week. The combination of timely reporting of diagnostic information plus thoughtful guidelines for clinicians can put facilities to their best use.

RECOGNITION, ISOLATION, AND TREATMENT

The most reliable approach to stopping the transmission of TB includes early recognition of active cases, their removal from contact with susceptible individuals, and the early initiation of antituberculous therapy.[13] By comparison, environmental controls and personal protective equipment, such as respiratory devices, are of secondary importance in the hierarchy of TB control (see Chapter 4).

Case recognition requires the education of staff regarding TB and populations at risk. The signs and symptoms of TB are not specific, but fever, cough, night sweats, hemoptysis, malaise, and weight loss of more than 2 weeks' duration are characteristic complaints of a person with active disease.[14] Apical infiltrates with cavitary lesions are common radiographic findings in reactivation disease. HIV-infected persons with low CD4 counts are most likely to develop active disease soon after becoming infected. Their radiographic findings are more frequently atypical (e.g., lower lobe or diffuse involvement).[5,15] A patient suspected of infectious TB based on clinical or radiographic data should be placed in special respiratory (acid-fast bacillus, or AFB) isolation until three negative results have been obtained from acid-fast smears. Failure to recognize the signs and symptoms of TB can lead to periods of unprotected exposure for health care workers and other patients. Criteria for discharge from special respiratory (AFB) isolation must be developed. The criteria will include not only when a patient with TB is deemed noninfectious (see below) but also when a patient with another respiratory disorder is put into isolation while the diagnosis of TB is being evaluated. Properly constructed respiratory isolation facilities should be available in all acute care facilities. However, the development of resistant strains of *M. tuberculosis* and concern about transmission in the hospital among patients and to health care workers may strain hospital resources. Thus, the development of practice guidelines for respiratory isolation is essential to focus the institutional response to this problem and appropriately allocate resources.

Efforts to identify cases of TB should begin at all patient entry points in a health care facility. Emergency departments, clinics, registration areas, and admissions offices seldom have adequate isolation facilities, and their common waiting areas can be sites in which multiple individuals can be exposed to a single active case of TB. Triage nurses and clerical workers should administer a simple set of questions regarding TB to patients at intake. Table 20-4 is an example of a triage policy in place at our institution. Individuals responding

---

TABLE 20-4. Guidelines for Triage of Patients in Outpatient Areas

1. Every patient entering the hospital through the admissions office, emergency room, clinics, and practices should be questioned regarding the presence of cough.
2. If cough is not identified by questioning or evaluation, proceed with appropriate work-up for patient.
3. If a patient has a productive cough of more than 2 weeks' duration, a mask should be placed on the patient. Patients at particular risk for TB include those on immunosuppressive medications (e.g., cyclosporine or steroids); HIV-infected persons; persons born in countries with high endemic rates of TB; alcoholics; and those with kidney failure, pulmonary disease, and other chronic debilitating conditions.
4. If circumstances in the emergency room permit, the suspected patient should be brought into the emergency room or walk-in clinic for more careful evaluation. If an isolation room is available, the suspected patient should be placed in a closed room, and all health care workers entering the room should wear TB masks. *This recommendation is not meant to subvert the triage of more critically ill patients.*
5. Patients identified as suspected of having TB at sites other than the walk-in clinic or emergency department should be evaluated at those sites to the extent that is feasible before referral for admission or emergency room evaluation.
6. If TB is a persistent concern after more thorough evaluation, the patient should have a chest radiograph performed as soon as possible and, if appropriate, be admitted to a negative pressure room for special respiratory (AFB) isolation in the hospital.
7. If, following more in-depth evaluation, the patient is thought not likely to have TB, precautions may be discontinued.

positively to questions regarding signs and symptoms of TB should be masked to prevent generation of infectious droplet nuclei, removed from common waiting areas, placed in an isolation setting if available, and undergo further evaluation for TB. Ideally, patients suspected of active TB should be immediately placed in a well-ventilated room capable of maintaining special respiratory (AFB) isolation precautions and undergo an expedited examination, including a chest radiograph. Since most outpatient facilities do not have ventilation adequate for TB control, control of the infectious source (i.e., placing a mask on the patient and preventing unprotected coughing and sneezing by use of a tissue or handkerchief) should be strongly emphasized in this setting. If admission is necessary, the patient should be promptly admitted to rooms specially designated for TB isolation.

Since the mid-1980s, the demographics of TB have shifted dramatically to the 25–45-year-old age group, particularly in the geographic areas hardest hit by the HIV pandemic.[14,16] In addition, Asians and Hispanics have case rates several-fold higher than those among whites. Despite these demographics, one cannot rely soley on demographic information to make decisions to admit and isolate patients for treatment of TB. These decisions must be based on clinical and radiographic suspicion of the disease. Many cases of TB will continue to occur among middle-aged and elderly individuals who develop reactivation disease following exposures decades ago. Substance abusers and immigrants from developing areas of the world with high endemic rates of TB are also in demographic groups in which TB should be considered. Underlying medical conditions, such as pulmonary diseases, pharmacologic immunosuppression, organ failure, and malnutrition, increase the risk of developing active TB following infection.[17]

If they are not severely ill, the care of patients with active pulmonary TB can be managed at home if they can be relied upon to take their medication from the outset and to avoid unexposed persons. Inpatient management ensures the opportunity to initiate therapy in a controlled setting while educating the patient regarding the disease and the importance of completing the therapy to ensure a cure.

During hospitalization, patients with active pulmonary TB should remain in special respiratory (AFB) isolation until they are no longer contagious. Most patients with susceptible strains of *M. tuberculosis* who are receiving appropriate therapy will be noninfectious within 2–3 weeks of the initiation of antituberculous therapy;[14] however, MDR strains may remain smear- and culture-positive for months, and 50 percent may never have negative culture results.[18] Treatment is considered in greater detail elsewhere in this volume (see Chapter 12). Treatment regimens should include four drugs initially in any region that has experienced greater than a 4 percent incidence of isoniazid resistance.[19] HIV-infected persons should be treated with the same regimen for susceptible strains but continue for 6 months following conversion of sputum smears. Therapy for resistant strains will be guided by susceptibilities and requires a minimum of 18 months of therapy. A decision to discontinue isolation must be based on definite clinical and laboratory evidence of response to treatment rather than an arbitrary duration of treatment.[13] Improvement in cough and constitutional symptoms should be observed before discontinuing isolation. Progressive improvement in sputum AFB should be observed in addition to the clinical signs of response to therapy. Patients with MDR TB should remain in respiratory isolation until the sputum is free of AFB. These recommendations will undoubtedly increase lengths of stay in the hospital because many patients with an effective response to therapy continue to have positive smear results for weeks, although with decreasing numbers of acid-fast organisms seen. Concern about premature discontinuation of isolation in geographic areas where MDR TB is prevalent has led to these more stringent guidelines. If directly observed therapy or other reliable follow-up can be arranged, patients with a good clinical response and improving AFB smear results can be discharged.

THE NONCOMPLIANT PATIENT

Maintaining hospital-based respiratory isolation for TB is a challenge to both clinicians and patients. The tedium of isolation and the pressure of extramural family concerns, financial and employment issues, and occasionally personality disorders will cause some patients to attempt to flee the hospital. Predictors of noncompliance are sometimes difficult to identify, although homelessness, drug or alcohol abuse, and mental illness are frequent culprits.[14] Efficient discharge planning may enhance compliance if impediments to compliance can be addressed before the patient is lost to follow-up. Solving these problems may not be possible, but recognizing them may enable remedies to be put in place (e.g., directly observed therapy) that result in better care for patients, improved compliance, and a higher level of protection against spread of TB for patients and staff.

Short of leaving the hospital against medical advice, many patients will find their confinement uncomfortable to the degree that they open doors and windows or walk in the corridor for comfort's sake. These maneuvers break the negative pressure containment of their isolation rooms and place those outside the room at risk of exposure. The first step in preserving the compliance of patients in isolation is to determine the root cause of their desire to break isolation precautions. In our experience, most patients will remain voluntarily and conform to isolation practices if an attempt is made to address the causes of their discomfort (i.e., boredom and isolation rooms that are uncomfortably warm). Attention to such matters as a comfortable environment and the provision of such amenities as video cassette players may alleviate some of the discomfort and boredom and improve patient compliance with isolation practices. Assurance of child care arrangements, flexibility by the care givers in the frequency of phlebotomy and sputum testing, and psychiatric intervention have proven effective in maintaining patients in isolation without quarantine. Such efforts should be exhausted before a legal remedy is sought. The emergence of MDR TB and the threat that it poses to immunocompromised and competent hosts alike makes the application of quarantine an occasional but necessary component of TB control.

Court-ordered detention for TB is carried out in some jurisdictions today in the same way that mental health commitments are implemented, with patients given the opportunity for due process to challenge the order. Most states possess the legal authority to detain patients for examination and care when they represent a threat to public health.[20] Fewer than half the states may impose treatment by statute, with confinement lapsing in most cases when the patient is no longer a threat to public health or is noncontagious. Thus, even when a court order has been obtained, patients often leave confinement when they are noncontagious and before they have completed therapy. Court-ordered incarceration and therapy should not be viewed as a large-scale remedy for the control of TB; rather, it should be seen as an act to protect the public health from an individual who cannot comply with treatment and who through casual contact is a threat to the health of others. The keys to overall control of TB remain much as they were nearly a century ago: the eradication of poverty, better housing, adequate nutrition, and access to health care.

TRANSITION TO OUTPATIENT CARE

Making the transition from the inpatient to the outpatient setting is a crucial link in the chain of care. Public health authorities should be advised of patients confirmed to have or suspected of having TB as early as possible during their hospitalization in order to provide sufficient time for making posthospital arrangements. If reporting is delayed until an isolate is confirmed as *M. tuberculosis*, the long interval between admission and confirmation of species may result in many patients' leaving the hospital prior to notification of the health department. In such cases, the best chance for continued compliance with therapy may be lost. Investigation of the obstacles to effective follow-up while the patient is still hospitalized may identify special needs that require directly observed therapy. The responsibility for notification and linkage to the health department is mandated by law and rests with physicians and laboratories, but is often overlooked by physicians and delayed until the isolate is confirmed as *M. tuberculosis*. This problem can be averted by having the person or group responsible for coordinating TB control activities within the institution notify health department personnel about patients on the basis of suspicion. In addition, the hospital TB coordinator must assure that an accurate summary of the patient's hospital course is provided to posthospital care givers before the first outpatient visit and that the patient is given written instructions regarding medications and the time and location of the patient's first appointment.

ENVIRONMENTAL CONTROLS

Environmental controls for TB include the engineering controls (room air exhaust systems, air filtration systems, and ultraviolet lights) and isolation rooms employed to interrupt disease transmission (see Chapter 4). Isolation practices for inpatient infectious disease control can be carried out in a variety of hospital settings. Special respiratory (AFB) isolation is a CDC category of isolation specifically designated for patients with active pulmonary TB who are known or presumed to be contagious.[21] The setting for this isolation category is a private room with special air-handling characteristics. The room air volume should be exchanged a minimum 6 times per hour.[13] Furthermore, the room should be at negative pressure relative to adjacent areas to prevent leakage of air containing infectious droplet nuclei outside the room, thereby preventing exposure of personnel and patients outside the room. Finally, the room air should be exhausted directly to the environment outside the hospital without recirculation indoors.[13] This external exhaust and resultant fresh air exchange protects visitors and workers who enter the room by removing infectious droplet nuclei over time. At a rate of 6 air changes per hour, room air will be decontaminated at 99.9 percent efficiency in slightly more than 1 h. The speed of air exchange can be increased until 15–20 air changes per hour are achieved, beyond which little additional benefit is obtained. It should be remembered that this means of air decontamination occurs at the cost of lost energy in externally ventilated cooled and/or heated air.

Special respiratory (AFB) isolation rooms should be designated with the assistance of hospital or extramural engineering personnel. Negative pressure rooms can be readily identified by the use of "smoke sticks," which demonstrate the direction of air flow. Smoke should be drawn under the door and into the room if it is at negative pressure to adjacent areas. Staff should be educated about the common daily occurrences that can overcome negative air pressure and reverse the direction of air flow. For example, open windows and room doors create drafts that draw air from the room. Open doors to stairwells, and elevator shafts and hallway fans may create sufficient drafts outside the room to overcome negative room air pressure. Wind currents on external building walls and southern exposures creating unequal heating may unexpectedly reverse the direction of air flow. Air exchange volumes should be checked quarterly by qualified personnel, and the system should be monitored on a daily basis for malfunctions. Following the identification and certification of rooms that meet the minimum standards for special respiratory (AFB) isolation (negative pressure plus six room air changes per hour), a list of those rooms should be disseminated to admitting and clinical personnel for use as the need arises.

The same standards of ventilation necessary for inpatient TB isolation rooms are needed in certain outpatient and diagnostic areas. High-risk procedure areas, such as bronchoscopy suites, aerosolized pentamidine administration areas, and sputum induction booths, should be held to this standard. Clinics and emergency departments are front-line areas where patients with undiagnosed active pulmonary TB may first seek care. Large-scale negative pressure ventilation in these departments may be impractical, but rooms should be designated in the outpatient areas where patients identified at triage as having potential cases of TB may be sequestered away from other patients and personnel while undergoing a more thorough evaluation. Infectious droplet nuclei can remain suspended in air for hours, and, as a result, susceptible individuals can be exposed to infectious particles when their source is no longer present. In crowded settings, such as emergency department waiting areas, the prompt evaluation of suspected patients may be impeded by the volume of patients and the higher priority given to more critically ill patients. Fortunately, prolonged exposure (usually weeks to months) is normally required for infection to occur. Nonetheless, the importance of source control in such settings should not be overlooked as a measure to prevent the spread of *M. tuberculosis*. A simple intervention, such as wearing a mask or using a tissue to control coughs and sneezes, can minimize the generation of infectious droplet nuclei.

The location of clinics and emergency departments within the hospital physical plant may preclude effective ventilation. In such cases, secondary environmental controls, such as ultraviolet C (UVC; 254 nm) lighting and high-efficiency particulate air (HEPA) filtration, should be employed.[22] UVC light placed within a room can achieve the equivalent effect of 25 room air exchanges per hour.[23-25] If placed within the ventilation duct work, UVC light will effectively decontaminate the volume of room air exhausted each hour.[24] UVC lighting should be mounted in such a way as to avoid potential occupational hazards to eyes and skin. UVC lighting is considered in greater detail in

Chapter 4. Room air can be effectively cleansed of infectious droplet nuclei through HEPA filtration and can be recirculated if decontamination is 99.9 percent efficient. HEPA filtration has been used to remove environmental molds from the ambient air of oncology units. Adequate maintenance is essential to the functioning of all environmental controls. Dusting of exhaust equipment and UVC lights in negative pressure rooms and periodic replacement of HEPA filters are mandatory to maintain the functioning and efficiency of these systems.

No absolute standard can be applied to all institutions in terms of the number of special respiratory (AFB) isolation rooms. In 1992, a survey of Philadelphia hospitals revealed that 10 major institutions possessed 188 special respiratory isolation rooms (P. J. Brennan, unpublished observation). This number, which represents only a portion of the city's hospitals and TB isolation facilities, would seem more than adequate for the needs of a city with 338 cases of active pulmonary TB in the year of the survey (Commonwealth of Pennsylvania Department of Health Data), given that most patients will be managed as outpatients for most of their illness. However, these rooms are often fully occupied to meet patients' needs other than TB isolation. For example, in institutions without dedicated HIV units, it is likely that the HIV case load, more than any other infectious disease, will occupy these rooms for reasons other than TB isolation. Private room demand, HIV case load, and other infectious disease isolation needs (e.g., methicillin-resistant *Staphylococcus aureus* and other epidemiologically significant organisms) divert these rooms to other purposes.

PERSONAL PROTECTIVE EQUIPMENT

Perhaps the most controversial aspect of recent guidelines for TB control has been the use of personal respiratory protection. Its use, as with isolation rooms, is predicated on the identification of a patient as a potential source of infection. Thus, the use of this equipment is part of the secondary line of defense following recognition and treatment. Surgical masks have long been the norm for worker protection against respiratory pathogens. These masks are not air filtration devices and, as worn by most workers, develop gaps at their margins that permit funnels of air to be inhaled. In 1990, the CDC and the National Institute of Occupational Safety and Health (NIOSH) advocated the use of an industrial hygiene product called the particulate respirator (PR) for respiratory protection against TB.[13] Particulate respirators are form-fitting devices worn over the face that are capable of filtering particles in the submicron range from the air. An infectious droplet nucleus is in the $1-5$ μm range.

This filtration capability and tight facial fit theoretically provide a greater level of respiratory protection against airborne infection. However, clinical studies comparing PRs with surgical masks have not yet been performed. In the absence of evidence supporting the efficacy of PRs (or the failure of surgical masks) in protection against tuberculous infection, the recommendation for their use has been implemented slowly in hospitals. The seal that the PRs create on the face is such that breathing may be difficult for individuals with marginal pulmonary function. The requirements of the Occupational Safety and Health Administration (OSHA) for their use includes medical screening to ensure the worker's ability to breathe while wearing one, fit testing, and training in their use.[13] The time and effort needed to carry out these requirements and the lack of convincing data supporting their efficacy have been important elements in the hesitancy of hospitals to embrace their use.

Several PRs are available through commercial manufacturers, but the requirements have been further complicated by conflicts in the standards that the CDC recommends as satisfactory and those that OSHA will require. CDC recommended a dust-mist respirator as adequate protection in its 1990 guidelines, whereas OSHA requires a higher level of protection, a dust-mist-fume respirator. The dust-mist respirator resembles a cupped surgical mask, while the dust-mist-fume device straps behind the head and has an exhalation valve on the front of the mask. The devices differ in their level of protection, with the dust-mist-fume respirator providing a tighter seal and thus somewhat better protection in theory (and much greater cost). As of April 1994, the issue of the most appropriate device for respiratory protection is unresolved. A draft revision of CDC's 1990 guidelines advocating even more stringent protection is now the subject of debate.

The conflicting guidelines from the federal agencies reflect the differing views of clinicians and nonclinicians in the perception of acceptable risk in the health care environment. Whereas most clinicians recognize and accept some level of personal risk in the care of patients, OSHA's position that there is no acceptable hazard in the work place has led to more stringent and cumbersome requirements. Insofar as OSHA is the government's enforcement arm for occupational safety, institutions can expect to be held to OSHA's standard. The hazard of MDR TB in OSHA Region II (New York City and New Jersey) has led the agency to require the use of powered, half-mask, HEPA filters to be worn by workers in that region in settings of high probability or known exposure to TB. These devices, referred to as powered air pressure respirators (PAPRs), provide a higher level of protection than even the dust-mist-fume respirators.

The current guidelines will affect hospitals in several ways. The increased cost of respiratory protection will be significant. The cost of a dust-mist respirator is approximately $1.00, versus $0.12 for a surgical mask. Based on an average 3-week hospitalization for TB for 20 TB patients in a year, a hospital will probably experience $10,000 per year in increased cost for respiratory protection of employees. Each PAPR may range in price from approximately $150 to >$350 dollars. Many such devices will be needed in geographic regions of even moderate TB prevalence, resulting in costs of tens of thousands of dollars. When one considers the excess use of these devices that will probably occur, as well as their use for the many patients who are admitted for TB but found not to have disease, the cost will be several-fold higher. In the first year of use at our institution, $60,000 in increased cost was incurred as a result of the switchover to a higher level of respiratory protection. The added cost of facility renovation for TB isolation needed in many institutions will easily carry the expense of TB control in hospitals during this era beyond the $100,000 range. Health care institutions can also expect OSHA to enforce the use of higher levels of respiratory protection under its "general duty clause" to provide a safe work environment. In light of the increased expenses, potential penalties, and limited data on the value of environmental and personal protection against TB, new clinical research is desperately needed to determine the safest, most cost-effective means of delivering inpatient TB care.

Federal guidelines in this area are likely to evolve as more information accumulates about the relative benefits of respiratory devices and environmental controls. Recommendations for respiratory protection are not likely to return to less stringent devices, such as surgical masks, in an era when MDR TB has become prevalent. Further regulatory action can be anticipated in the near future in the area of respiratory devices and work place protection against TB akin to OSHA's blood-borne pathogen standard.

TUBERCULIN SKIN TESTING OF HEALTH CARE WORKERS

Skin test conversions among health care workers in many fields have become increasingly common.[2,3,5,9,26] In recent nosocomial outbreaks of MDR TB, at least 17 workers have developed clinical tuberculosis.[5] Six workers, all with immunity compromised by HIV or other conditions, died of MDR TB. To assess the efficacy of a hospital's infection control procedures for TB, the periodic tuberculin testing of health care workers is essential. The details of the Mantoux test are discussed in greater detail in Chapter 5.

All job classifications in a hospital should be stratified for TB exposure risk in order to determine the frequency of skin testing for each employee. Workers in high-exposure positions, such as emergency department personnel and pulmonary personnel, should be screened twice yearly. All other personnel should be tested at least annually.

Screening programs in large institutions may be needed to perform 5000 to 10,000 skin tests annually. Such an effort requires dedicated individuals whose responsibility is to see that the program moves forward. Testing at the work site enables employees to be screened without loss of time from work but involves more advance planning prior to a tester's site visit. The equivalent of one to two full-time employees may be needed to perform all the tasks necessary to manage a hospital's TB screening program. Table 20-5 lists the needs of a hospital-based tuberculin skin testing program. In addition, screening programs for employees with occupational exposures must provide follow-up and prophylaxis or treatment if indicated at no cost to the employee.

In institutions without active testing programs, the issue of whether to perform booster testing (Chapter 5) will have to be addressed in the first year of the program. If applied to all employees, twice as many tests will have to be performed and interpreted in the first year as in subsequent years. In individuals whose immunity from a remote infection has waned, a positive test result may be obtained when a second tuberculin test is performed within a few weeks of the first. This is more likely to be seen in individuals older than age 55, although there are no good data on the frequency of the booster phenomenon in younger persons. Performing booster testing is the best way to establish an accurate hospital-wide baseline for tuberculin reactivity. If booster testing is not performed, some infected individuals who have negative test results may not receive prophylaxis when indicated for underlying medical conditions; conversely, boosted individuals may be perceived in later testing to be new conversions, representing recent infection, and receive prophylaxis inappropriately. When a baseline frequency of tuberculin reactivity has been established, each new conversion within a department should be investigated and an attempt made to explain it. Clusters (more than one) or conversions in one area suggest deficiencies in disease recognition or infection control practices.

TABLE 20-5. Institutional Needs for Tuberculin Skin Testing Program

Hospital policy requiring employee testing
Hospital enforcement mechanism for testing program
Centralized testing responsibility (e.g., occupational health service or infection control office)
Sufficient staffing to carry out program
Data base for tracking employees

SUMMARY

The new epidemic of TB comes at a particularly vulnerable time for hospitals with large inpatient populations of susceptible patients and shrinking health care dollars for implementing controls. The inpatient management of TB requires the coordinated efforts of hospital personnel in a wide variety of roles. Education of staff so that TB is recognized, isolated, and treated early is paramount in the control of disease. Environmental controls and personal protective equipment are secondary lines of defense but may provide protection against contagious persons when disease is recognized.

REFERENCES

1. Centers for Disease Control Advisory Committee for the Elimination of Tuberculosis: A strategic plan for the elimination of tuberculosis in the United States. *MMWR* 38(suppl S3), 1989; and Centers for Disease Control: Prevention and control of tuberculosis in U.S. communities with at-risk minority populations and among homeless persons. *MMWR* 41: 1, 1992.
2. Edlin BR, Tokars JI, Greico MH, et al: An outbreak of multidrug-resistant tuberculosis among hospitalized patients with the acquired immunodeficiency syndrome. *N Engl J Med* 326:1514, 1992.
3. Fischl MA, Uttamchandani RB, Daikos GL, Poblete RB, et al: An outbreak of tuberculosis caused by multiple-drug-resistant tubercle bacilli among patients with HIV infection. *Ann Intern Med* 117:177, 1992.
4. Daley CL, Small PM, Schecter GF, et al: An outbreak of tuberculosis with accelerated progression among persons infected with the human immunodeficiency virus. *N Engl J Med* 326:231, 1992.
5. Dooley SW, Jarvis WR, Martone WJ: Multi-drug resistant tuberculosis. *Ann Intern Med* 117:257, 1992.
6. Centers for Disease Control: *Mycobacterium tuberculosis* transmission in a health clinic: Florida, 1988. *MMWR* 38:256, 1989.
7. LeClair JM: Airborne transmission of chickenpox in a hospital. *N Engl J Med* 302:450, 1980.
8. Ramirez JA, Anderson P, Herp S, Raff MJ: Increased rate of tuberculin skin test conversion at a university hospital. *Infect Control Hosp Epidemiol* 13:579, 1992.
9. Pearson ML, Jereb JA, Frieden TR, Crawford JT, Davis BJ, Dooley SW, Jarvis WR: Nosocomial transmission of multidrug-resistant *Mycobacterium tuberculosis*: a risk to patients and health care workers. *Ann Intern Med* 117:191, 1992.
10. Mahmoudi A, Iseman MD: Pitfalls in the care of patients with tuberculosis: common errors and their association with the acquisition of drug resistance. *JAMA* 270:65, 1993.
11. Brudney K, Dobkin J: Resurgent tuberculosis in New York City. *Am Rev Respir Dis* 144:745, 1991.
12. Centers for Disease Control: National action plan to combat multidrug-resistant tuberculosis. *MMWR* 41:5, 1992.

13. Centers for Disease Control: Guidelines for preventing the transmission of tuberculosis in health-care settings, with special focus on HIV-related issues. *MMWR* 39:1, 1992.
14. American Thoracic Society: Control of tuberculosis in the United States. *Ann Rev Respir Dis* 146:1623, 1992.
15. Sunderam G, McDonald RJ, Maniatis T, Oleske J, Kapilla R, Reichman LB: Tuberculosis as a manifestation of the acquired immunodeficiency syndrome (AIDS). *JAMA* 256:362, 1986.
16. Frieden TR et al: The emergence of drug-resistant tuberculosis in New York City. *N Engl J Med* 328:521, 1993.
17. Centers for Disease Control and American Thoracic Society: *Core Curriculum on Tuberculosis*. CDC Publications, 1991.
18. Goble M et al: Treatment of 171 patients with pulmonary tuberculosis resistant to isoniazid and rifampin. *N Engl J Med* 328:527, 1933.
19. Centers for Disease Control: Initial therapy in the era of multidrug resistance: recommendations of the Advisory Council for the Elimination of Tuberculosis. *MMWR* 42:1, 1993.
20. Gostin LO: Controlling the resurgent tuberculosis epidemic. *JAMA* 269:255, 1993.
21. Centers for Disease Control: *CDC Guideline for Isolation Precautions in Hospitals*. CDC Publications, 1982.
22. Iseman MD: A leap of faith: what can we do to curtail intrainstitutional transmission of tuberculosis? *Ann Intern Med* 117:251, 1992.
23. Nardell EA: Dodging droplet nuclei. *Am Rev Respir Dis* 142:501, 1990.
24. California Department of Health Services: *Using Ultraviolet Radiation and Ventilation to Control Tuberculosis*. California Department of Health, 1990.
25. Nardell EA, Keegan J, Cheney SA, Etkind SC: Airborne infection. *Am Rev Respir Dis* 144:302, 1991.
26. Frampton MW: An outbreak of tuberculosis among hospital personnel caring for a patient with a skin ulcer. *Ann Intern Med* 117:312, 1992.

CHAPTER 21

The Strategic Plan to Eliminate Tuberculosis in the United States and the National Action Plan to Combat Multidrug-Resistant Tuberculosis

ALAN R. HINMAN / JAMES M. HUGHES

HISTORY

From the late 1800s to the 1940s, the primary method of tuberculosis (TB) control was the isolation of infected individuals in special sanatoriums until death or until the disease went into remission. In the early part of this century, TB control was largely a voluntary movement at the state and local level. With urging from the Society for the Prevention of Tuberculosis, established in 1904, programs were set up and supported by local health departments. With the advent of antibiotics in the 1940s and multiple drug regimens for TB in the early 1950s, effective treatment for TB became possible. The Public Health Service (PHS) became involved in the evaluation of antibiotics such as strep-tomycin, para-aminosalicylic acid (PAS), and isoniazid both in the United States and in post–World War II Europe. At that time, treatment still involved a long stay in a TB sanatorium with additional treatment and lifetime follow-up after discharge.

In 1944, Congress passed the Public Health Service Act, establishing the Division of Tuberculosis Control. The act authorized grants to states for TB control. By the end of the war, PHS had organized TB support teams available to population centers of more than 100,000 to supply radiology teams and case-finding staff. By 1953, some 20 million people in 20 cities had been examined. With better living conditions and antibiotics available to treat TB, fewer cases were being found. So, with a low yield of new cases, rising costs due to inflation, and growing concern about exposure to x-rays, this program was discontinued.

339

By the 1960s, it was becoming obvious that long-term isolation of patients with active disease was not necessary to protect the patient and the community. The PHS began to recommend states close their sanatoriums and have patients receive all or most of their treatment on an outpatient basis. This represented a potential savings of almost $400 million to state and local governments. With the closing of sanatoriums around the nation, an increased need for health department follow-up was generated.[1] In the early 1960s, 75,000–100,000 patients needing outpatient follow-up services were being carried on health department case registers. In addition, an average of five contacts for each new case had to be identified and tested, and those found to be infected had to be placed on preventive treatment. This necessitated assistance from the PHS.

In 1959, in Harriman, New York, a group of TB experts met to take stock of the nation's TB control efforts and develop standards for evaluating TB control programs. This came to be known as the Arden House Conference, after the conference center in which it was held. These experts recommended *eradication* of the disease, with drug treatment as the main tool for public health TB programs. This group made 11 secondary recommendations, concentrating largely on making treatment feasible and efficient. These recommendations have led to the current approach to TB prevention and control in the United States, which has two major components: (1) identification and treatment of persons with TB disease (which both cures their infection and prevents transmission to others) and (2) identification and treatment of those with TB infection (to prevent their subsequently developing the disease).

Since the duration of the treatment for both disease and inactive infection is at least 6 months, patients' adherence to therapy is a major problem. Fortunately, directly observed therapy (DOT), in which a health worker personally gives medication to the patient and observes that it it taken, has been shown to be a highly effective way of assuring completion of therapy.[2]

On November 1, 1960, the Tuberculosis Branch, Division of Special Health Services, Bureau of State Services, was organizationally transferred to the Communicable Disease Center (CDC, now the Centers for Disease Control and Prevention). The branch remained in Washington. In response to the Surgeon General's Task Force on Tuberculosis, federal TB project grants were initiated. These grants reached a peak level of $20 million in 1968 (see Table 21-1 for complete funding history). Along with this granting of funds, the role of the CDC has been to provide national leadership in the development and implementation of effective strategies designed to interrupt the transmission of TB and ultimately eliminate the disease. The CDC has established policies and guidelines for TB control programs in conjunction with the American Thoracic Society. An important function of the CDC has been to gather data on the disease to define the overall TB problem and further elucidate specific issues. The CDC has provided consultative visits by head-quarters staff to local programs, and, in some areas, direct long-term assignments of CDC staff are made to assist in program implementation. In addition, training courses for TB workers are provided through both field and head-quarters staff. The CDC has directed special emphasis toward the emerging problems of drug resistance, refugee health, undocumented aliens, and cooperative border activities.

Much of the CDC's direct assistance to state and local health departments has been in the form of public health advisors. These federal employees are assigned, upon request, to areas that have the highest number of cases or have unique and complicated problems, such as drug-resistant TB. These assignees bring with them expertise in program, operational, and epidemiologic skills that the health departments are not otherwise able to procure. These advisors are assigned "in lieu of cash," and their salaries are paid with cooperative agreement funds.

By the late 1960s, categorical TB project grants began to be phased out in favor of general public health formula grants under section 314(d) of the Public Health Service Act. With these new grants, there was no requirement that any funds be used for TB control. Under this formula funding, many health departments redistributed funds away from TB programs. Categorical grants were eliminated after fiscal year 1971 and reinstituted in fiscal year 1982. During the late 1960s and early 1970s, virtually all TB sanatoriums were closed. Unfortunately, the savings realized by this action were not matched by a redirection of funds to establish the outpatient management system. Nonetheless, TB rates continued to decline.

STRATEGIC PLAN FOR ELIMINATION OF TB IN THE UNITED STATES

Because of the favorable trends in TB incidence in the United States in the early and mid-1980s, Dr. James O. Mason, then director of the CDC, challenged the public health community to eliminate TB from the country. The Advisory Committee on the Elimination of Tuberculosis was formed and in 1989 released the Strategic Plan for Elimination of Tuberculosis in the United States.[3] The plan defined the target as an incidence of TB of less than one case per million population by the year 2010. An interim target for the year 2000 was an incidence of 35 cases per million. The plan decribed three components: more effective use of existing prevention and control methods; development and evaluation of new prevention, diagnostic, and treatment technologies; and

TABLE 21-1. CDC History of TB Funding, 1944–1993 in Thousands of Dollars

Fiscal Year	Formula Grants	Project Grants	Emergency Grants	Program Operations*	TB-HIV	Total CDC
1944	197					
1945	2,086					
1946	6,026					
1947	8,433					
1948	8,300					
1949	9,457					
1950	9,637					
1951	9,258					
1952	8,599					
1953	8,047					
1954	5,988					
1955	6,004					
1956	6,046					
1957	6,575					
1958	6,983					
1959	6,439					
1960	4,000					4,000
1961	4,000					4,000
1962	3,500	500				4,000
1963	3,250	1,250				4,500
1964	2,900	1,606				4,506
1965	3,000	5,000				8,000

Year						
1966	3,000	9,700				12,700
1967	3,000	14,950				17,950
1968		16,016				16,016
1969		20,266				20,266
1970		3,297				3,297
1971		5,300				5,300
1972–1979						0†
1980				3,600		3,600
1981				3,700		3,700
1982		1,000		4,000		5,000
1983		5,000		4,000		9,000
1984		5,000		4,200		9,200
1985		4,950		4,300		9,250
1986		4,785		4,400		9,185
1987		7,000		4,600		11,600
1988		6,702		5,200	2,000	13,902
1989		6,622		5,200	8,909	20,731
1990		8,335		5,300	8,898	22,533
1991		9,109		5,372	10,793	25,274
1992		15,321		5,372	25,793	46,486‡
1993		34,347	39,283	5,205	25,463	104,298
1994		111,500		5,269	25,463	142,232

*Program operations support not tracked for fiscal years 1944–1979.

†No categorical grants in fiscal years 1972–1982.

‡Includes $15 million in redirected HIV funds.

technology assessment and transfer. These components and their various parts are described below.

Component 1 is the more effective use of existing prevention and control methods, including

1. Improving surveillance to ensure that all persons with signs and symptoms suggestive of TB are evaluated promptly, that all suspected or diagnosed cases are reported promptly to health departments, and that active, population-specific case finding, screening, and preventive intervention programs are established and maintained by health departments
2. Improving case prevention by ensuring that all persons have the results of at least one tuberculin skin test (TST) recorded, that periodic TST programs are conducted among persons at high occupational risk for exposure to TB (e.g., staff in TB clinics, mycobacteriology laboratories, shelters for the homeless, correctional institutions, and health care institutions), and that persons with recently acquired TB infection are promptly evaluated and treated appropriately with DOT (if needed) to ensure they complete a course of treatment
3. Improving disease containment by ensuring that patients with TB receive an appropriate therapy regimen and that they are followed to ensure they are adequately treated, using DOT if necessary
4. Program assessment and evaluation to ensure that TB programs are making satisfactory progress toward the goal of elimination

Component 2 is the development and evaluation of new prevention, diagnostic, and control methods. This component includes

1. Improving methods for preventing disease in infected persons by developing shorter, safer, more effective, and more economical means of preventing progression from asymptomatic infection to disease in infected persons
2. Improving methods of identifying infected persons at risk of developing disease
3. Improving methods of preventing infection or the establishment of infection in various body sites through research on immune mechanisms and new vaccines as well as environmental approaches to reduce risk of exposure
4. Improving methods of treating disease through extensive research to screen antimicrobial agents for anti-tuberculous activity, developing improved delivery systems, and behavioral research to improve adherence to drug regimens
5. Improving methods of diagnosing disease through research to develop new techniques that would make it possible to identify *Mycobacterium*

tuberculosis much more rapidly than is currently possible through technology such as DNA probes, polymerase chain reaction, and so on

Component 3, technology assessment and transfer, involves rapid dissemination and implementation of new knowledge, including both provider and public education, increased collaboration between public and private sectors, and increased partnerships with nongovernmental organizations.

The elimination plan was endorsed by the Secretary of Health and Human Services, Louis B. Sullivan, M.D., and also gained wide support from groups such as the American Lung Association, the American College of Physicians, the American Medical Association, and the American Public Health Association. The National Coalition to Eliminate Tuberculosis was formed to support the elimination activities through education of the public, health professionals, and policymakers. The coalition now includes approximately 60 organizations.

At the time of development of the elimination plan, it was estimated that it would take approximately $40 million each year in federal TB prevention and control funds to support the federal share of the effort, primarily supporting surveillance and investigation of disease, and support for outreach workers to provide DOT. An additional (unspecified) amount would be required for the research necessary to develop new technologies. Although appropriations in support of TB prevention and control increased from $8.3 million in fiscal year 1990 to $9.1 million in 1991 and $15.3 million in 1992, the projected level for full support was not reached (Table 21-1).

During this period, approximately $9–$10 million per year in human immunodeficiency virus (HIV) prevention funds also was spent in support of HIV-TB activities, including studies of the effectiveness of treatment and chemoprophylaxis in dually infected individuals and provision of TB evaluation for clients in drug treatment and HIV counseling and testing settings. During fiscal year 1992, an additional $15 million in HIV funds was redirected to help address the outbreaks of multidrug-resistant (MDR) TB. This included support to upgrade state and territorial health department mycobacteriology laboratories.

NATIONAL ACTION PLAN TO COMBAT MDR TB

In late 1991, CDC Director William H. Roper established a task force to address the issue of MDR TB. We cochaired the task force, which had membership from all the federal agencies involved in TB activities, including all relevant parts of the PHS–Agency for Health Care Policy Research (AHCPR); the Alcohol, Drug Abuse and Mental Health Administration

(ADAMHA, now the Substance Abuse and Mental Health Services Administration, or SAMHSA); the CDC; the Food and Drug Administration (FDA); the Health Resources and Services Administration (HRSA); the Indian Health Service (IHS); the National AIDS Program Office (NAPO); the National Institutes of Health (NIH), as well as the Health Care Financing Administration (HCFA), the Bureau of Prisons (BOP), the Department of Housing and Urban Administration (HUD), the Department of Veterans Affairs (VA), and the Occupational Safety and Health Administration (OSHA).

One of the first activities of the TB task force was to organize a conference in Atlanta, January 22–23, 1992, on meeting the challenge of MDR TB.[4] The conference was attended by more than 400 persons, who concluded that existing tools for diagnosis, management of patients, and infection control must be more thoroughly implemented and that research to develop new approaches to diagnosis and therapy was critically needed. Discussions at this conference provided important direction to the next activity of the task force, which was to produce the National Action Plan to Combat Multidrug-Resistant Tuberculosis, first released in April 1992.[5]

The action plan, which elaborates on the Strategic Plan to Eliminate Tuberculosis, has guided governmental activities since its release. It identified 38 specific problems in 9 major areas, defined objectives to address each of the problems, described implementation steps to achieve the objectives, identified the responsible organizations for carrying out those implementation steps, and gave starting dates for each of them. The 9 primary areas of activity described in the action plan were (1) surveillance and epidemiology; (2) laboratory diagnosis; (3) management of patients; (4) screening and preventive therapy; (5) infection control; (6) outbreak control; (7) program evaluation; (8) information dissemination, training, and education; and (9) research. Table 21-2 summarizes the problem statements and the objectives. The plan is intended as a blueprint for action by federal agencies. However, many of the implementation steps depend on the cooperation of state and local official health agencies as well as the private medical care sector and voluntary and community-based organizations.

Following publication of the plan, a more detailed implementation plan was developed by the task force. It outlines 219 implementation steps, identifies the responsible organizations, provides a time frame, and indicates the relative priority of each of the steps. At the time the plan was completed, it was estimated that it might cost approximately $515 million per year to fully implement it. However, that estimate included funding for a policy that was proposed for *consideration*, not as a recommendation: federal purchase and distribution of all anti-tuberculous drugs. This step alone would cost an estimated $75 million per year. It should be noted that the funding estimates did not include payment for inpatient services, renovation of isolation facilities, and so on.

The federal appropriation for support of TB prevention and control activities in fiscal year 1993 was $104 million; approximately $40 million more than the total expended in fiscal year 1992 (Table 21-1). In addition, approximately $35 million were spent by the NIH on TB-related research in fiscal year 1993. The appropriation for TB prevention and control at the CDC for fiscal year 1994 is approximately $142 million, with an additional approximately $45 million for research activities through the NIH.

The fiscal year 1993 appropriation included approximately $34 million to support basic prevention and control activities, such as surveillance, DOT, and laboratory activities. Approximately $25 million were used for HIV-TB activities, including expanded support for TB screening and management in drug treatment centers and correctional facilities.

Approximately $39 million was appropriated for emergency grants to the most heavily affected areas. Of this, $35 million was awarded to the six states that reported the largest number of cases in 1991 (California, Florida, Georgia, New Jersey, New York, and Texas) and the seven localities that reported the most cases (Chicago, Houston, Los Angeles, New York City, Philadelphia, San Diego, and San Francisco). Approximately 50 percent of the total was awarded to New York City, which has been most heavily affected. The remainder of these funds were designated to support three "model" TB programs, which combined service delivery, training, and research.

The recent resurgence in TB incidence has been ascribed to four major factors, as described elsewhere in this text (see Chapters 1, 14, 15, and 18): (1) deterioration of the public health infrastructure, (2) immigration from countries with a high prevalence of TB, (3) the HIV epidemic, and (4) outbreaks of TB, especially MDR TB. The additional federal support being made available for TB prevention and control activities should provide a major boost to the deteriorated TB public health infrastructure in the United States, but it is clear that federal funds alone cannot do the job. Significant commitments must also be made at the state and local levels.

Although the emergence of MDR TB has posed a significant problem in some areas of the country, it must be remembered that approximately 40 percent of all counties in the United States are free of reported TB and that in 25 states and the District of Columbia the reported incidence in 1992 was lower than that in 1991. In these areas, continuation of currently successful approaches is warranted. In areas that are particularly affected by immigration, HIV-TB, and/or MDR TB, intensified activities will be needed. The additional federal resources being made available should significantly help in this endeavor. Our experience to date in investigating MDR TB outbreaks in

TABLE 21-2. National Action Plan to Combat MDR TB

Problem	Objective
Surveillance and Epidemiology	
1. National surveillance systems are inadequate to accurately determine the frequency and patterns of drug-resistant TB.	1. Develop nationwide surveillance systems to determine drug susceptibility patterns of persons with active TB.
2. Hospitals, correctional facilities, and other institutional settings have been the focus of outbreaks of MDR TB. The extent of MDR TB transmission in the community has not been well studied. Epidemiologic studies and surveillance data are needed to assess the risk of infection and disease and factors promoting TB transmission in institutional settings, as well as the extent of community transmission.	2. Conduct epidemiologic investigations and studies to better define the scope and magnitude of the problem, to identify risk factors for transmission of TB in special settings, and to define the extent of MDR TB transmission in the community.
3. Certain subgroups of the population, including workers and clients of some service occupations, are at increased risk of TB. Data are needed to assess the risks and patterns of *M. tuberculosis* infection and active TB (both MDR TB and drug-sensitive TB) among both workers and nonworkers in settings where there is a risk of TB transmission.	3. Determine the patterns of TB disease and infection among workers and nonworkers in settings where there is a risk of TB transmission and characterize current programs for TB infection screening and infection control in these settings.
4. Persons with HIV infection have been the focus of the recent MDR TB outbreaks. However, the impact of HIV infection on TB trends has not been well characterized. Information is needed to assess the impact of HIV infection on recent trends in TB disease and infection, including MDR TB, in the United States.	4a. Characterize HIV infection status in persons with TB and forecast the effect of HIV on future TB trends. b. Study drug susceptibility patterns, treatment, and risk factors for TB in HIV-infected persons and perform surveillance of skin test reactivity, anergy testing, and use of preventive therapy for persons with HIV infection.
Laboratory Diagnosis	
5. The most rapid currently available laboratory technologies to identify MDR TB are not in	5. Increase the awareness and understanding of MDR TB in the laboratory community, and

TABLE 21-2 *(Continued).* **National Action Plan to Combat MDR TB**

Problem	Objective
Laboratory Diagnosis	
widespread use in state and local health department laboratories.	upgrade state and local public health laboratory mycobacteriology capacity.
6. Current laboratory capacity to track and characterize the epidemic of MDR TB may not be adequate as the outbreak spreads to more geographic areas.	6. Enhance laboratory capacity to support outbreak investigations and special studies of MDR TB.
7. Approximately 700,000 aliens apply for permanent resident status annually. Under provisions of the Immigration and Naturalization Act, each of these individuals must receive a medical examination that includes an examination for TB. The quality of laboratories used by examining physicians abroad may not be adequate to perform sputum smear examinations to identify infectious TB or to perform drug susceptibility tests.	7. Evaluate the ability of these overseas screening laboratories to detect acid-fast bacilli, identify *M. tuberculosis,* and carry out drug susceptibility tests and enhance their capability as needed.
Patient Management	
8. TB treatment must be given for a minimum of 6–9 months. If TB patients do not complete therapy, they may not be cured, and if they take medications incorrectly, their organisms may develop drug resistance. Therefore, TB patients need some degree of supervision to ensure compliance with and completion of therapy.	8. Provide guidance regarding a stepwise approach to assure completion of therapy for all TB patients, with particular emphasis on implementation of DOT.
9. Approximately 700,000 aliens apply for immigrant visas abroad annually. Many of these applicants are residing in countries with a high incidence of MDR TB because of inadequate programs to manage and treat persons with TB.	9. Evaluate the feasibility of establishing DOT programs in four or five of the high-volume immigration countries with a high incidence of TB to decrease the likelihood of introduction of MDR TB to the United States.
10. There are few inpatient facilities available for long-term treatment of complicated TB cases,	10. Explore varying options for long-term institutionalization of TB patients, including patients

(continued)

TABLE 21-2 (Continued). National Action Plan to Combat MDR TB

Problem	Objective
Patient Management	
particularly patients with MDR TB, and many areas do not have a method of paying for these services.	with MDR TB, and assist health departments in securing Medicare, Medicaid, and other funds for financing institutional care.
11. Many TB patients do not have health insurance. Local health department budgets have difficulty providing adequate services to all who need them. This may cause breaks in the continuity of care, which may lead to the development of drug-resistant disease.	11. Find means of paying for outpatient services to persons who do not have third-party coverage.
12. TB patients, particularly those with MDR TB, often require specialized services that are difficult to provide in all acute-care hospitals and outpatient clinics.	12. Evaluate feasibility of developing specialized inpatient and outpatient TB treatment units and developing regional inpatient treatment centers.
13. Drugs needed to treat TB, particularly those needed to treat MDR TB, are often unavailable, and the cost of some of these drugs is high, which may be an obstacle to effective treatment of patients.	13. CDC, FDA, pharmaceutical manufacturers, and others will work together to assure an ongoing supply of currently licensed antituberculous drugs at acceptable cost.
14. Laws, regulations, and/or procedures for the quarantine, detention, reporting, and treatment of patients may be out of date or inadequate as epidemiology of TB continues to evolve.	14. Develop guidelines and recommendations that address legal issues of TB control.
15. Homeless TB patients are often not able to complete TB therapy because of lack of stable housing and need for other social services. This may lead to the development of drug-resistant disease.	15. TB patients who are homeless, have unstable living arrangements, or lack essential social services will have access to housing for the duration of their TB treatment and will receive assistance with social services.
16. TB among migrant and seasonal farm workers may be undiagnosed and inadequately	16. Coordinate public health systems so that migrant and seasonal farm workers will have access to

TABLE 21-2 (Continued). **National Action Plan to Combat MDR TB**

Problem	Objective
Patient Management	
treated because of lack of stable housing, the unique work situation, and geographic mobility. This may lead to the development of drug-resistant disease.	diagnosis and treatment.
17. TB patients who have substance abuse problems are likely to be noncompliant with TB therapy and may develop drug-resistant disease as a result.	17a. Improve patients' compliance with antituberculous regimens among substance abusers in drug abuse treatment centers.
	b. Improve patients' compliance with antituberculous regimens among substance abusers not in drug abuse treatment programs.
18. Approximately 700,000 aliens apply for permanent resident status annually. A large percentage of these applicants come from countries where TB (including MDR TB) is common. Under provisions of the Immigration and Naturalization Act, many aliens with active TB are admitted to the United States with a waiver of excludability. Upon arrival at a U.S. port of entry (POE), CDC staff notifies state and local health authorities at the aliens' final destination of the aliens' arrival. However, CDC does not have staff at all of the major POEs and must rely on the Immigration and Naturalization Service staff to provide copies of the aliens' medical documentation so that health authorities can be notified. Consequently, documentation on some aliens arriving with TB is missed. This leads to breaks in continuity of care and may result in the development of drug-resistant disease.	18. Improve the process of notifying state and local health departments of aliens arriving with TB.

(continued)

TABLE 21-2 *(Continued).* National Action Plan to Combat MDR TB

Problem	*Objective*
Screening and Preventive Therapy	
19. There is no standard approach to the evaluation and management of persons exposed to MDR TB.	19. Develop and publish an approach to the evaluation and management of persons exposed to MDR TB.
20. Many persons in populations at high risk for TB may also be at risk for noncompliance with therapy if active TB develops. This may lead to the development of drug-resistant TB.	20. Implement screening and preventive therapy programs, including supervised preventive therapy, in populations at high risk for both TB and noncompliance.
Infection Control	
21. Various infection control strategies are available to prevent TB transmission in institutional settings. The effectiveness and feasibility of these strategies are not well characterized, and they are not consistently implemented.	21. Assess the effectiveness and feasibility of various infection control strategies in institutional settings (e.g., health care facilities, substance abuse clinics, residential treatment centers, shelters for the homeless, and correctional facilities) and ensure that appropriate procedures are implemented through educational and regulatory approaches.
22. Tuberculin skin testing of workers in settings where there is a risk of TB transmission is very important. Skin testing identifies workers who are infected with *M. tuberculosis* and need to be evaluated for active TB and for preventive therapy. It also serves as an indicator of the effectiveness of infection control practices. However, tuberculin skin testing programs are not consistently implemented.	22. Ensure that adequate tuberculin skin testing programs for workers are in place in settings where there is a significant risk of TB transmission.
Outbreak Control	
23. The control of MDR TB outbreaks is costly and complex, requiring close collaboration among local, state, and federal health officials and others (e.g., hospital officials, correctional facility officials, and technical consultants).	23. Facilitate collaboration of various officials and organizations for controlling MDR TB outbreaks.

TABLE 21-2 (Continued). National Action Plan to Combat MDR TB

Problem	Objective
Program Evaluation	

Problem	Objective
24. Some TB control programs may not be effective in managing TB patients, which may lead to the development of drug-resistant disease. There is a need for assessing the quality of TB control (including health department infrastructure, facilities, priorities, etc.).	24. The CDC, in conjunction with other agencies (e.g., American Lung Association, and other members of the National Coalition for Elimination of TB), will assist state and local health departments in assessing the adequacy of their TB control programs.
25. Poor compliance with prescribed treatment promotes the development of drug-resistant strains of *M. tuberculosis*, which may lead to outbreaks of MDR TB. Programs do not currently collect and analyze data on treatment outcomes that would identify populations at high risk for treatment failure.	25. Assess program performance by collecting information on treatment outcomes of TB patients on an individual case basis, which will allow more effective targeting of resources.

Information Dissemination, Training, and Education	
26. There is a lack of expertise regarding treatment of TB, especially treatment of MDR TB, in many parts of the United States.	26. Develop a cadre of health care professionals with expertise in the management of TB, including MDR TB.
27. Nosocomial transmission of TB to health care workers and patients is occurring. Such transmission is preventable if recommended infection control practices are implemented.	27. Disseminate information on the prevention of TB transmission to individuals and facilities that provide services to persons with TB or to persons at high risk for TB.
28. A critical need exists for trained researchers to develop the new diagnostic assays, therapeutic agents, and vaccines to meet present and future TB public health needs.	28. Train adequate numbers of researchers to effectively respond to TB research needs.
29. Mycobacteriology laboratory personnel may not be familiar with state-of-the-art TB diagnostic technologies and reporting practices.	29. Provide training and evaluation of clinical mycobacteriology laboratory personnel in new diagnostic techniques for TB.
30. Strategies for training and delivering TB information and education to health professionals and others have been inadequate.	30. Develop an integrated system for professional information and communication on TB.

(continued)

TABLE 21-2 (Continued). National Action Plan to Combat MDR TB

Problem	Objective
Research	
31. Research on TB needs to be conducted and promoted by a variety of agencies, including CDC, NIH, FDA, and others. Coordination of research efforts among these agencies will be important in ensuring that critical knowledge gaps are addressed effectively.	31. Develop a mechanism for coordinating TB research activities among the various involved agencies.
32. There is a critical lack of knowledge about the basic characteristics of *M. tuberculosis* (e.g., growth, physiology, biochemistry, genetics, and molecular biology). This knowledge gap is a barrier to the development of new treatment and control modalities.	32. Provide increased support for basic research on the biology of *M. tuberculosis* and the host responses to infection.
33. Existing diagnostic methods to identify persons with drug-resistant TB are very slow, impeding treatment and control efforts.	33. Develop and evaluate new technology to rapidly and reliably diagnose cases of TB and identify drug susceptibility patterns.
34. Existing methods of identifying latent TB infection, especially in persons who are immunosuppressed, lack sensitivity and specificity.	34. Develop and evaluate new technologies to rapidly and reliably identify latent tuberculous infection in both immunocompetent and immunosuppressed persons.
35. Currently available drugs are not sufficiently effective in treating MDR TB. The duration of therapy required to treat TB with currently available drugs leads to noncompliance with therapy and development of drug-resistant disease.	35. Encourage the development and evaluation of new drugs and modalities to treat and prevent MDR TB, as well as to reduce the duration of therapy required to cure drug-susceptible TB.

hospitals and correctional facilities indicates that in each there have been significant deficiencies in carrying out existing recommendations for prevention of nosocomial transmission. Where aggressive steps have been taken to implement currently recommended approaches, evidence indicates that transmission to other patients and health care workers has been curtailed.

Consequently, even though the reported incidence of TB continues to rise in the United States as a result of identifiable problems, we remain optimistic that the elimination target can be achieved if aggressive prevention and control strategies are effectively implemented, although it may be slightly delayed.

ACKNOWLEDGMENTS

The authors wish to acknowledge the invaluable assistance of Dixie Snider and Carmine Bozzi in summarizing the history of TB control efforts in the United States.

REFERENCES

1. National Tuberculosis and Respiratory Disease Association: Standards for tuberculosis treatment in the 1970s: a statement by the Ad Hoc Committee on Quality Care for Tuberculosis. *Am Rev Respir Dis* 102:992, 1970.
2. American Thoracic Society: Intermittent chemotherapy for adults with tuberculosis. *Am Rev Respir Dis* 110:374, 1974.
3. Centers for Disease Control: A strategic plan for the elimination of tuberculosis in the United States. *MMWR* 38(suppl S-3):1, 1989.
4. Hinman AR, Hughes JM, Snider DE Jr, Cohen ML: Meeting the challenge of multidrug-resistant tuberculosis: summary of a conference. *MMWR* 41(RR-11):49, 1992.
5. Centers for Disease Control: National action plan to combat multidrug-resistant tuberculosis. *MMWR* 41(RR-11):1, 1992.

PART VI

Nontuberculous Mycobacterial Diseases

CHAPTER 22

Slowly Growing Nontuberculous Mycobacterial Disease

DONALD D. PETERSON

Mycobacteria other than *Mycobacterium tuberculosis* have traditionally been divided into the slow-growing (Runyon groups I, II, and III) and rapid-growing nontuberculous mycobacteria (Runyon group IV), as discussed in Chapter 3.

Among the important overall differences are that nontuberculous mycobacteria are not contagious, thus eliminating many of the public health issues raised by tuberculosis (TB), and that they usually cause more indolent syndromes, which paradoxically can make diagnostic and management issues more difficult in individual cases. The lack of contagiousness has meant that patients with atypical mycobacterial infection are not reported to public health departments, and, thus, statistics concerning incidence are sparse and incomplete, as are data concerning the natural history of infection.

The most common pulmonary pathogens among the nontuberculous mycobacteria are *Mycobacterium avium*, *Mycobacterium intracellularae*, and *Mycobacterium kansasii*, all slow-growing mycobacteria. The first two will be lumped under the term *M. avium* complex and will be the subject of most of this chapter, since recent studies have emphasized the increased frequency of this infection in the normal host.[1-5] The important issue of *M. avium* infection in patients with acquired immune deficiency syndrome (AIDS) is addressed in Chapter 24.

M. AVIUM COMPLEX

Epidemiology

Pulmonary infections with *M. avium* complex probably occur worldwide, as indicated by reports from Japan[6] and South Africa,[7] although the very limited data available suggest that prevalence rates may vary markedly. In the United States, the incidence of pulmonary infection with *M. avium* complex seems to be correlated with frequency of isolation of the organism from environmental water sources, especially fresh water and brackish water in warmer climates.[8] Some plasmid-containing strains are more virulent and are most often the ones associated with disease in humans. In addition, they have been isolated from environmental aerosols rather than from dust and soil.[9] Although rates of skin test reactivity are highest in southeastern farmers,[9] the water supply in some northeastern cities and, indeed, in many hospitals has been found to be contaminated with *M. avium* complex, with particularly high concentration rates for hot water systems and shower heads,[10] thus leading to speculation that the route of entry in some cases may be through aerosolization while showering.

Patients with *M. avium* complex infection are generally divided into three main groups (Table 22-1):

1. Patients with preexisting chronic lung diseases, such as chronic obstructive lung disease, or scarring from various types of previous lung injury, including infection with *M. tuberculosis*, often develop *M. avium* complex infection. The majority of such cases occur in men, probably because of their greater incidence of chronic lung disease from various causes.
2. More recently, a growing number of cases have been recognized in healthy elderly people with no evidence of preexistent lung disease. This syndrome is more common in elderly women, even more so than can be accounted for by gender-related survival differences. The relative number of such infections identified may be similar to that for the first group.
3. Patients with AIDS show the highest predisposition to infection with *M. avium* complex. The proportion of patients in this group relative to the first two groups varies markedly from laboratory to laboratory and

TABLE 22-1.   Characteristics of Patients with Pulmonary Infection Caused by *M. avium* Complex

Group	Predisposing Condition	No. of Patients	Age, Years*	Male/Female, %
1	Underlying chronic lung disease or lung scarring	64	64.7 ± 14	50/50
2	No underlying chronic lung disease or lung scarring	21	66.1 ± 9.6	19/81
3	AIDS	34	38 ± 12	94/6

*Age plus or minus the standard deviation.

Source: Used with permission. From Prince et al.[1]

practice to practice, depending on the incidence of AIDS in the community.

As of 1980, atypical mycobacteria accounted for approximately one-third of pathogenic mycobacterial isolates.[11] Although the overall incidence of TB in the United States is now rising, as discussed in Chapter 1, the current proportion of mycobacterial disease due to atypical mycobacteria is approximately 50 percent.[12] Since many communities have been relatively less affected by the causative factors in the rise in TB, such as AIDS, new infections with *M. avium* complex may be diagnosed more frequently than TB in many hospitals.[1,3]

Pathophysiology

The route of entry for pulmonary infection with *M. avium* complex is presumed to be inhalational, although this is difficult to establish with certainty. Environmental factors are likely to be important, as discussed above. Person-to-person transmission has never been demonstrated. Given the presumably high rate of exposure compared to the low rate of infection with *M. avium* in the normal host, as well as its predominance in the United States in elderly white women, some type of subtle impairment in host defense has been suspected but thus far only vaguely characterized.[13] Additional evidence for the hypothesis of impaired host defense is provided by tendency for *M. avium* complex infections to afflict women with mild chest wall deformities due to pectus excavatum or scoliosis,[14] suggesting that the predisposition may be an associated genetic impairment in defense mechanisms rather than the relatively mild structural derangement of the thoracic cage.

The frequent establishment of asymptomatic infection with *M. avium* is shown through epidemiological studies employing skin testing. Since population screening with skin testing for atypical mycobacteria is not routinely performed, little is known about whether the initial infection and later stages mirror the pathophysiology of infection with *M. tuberculosis* (e.g., with asymptomatic persistence of organisms in the lungs and eventual reactivation). Thus, it is uncertain whether the recent rise in incidence of *M. avium* complex disease is due to new infection, due to reactivation of dormant primary disease, or possibly even artifactual because of poor recognition of this disease in the past.

Clinical Presentation

In immunocompetent patients, the clinical presentation of pulmonary infection with *M. avium* complex (Table 22-2) is generally similar whether the patients are categorized as "normal hosts" or patients with preexisting pulmo-

TABLE 22-2. Clinical Characteristics of Patients Without Predisposing Conditions Who Had Pulmonary Disease Caused by *M. avium* Complex

Characteristic	No./Total Patients, %
Female	17/21 (81)
Cough or sputum	18/21 (86)
Fever	3/21 (14)
Weight loss	3/21 (14)
Hemoptysis	3/21 (14)
Positive Mantoux test results	3/14 (21)*
Local radiographic pattern	5/21 (23)
Diffuse radiographic pattern	16/21 (76)

*Fourteen patients were tested.
Source: Used with permission. From Prince et al.[1]

nary disease, although the eventual course and consequences of the disease may be affected by the patient's preexisting pulmonary condition. The most common symptoms are cough and sputum production, with the sputum often being purulent. Since chronic cough is such a nonspecific symptom, the patient or the treating physician may ignore the problem for years until the cough becomes more troubling or until a chest radiograph, taken for other reasons, discloses an abnormality. In a group of patients with no underlying pulmonary disease, the mean duration of symptoms before diagnosis was 26 weeks.[1] Hemoptysis occurs in a minority of patients and is usually low-grade, rarely leading to surgical intervention for control of bleeding. Fever, dyspnea, and chest pain are uncommon unless caused by other processes.

M. avium complex infection may also present as an asymptomatic pulmonary nodular infiltrate that has been surgically resected because of the suspicion that the patient has carcinoma of the lung. With advances in less invasive diagnostic techniques over the last 15 years, this scenario has become less frequent.

On the other hand, an important subgroup of patients presents with more rapidly evolving disease (several months to several years) characterized by progressive cough and sputum production, gradual debilitation, low-grade fever, and eventually dyspnea due to widespread pulmonary involvement. These patients may develop bronchiectasis, with episodic exacerbations due to bacterial superinfection, particularly with *Pseudomonas* species. In some patients who present with clinical evidence of bronchiectasis involving many areas of the lungs, the isolation of both *M. avium* complex and gram-negative bacteria makes it difficult to draw any conclusion as to whether the original problem was bronchiectasis of unknown cause, with subsequent colonization or infection with *M. avium* complex, or widespread pulmonary infection with *M. avium* complex causing the bronchiectasis.

When patients with preexisting pulmonary disease develop *M. avium* complex infection, the symptoms are often overlooked or mistakenly ascribed to the previous condition, particularly in the case of patients with scarring from previous infection with *M. tuberculosis*. Other types of chronic respiratory compromise predisposing to infection with *M. avium* complex include chronic obstructive pulmonary disease, cystic fibrosis,[15] bronchiectasis, silicosis, pulmonary fibrosis, and deformities of the thoracic cage, such as pectus excavatum and mild scoliosis, particularly in women.[14]

Radiographic Presentation

Before 1985, available information suggested that the atypical mycobacteria usually caused upper lobe cavitary disease without any difference in radiographic appearance from disease due to *M. tuberculosis*. However, a strict definition of atypical mycobacterial infection and the increase in the number of patients diagnosed through means such as bronchoscopy and needle biopsy have recently modified this belief substantially.[1,3] Although chest radiographs of patients with previously normal lungs who develop *M. avium* complex disease resemble radiographs of reactivation TB in approximately 50 percent of cases, the other half show one or more nodular infiltrates, with the presentation varying widely from that of the asymptomatic solitary nodule mimicking lung cancer to multiple nodular infiltrates in all lung zones. Infiltrates due to *M. avium* complex disease frequently involve the anterior segments of the upper lobes, the right middle lobe, the lingula, or the basilar segments of the lower lobes, all relatively unusual locations for reactivation TB. Occasionally, a predominantly upper-lobe focus is seen in association with multiple smaller upper and lower lobe nodular infiltrates. Noncavitary disease isolated to the lingula and/or right middle lobe may be particularly frequent in elderly women and has been termed the Lady Windermere syndrome,[16] because of a supposition that the fastidious refusal to cough up phlegm may have some pathogenetic significance; however, the clinical and demographic characteristics of such patients appear to match the overall pattern seen with *M. avium* complex infection, making this supposition quite doubtful.

Comparison of radiographic findings in infection due to *M. avium* complex and *M. tuberculosis* is complicated by the fact that many patients presenting with TB in the United States today have radiographic findings previously considered unusual for TB.[3] Cavitation occurs in approximately half of *M. avium* complex infections,[1,3] less often than had been shown in studies relying on positive sputum smear and culture results for diagnosis. Although cavities tend to be smaller and more thin-walled than in patients with TB,[3] the degree of overlap negates clinical utility for this statistical difference. Cavities may be solitary, with little apparent associated infiltrate. Pleural effusions are occasionally noted but are usually small unless complicated by bacterial super-infection associated with bronchopleural fistula. Miliary disease due to *M. avium* complex in the normal host is rare and should prompt a search for underlying immunodeficiency.

Computed tomograms of the chest are often helpful in detecting the presence of multiple areas of involvement and subtle cavitation strongly suggestive of granulomatous infection (Fig. 22-1). Alternatively, they may be used to provide additional evidence of localized disease in a patient being considered for surgical resection of known *M. avium* complex pulmonary infection.

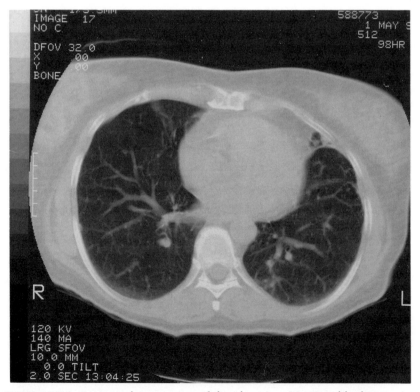

FIGURE 22-1. Computed tomograms of the chest in a 72-year-old white woman with chronic cough and purulent sputum, demonstrating typical bilateral nodular infiltrates.

Mediastinal adenopathy is rarely noted and may be a sign of primary progressive infection unless present for other reasons.

The tendency of *M. avium* complex disease to complicate many chronic lung conditions leads to a wide variety of additional radiographic presentations, including patients with *M. avium* complex infection and scarring from previous TB. Progressive pulmonary disease may produce a generalized reticulonodular cystic pattern, reflecting large numbers of small cavities and/or development of bronchiectasis.

Diagnostic Methods

Sputum examination and culture for acid-fast bacteria remain key elements in establishing the diagnosis in many clinical settings. However, a considerable percentage of cultures testing positive for *M. avium* complex will reflect contamination in the laboratory or colonization of the patient without actual disease. This percentage will vary widely, depending on the laboratory, the prevailing practice in the local community regarding the number of specimens sent for culture in various types of patients, and the actual incidence of *M. avium* complex disease. Thus, a laboratory that processes a large proportion of specimens from patients unlikely to have mycobacterial infection will have a much higher false-positive rate of culture.

To help establish the significance of positive culture results, confirmatory evidence is sought in a number of ways. First, the clinical presentation or chest radiograph of the patient should be such as to make the diagnosis plausible and worth further pursuit. Acid-fast smear positivity usually reflects a higher number of organisms present and is often reported semiquantitatively; thus, a smear showing a large number of organisms gives additional credence to the diagnosis of mycobacterial infection. Repeated sputum culture positivity makes laboratory contamination much less likely as a cause of the positive culture results, allowing for the possibility that the patient simply has colonization with *M. avium* complex, especially if chest radiographs are compatible with scarring from previous diseases.

Skin testing is not generally useful in diagnosis of atypical mycobacterial infections, since the high background rate of skin test positivity greatly lowers the predictive value of a positive skin test in a patient suspected of having mycobacterial disease. A recent study[12] failed to demonstrate the utility of skin tests for atypical mycobacteria, partly because purified protein derivative B (PPD-B), the reagent prepared to elicit reactions in patients with *M. avium* complex infection, actually caused positive reactions of equal size in patients with TB. In selected circumstances, such as the convincing demonstration of acid-fast organisms in biopsy specimens without appropriate culture confirmation or clinical presentations very suggestive of mycobacterial infection, skin testing with standard intermediate-strength PPD-S for TB may help guide clinical decisions.

Bronchoscopy often provides the initial evidence of infection with *M. avium* complex, since it is frequently used to evaluate pulmonary nodules or persistent infiltrates of unknown cause. In patients with compatible clinical characteristics, positive acid-fast smear and culture results are likely to reflect actual disease, but results must still be interpreted with the above-mentioned caveats regarding colonization or contamination during processing of sputum specimens. For example, contamination of the bronchoscope was recently described as a cause of a "pseudoepidemic" of atypical mycobacterial infections.[17]

Ideally, infection with *M. avium* complex would be established by both positive culture results and demonstration on biopsy of caseating granulomata in lung tissue, with acid-fast smear results being positive for the lung tissue. Bronchoscopy with washings or lavage for smears and cultures and transbronchial biopsies for pathology stains frequently provide this evidence,[1] depending on the size and location of infiltrates, activity of disease, and technical factors related to the skill of the bronchoscopist and the handling of specimens. Percutaneous needle aspiration and/or biopsy can provide material for smears and cultures, and perhaps a small core biopsy for histological examination, depending on the technique employed. In this situation, the main issue often is to diagnose or exclude carcinoma of the lung, but positive evidence of granulomatous infection may be obtained if specimens are processed with this consideration in mind. Open lung biopsy is likely to be employed, not in a patient suspected of having granulomatous disease, but, rather, in a patient with a nodule or nodular infiltrate with a significant clinical suspicion of malignancy, generally after some of the above-mentioned diagnostic methods have failed to provide enough evidence to avoid a surgical approach. In some cases, rigid thoracoscopy may be able to provide the diagnosis with less morbidity than standard thoracotomy.

Unfortunately, despite the diagnostic techniques outlined above, a frequent scenario is the demonstration of positive acid-fast smear results from a patient who clinically has disease compatible with either TB or atypical mycobacteria. Given the approximately equal incidence of these diseases, many public health dollars are wasted in infection control measures and contact tracing for patients eventually proven 3–6 weeks later to have atypical mycobacterial disease, not to mention the considerable anxiety generated during this period among family, friends, and healthcare workers. Therefore, effort is continuing to find more rapid methods of diagnosis using culture, serologic, and DNA probe techniques (see Chapters 3 and 16).

Clinical Course and Treatment

The natural history of untreated infection with *M. avium* complex in the normal host is extremely variable. At one end of the spectrum, the patient with an asymptomatic nodular infiltrate proven to be due to *M. avium* complex infection at the time of thoracotomy for suspected lung cancer may have previous chest radiographs demonstrating gradual enlargement of the lesion over years, sometimes with periods of stability lasting years or even temporary partial resolution of radiographic findings. In fact, "tuberculomas" are usually found to be due to infection with *M. avium* rather than *M. tuberculosis*[20] when appropriate culture results are obtained. When asymptomatic localized disease is detected in this manner, cure is generally provided by the surgical resection without the need for chemotherapy.[20,21] In all likelihood, many such patients never would have developed symptomatic disease. At the other end of the spectrum, the patient presenting with extensive bilateral infiltrates and debilitation has a guarded prognosis, even with treatment with a multidrug regimen.[1] A recent report[22] suggested a better prognosis for patients infected with *M. intracellularae* than with *M. avium* but was based on small numbers with considerable overlap among groups, with most patients falling into the intermediate category of stable or slowly progressive disease.

Most isolates of *M. avium* complex are resistant or relatively resistant to many of the drugs generally effective for treatment of *M. tuberculosis*, including isoniazid and pyrazinamide, which are in the currently recommended three-drug regimen for treatment of non–drug-resistant TB. Therefore, the 1990 recommendations of the American Thoracic Society[23] are frequently modified to delete isoniazid and pyrazinamide.[24] Treatment regimens usually include four or even five drugs, with the organism typically having demonstrated partial resistance in vitro to some of them. However, treatment is usually initiated on the basis of positive smear results and is therefore often directed against *M. tuberculosis*, given the difficulty in distinguishing these infections clinically. Three to six weeks later, following the culture confirmation of *M. avium* complex, the decision can be made to follow the American Thoracic Society recommendations to use isoniazid, rifampin, ethambutol, and streptomycin or to modify the regimen as mentioned above, with possible further changes pending analysis of drug sensitivities of the isolate. Paradoxically, many patients respond favorably to initial therapy despite in vitro resistance of the organism to the individual drugs in the treatment regimen. Because of historical data indicating a favorable response of many *M. avium* complex patients treated with standard antituberculous chemotherapy despite in vitro resistance; because of difficulties in establishing standardized, reliable susceptibility testing; and because of the paucity of data regarding the eventual outcome of infection with *M. avium* complex, the usefulness of sensitivity testing for guiding initial treatment has been questioned.[25] Certainly, quantitative assessments of drug activity and the study of synergistic drug interactions hold future promise in making therapy more effective and rational.[24,25]

In addition to the four-drug regimen of isoniazid, rifampin, ethambutol, and streptomycin, other frequently used drugs include second-line antituberculous agents, such as clofazimine, ethionamide, amikacin, and even cycloserine, with considerable risk of toxicity. Among the newer antibiotics, the macrolides (e.g., clarithromycin) and the quinolones (e.g., ciprofloxacin) have demonstrated efficacy and are often the first drugs begun if the infection is known to be due to *M. avium* complex rather than *M. tuberculosis* at the time of initiation of treatment. In such situations, a frequently chosen four-drug regimen is clarithromycin, ciprofloxacin, rifampin, and ethambutol, with modifications made following results of sensitivity testing.

Side effects usually cause at least one alteration in the planned treatment regimen;[26] given the relative indolence of the infection in most patients, a practical approach is to start with one or two drugs and add the others at weekly intervals rather than attempting to begin all drugs simultaneously, as is usually done in more standardized regimens for TB. Assuming a favorable clinical response, the regimen for the treatment of *M. avium* complex is usually continued for 18–24 months. Even then there is a significant chance of relapse, most likely because of the persistence of viable organisms in the lungs or, alternatively, perhaps because of reinfection due to continued environmental exposure to *M. avium* complex. A recent report[18] indicated that the prognosis may be more favorable than previously suggested and promoted the concept that longer-term treatment (up to 7 years) may not only reduce the chances of relapse but may also slow disease progression in apparent nonresponders. In fact, for some patients with *M. avium* complex disease presenting with minimal symptoms (usually chronic bronchitis), careful follow-up without initiation of treatment is a reasonable option (Fig. 22-2). A recent community-based report[19] also suggests a much more favorable prognosis than has been derived from studies drawn from academic referral settings; patients generally had less advanced disease at the time of presentation, and the large majority responded well to chemotherapy with three- to five-drug regimens or to surgery when appropriate.

Because of the potentially adverse effects and the cost of drug treatment, along with the possibility of nonresponse or eventual relapse, surgical resection is often advocated when disease is localized to a single lobe.[4,20] Computed tomography should be used to ensure that the patient does not actually have small nodular infiltrates elsewhere, a frequent finding even when routine chest radiographs suggest a single focus of disease. In addition, once general criteria

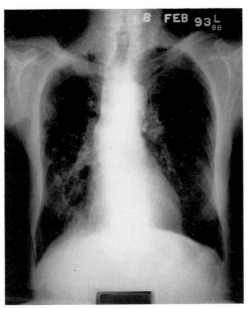

FIGURE 22-2. Chest radiograph of an 88-year-old man with chronic cough and sputum production. Symptoms and radiographic findings have fluctuated over at least 8 years, with excellent functional status at present, after never having been treated.

for surgical resection (including functional status, other medical conditions, and pulmonary reserve) are applied, most patients are eliminated from consideration for surgical treatment. The remaining subgroup is likely to be much less symptomatic and is more likely to respond to a multiple-drug regimen than is the group with bilateral disease,[1] thus fulfilling the old adage that the operation is most likely to be tolerated by and to be beneficial for those who need it the least. Ideally, patients should have 2–3 months of chemotherapy before surgery, hopefully with conversion to negative smear results. An additional 2–3 months of chemotherapy should be continued after surgery.

Despite the apparent risks, surgery can indeed offer the hope of cure in some patients and should be considered an important option in the management of symptomatic localized disease, particularly when response to drug treatment is suboptimal or when drug regimens are not tolerated by the patient. Occasionally, even pneumonectomy may be considered in carefully selected patients (Fig. 22-3). However, pneumonectomy in patients with continued acid-fast sputum positivity carries a high risk of eventual development of bronchopleural fistula;[4] this often fatal complication is apparently

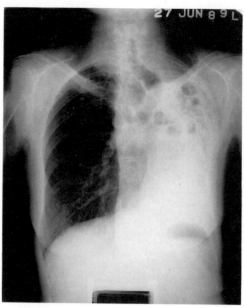

FIGURE 22-3. Chest radiograph of a 67-year-old white woman with previous left upper lobe destruction by TB 40 years ago and now with left lower lobe consolidation due to *M. avium* complex disease. Because of persistent cough, sputum, and weight loss without response to a four-drug regimen, she underwent left pneumonectomy, with eventual cure and return to normal functional status following a protracted and complicated postoperative course.

more common in patients with bacterial superinfection undergoing right pneumonectomy. Whether earlier pulmonary resection performed on a much larger fraction of the patients with *M. avium* complex infection would improve overall survival rates is speculative.

Patients who have progressive disease due to *M. avium* complex may eventually develop weight loss and debilitation due to extensive pulmonary involvement with respiratory insufficiency and generalized bronchiectasis, often complicated by chronic bronchial superinfection with *Pseudomonas aeruginosa*. Other potentially serious complications include hemoptysis, empyema, and bronchopleural fistula.

M. KANSASII

M. kansasii is much less prevalent in environmental water samples than is *M. avium* complex and is seen as a cause of disease predominantly in the midwestern United States and some southern states. Contamination of laboratory specimens with *M. kansasii* and colonization of the lungs occur rather infrequently; thus, most laboratory isolations reflect actual disease.[27] Given this initial difference, the same general principles guide clinical assessment of patients with *M. kansasii*, since the syndromes it causes are similar. Pulmonary infections are distributed among normal hosts and patients with various types of chronic lung disease (usually older white males) but are unusual in patients with AIDS. Compared to *M. tuberculosis*, *M. kansasii* often causes cavities that are thin-walled, with relatively little surrounding parenchymal infiltration. Disseminated infection is rare and generally requires some type of underlying immunosuppression.

Treatment of *M. kansasii* with standard antituberculous therapy is generally successful despite frequent partial or total resistance to isoniazid. Rifampin is considered the most important drug in the typical three-drug regimen also including isoniazid and ethambutol. Treatment is usually continued for 12–24 months. Surgery is rarely considered a treatment option because of the good response of *M. kansasii* to pharmacological therapy.

REFERENCES

1. Prince DS, Peterson DD, Steiner RM, Gottlieb JE, Scott R, Israel HL, Figueroa WG, Fish JE: Infection with *Mycobacterium avium* complex in patients without predisposing conditions. *N Engl J Med* 321:863, 1989.
2. Iseman MD: *Mycobacterium avium* complex and the normal host: the other side of the coin. *N Engl J Med* 321:896, 1989.
3. Albelda SM, Kern JA, Marinelli DL, Miller WT: Expanding spectrum of pulmonary disease caused by nontuberculous mycobacteria. *Radiology* 157:289, 1985.
4. Pomerantz M, Madsen L, Goble M, Iseman M: Surgical management of resistant mycobacterial tuberculosis and other mycobacterial pulmonary infections. *Ann Thorac Surg* 52: 1108, 1991.
5. Contreras MA, Cheung OT, Sanders DE, Goldstein RS: Pulmonary infection with nontuberculous mycobacteria. *Am Rev Respir Dis* 137:149, 1988.
6. Tsukamura M, Kita N, Shimoide H, Arakawa H, Kuze A: Studies on the epidemiology of nontuberculosis mycobacteriosis in Japan. *Am Rev Respir Dis* 137:1280, 1988.
7. Plit ML, Woolf M, Miller GB: Pulmonary non-tuberculous mycobacterial disease. *S Afr Med J* 74:217, 1988
8. Falkinham JO, Parker BC, Gruft H: Epidemiology of infection by nontuberculous mycobacteria. *Am Rev Respir Dis* 121:931, 1980.
9. O'Brien RJ: The epidemiology of nontuberculous mycobacterial disease. *Clin Chest Med* 10:407, 1989.
10. duMoulin GC, Stottmeier KD, Pelletier PA, Tsang AY, Hedley-Whyte J: Concentration of *Mycobacterium avium* by hospital hot water systems. *JAMA* 260:1599, 1988.
11. Good RC, Mastro TD: The modern mycobacteriology laboratory: how it can help the clinician. *Clin Chest Med* 10:315, 1989.
12. Huebner RE, Schein MF, Cauthen GM, Geiter LJ, Selin MJ, Good RC, O'Brien RJ:

Evaluation of the clinical usefulness of mycobacterial skin test antigens in adults with pulmonary mycobacterioses. *Am Rev Respir Dis* 145:1160, 1992.

13. Tsuyuguchi I, Shiratsuchi H, Okuda Y, Yamamoto Y: An analysis of in vitro T cell responsiveness in nontuberculous mycobacterial infection. *Chest* 94:822, 1988.

14. Iseman MD, Buschman DL, Ackerson LM: Pectus excavatum and scoliosis: thoracic anomalies associated with pulmonary disease caused by *Mycobacterium avium* complex. *Am Rev Respir Dis* 144:914, 1991.

15. Aitken ML, Burke W, McDonald G, Wallis C, Ramsey B, Nolan C: Nontuberculous mycobacterial disease in adult cystic fibrosis patients. *Chest* 103:1096, 1993.

16. Reich JM, Johnson RE: *Mycobacterium avium* complex pulmonary disease presenting as an isolated lingular or middle lobe pattern: the Lady Windermere syndrome. *Chest* 101: 1605, 1992.

17. Gubler JGH, Salfinger M, Von Graevenitz A: Pseudoepidemic of nontuberculous mycobacteria due to a contaminated bronchoscope cleaning machine. *Chest* 101:1245, 1992.

18. Hornick DB, Dayton CS, Bedell GN, Fick RB: Nontuberculous mycobacterial lung disease: substantiation of a less aggressive approach. *Chest* 93:550, 1988.

19. Reich JM, Johnson RE: *Mycobacterium avium* complex pulmonary disease: incidence, presentation, and response to therapy in a community setting. *Am Rev Respir Dis* 143:1381, 1991.

20. Teirstein AS, Damsker B, Kirschner PA, Krellenstein DJ, Robinson B, Chuang MT: Pulmonary infection with *Mycobacterium avium-intracellulare*: diagnosis, clinical patterns, treatment. *Mt Sinai J Med* 57:209, 1990.

21. Davidson PT: The diagnosis and management of disease caused by *M. avium* complex, *M. kansasii*, and other mycobacteria. *Clin Chest Med* 10:431, 1989.

22. Yamori S, Tsukamura M: Comparison of prognosis of pulmonary disease caused by *Mycobacterium avium* and by *Mycobacterium intracellulare*. *Chest* 102:89, 1992.

23. American Thoracic Society: Official statement on diagnosis and treatment of disease caused by nontuberculous mycobacteria. *Am Rev Respir Dis* 142:940, 1990.

24. Heifets LB, Iseman MD: Individualized therapy versus standard regimens in the treatment of *Mycobacterium avium* infections. *Am Rev Respir Dis* 144:1, 1991.

25. Wallace RJ, Glassroth J, O'Brien R: A plea for clinical trials to resolve the issue of optimal therapy in the treatment of *Mycobacterium avium* infection. *Am Rev Respir Dis* 144:3, 1991.

26. Davidson PT, Khanijo V, Goble M, Moulding TS: Treatment of disease due to *Mycobacterium intracellulare*. *Rev Infect Dis* 3:1052, 1981.

27. Lillo M, Orengo S, Cernoch P, Harris RL: Pulmonary and disseminated infection due to *Mycobacterium kansasii*: a decade of experience. *Rev Infect Dis* 12:760, 1990.

CHAPTER 23

Syndromes, Diagnosis, and Treatment of Rapidly Growing Mycobacteria

PAUL W. WRIGHT / RICHARD J. WALLACE, JR.

During the past decade, rapidly growing mycobacteria (RGM) have been increasingly recognized as pathogens in infections involving the skin,[1] soft tissue,[2] bones and joints,[2] lungs,[3] cornea,[4] postsurgical sites (nosocomial),[5] and bloodstream.[6] The RGM are nontuberculous mycobacteria (NTM) that are easily recovered from the environment. They grow readily in 3–5 days (by definition, they produce visible individual colonies in <7 days) on both standard mycobacterial media, such as Löwenstein-Jensen (L-J) medium, and on 5 percent sheep's blood agar and chocolate agar. The RGM stain both as acid-fast organisms and as gram-positive rods, the latter in a beaded pattern that may be confused with aerobic diphtheroids. However, they stain relatively poorly by either method in tissues or drainage and hence may be missed unless cultures are performed.

The RGM are a highly diversified, heterogeneous, and complex group of organisms that vary in pathogenicity from mere saprophytes to pathogens causing significant illness. They currently comprise 23 recognized species, with a number of other taxonomic groups not yet sufficiently characterized. The vast majority (95 percent) of RGM human infections are due to the *Mycobacterium fortuitum* and the *Mycobacterium chelonae* groups, sometimes referred to as the *M. fortuitum* complex. Other RGM, which rarely cause disease, include *Mycobacterium smegmatis*, *Mycobacterium flavescens*, *Mycobacterium neoaurum*, *Mycobacterium thermoresistibile*, and unnamed and less well-characterized groups, such as the *M. chelonae*-like organism (MCLO). Species of RGM that form pigmented colonies include *Mycobacterium vaccae*, *M. flavescens*, *Mycobacterium gadium*, and *M. neoaurum*. Nonpigmented species of RGM include the *M. fortuitum* complex and *M. smegmatis*.

HISTORY

One of the earliest reports of RGM occurred in 1903 when Friedmann isolated *M. chelonae* from the lungs of two sea turtles (*Chelona corticata*), from which its name is derived.[1] Friedmann felt that his organism was not pathogenic and developed the so-called "turtle vaccine" to prevent human tuberculosis (TB).[2] Friedmann was not proven wrong until 50 years later when *M. chelonae* was recovered from the tissues of a patient with a septic knee and associated gluteal abscess.[3]

   M. fortuitum was isolated from frogs in 1905 and initially named *Mycobacterium ranae*.[4] In 1938, da Costa Cruz recovered an organism he named *M. fortuitum* from a "cold" injection abscess of the deltoid muscle of a 25-year-old woman who had received a vegetable abstract injection containing vitamins A and D.[5] The two isolates were subsequently shown to be identical, with the epithet *M. fortuitum* being retained over *M. ranae* despite the lack of historical precedent. In 1970, a clinical study by Hand and Sanford from Texas clearly established the pathogenicity of *M. fortuitum*.[7] Since that time, the number of reports has markedly increased.

TAXONOMY

The nomenclature of the RGM continues to be complex and rapidly evolving due to the large number of taxonomic groups and the only recent recognition that some of them are pathogens. Table 23-1 lists the current and former names of the RGM most commonly associated with human disease.

   The *M. fortuitum* complex is separated from the other RGM by their degradation of para-aminosalicylic acid, growth on MacConkey agar without crystal violet, growth in the presence of hydroxylamine HCl, a positive rapid (3-day) arylsulfatase test result,[8] and the demonstration of unique patterns of mycolic acid esters on high-performance liquid chromatography (HPLC). The *M. chelonae* group consists of taxonomic groups that are resistant to polymyxin B, fail to reduce nitrate, and do not take up iron. This group includes *M. chelonae* and *Mycobacterium abscessus*. The *M. fortuitum* group consists of taxonomic groups that are susceptible to polymyxin B, reduce nitrate, and incorporate iron into their colonies when grown on ferric ammonium citrate (iron uptake). This group includes *M. fortuitum*, *Mycobacterium peregrinum*, and *M. fortuitum* third biovariant complex. Kusunoki[9] recently separated *M. chelonae*, *M. abscessus*, *M. fortuitum*, and *M. peregrinum* into distinct species (their previous status was that of subspecies or biovariants) by showing that they were <70 percent similar when compared by use of genomic DNA-

TABLE 23-1   Nomenclature Changes in the RGM

Current Designation	Former Designation
M. fortuitum	M. fortuitum, M. ranae, M. fortuitum biovariant fortuitum
M. peregrinum	M. peregrinum, M. fortuitum biovariant peregrinum
M. fortuitum third biovariant complex	Bonicke group C, M. fortuitum third biovariant
Sorbitol-positive group	
Sorbitol-negative group	
M. abscessus	M. abscessus, M. chelonae subspecies abscessus
M. chelonae	M. friedmanii, M. chelonei, M. chelonae subspecies chelonae
M. chelonae- like organism (MCLO)	M. chelonei-like organism (MCLO)
M. smegmatis	M. smegmatis

DNA homology studies (quantitative hybridization). Clinically, these organisms differ from each other in disease presentation and antibiotic susceptibility patterns. Separation of the *M. fortuitum* group and the *M. chelonae* group to the species level requires studies on the utilization of various carbohydrates as sole carbon sources (mannitol, inositol, and citrate). *M. chelonae* and *M. abscessus*, but not the individual species in the *M. fortuitum* group, can also be separated by HPLC. Since not all laboratories perform species-level identification, clinicians should determine whether an organism identified as *M. chelonae* is a member of that species or of the group that contains both *M. abscessus* and *M. chelonae*.

EPIDEMIOLOGY

RGM are commonly recovered from water (including tap water), soil, dust, and aerosols.[10] Wolinsky and Rynearson[11] recovered NTM from 82 percent of soil samples collected from four eastern states, with RGM being recovered in two-thirds of these samples. RGM have been recovered from tap water,[12] natural water,[12] and biofilm.[13,14] Although RGM are recovered from clinical samples in all parts of the United States, the southeastern coastal states, from Georgia to Texas, appear to be the most endemic areas. Most cases of disease are community-acquired and sporadic, although nosocomial infections do occur, especially in association with the use of long-term catheters and exposure to tap water.

Little is known about how patients acquire NTM infection, but it is generally believed that most infections arise from environmental exposure to the organism. In the case of nosocomial infections, many occur following surgical procedures in which the patients are infected from an unknown source or through contaminated water or solutions, especially tap water. The recent use of pulsed field gel electrophoresis for determining genomic DNA large restriction fragment patterns (i.e., DNA fingerprinting) of mycobacteria has allowed the identification of specific strains and thus allowed for better epidemiologic investigation of nosocomial outbreaks.[15]

In national survey studies during 1979 and 1980, the NTM accounted for one-third of all pathogenic mycobacterial isolates sent to state laboratories (*Mycobacterium tuberculosis* accounted for the other two-thirds).[15] Of these NTM isolates, *M. fortuitum* was the second-commonest isolate (19 percent), with *Mycobacterium avium* complex (60 percent) being first. In 1988, Tsukamura[16] reported a substantial increase in the number of cases of disease due to *M. fortuitum* complex in Japan. In a study of 513 isolates of NTM in patients testing negative for human immunodeficiency virus (HIV) in Switzerland, Debrunner et al.[17] reported that 10 percent of the isolates were RGM.

CLINICAL MANIFESTATIONS

Skin, Soft Tissue, and Bone

Cutaneous, soft tissue, and bone disease account for the majority (59 percent) of infections due to RGM.[18] Community-acquired skin and soft tissue illness results from puncture wounds or trauma that results in open wounds or fractures. The host typically is an adult in good health. Children seem to be involved less frequently, despite their higher exposure to trauma.

Symptoms typically develop 4–8 weeks following the injury but may be delayed up to 6 months or even years after the injury. Pain and swelling around the site of trauma, with mild serous drainage, are the usual presenting symptoms. The illness usually has an indolent course, with significant fever (>101°F.) or systemic symptoms being rare. Regional lymphadenitis and widely dispersed, nodular skin lesions (disseminated disease) are uncommon but do occur.[19]

The diagnosis of RGM infection should be suspected in a patient presenting with such a history of a serous draining infection with a delayed onset from time of injury. Definitive diagnosis is accomplished by culturing the organism. Usually, the organism is *M. fortuitum* or the third biovariant complex of *M. fortuitum* (two-thirds of the time), while the remainder is primarily *M. abscessus*. When the discharge from a wound infected with a RGM is stained with acid-fast or Gram's stains, only a moderate number of inflammatory cells are usually seen, typically without organisms. The organism usually can be cultured from a vigorous swab of the wound, but occasionally it is necessary to perform a tissue biopsy for a successful culture.

In a study[20] of 85 clinical isolates of *M. fortuitum* third biovariant complex, most infections (76 percent) involved cutaneous tissue, soft tissue, or bone. These infections usually occurred after penetrating metal injuries or open fractures. The most common sites of injury involved the feet, legs, and arms, with a nail puncture wound to the foot being the classic injury. Patients typically presented with cellulitis or abscesses 4–6 weeks after their initial injury.

Unlike infections due to other RGM species, cutaneous infections due to *M. chelonae* are usually associated with the chronic use of low-dose corticosteroids. A history of trauma is often absent. In a series of 100 cutaneous, soft tissue, or bone isolates, the most common clinical presentation of infection with *M. chelonae* (53 percent) involved disseminated cutaneous disease. This illness is characterized by multiple nodular draining skin lesions, usually of the lower extremity. Other forms of disease included localized cellulitis, abscess, or bone infection (35 percent), with the remainder (12 percent) due to vascular access and peritoneal catheter infections.[21] Most patients were immunosuppressed, with 92 percent of patients having disseminated cutaneous disease and 62 percent of all patients with *M. chelonae* receiving corticosteroid therapy. Underlying diseases commonly associated with disseminated infection included organ transplantation (25 percent), rheumatoid arthritis (25 percent), and other autoimmune disorders (26 percent).

M. smegmatis was first reported as a human pathogen involving skin, soft tissue, and/or bone in 1988 when the clinical presentations of 22 human isolates (from 21 patients; 1 patient had 2 different strains) from the southern United States and Australia were reported.[22] While disease due to this organism is rare, greater interest in separating the specific species of RGM causing disease rather than grouping them all as *M. fortuitum* complex appears to be the major reason for identifying this organism as a definite human pathogen. Of the 21 patients involved, 19 had skin, soft tissue, or bone infections (similar to those seen with other RGM species), while the remainder had chronic respiratory infections. Seven patients with *M. smegmatis* infection had undergone cardiac surgery, five had localized trauma, and one had a long-term intravenous catheter. No cases were associated with the urinary tract, despite the species name.

Pulmonary Disease

The number of patients diagnosed with lung infections due to RGM has increased markedly in the last decade. This increase probably stems from a greater suspicion, recognition, and understanding of the pulmonary role of the RGM, but it could possibly also represent an increase in disease occurrence. In a recently published report[23] of 154 cases of RGM lung disease, most infection was due to *M. abscessus* (82 percent); followed by *M. fortuitum* (13 percent), *M. fortuitum* third biovariant complex (2 percent), *M. peregrinum* (1 percent), *M. smegmatis* (1 percent), *M. chelonae* (<1 percent), and *M. chelonae*-like organisms (MCLOs; <1 percent).

The typical patient with rapidly growing mycobacterial lung disease is a white (83 percent) female (65 percent) nonsmoker (66 percent) over 50 years of age (mean age of onset, 54 years).[23,24] Although one-third of these patients have no identifying underlying disorder, predisposing illnesses include previous mycobacterial lung disease, bronchiectasis, cystic fibrosis, coexistent *M. avium* complex disease, exogenous lipoid pneumonia, and gastroesophageal disorders, such as achalasia with chronic vomiting. Corticosteroids, immunosuppressive drugs, and HIV infection do not seem to predispose patients to pulmonary infection with RGM.

Most patients with pulmonary infection due to RGM initially present only with cough (71 percent) and weakness or fatigue.[23] Less than 20 percent of patients present with the expected symptoms of fever, sputum production, hemoptysis, weight loss, and dyspnea; however, these constitutional symptoms become much more frequent with disease progression. The time from onset of first symptoms to the first positive culture result averages 26 months. The natural history of disease is that of a more slowly progressive and usually much less aggressive illness than that caused by other pulmonary mycobacterial pathogens. However, in the report of 154 patients cited above, 14 percent died as a consequence of their RGM lung disease and respiratory failure. All but one of these deaths were due to infection with *M. abscessus*.[23]

The radiographic pattern of RGM lung disease differs from that of TB and pulmonary disease due to *M. avium* complex and *Mycobacterium kansasii*. Cavitary disease is uncommon (16 percent).[23] Multilobar disease occurs in half the cases, and 77 percent of these cases have bilateral involvement. The pattern of infiltrates is evenly divided among interstitial (37 percent), interstitial and/or alveolar (40 percent), and reticulonodular (36 percent). The upper lobes (right 77 percent, left 61 percent) were most commonly involved with infiltrates.

Laboratory diagnosis should be based on isolating the organisms from either two or more sputum or bronchoscopic specimens (preferably acid-fast smear-positive) or one biopsy specimen. Radiographic criteria for diagnosis are based on the presence of cavitary or noncavitary infiltrates that cannot be explained by alternative diagnoses other than bronchiectasis. Clinical criteria require the presence of a pulmonary disease symptom, such as cough, sputum production, fever, hemoptysis, dyspnea, or weight loss.[23]

Lymph Node Disease

Most mycobacterial lymphadenitis is due to infection from *M. tuberculosis*, *M. avium* complex, or *Mycobacterium scrofulaceum* rather than RGM. The RGM most commonly associated with lymph node disease are *M. fortuitum*,[7,18,25] *M. abscessus*,[26,27] *M. chelonae*,[21] and *M. smegmatis*.[22] Cervical lymphadenitis is the most common site of RGM lymph node disease, which is often associated with previous dental or oral procedures. Inguinal adenitis with fistulous drainage can also be seen, perhaps reflecting the frequency of lower-extremity involvement with cutaneous or bone infections. In a report[18] of 125 cases of RGM infection, only 4 cases of lymphadenitis were reported, and they were from cervical lymph nodes from which *M. fortuitum* was isolated.

Diagnosis is accomplished by isolating the RGM from lymph node culture by means of biopsy, aspiration, or directly from node drainage.

Osteomyelitis and Joint Disease

Sternum infections following cardiac surgery were initially the most commonly recognized and reported bone infection due to RGM.[28] Eighty-nine percent of RGM isolates recovered from post–cardiac surgery infections involved the sternum. Nearly two-thirds of these isolates were *M. fortuitum*, 13 percent were *M. abscessus*, and 13 percent were *M. smegmatis*.[28] With a decline in the numbers of these cases, osteomyelitis following penetrating trauma or open fractures of the lower extremity has become the most common type of bone infection. These infections are usually caused by *M. fortuitum*,[18] *M. abscessus*,[18] and *M. fortuitum* third biovariant complex.[20] Synovitis due to the *M. fortuitum* group[2] and the *M. chelonae* group[29] has been occasionally reported.

Disseminated Disease Not HIV-Related

Disseminated cutaneous disease due to RGM occasionally occurs in immunosuppressed patients with chronic renal failure, renal transplantation, or corticosteroid therapy. Although an early study showed 80 percent of cases to be due to *M. abscessus*,[18] recent studies have suggested a predominance of *M. chelonae*.[30-32] One of these studies[31] identified two disease syndromes:

one group with widespread, multiorgan involvement, having a survival rate of only 10 percent, and a second group with primarily skin manifestations, having a 90 percent survival rate. Patients from the first group with disseminated cutaneous infection were seriously ill, with rapidly fatal (usually malignant) disorders, such as acute leukemia or stage 4 lymphoma. These patients presented with fever and other systemic symptoms and had positive blood and bone marrow culture results in addition to positive skin culture results. This syndrome is uncommon and often caused by *M. abscessus*. The majority of cases fell into the second group. These patients had chronic, generally nonfatal disorders, such as a connective tissue disease or organ transplantation that required chronic corticosteroid use. The patients were not constitutionally ill and presented with multiple subcutaneous nodular lesions, often on the extensor surfaces of the arms and legs. These lesions have been referred to as "pseudoerythema nodosum," but, unlike erythema nodosum, they eventually necrose and drain a serous fluid. By applying pressure to the lesion, a thick, cheeselike material could usually be expressed. Blood and bone marrow culture results were negative, and the causative organism was usually *M. chelonae*. Most of the seriously ill patients died despite therapy, while the patients in the group with only skin nodules generally had a benign course, even without appropriate drug therapy. Our experience supports the recognition of these two syndromes of disseminated disease.

Renal transplantation complicated by disseminated infection due to the *M. chelonae* group has been studied in more detail than have other predisposing illnesses.[32] Such patients typically present with a clinically distinctive syndrome characterized by indolent, tender, erythematous nodules on the lower extremities (or sometimes involving the upper extremities), placing them in the benign disease group. Diagnosis usually requires tissue biopsy followed by culture with incubation up to a month. Therapy consists of surgical excision and long-term antibiotic therapy, with some patients experiencing a chronic, relapsing course. Identification of the organism to subspecies was accomplished in one study[32] in only two of seven cases: one case of *M. chelonae* and one of *M. abscessus*. However, the provided antimicrobial susceptibilities suggested that most unidentified isolates were *M. chelonae*.

Disease Associated with HIV Infection

RGM infection rarely occurs in patients with HIV infection. In a series from Brooklyn, an area highly endemic for acquired immune deficiency syndrome (AIDS), only 5 of the 34 patients from whom *M. fortuitum* complex was isolated were infected with HIV.[33] Two isolates were obtained from cervical lymph nodes, while the remaining 2 were isolated from pleural fluid and sputum. Recent literature reveals 7 other cases of HIV-positive patients with disease due to *M. fortuitum*: 6 cases of disseminated disease[34-36] and 1 case of right middle lobe syndrome.[37]

Bacteremia and Catheter Sepsis

Mycobacteremia due to *M. fortuitum*, *M. abscessus*, *M. chelonae*, and, rarely, other RGM occurs most often (87 percent)[18] in immunosuppressed patients on long-term catheters, such as those receiving hemodialysis (end-stage renal disease)[38] or long-term central venous catheter therapy (especially cancer patients).[39] Rarely, the mycobacteremia occurs as a consequence of open-heart surgery (e.g., prosthetic valve endocarditis or sternal wound infection),[18] disseminated infection in patients with acutely fatal diseases, or chronic corticosteroid therapy (e.g., for connective tissue disease).[40] One study of a nosocomial epidemic among hemodialysis patients reported 24 cases of infection due to *M. abscessus*, of which 18 were recovered from blood cultures. The mortality rate among these patients was approximately 50 percent.[38] In a study of 125 cases of disease due to RGM, 13 cases had positive blood culture results: *M. abscessus* (9 cases), *M. fortuitum* (3 cases), and *M. fortuitum* third biovariant (1 case).[18] Four cases of *M. fortuitum* bacteremia were reported in 36 patients with AIDS who underwent fiberoptic bronchoscopy.[36] *M. fortuitum* bacteremia has been reported[39] in 4 patients with cancer and long-term venous catheters. Three of these patients had polymicrobial sepsis, but none had evidence of infection, such as phlebitis or cellulitis, around the insertion sites of their intravenous catheters. However, in a more recent report from the same hospital, of 15 cancer patients with catheter-related infections due to *M. fortuitum* complex, 11 had bacteremia, while 4 had catheter-site infections. Nine infections were due to the *M. fortuitum* group and 6 to the *M. chelonae* group.[41] An unusual syndrome of hepatomegaly, right upper quadrant tenderness, marked elevation of hepatic alkaline phosphatase, granulomas on liver biopsy, with positive hepatic culture results has been described in some of the patients with catheter sepsis.[42] Successful treatment of these infections required catheter removal, appropriate antibiotic therapy based on in vitro susceptibilities, and surgical resection of the catheter tunnel infection when present.

Other Nosocomial Infections

Nosocomial infections due to RGM have been associated not only with long-term central intravenous catheters[43] but also with continuous ambulatory peritoneal dialysis catheters,[44] postsurgical wound infections,[45,46] and chronic hemodialysis.[38] Peritonitis[44] in patients receiving continuous peritoneal dialysis has been caused by *M. chelonae* (three cases) and *M. fortuitum* (two cases).

Peritonitis has also been associated with infection due to *M. chelonae*-like organisms (MCLOs) in patients receiving intermittent peritoneal dialysis.

Postsurgical wound infections due to RGM are recognized most commonly following augmentation mammaplasty[45] or cardiac bypass surgery.[46] Of 37 cases[47] of RGM infections associated with augmentation mammaplasty, 70 percent were due to *M. fortuitum*, 14 percent to *M. fortuitum* third biovariant complex, and 11 percent to *M. abscessus*. Breast infections due to RGM but not associated with augmentation mammaplasty were essentially due to the same organisms. In a series[28] of 89 isolates of RGM isolated from cardiac-bypass–related infections, 8 taxonomic groups (probable species) were identified. The majority (72 percent) of them were *M. fortuitum*, while *M. abscessus* and *M. smegmatis* each represented 11 percent of the isolates. Fifty percent of the cases came from Texas, and 80 percent originated from southern coastal states.

Less frequently, sporadic surgical wound infections can occur after almost any type of surgery.[18] Epidemic nosocomial infections have been reported in association with facial reconstructions, podiatry procedures, and needle injections.

Recently, a number of pseudo-outbreaks of lung disease have been reported in association with the use of fiberoptic bronchoscopes contaminated with *M. abscessus*. Most of these outbreaks have been secondary to contaminated automated bronchoscope washing machines that used tap water for the rinsing of bronchoscopes.[14]

THERAPY

Treatment of RGM infections is a considerable challenge for a number of reasons:

1. There are at least eight species of pathogenic RGM, which have different and somewhat variable drug susceptibilities.
2. These various species present in a wide array of clinical syndromes and vary in their morbidity from infections that spontaneously resolve without therapy to fatal infections that fail to respond to antibiotic and/or surgical therapy.
3. Different infection sites due to the same pathogen may require different plans of therapy.
4. There are no controlled clinical trials that would help determine the appropriate choice of antibiotics, length of therapy, and use of adjunctive therapy such as surgery. The outbreaks of *M. abscessus* sternal wound infections following cardiac surgery in the early 1980s[46,48,49] resulted in

a fatal outcome in one out of three cases despite antibiotic therapy. Apparently, this mortality rate is considerably less today because of the earlier recognition of clinical disease and greater experience in treating such cases with a better choice of antibiotics.

5. The RGM are not susceptible to the first-line antituberculous drugs (except for the susceptibility of *M. smegmatis* to ethambutol) and require in vitro susceptibility studies. These studies must be performed in laboratories having specialized mycobacterial capabilities.

6. With the proliferation of new antibiotics, many of them have not yet been studied for their potential for treating RGM.

Although there are no controlled studies of the treatment of infections due to the RGM, clinical experience appears to support the reliability of in vitro antibiotic susceptibility studies, especially with skin and soft tissue infections.[20,32,41,50,51] In general, the *M. fortuitum* group responds well to several oral and injectable antibiotics (Table 23-2). The percentage of *M. fortuitum* isolates susceptible to antibiotics are as follows: ciprofloxacin (100 percent),[51] ofloxacin (100 percent),[51] sulfamethoxazole (95 percent),[53] amoxicillin-clavulanic acid (90 percent),[54] doxycycline (44 percent),[53] clarithromycin (81 percent),[52] erythromycin (1 percent),[53] imipenem (100 percent),[54] amikacin (100 percent),[53] cefoxitin (70 percent),[53] and cefmetazole (100 percent).[54] Even though *M. fortuitum* has excellent susceptibility to ciprofloxacin and ofloxacin, these drugs should not be used in single-drug coverage because of the risk of developing mutational resistance.[51] *M. fortuitum* produces β-lactamase, which appears to be responsible for some degree of resistance to the β-lactam antibiotics.[55] Imipenem has greater activity against *M. fortuitum* (100 percent susceptible at a MIC of 8 μg/ml) than do other β-lactams, such as cefmetazole, cefoxitin, and amoxicillin-clavulanic acid.[54]

In comparison to *M. fortuitum*, *M. peregrinum* seems to be slightly more susceptible to antibiotic therapy, while *M. fortuitum* third biovariant complex is slightly more resistant (Table 23-2). *M. peregrinum* is usually susceptible to clarithromycin (100 percent),[52] sulfamethoxazole (100 percent),[53] doxycycline (63 percent),[53] cefoxitin (100 percent),[53] amikacin (100 percent),[53] ciprofloxacin (100 percent),[51] and ofloxacin (100 percent).[51] *M. fortuitum* third biovariant complex is usually susceptible (100 percent) to imipenem, amikacin, gentamicin, ciprofloxacin, and sulfamethoxazole.[20] The sorbitol-positive group is resistant to conventional doses of the macrolides, including clarithromycin, while the sorbitol-negative isolates are susceptible.[52]

A limited number of patients with *M. smegmatis* infection have been treated with antibiotics according to in vitro susceptibility tests (rather than standard antituberculous therapy) and have responded well to this therapy. Some were treated surgically as well. This organism is usually susceptible to

TABLE 23-2 Recommended Drugs for Commonly Encountered Species of RGM

Organism	Oral Drugs	Parenteral Drugs	Alternative Drugs	Potential Surgical Benefit
M. fortuitum	Sulfamethoxazole, ciprofloxacin or ofloxacin, clarithromycin (81 percent susceptible)	Amikacin, imipenem	Doxycycline or minocycline, (50 percent susceptible)	+
M. fortuitum (third biovariant) sorbitol-positive	Ciprofloxacin or ofloxacin, sulfamethoxazole	Imipenem, amikacin		+
M. fortuitum (third biovariant) sorbitol-negative	Ciprofloxacin or ofloxacin, sulfamethoxazole, clarithromycin	Imipenem, amikacin	Cefoxitin, azithromycin (?)	+
M. chelonae	Clarithromycin	Imipenem, amikacin, tobramycin	Azithromycin (?), doxycycline or minocycline, (26 percent susceptible), ciprofloxacin (19 percent susceptible)	++

M. abscessus Skin	Clarithromycin	Imipenem, amikacin	Azithromycin (?), cefoxitin (70 percent susceptible)	++
Lung	Clarithromycin	Amikacin, imipenem	Azithromycin (?), cefoxitin	++++
M. chelonae-like organism (MCLO)	Clarithromycin, ciprofloxacin or ofloxacin, amoxicillin-clavulanic acid, trimethroprim-sulfamethoxazole	Amikacin, imipenem, cefoxitin	Doxycycline (or minocycline, 50 percent susceptible), azithromycin	++
M. smegmatis	Ciprofloxacin or ofloxacin, sulfamethoxazole, doxycycline or minocycline, ethambutol	Imipenem, amikacin	Clarithromycin (some isolates are resistant)	++

ciprofloxacin (100 percent),[51] ofloxacin (100 percent),[51] amikacin (90 percent),[22] imipenem (90 percent),[22] doxycycline (90 percent),[22] sulfamethoxazole (90 percent),[22] and ethambutol (90 percent).[22]

The *M. chelonae* group is more resistant to oral antibiotics than the *M. fortuitum* group. *M. abscessus* is usually susceptible to clarithromycin (100 percent),[52] cefoxitin (82 percent),[54] amikacin (98 percent),[53] and tobramycin (59 percent).[53] *M. chelonae* is usually susceptible to clarithromycin (100 percent),[21] erythromycin (80 percent),[52] amikacin (97 percent),[53] tobramycin (100 percent),[53] doxycycline (26 percent),[21,53] ciprofloxacin (19 percent),[21,51] and imipenem (73 percent).[54] Recent studies have suggested that clarithromycin (500 mg twice a day) is highly effective in treating infections due to this species and is considered the drug of choice.[32] *M. chelonae*-like organisms (MCLOs) are susceptible to ciprofloxacin,[51] ofloxacin,[51] amoxicillin-clavulanic acid, clarithromycin,[52] amikacin, imipenem, and cefoxitin.

Antibiotic therapy usually requires a minimum of 4 months' therapy for localized skin and soft tissue infections, while disseminated (cutaneous) infections and bone infections probably require 6 months of therapy. The required duration of therapy for pulmonary infection is unknown but is probably 6–12 months. *M. fortuitum* pulmonary disease usually responds adequately to antibiotic therapy alone. However, pulmonary disease due to *M. abscessus* infection is very difficult to treat and almost always requires surgical resection of localized disease for successful management.[23] However, with the use of clarithromycin, the prognosis may be better. Since pulmonary *M. abscessus* infections are often indolent and slowly progressive, bilateral and diffuse disease may be best managed conservatively, with only observation or antibiotic therapy. Soft tissue infection often requires surgery if the disease is extensive, involves abscess formation, or requires difficult drug therapy. Foreign bodies, such as breast implants and percutaneous catheters, almost always must be removed for resolution of the infection.

REFERENCES

1. Cobbett L: An acid-fast bacillus obtained from a pustular eruption. *Br Med J* 2:158, 1918.
2. Moore M, Frerichs JB: An unusual acid-fast infection of the knee with subcutaneous abscess-like lesions of the gluteal region. *J Invest Dermatol* 20:133, 1953.
3. Awe RJ, Gangadharam PR, Jenkins DE: Clinical significance of *Mycobacterium fortuitum* infections in pulmonary disease. *Am Rev Respir Dis* 108:1230, 1973.
4. Turner L, Stinson I: *Mycobacterium fortuitum* as a cause of corneal ulcer. *Am J Ophthalmol* 60:329, 1965.
5. Hoffman PC, Fraser DW, Robicsek F, O'Bar PR, Mauncey CU: Two outbreaks of sternal wound infections due to organisms of the *Mycobacterium fortuitum* complex. *J Infect Dis* 143:533, 1981.

6. Pottage JC Jr, Harris AA, Trenholme GM, Levin S, Kaplan RL, Feczko JM: Disseminated *Mycobacterium chelonei* infection: a report of two cases. *Am Rev Respir Dis* 126:720, 1982.

7. Hand WL, Sanford JP: *Mycobacterium fortuitum*: a human pathogen. *Ann Intern Med* 73:971, 1970.

8. Kirschner P, Kiekenbeck M, Meissner D, Wolters J, Böttger EC: Genetic heterogeneity within *Mycobacterium fortuitum* complex species: genotypic criteria for identification. *J Clin Microbiol* 30:2772, 1992.

9. Kusunoki S, Ezaki T: Proposal of *Mycobacterium peregrinum* sp. nov., nom. rev., and elevation of *Mycobacterium chelonae* subsp. *abscessus* (Kubica et al.) to species status: *Mycobacterium abscessus* comb. nov. *Int J Syst Bacteriol* 42:240, 1992.

10. O'Brien RJ: The epidemiology of nontuberculous mycobacterial disease. *Clin Chest Med* 10:407, 1989.

11. Wolinsky E, Rynearson TK: Mycobacteria in soil and their relation to disease-associated strains. *Am Rev Respir Dis* 97:1032, 1968.

12. Wallace RJ Jr: Nontuberculous mycobacteria and water: a love affair with increasing clinical importance. *Infect Dis Clin North Am* 1:677, 1987.

13. Schulze-Röbbecke R, Janning R, Fischeder R: Occurrence of mycobacteria in biofilm samples. *Tubercle Lung Dis* 73:141, 1992.

14. Fraser VJ, Jones M, Murray PR, Medoff G, Zhang Y, Wallace RJ Jr: Contamination of flexible fiberoptic bronchoscopes with *Mycobacterium chelonae* linked to an automated bronchoscope disinfection machine. *Am Rev Respir Dis* 145:853, 1992.

15. Hector JS, Pang Y, Mazurek GH, Zhang Y, Brown BA, Wallace RJ Jr: Large restriction fragment patterns of genomic *Mycobacterium fortuitum* DNA as strain-specific markers and their use in epidemiologic investigation of four nosocomial outbreaks. *J Clin Microbiol* 30:1250, 1992.

16. Tsukamura M, Kita M, Shimoide H, Arakawa H, Kuze A: Studies on the epidemiology of nontuberculous mycobacteriosis in Japan. *Am Rev Respir Dis* 137:1280, 1988.

17. Debrunner M, Salfinger M, Brändli O, von Graevenitz A: Epidemiology and clinical significance of nontuberculous mycobacteria in patients negative for human immunodeficiency virus in Switzerland. *Clin Infect Dis* 15:330, 1992.

18. Wallace RJ Jr, Swenson JM, Silcox VA, Good RC, Tschen JA, Stone MS: Spectrum of disease due to rapidly growing mycobacteria. *Rev Infect Dis* 5:657, 1983.

19. Nelson BR, Rapini RP, Wallace RJ Jr, Tschen JA: Disseminated *Mycobacterium chelonae* ssp. *abscessus* in an immunocompetent host and with a known portal of entry. *J Am Acad Dermatol* 20:909, 1989.

20. Wallace RJ Jr, Brown BA, Silcox VA, Tsukamura M, Nash DR, Steele LC, Steingrube VA, Smith J, Sumter G, Zhang Y, Blacklock Z: Clinical disease, drug susceptibility, and biochemical patterns of the unnamed third biovariant complex of *Mycobacterium fortuitum*. *J Infect Dis* 163:598, 1991.

21. Wallace RJ Jr, Brown BA, Onyi GO: Skin, soft tissue, and bone infections due to *Mycobacterium chelonae chelonae*: importance of prior corticosteroid therapy, frequency of disseminated infections, and resistance to oral antimicrobials other than clarithromycin. *J Infect Dis* 166:405, 1992.

22. Wallace RJ Jr, Nash DR, Tsukamura M, Blacklock ZM, Silcox VA: Human disease due to *Mycobacterium smegmatis*. *J Infect Dis* 158:52, 1988.

23. Griffith DE, Girard WM, Wallace RJ Jr: Clinical features of pulmonary disease caused by rapidly growing mycobacteria: an analysis of 154 patients. *Am Rev Respir Dis* 147:1271, 1993.

24. Griffith DE, Wallace RJ Jr: Pulmonary disease due to rapidly growing mycobacteria. *Semin Respir Med* 9:505, 1988.

25. Wells AQ, Agius E, Smith N: *Mycobacterium fortuitum*. *Am Rev Tuberc* 72:53, 1955.

26. Morris CA, Grant GH, Everall PH, Myres TM: Tuberculoid lymphadenitis due to *Mycobacterium chelonei*. *J Clin Pathol* 26:422, 1973.
27. Zina AM, Depaoli M, Bossano AI: Cutaneous-mucous infection with lymphadenopathy caused by *Mycobacterium chelonei*. 160:376, 1980.
28. Wallace RJ Jr, Musser JM, Hull SI, Silcox VA, Steele LC, Forrester GD, Labidi A, Selander RK: Diversity and sources of rapidly growing mycobacteria associated with infections following cardiac surgery. *J Infect Dis* 159:708, 1989.
29. Sutker WL, Lankford LL, Tompsett R: Granulomatous synovitis: the role of atypical mycobacteria. *Rev Infect Dis* 5:729, 1979.
30. Wallace RJ Jr: The clinical presentation, diagnosis, and therapy of cutaneous and pulmonary infections due to the rapidly growing mycobacteria, *M. fortuitum* and *M. chelonae*. *Clin Chest Med* 10:419, 1989.
31. Ingram CW, Tanner DC, Durack DT, Kernodle GW Jr, Corey GR: Disseminated infection with rapidly growing mycobacteria. *Clin Infect Dis* 16:463, 1993.
32. Cooper JF, Lichtenstein MJ, Graham BS, Schaffner W: *Mycobacterium chelonae*: a cause of nodular skin lesions with a proclivity for renal transplant recipients. *Am J Med* 86:173, 1989.
33. Shafer RW, Sierra MF: *Mycobacterium xenopi*, *Mycobacterium fortuitum*, *Mycobacterium kansasii*, and other nontuberculous mycobacteria in an area of endemicity for AIDS. *Clin Infect Dis* 15:161, 1992.
34. Sack JB: Disseminated infection due to *Mycobacterium fortuitum* in a patient with AIDS. *Rev Infect Dis* 12:961, 1990.
35. Rodrigueq-Barradas MC, Clarridge J, Darouiche R: Disseminated *Mycobacterium fortuitum* disease in an AIDS patient. *Am J Med* 93:473, 1992.
36. Tenholder MF, Moser RJ III, Tellis CJ: Mycobacteria other than tuberculosis. *Arch Intern Med* 148:953, 1988.
37. Lambert GW, Baddour LM: Right middle lobe syndrome caused by *Mycobacterium fortuitum* in a patient with human immunodeficiency virus infection. *South Med J* 85:767, 1992.
38. Nontuberculous mycobacterial infections in hemodialysis patients. *MMWR* 32(18):244, 1983.
39. Hoy JF, Rolston KVI, Hopfer RL, Bodey GP: *Mycobacterium fortuitum* bacteremia in patients with cancer and long-term venous catheters. *Am J Med* 83:213, 1987.
40. Pierce PF, DeYoung DR, Roberts GD: Mycobacteremia and the new blood culture systems. *Ann Intern Med* 99:786, 1983.
41. Raad II, Vartivarian S, Khan A, Bodey GP: Catheter-related infections caused by the *Mycobacterium fortuitum* complex: 15 cases and review. *Rev Infect Dis* 13:1120, 1991.
42. Brannan DP, DuBois RE, Ramirez MJ, Ravry MJR, Harrison EO: Cefoxitin therapy for *Mycobacterium fortuitum* bacteremia with associated granulomatous hepatitis. *South Med J* 77:381, 1984.
43. Flynn PM, Hooser BV, Gigliotti F: Atypical mycobacterial infections of Hickman catheter exit sites. *Pediatr Infect Dis J* 7:510, 1988.
44. Merlin TL, Tzamaloukas AH: *Mycobacterium chelonae* peritonitis associated with continuous ambulatory peritoneal dialysis. *Am J Clin Pathol* 91:717, 1989.
45. Clegg HW, Foster MT, Sanders WE Jr, Baine WB: Infection due to organisms of the *Mycobacterium fortuitum* complex after augmentation mammaplasty: clinical and epidemiologic features. *J Infect Dis* 147:427, 1983.
46. Hoffman PC, Fraser DW, Robicsek F, O'Bar PR, Mauney CU: Two outbreaks of sternal wound infections due to organisms of the *Mycobacterium fortuitum* complex. *J Infect Dis* 143:533, 1981.
47. Wallace RJ Jr, Steele LC, Labidi A, Silcox VA: Heterogeneity among isolates of RGM responsible for infections following augmentation mammaplasty despite case clustering in Texas and other southern coastal states. *J Infect Dis* 160:281, 1989.

48. Szabo I, Sárközi K: *Mycobacterium chelonei* endemy after heart surgery with fatal consequences. *Am Rev Respir Dis* 121:607, 1980.
49. Hoffman PC, Fraser DW, Robicsek F, O'Bar PR, Mauney CU: Two outbreaks of sternal wound infections due to organisms of the *Mycobacterium fortuitum* complex. *J Infect Dis* 143:533, 1981.
50. Wallace RJ Jr, Swenson JM, Silcox VA, Bullen MG: Treatment of non-pulmonary infections due to *Mycobacterium fortuitum* and *Mycobacterium chelonei* on the basis of in vitro susceptibilities. *J Infect Dis* 152:500, 1985.
51. Wallace RJ Jr, Bedsole G, Sumter G, Sanders CV, Steele LC, Brown BA, Smith J, Graham DR: Activities of ciprofloxacin and ofloxacin against rapidly growing mycobacteria with demonstration of acquired resistance following single-drug therapy. *Antimicrob Agents Chemother* 34:65, 1990.
52. Brown BA, Wallace RJ Jr, Onyi GO, De Rosas V, Wallace RJ III: Activities of four macrolides, including clarithromycin, against *Mycobacterium fortuitum*, *Mycobacterium chelonae*, and *M. chelonae*-like organisms. *Antimicrob Agents Chemother* 36:180, 1992.
53. Swenson JA, Wallace RJ Jr, Silcox VA, Thornsberry C: Antimicrobial susceptibility of five subgroups of *Mycobacterium fortuitum* and *Mycobacterium chelonae*. *Antimicrob Agents Chemother* 28:807, 1985.
54. Wallace RJ Jr, Brown BA, Onyi GO: Susceptibilities of *Mycobacterium fortuitum* biovar. *fortuitum* and the two subgroups of *Mycobacterium chelonae* to imipenem, cefmetazole, cefoxitin, and amoxicillin-clavulanic acid. *Antimicrob Agents Chemother* 35:773, 1991.
55. Nash DR, Wallace RJ Jr, Steingrube VA, Udou T, Steele LC, Forrester GD: Characterization of beta-lactamases in *Mycobacterium fortuitum* including a role in beta-lactam resistance and evidence of partial inducibility. *Am Rev Respir Dis* 134:1276, 1986.

CHAPTER 24

Diagnosis and Treatment of Nontuberculous Mycobacterial Infections in Patients with AIDS

C. ROBERT HORSBURGH, JR.

Infections with nontuberculous mycobacteria are the most common bacterial infections of patients with acquired immune deficiency syndrome (AIDS) in the developed world, occurring in 15–24 percent of patients.[1] Nearly all of these infections are due to organisms of the *Mycobacterium avium* complex (MAC). This complex includes *M. avium*, *Mycobacterium intracellulare*, and *Mycobacterium scrofulaceum*; the overwhelming majority of infections are due to *M. avium*.[1,2] Other nontuberculous mycobacteria causing disseminated disease in patients with AIDS include *Mycobacterium kansasii*, *Mycobacterium genavense*, and *Mycobacterium haemophilum*.[3–6] Case reports have also appeared of disseminated infection with *Mycobacterium fortuitum*, *Mycobacterium terrae*, *Mycobacterium gordonae*, *Mycobacterium marinum*, *Mycobacterium malmoense*, and *Mycobacterium xenopi*. In general, the clinical presentation of and therapy for these infections are similar to those of disseminated MAC disease. It is surprising to note that neither the incidence nor the clinical course of infection with *Mycobacterium leprae* appear to be altered by infection with HIV.

Disseminated MAC infection occurs with equal frequency in men and women.[7] There is a slightly decreased frequency in Hispanics and decreased frequency with increasing age. All HIV transmission categories (homosexual, intravenous drug user, heterosexual, and blood product recipient) are affected equally. With over 250,000 AIDS cases now reported, estimates of disseminated MAC in the United States range from 38,000–60,000.

Such infections have become increasingly frequent as the AIDS epidemic has matured. This is because the risk of MAC infection increases as the CD4+ cell count decreases, and more patients now survive to a point where they have low counts and are susceptible to MAC.[1,8] Nearly all MAC infections occur in persons with <50 CD4+ cells (shown schematically in Fig. 24-1).

Disease occurs after exposure to MAC in the environment, although the

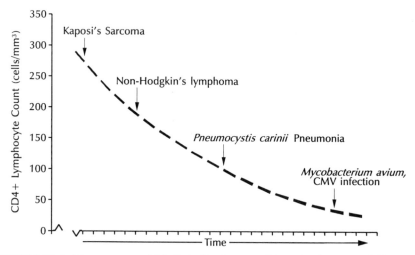

FIGURE 24-1. Occurrence of AIDS, indicating conditions in the natural history of HIV infection, by CD4+ cell count.

specific reservoirs and modes of exposure are not known.[1] Infection can be acquired through the respiratory or gastrointestinal tract, with the latter by far the most common. Localized disease in either the respiratory or gastrointestinal tract soon disseminates, with involvement of blood, bone marrow, liver, spleen and lymph nodes.[9,10] Because of the rapid dissemination of MAC, therapeutic strategies for localized and disseminated MAC disease are the same.

Disease in children is similar to that in adults, although the frequency is less, presumably due to the fact that the AIDS epidemic in children is more recent and therefore fewer HIV-infected children have reached the low CD4+ cell levels that put them at risk for MAC infection.[11] Disseminated MAC is more common in children who acquired HIV through blood product administration, but this is thought only to reflect the lower CD4+ cell levels in this group. In children, as in adults, persons with <50 CD4+ cells per cubic millimeter are at highest risk of acquiring MAC, although in children <1 year of age, this is less reliable, since normal lymphocyte counts are much higher in these children.

Untreated MAC infection is significantly associated with shortened survival (4 months versus 11 months; Fig. 24-2).[12-14] Treatment of patients with disseminated MAC disease with antimycobacterial agents, on the other hand, is associated with survival similar to that of patients with AIDS but without MAC.[12,15]

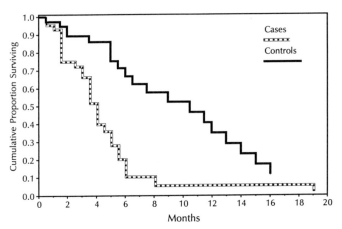

FIGURE 24-2. Survival of patients with HIV infection with and without disseminated MAC infection, matched by CD4+ cell count. Survival of patients with MAC is shown with a dotted line; survival of control subjects is shown with a solid line.

DIAGNOSIS

Localized infection of the gastrointestinal tract or the lung with MAC may occur, leading to pneumonia or localized gastrointestinal disease. MAC pneumonia, occurring in 16 percent of cases of disseminated MAC disease,[15] can be diagnosed by sputum smear (although smear results are rarely positive) or culture in the presence of pulmonary infiltrates, but care must be taken to exclude other causes of such infiltrates; this usually requires bronchoalveolar lavage or lung biopsy. Moreover, coexistence of MAC pneumonia with other pneumonias, such as *Pneumocystis carinii* pneumonia, must be considered. Histologic examination shows granulomatous disease or infiltration with mycobacteria in which case granulomas may be absent. Radiographic presentations have not been well-studied, but cavitation may occur. Concurrent blood cultures should be obtained to determine whether disease has disseminated. Positive culture results for sputum in the absence of a pulmonary infiltrate represent colonization with MAC. In patients with human immunodeficiency virus (HIV) infection and <50 CD4+ cells, such colonization predicts subsequent disseminated disease.[16]

MAC gastrointestinal disease, manifested by diarrhea, abdominal pain, and/or wasting syndrome, can be diagnosed only by endoscopic biopsy of either the small intestine or the colon.[9,17] Histologic examination shows infiltration of gut tissue with mycobacteria. Because disease may be focal, a negative biopsy result does not exclude disease, and obtaining multiple specimens is recommended. Stool cultures and smears are of little help, since they are insensitive; a positive stool smear result is seen only with extensive disease, when dissemination has invariably occurred. A positive stool culture result, on the other hand, can represent colonization rather than disease, although most such patients progress to disseminated MAC infection within a few months. No consistent radiographic pattern has been reported, although thickening of the duodenum or multiple enlarged abdominal lymph nodes on computed tomographic (CT) scan should raise clinical suspicion. Some authors have reported a syndrome of MAC disease limited to the liver, often with elevated alkaline phosphatase levels, but liver biopsy is necessary to establish this diagnosis.

The diagnosis of disseminated MAC disease is most commonly made by culture of the organism from blood.[18] A single blood culture is adequate, although low levels of bacteremia may be below the limit of detection of the test. For this reason, we follow a patient whose initial blood culture result is negative with monthly blood cultures if the index of suspicion for disseminated MAC is high and other explanations for the clinical picture are not found. In addition to blood, any sterile site culture that grows MAC is considered evidence for disseminated MAC. Such sites include bone marrow, lymph node, and liver biopsy; however, none of these offers an advantage in diagnosis over blood culture. Culture of MAC from sputum, bronchoalveolar lavage, stool, or gastrointestinal biopsy does not indicate dissemination, although a positive culture result from both the gastrointestinal and the respiratory tract is strongly suggestive of disseminated MAC; a blood culture should be obtained to confirm the diagnosis. Blood cultures should include a step in which blood leukocytes are lysed,[19,20] since mycobacteria in blood are largely, if not entirely, within these cells. The lysed cells are then cultured on solid or liquid media. Liquid media may allow more rapid identification of mycobacteremia, while solid media allow quantification of the levels of mycobacteremia. Such levels are used by some clinicians to assess the response to therapy; initial levels of mycobacteremia have also been shown to predict survival.[15] Culture in liquid media will usually reveal mycobacteria in 2 weeks, while solid media require about 3 weeks. Cultures should be observed for 6 weeks before reporting a negative result. Mycobacteria recovered are speciated by biochemical tests or, more commonly, by DNA probes.

The most common presentation of disseminated MAC disease is fevers and night sweats, with or without weight loss, in a patient with <100 CD4+ cells per cubic millimeter. A subset of patients will present with severe anemia (hematocrit <26%) without fevers or night sweats.[12] Thus, it is important to look for MAC in patients with such anemia. Other signs and symptoms that may occur, singly or in concert, are hepatosplenomegaly, diarrhea, and elevated alkaline phosphatase levels.[21,22] While many of these signs and symptoms are not specific for disseminated MAC, they are significantly associated with it, and the occurrence of any one of them (in a patient with <100 CD4+ cells) should prompt an investigation for MAC.[22] On the other hand, the occurrence of disseminated MAC without at least one of these signs or symptoms is extremely rare.

THERAPY FOR MAC DISEASE

Disseminated MAC is a chronic disease with a prolonged course. It is therefore not imperative to begin therapy before culture results are obtained, although some clinicians prefer to treat presumptively, pending the results of culture. Presumptive treatment without culture is to be avoided, since many other conditions may mimic the symptoms of MAC and could be missed. Patients with MAC rarely require hospitalization for treatment of their illness and can be followed as outpatients.

Four-drug regimens for therapy of disseminated MAC disease have shown symptomatic improvement and decreases in levels of mycobacteremia in most patients.[23,24] These regimens contain rifampin, ethambutol, ciprofloxacin, and clofazimine or amikacin. More recently, two macrolide agents, clarithromycin and azithromycin, have become available and have been shown to have excellent in vitro and in vivo activity against MAC.[25-27] It is now recommended that all patients with disseminated MAC receive one of these agents as part of a multidrug treatment regimen. Treatment should be initiated with at least two, and preferably three, antimycobacterial agents, including one macrolide (Table 24-1). Single-agent therapy with macrolides (or other agents) is contraindicated due to the emergence of resistant organisms and subsequent clinical failure of the regimen.[27] At least one additional agent should be administered with the macrolide in an effort to prevent emergence of resistance, although this may still occur despite combination therapy. For patients who do not tolerate a macrolide or whose MAC isolate is not susceptible to macrolides, one of the four-drug nonmacrolide regimens noted above should be used.[23,24] Therapy is continued for the life of the patient.

Resistance to antimycobacterial agents may occur for several reasons. First, as in tuberculosis (TB), a few MAC isolates will be resistant to any of the antimycobacterial agents at the beginning of therapy. Single-agent therapy will eliminate susceptible organisms, allowing emergence of a subpopulation of resistant ones. Use of a second agent can prevent this phenomenon. However, with a large initial burden of organisms, isolates with resistance to more than one agent may be present, necessitating therapy with more drugs.

TABLE 24-1 Antimicrobial Agents Used in Treatment of MAC Infection

Drug	Recommended Dose	Prominent Adverse Reactions
Macrolides		
Clarithromycin	500 mg twice a day	Nausea, abdominal pain,
Azithromycin	500 mg per day	diarrhea, hepatotoxicity
Rifamycins		
Rifampin	600 mg per day*	Rash, hepatotoxicity,
Rifabutin	450–600 mg per day*	neutropenia, orange urine, uveitis
Aminoglycosides		
Amikacin	10–15 mg/kg per day*	Ototoxicity, nephrotoxicity
Quinolones		
Ciprofloxacin	500–750 mg twice a day	Nausea, abdominal pain,
Ofloxacin	400 mg twice a day	diarrhea, rash
Other compounds		
Ethambutol	800–1200 mg per day*	Nausea, abdominal pain, changes in visual acuity
Clofazimine	100 mg per day	Skin hyperpigmentation, nausea, abdominal pain

Note: All drugs are administered by mouth with the exception of amikacin (intravenous).
*May administer in divided doses.

Choosing the optimal regimen for an individual patient is problematic. Studies of MAC infection in persons without AIDS and a few case reports in patients with AIDS have suggested that the results of in vitro susceptibility tests may be useful in selection of antimycobacterial agents.[1] However, such results have not been demonstrated to be associated with improved outcome in any prospective studies, and results are often not available until 4–8 weeks after diagnosis. Moreover, there is no general agreement on the best methods of performing the testing and no generally accepted guidelines for defining a "susceptible" organism. Nonetheless, most clinicians agree that the antimycobacterial agents shown in Table 24-1 are those to which MAC organisms are most likely to be susceptible.[1,28]

In addition, some drug combinations may act synergistically against MAC. In vitro evidence suggests such energy may occur between macrolides and ethambutol, between ethambutol and rifamycins, and between clofazimine and fluoroquinolones. However, the clinical relevance of such synergy remains to be demonstrated.

While the slow growth rate of MAC would suggest that the antimycobacterial could be given as a single daily dose, this is rarely possible. Many patients have difficulty tolerating a single daily dose, and twice-daily dosing is the rule rather than the exception. Similarly, while daily intravenous dosing of amikacin is given for the first 4 – 8 weeks, cumulative otoxicity and nephrotoxicity usually lead to eventual dose reduction. Some clinicians go to thrice-weekly dosing after 4 – 8 weeks, although no data are available to confirm the utility of this regimen. Higher doses of ethambutol (to 25 mg/kg) may be beneficial but require monitoring for the development of optic neuritis.

Selection of treatment regimens for children with MAC should follow the same principles as outlined for adults, with appropriate reduction in doses on a per-kilogram basis. However, the use of fluoroquinolones is generally avoided due to the potential for erosion of cartilage in growing bone.

OTHER NONTUBERCULOUS MYCOBACTERIAL INFECTIONS IN PATIENTS WITH AIDS

Several species of nontuberculous mycobacteria, notably *M. genavense* and *M. malmoense*, are closely related to *M. avium* and do not require a different treatment strategy. However, other nontuberculous mycobacteria require a different approach. Disease due to *M. kansasii*, which may be localized to the lungs without dissemination[6] or may be disseminated, should be treated with a regimen that includes isoniazid, ethambutol, and rifampin. If the patient cannot tolerate these or does not respond clinically, an aminoglycoside or a quinolone may be added. As with MAC, there is no consensus on the usefulness of in vitro susceptibility testing in selection of regimens for individual patients.

M. haemophilum infection often presents initially as single or multiple skin lesions.[4] Optimal treatment regimens have not been defined for either localized or disseminated disease. Susceptibility in vitro has been reported with rifampin, quinolones, macrolides, and amikacin.

TOXICITY OF ANTIMYCOBACTERIAL AGENTS

Common side effects of the macrolides are gastrointestinal pain, nausea, vomiting, and possible ototoxicity (Table 24-1). Ethambutol and the rifamycins may also cause gastrointestinal pain, nausea, and vomiting, and the rifamycins may cause rash or leukopenia. When possible drug effects occur, it is often difficult to know which is the likely offending agent, and it may be necessary to stop all agents and rechallenge consecutively. In some cases, increased abdominal pain may not be toxicity but, rather, the result of progression of the underlying MAC disease, indicating the need for a change in the antimycobacterial regimen.

It is also important to consider the effects of the antimycobacterial agents on other medicines the patient may be taking. Rifamycins may decrease serum levels of other concomitant medications, such as ketoconazole and methadone. Clarithromycin and zidovudine doses should not be taken at the same time, because concomitant administration leads to lowered serum zidovudine concentrations. This problem can be avoided by leaving a period of at least 2 h between administration of the two agents. Patients taking rifabutin also have lower levels of zidovudine in the blood, although the clinical significance of this phenomenon is unclear. Coadministration of clofazimine and rifampin has been reported to lead to lower rifampin levels. Conversely, antacids may decrease absorption of macrolides, aluminum salts may decrease absorption of ethambutol, and ketoconazole may decrease absorption of rifamycins. Rifabutin has been associated with uveitis when taken with macrolides or fluconazole.

Toxicities of antimycobacterials may also add to similar toxicities due to other agents. Potential examples of this would be gastrointestinal intolerance of clarithromycin, ciprofloxacin, and rifampin (and possibly ethambutol and clofazimine as well); ototoxicity of clarithromycin and aminoglycosides; and peripheral neuritis of didanosine, zalcitadine, and ethambutol.

If side effects require discontinuation of a macrolide (clarithromycin or azithromycin), the other macrolide can be substituted, since they have different toxicity profiles. On the other hand, the two currently available rifamycins (rifampin and rifabutin) are closely related, and toxicity to one may predict toxicity to the other, although data are lacking on the frequency of this occurrence.

MANAGEMENT OF PATIENTS

Patients should be followed with monthly blood cultures. In our clinic, we follow quantitative cultures to give an indication of response or failure in a more timely fashion, since higher initial levels of bacteremia take longer to clear. Successful therapy will result in negative blood culture results in 1–3 months; the time to a negative culture result depends on the initial level of bacteremia, the dose of the drug tolerated, and the susceptibility of the organism. Blood cultures that become positive after having been negative are associated with clinical relapse and may indicate development of in vitro resistance to antimycobacterial agents, particularly the macrolides.

Serum drug levels of antimycobacterial agents may be diminished in patients with disseminated MAC.[29] This is particularly true of agents absorbed from the intestine, such as rifampin, ethambutol, ciprofloxacin, and clofazimine, where serum levels rarely reach the normal range. Clarithromycin levels are also decreased; no data are available on azithromycin levels. However, many patients respond to therapy despite low serum drug levels, and there is no indication for routine monitoring of these levels. For patients who do not respond to therapy and appear to have severely impaired drug absorption, there may be a role for intravenous therapy, at least for a limited period of time.

Symptomatic responses may occur, even in the absence of clearing of bacteremia, and may be related to decreased serum levels of inflammatory mediators such as interleukin 1 or tumor necrosis factor. Fevers and night sweats respond the most frequently to antimycobacterial therapy, followed by stabilization of weight or weight gain. Diarrhea also responds frequently, while improvement in anemia, hepatosplenomegaly, or alkaline phosphase elevations are seen less often.

Anemia should be treated symptomatically; we have found that a hemoglobin level of <8.0 mg/dl or a hematocrit of <24 percent usually indicates the need for a transfusion. We transfuse patients with MAC and anemia with 2 units of blood whenever these thresholds are reached; this usually results in a transfusion every 6–8 weeks. Some authors have suggested a role for erythropoietin in treatment of anemia in these patients, although in our clinic endogenous erythropoietin levels are often markedly elevated. Nonetheless, in some patients, erythropoietin may decrease transfusion requirements.

PROPHYLAXIS

The elevated risk of persons with HIV infection and low CD4+ cell counts for MAC has led to trials of antimycobacterial prophylaxis to prevent MAC. To date, only one agent, rifabutin, has been shown to be effective for such prophylaxis. In two large trials using 300 mg orally per day, a >50 percent reduction of MAC bacteremia was seen in patients receiving rifabutin compared to those receiving placebo.[30,31] On the basis of these results, the U.S. Public Health Service has recommended rifabutin prophylaxis for all persons who have <100 CD4+ cells per cubic millimeter. In addition, clarithromycin and azithromycin are assumed to be useful as prophylaxis against MAC, and studies are in progress to test their effectiveness.

Several precautions should be taken when administering rifabutin prophylaxis. First, clinicians must ensure that persons given rifabutin prophylaxis do not have unrecognized TB, since treatment with rifabutin alone could lead to drug-resistant TB. Second, since rifamycins may alter levels of other drugs in the patient's regimen, persons on rifabutin should be monitored to detect decreases in antifungals, antivirals, or methadone. Third, persons who already have a complex regimen of therapeutic agents may demonstrate decreased adherence when another agent is prescribed. Thus, the potential benefit of MAC prophylaxis must be weighed against the need for other agents in patients with advanced AIDS.

REFERENCES

1. Horsburgh CR: *Mycobacterium avium* complex infection in the acquired immunodeficiency syndrome. *N Engl J Med* 324:1332, 1991.
2. Ellner JJ, Goldberg MJ, Parenti DM: *Mycobacterium avium* infection with AIDS: a therapeutic dilemma in rapid evolution. *J Infect Dis* 163:1326, 1991.
3. Bottger EC, Teske A, Kirschner P, et al: Disseminated "*Mycobacterium genavense*" infection in patients with AIDS. *Lancet* 340:76, 1992.
4. Straus WL, Ostroff SM, Jernigan DB, et al: Clinical and epidemiologic characteristics of *Mycobacterium haemophilum*, an emerging pathogen in immunocompromised patients. *Ann Intern Med* 120:118, 1994.
5. Valainis GT, Cardona LM, Greer DL: The spectrum of *Mycobacterium kansasii* disease associated with HIV-1 infected patients. *J Acquire Immune Defic Dis* 4:516, 1991.
6. Levine B, Chaisson RE: *Mycobacterium kansasii*: a cause of treatable pulmonary disease associated with advanced human immunodeficiency virus infection. *Ann Intern Med* 114:861, 1991.
7. Horsburgh CR, Selik RM: The epidemiology of disseminated nontuberculous mycobacterial infection in the acquired immunodeficiency syndrome (AIDS). *Am Rev Respir Dis* 139:4, 1989.
8. Nightingale SD, Byrd LT, Southern PM, et al: Incidence of *Mycobacterium avium-intracellulare* complex bacteremia in human immunodeficiency virus-positive patients. *J Infect Dis* 165:1082, 1992.
9. Gray JR, Rabeneck L: Atypical mycobacterial infection of the gastrointestinal tract in AIDS patients. *Am J Gastroenterol* 84:1521, 1989.
10. Tenholder MF, Moser RJ, Tellis CJ: Mycobacteria other than tuberculosis: pulmonary involvement in patients with acquired immunodeficiency syndrome. *Arch Intern Med* 148:953, 1988.
11. Horsburgh CR, Caldwell MB, Simonds RJ: Epidemiology of disseminated nontuberculous mycobacterial disease in children with acquired immunodeficiency syndrome. *Pediatr Infect Dis J* 12:219, 1993.
12. Horsburgh CR, Havlik JA, Ellis DA, et al: Survival of AIDS patients with disseminated *Mycobacterium avium* complex infection with and without antimycobacterial chemotherapy. *Am Rev Respir Dis* 144:557, 1991.

13. Jacobson MA, Hopewell PC, Yajko DM, et al: Natural history of disseminated *Mycobacterium avium* complex infection in AIDS. *J Infect Dis* 164:994, 1991.

14. Chaisson RE, Moore RD, Richman DD, et al: Zidovudine Epidemiology Study Group: Incidence and natural history of *Mycobacterium avium* complex infections in patients with advanced human immunodeficiency virus disease treated with zidovudine. *Am Rev Respir Dis* 146:285, 1992.

15. Horsburgh CR, Metchock B, Gordon SM, et al: Predictors of survival of patients with AIDS and disseminated *Mycobacterium avium* complex disease. J Infect Dis 1994 (in press).

16. Chin DP, Hopewell PC, Yajko DM, et al: Mycobacterium avium complex in the respiratory or gastrointestinal tract and the risk of MAC bacteremia in patients with human immunodeficiency virus infection. *J Infect Dis* 169:289, 1994.

17. Monsour HP, Quigley EMM, Markin RS, et al: Endoscopy in the diagnosis of gastrointestinal *Mycobacterium avium-intracellulare* infection. *J Clin Gastroenterol* 13:20, 1991.

18. Yagupsky P, Menegus MA: Cumulative positivity rates of multiple blood cultures for *Mycobacterium avium-intracellulare* and *Cryptococcus neoformans* in patients with the acquired immunodeficiency syndrome. *Arch Pathol Lab Med* 114:923, 1990.

19. Gill VJ, Park CH, Stock F, et al: Use of lysis-centrifugation (isolator) and radiometric (BACTEC) blood culture systems for the detection of mycobacteremia. *J Clin Microbiol* 22:543, 1985.

20. Salfinger M, Stool EW, Piot D, Heifets L: Comparison of three methods for the recovery of *Mycobacterium avium* complex from blood specimens. *J Clin Microbiol* 26:1225, 1988.

21. Hawkins CC, Gold JWM, Whimbey E, et al: *Mycobacterium avium* complex infections in patients with acquired immunodeficiency syndrome. *Ann Intern Med* 105:184, 1986.

22. Havlik JA, Horsburgh CR, Metchock B, et al: Disseminated *Mycobacterium avium* complex infection: clinical identification and epidemiologic trends. *J Infect Dis* 165:577, 1992.

23. Chiu J, Nussbaum J, Bozzette S, et al: Treatment of disseminated *Mycobacterium avium* complex infection in AIDS with amikacin, ethambutol, rifampin, and ciprofloxacin. *Ann Intern Med* 113:358, 1990.

24. Kemper KA, Meng T-C, Nussbaum J, et al: Treatment of *Mycobacterium avium* complex bacteremia in AIDS with a 4-drug oral regimen. *Ann Intern Med* 116:466, 1992.

25. Young LS, Wiviott L, Wu M, et al: Azithromycin for treatment of *Mycobacterium avium-intracellulare* complex infection in patients with AIDS. *Lancet* 338:1107, 1991.

26. Dautzentberg B, Truffot C, Legris S, et al: Activity of clarithromycin against *Mycobacterium avium* infection in patients with the acquired immune deficiency syndrome. *Am Rev Respir Dis* 144:564, 1991.

27. Chaisson RE, Benson CA, Dube M, et al: Clarithromycin for disseminated *Mycobacterium avium* complex in AIDS patients (abstract). Abstracts of the Eighth International Conference on AIDS/STD World Congress, vol 2. Amsterdam, p WeB 1052.

28. Heifets LB, Iseman MD: Choice of antimicrobial agents for *M. avium* disease based on quantitative tests of drug susceptibility. *N Engl J Med* 323:419, 1990.

29. Gordon SM, Horsburgh CR, Peloquin CA, et al: Low serum levels of oral antimycobacterial agents in patients with disseminated *Mycobacterium avium* complex disease. *J Infect Dis* 168:1559, 1993.

30. Nightingale SD, Cameron DW, Gordin FM, et al: Two controlled trials of rifabutin prophylaxis against *Mycobacterium avium* complex infection in AIDS. *N Engl J Med* 329:828, 1993.

31. Masur H, Public Health Service Task Force on Prophylaxis and Therapy for *Mycobaterium avium* Complex: Recommendations on prophylaxis and therapy for disseminated *Mycobacterium avium* complex disease in patients infected with the human immunodeficiency virus. *N Engl J Med* 329:895, 1993.

Index

403

meningitis in, 139–140
Mycobacterium avium complex disease in:
epidemiology, 392
treatment, 397
preventive treatment in, 137, 141
contacts, 98
duration of therapy, 96, 100
excluding active TB prior to, 101–102
rates for developing TB in reactors, 90–91
treatment of TB in, 137–141
bone and joint disease, 139
corticosteroids, 141
dosage recommendations, 192t
drug-resistant disease, 140
extrapulmonary disease, 138–140
meningitis, 139–140
options for initial therapy, 199t
pulmonary disease, 137–138
direct observation, 138
with HIV infection, 138
INH and rifampin two-drug regimen, 137
INH and rifampin with pyrazinamide, 138
tuberculin skin test in, 85–86
in diagnosis of TB, 133–135, 134–135t
interpretation of reaction, 134–135, 134–134t
limitations with multiple-puncture test, 133
tuberculosis in, 129–142
cervical lymphadenitis, 132–133
clinical manifestations, 132–133
coexistence with HIV infection, 131
diagnosis (*See under* diagnosis of TB in *above*)
epidemiology, 129–131
extrapulmonary disease, 132
in foreign-born, 131
increasing incidence, 129, 131
meningitis, 132, 139–140
(*See also* Meningitis)
pleural effusion, 132
progressive primary pulmonary disease, 132
radiographic findings, 132
risk of disease in untreated infection, 129
treatment (*See under* treatment of TB in *above*)
Ciprofloxacin, 196
adverse effects, 305t, 306, 396t
dosage recommendations: for initial treatment of TB, 192t
in multidrug-resistant TB, 305t
in HIV-infected patient, 233

in *Mycobacterium avium* complex disease, 368, 396t
Clarithromycin:
adverse effects, 396t
in *Mycobacterium abscessus* infection, 386
in *Mycobacterium avium* complex disease, 368, 395, 396t
in *Mycobacterium chelonae* infection, 386
zidovudine interaction with, 398
Clofazimine:
adverse effects, 305t, 306, 396t
dosage recommendations: for initial treatment of TB, 191, 192t
in multidrug-resistant TB, 305t, 306
in *Mycobacterium avium* complex disease, 396t
rifampin interaction with, 398
Compliance (*see* Noncompliance)
Computed tomography:
in bone and joint TB, 285, 286f
for CNS tuberculoma, 164–165
in *Mycobacterium avium* complex disease, 364–365, 364f
in pulmonary tuberculosis, 278f, 284–285, 284f
in renal tuberculosis, 286
in tuberculous meningitis, 163–164
Contacts:
BCG vaccination studies in, 119, 120t
INH preventive therapy for, 98
investigation as diagnostic tool, 136
Convection, and TB transmission, 59
Conversion, 85
Convertor, 89
preventive therapy for, 99
(*See also* Tuberculin skin test)
Cord factor, and *M. tuberculosis* virulence, 20
Corticosteroids:
in extrapulmonary TB, 183
M. chelonae skin infection associated with, 377
rifampin interaction with, 193
suppression of immunological rebound phenomena, 218
in tuberculosis therapy, 204
in children, 141
in meningitis, 167
Costs:
of isoniazid prophylaxis, 95, 96
for National Action Plan to Combat Multidrug-Resistant Tuberculosis, 346–347
for strategic plan to eliminate TB in US, 342–343t, 345